Speaking Clearly
Improving Voice and Diction

THIRD EDITION

Speaking Clearly

Improving Voice and Diction

JEFFREY C. HAHNER
Pace University

MARTIN A. SOKOLOFF
Pace University

SANDRA L. SALISCH
Pace University

McGraw-Hill, Inc.

New York   St. Louis   San Francisco   Auckland   Bogotá
Caracas   Hamburg   Lisbon   London   Madrid   Mexico   Milan
Montreal   New Delhi   Paris   San Juan   São Paulo
Singapore   Sydney   Tokyo   Toronto

34567890 DOC/DOC 9987654321

ISBN 0-07-557316-4

This book was set in Bookman Light by University Graphics, Inc.
The editors were Hilary Jackson and Fred H. Burns;
the designer was Wanda Siedlecka;
the production supervisor was Birgit Garlasco.
R. R. Donnelley & Sons, Inc. was printer and binder.

Library of Congress Cataloging-in-Publication Data

Hahner, Jeffrey C.
    Speaking clearly: improving voice and diction / Jeffrey C.
Hahner, Martin A. Sokoloff, Sandra L. Salisch. — 3rd ed.
        p.   cm.
    Rev. ed. of: Speaking clearly / Jeffrey C. Hahner . . . [et al.]
2nd. ed. © 1986.
    ISBN 0-07-557316-4
    1. Speech.   2. Voice.   3. Communication.   4. English language—
Diction.   5. English language—Phonetics.   I. Sokoloff, Martin A.
II. Salisch, Sandra L.
PN4121.H17   1990
808.5—dc20   89-39286

Permission/acknowledgments follow the index.

Once again, we thank our families, especially Bette and Tim Hahner, Vivienne Sokoloff, and Jeannette Salisch.

Contents

Chapter Three
The Sounds of American English   29

PART TWO
DICTION   45

Chapter Four
Improving Voice and Diction: The Basics   47

Chapter Five
Diction: The Consonants   53

Chapter Six
Diction: The Vowels and Diphthongs   190

PART THREE
VOICE

Chapter Seven
Voice Production

GUIDE TO VOICE PRODUCTION EXERCISES

*Included under vowels

Chapter Eight
Vocal Expressiveness 276

Preface

Taking (and teaching) a college course in voice and diction can often be a real challenge. Many students who enroll with high hopes for dramatic changes in speech don't achieve those changes or find that they are, at most, very temporary. One of the main reasons for this is lack of time; students usually have been speaking for at least seventeen years and would like to change their way of speaking in just one short semester or one even shorter summer session. Furthermore, they aren't going to attempt this in a one-to-one setting with an instructor but on a time-sharing basis in the classroom. Also, it's probably not the only course the students are taking at the time, and all the other pressures of life also make themselves felt and compete for the students' attention. In addition, the students frequently feel uncomfortable about carrying over what they're learning in class to everyday communication situations. So if taking (and teaching) a course in voice and diction is a challenge, it's because conditions are far from ideal.

Our purpose in writing this book is to eliminate some of the obstacles to success in voice and diction courses, and to increase the chances for the significant, lasting changes in voice and diction that most students seek.

This book is the result of over twenty years of teaching voice and diction courses to thousands of students. During that time we've been able to identify many of the factors that spell success in speech improvement. We've pooled our knowledge, our experience, and the materials that we've developed over the years to provide a book that capitalizes on the success factors. This book brings you the things we do that *work:* specific materials and approaches we use that have proven themselves effective in the classroom.

One such approach is the use of voice and diction drills that are presented in increasing order of difficulty. Our drills distinguish between the less and more difficult productions of a given sound and prevent students from trying to progress too rapidly or starting at levels inappropriate for beginners. These drills give the students early rewards and help them to develop a healthy, positive attitude. Along this line, we've tried to avoid the use of tongue-twisters. The sentences in the drills are designed to present the target sounds at a frequency close to that of normal conversation. Words are familiar, and they can be phased into the students' everyday conversations.

We have also kept in mind the fact that students of voice and diction sometimes find it awkward or embarrassing to drill aloud on materials that, while providing ample practice on target sounds, may not make sense as far as content is concerned. Since students tend to resist using practice materials that sound "silly," we've made every effort to create materials that students can feel comfortable practicing, either alone or as part of a classroom group.

As voice and diction instructors and speech pathologists, we've found it extremely helpful to use ear-training techniques to help our students develop accurate auditory "pictures" of the correct production of target sounds. In this way, students can learn to monitor and correct their own productions of the sounds as well as learn to produce the sounds more easily. We have provided, in Chapter 4, an outline of the step-by-step ear-training process that can be applied in the classroom by the instructor or individually by the students as an out-of-class assignment. It is also possible to use the ear-training steps as a means to assess each student's ability to discriminate between standard and nonstandard productions of target sounds.

In many cases, students who have particularly hard-to-correct problems need additional help. We've provided Appendix B as a special section that covers, in a step-by-step way, such problems as lingual and lateral lisps. We've tried to give the students some self-help measures and provide carry-over materials for students who are concurrently engaged in speech therapy. In addition, we've tried to offer guidance to instructors who may feel unsure of themselves in these more specialized areas. Students who use Appendix B can be assigned practice on their own, thus allowing more class time for activities involving larger numbers of students.

This book also addresses two other major concerns. One is our belief that students in beginning courses in voice and diction ought to gain a certain sense of perspective as to where their own vocal and articulatory styles fit into their overall communication styles. For example, we consider paralinguistic elements such as loudness, rate, intonation, and voice quality to be essential aspects of a person's nonverbal communication. Accordingly, Chapters 7 and 8 are devoted to voice production and vocal expressiveness. But there are other nonverbal elements, such as kinesics and proxemics, that also are an important part of a person's total communication package. Appendix C completes the perspective on aspects of nonverbal communication.

We have found that significant numbers of beginning students in voice and diction have a high degree of apprehension about the course in general, and they suffer varying degrees of stagefright when asked to read or speak aloud in the classroom. We have included Appendix A to give students information about the nature and causes of stagefright and to provide them with concrete ways to manage stagefright successfully.

This is the third edition of *Speaking Clearly.* We wrote the first edition because we wanted to share what we do in teaching voice and diction. The second edition went beyond our own classrooms and incorporated many suggestions from users of the first edition. The most notable feature of the second edition was the sizable increase in drill materials. We also made layout improvements that made drills easier to find and to read aloud and provided a set of audio cassettes that allowed students to practice the consonant and vowel drills and exercises at home or in a language lab setting.

This edition draws even more on user suggestions. In particular, we've added a considerable number of new drills and many ''challenge'' sentences and materials. We've expanded coverage of voice, and we've organized readings in a systematic and more useful way. The revised layout and new drill and exercise heads make a much clearer distinction between exercises and text. Many users requested more coverage of regional and non-native dialects, so we added Appendix D, which is a guide to the features of individual dialects and where to find materials on each particular dialect. The section ''Dealing with Nervousness'' is now Appendix A, a move requested by many users.

The cassette tapes we provided to each adopter of the second edition proved to be both a blessing and a plague. The tapes were extremely popular and useful, but some instructors did not have the facilities available to make copies for their students. We also had numerous requests for tapes from students using the book who had not enrolled in formal courses and wished to study on their own. To remedy the problem of availability, we have added a channel of distribution suggested by many users. Although instructors will still receive a set of cassettes gratis, the tape program will now be sold separately in bookstores. The tapes have been revised and now come with a user's guide.

The last major change is one which users overwhelmingly requested—an instructor's manual. The manual provides many suggestions and ideas for implementing the procedures and materials provided in the text, as well as sample course outlines, quizzes, homework assignments, projects, classroom exercises, and advice on grading.

The manuscript was reviewed by several of our colleagues who provided very helpful critiques. They were Mary Barrett, Edgecombe Community College; Donald Bristow, Central State University; Charles Hukill, McMurry College; Janet Keys, University of Alabama, Birmingham; F. Fulton Ross, Hunter College; Louis Rosso, Winthrop College; Carole Tallant, University of North Carolina, Wilmington; and Florence Wolff, University of Dayton.

Finally, we couldn't have accomplished the finished text without the patience, understanding, and flexibility of our editors, Hilary Jackson and Fred Burns.

Jeffrey C. Hahner
Martin A. Sokoloff
Sandra L. Salisch

Part One

INTRODUCTION TO SPEECH COMMUNICATION

Why do you communicate? *How* do you do it? Why do some people communicate more effectively than others? How can I gain more self-confidence? How can I become a more effective speaker?

These are typical of the questions asked by people like you who are about to start working on voice and diction. Part I of this book will answer these and other questions you may have and start you on the way to *speaking clearly.*

Chapter One

Overview

Recently a series of employment interviews was held on our campus. Several seniors who were considered to be likely candidates for jobs with highly rated accounting firms appeared for their interviews. They were all shined and polished, and they had boned up on all they should know to make favorable impressions on the interviewers. Their academic credentials were highly suitable; they were all set. What happened? You guessed it! They failed the interviews.

Why? The interviewers told the Director of our Career Planning Center that the speech patterns of those students were more appropriate for manual laborers than professional accountants, and that these particular students would not be considered for employment.

Consider this case: one of our students in a voice and diction class, a rather petite young woman, made her first tape recording. This woman was also a student teacher, and during the conference that followed the recording session, she complained that she was having trouble maintaining discipline in her student teaching assignment. She said that she was assigned to teach several high school English classes and that most of the students towered over her physically. They paid little attention to her instructions, and she was feeling increasingly frustrated. She had never heard herself on tape before, and when she did, she realized that her voice was quite high-pitched and weak. She said, "I sound just like a little girl." After some voice retraining she returned to class. She found that with her "new" voice she was able to get her students' attention and really get down to the business of teaching.

These incidents, and many others like them, are familiar to anyone who is trained to observe the way people speak. As you think over some of your own communication history, you can probably remember several times when you made snap judgments about people solely on the basis of how they presented themselves through speaking. In other words, *how* a person says something, rather than *what* that person says, forms a lasting impression. You form these impressions because you've come to believe that a person's personality is reflected in the way he or she speaks. What if your first impression is wrong? If your relationship with that individual continues, it will take a long time for you to change your opinion.

A person's communication patterns are usually very informative as to what kind of person he or she is. We can tell a good deal about someone by the way he pronounces words; from the loudness, quality, and inflection of his voice; the way he uses gestures; the way he stands; what he does with his eyes and face. We make judgments mostly without being aware of the basis on which we are making them; but we make them just the same.

For most of us, the truth is we have not one but several styles of communicating. For example, we usually talk quite differently when we're speaking with our friends than we do when we're being interviewed for a job. Chances are in any of these situations we're trying to make a good impression and get the other person to respond to us in a favorable way.

"But," you may say, "I've been talking all my life, and I haven't had any trouble. Why should I study speech? What will it do for me?" The answers to these questions—the reasons for studying speech—will, of course, vary from student to student. For one student the reason might be a desire to communicate effectively. You may have no difficulty communicating in the specific geographic and social environment called home, but in a different environment, your present speech patterns might be so different from those around you that people pay more attention to the *way* you speak than to *what* you have to say. For another student the reason might be a wish to make a good impression. It may be that your present speech patterns could, at one time or another, prevent you from getting that job you're after, that promotion you deserve, that date with that person who is so special to you.

Perhaps it is the way you pronounce certain words or how loudly you speak or the quality of your voice or some other aspect of your speech that, in some way, prevents your communication from being as effective as you would like. The result is you may not be successful in getting the desired response from those with whom you are communicating.

Once they've thought about these reasons, most of our students say, "Okay, you've convinced me. But I *can't* change the way I speak; I'm too old! I'd just be wasting my time." We don't agree! First, you don't have to learn to speak all over again. You only have to add another speaking style to those you already possess, to be used when it's appropriate for the particular speaker, listener, or occasion. Second, the ability to learn new speech patterns doesn't depend on your age but on your motivation. It's simply a matter of learning new muscle habits and developing dormant listening skills. If you *want* to do it, you *can!* How long it takes you to improve your speech depends on how badly you want to do it and the amount of time you're willing to spend on practice.

THE COMMUNICATION PROCESS

Now is a good time to talk about communication: what it is, how it operates, and what influence your speech has on your communication and its effectiveness.

Communication is the process whereby an idea, thought, or feeling that arises in the mind of one person is conveyed to the mind of someone else. For example, say there's someone that you enjoyed meeting. You might want to convey to him or her this message: "I like you, and I would like a chance to get to know you better."

The first step in the process would be for your brain to reach back into its file of experiences and dig out the words that would best express the idea. To come up with the appropriate words, your brain would probably review a number of different ways to express the same idea and, based on your attitudes, values, and past experiences, select those words you think would result in the most effective, least risky way of conveying your message.

The next step would be for your brain to regulate the various structures and muscles your body uses to produce speech so that you could transmit the words of your message. These words, when spoken, exist in the form of sounds or vibrations of the air molecules surrounding you. When these vibrations reach the ear of another person (such as the person you intended should hear them), the vibrations change into nerve impulses that travel to the brain where they are translated into ideas.

So at this point, you have directed a message toward a person you'd like to get to know better, and you hope that person shares your feeling. But then you get a response far from the one you were hoping for. Why might this have happened? Chances are you were a victim of communication noise.

Noise

In an ideal situation, the message created in the brain of the other person would be exactly the same as the one that originated in yours. Most of the time this doesn't happen, though, because of a number of factors that operate in almost all communication situations. These factors are frequently called barriers to communication or simply noise. Noise exists in human speech communication because, at this time, we have no way to link the speaker's brain directly to the listener's. In a way, we could compare you and your listener to a television station and a TV set; they're miles apart, but an attempt is made to have a picture appear on the TV set that is the same as the one in the studio. When the picture is different, it's because of noise. The noise could be generated at the source ("Please stand by . . ."), by something between your set and the studio (an electrical storm), or by something wrong inside your TV set (crossed wires). Similarly, speech communication noises exist: environmental, listener-generated, and speaker-generated.

ENVIRONMENTAL NOISE

Just as a TV signal can be distorted while it's traveling between the studio and your set at home, so can your communication be subjected to distortion from noise between you and your listener.

The noise may be *acoustic*, that is, other sounds (not generated by speaker or listener) that block out speech or make hearing difficult. It is hard to understand conversations at a loud party, for example. For the same reason, people who live near busy airports learn to lip-read and use it to make themselves understood every time a jet takes off. The effect of acoustic noise on speech is that if you hear the words at all, you still can't be sure you heard them correctly.

There are *visual* noises, too. Have you ever sat in a classroom trying to pay attention to a lecture or discussion while your eyes and mind kept straying through the window to something happening outside? That something outside the window is a visual noise. (We also use, however, the visual sense to help us understand speech; there's less chance of error when you can see the speaker's lips.)

These are just a few illustrations of how environmental factors can disrupt communication or at least make it more difficult.

LISTENER-GENERATED NOISE

The receiver of the communication, though, can also be at fault. Think, for a moment, about all the factors you bring to each communication situation and how they might affect the way you listen to, understand, and integrate what someone is saying to you. How do you feel about the speaker, for instance? Do you like, respect, or admire that person? If so, you are much more likely to be open and receptive to what that person has to say. If you dislike, fear, or distrust the speaker, chances are you won't accept or agree with very much of what he or she says. How do you feel about the way the other person talks? Does that particular accent or way of pronouncing words turn you off?

Another factor to consider is how you feel about the subject you are talking about. Do you have a lot of fixed ideas, attitudes, or values about the subject? Is it something that you feel very strongly about? It's likely that if your answers to the last two questions are yes, your mind will be fairly closed to ideas or attitudes that differ from yours.

Do you react emotionally to certain words or phrases that have strong associations for you? How would you feel, for instance, if someone called you or your ideas dumb, communistic, "reactionary"? How willing would you be to listen objectively to that person?

These are all examples of factors existing within the listener that may increase or diminish the likelihood of effective communication taking place.

SPEAKER-GENERATED NOISE

Speakers can create noise that interferes with accurate message transmission through a number of different types of behaviors. Disturbing *linguistic behaviors* can constitute "noise" experienced as faulty grammar or *syntax*, incorrect word choices, or faulty production of any of the sounds that make up the words. *Paralinguistic behaviors* might include such interferences as uneven loudness, rate, or rhythm; inappropriate pitch or stress patterns; and unusual or abnormal voice qualities. *Extraverbal behaviors* can also cause problems; your gestures or facial expressions might not be appropriate for your message. All these behaviors can take the attention of your listener away from *what* is being said and focus it on *how* it is being said.

In this text, we deal primarily with the behaviors that constitute speaker-generated noise: those parts of your speech pattern that may call attention to themselves or in some way make your message hard to understand or cause your listener to misinterpret your message. We'll present both theory and practical exercises to help you eliminate such noise and to help you make your spoken communication more effective.

HOW TO USE THIS BOOK

This book contains a wide variety of materials related to voice and diction. First, browse through the entire book. See how it's laid out, what's covered in each appendix, how the index is organized. Once you're familiar with the book, you can use it more effectively.

Chapters

Each chapter is a complete unit in itself and can be used separately. This means your instructor can assign chapter readings in whatever order he or she prefers.

CHAPTER 2

Chapter 2 deals with the theory of speech—the anatomy and physiology—and requires no drill materials. This chapter will provide you with a basic understanding of how and why the vocal mechanism works the way it does and may make *speaking clearly* easier for you.

CHAPTER 3

Chapter 3 presents the theory as well as practical applications of the International Phonetic Alphabet (I.P.A.) for the purpose of teaching you the component sounds of American English. The drill materials in Chapter 3 will help you master the dual skills of transcribing in I.P.A. and reading orally from I.P.A. symbols. Chapter 3 also provides the framework for Chapters 5 and 6.

CHAPTER 4

Chapter 4 is very short but extremely important. This is a how-to chapter that shows you the steps to improving voice in diction. It's similar to the set of instructions that helps you assemble a bicycle. If you don't read the instructions in advance, you might assemble the bike incorrectly. In any case, it will probably take you longer to get it right.

Chapter 4 has a section with the strange title of ''Ear Training'' designed to help you to improve your auditory discrimination. Read this section thoroughly and make sure to do the exercises. You'll find them effective in teaching you the differences between the standard and nonstandard sounds of our language.

Finally, Chapter 4 has a set of warm-up exercises that will help you make your practice sessions more effective.

CHAPTERS 5 AND 6

Chapters 5 and 6 (the longest in the book) present theory and drills on all the component sounds of American English. Wherever possible, we have arranged the drills according to level of difficulty. This allows you to practice with less or more difficult materials, depending on your level of skill at producing the particular sound.

We have tried to design our practice sentences so that they are close to what people might say in normal conversation. We have made every effort to avoid "loading" each sentence with words containing the sound being practiced. Our clinical experience has shown us that loaded sentences (tongue twisters) are not particularly useful in helping you correct misarticulated sounds. They can be useful in "fine tuning," so you'll find some in the challenge materials for some sounds.

CHAPTERS 7 AND 8

In Chapters 7 and 8, guided activities for voice analysis and improvement are alternated with theory about effective voice characteristics. We have divided instructions for carrying out vocal exercises and activities according to the level of difficulty for self-directed student practice.

Appendixes

APPENDIX A

The thought of speaking aloud in class or before a group makes many people uncomfortable. If you feel that way, we strongly recommend that you read Appendix A. It deals with reducing stagefright and anxiety. Read Appendix A and try the practice activities according to your own needs or as your instructor assigns.

APPENDIX B

Appendix B covers special explanations and drills for some hard-to-correct speech problems. Your instructor may suggest that you use this section, or you may want to use it on your own if you're having trouble with the sounds this section covers.

APPENDIX C

The subject of this Appendix is nonverbal communication, and it will help you become aware of some of the barriers to communication that may be generated by poor nonverbal or extraverbal behaviors on the part of the speaker. Here, again, we have alternated explanatory materials on theory with specific suggestions for exercises you can do, either in class or outside class, to reinforce and clarify the theory.

APPENDIX D

Appendix D covers dialects—the ways American English is spoken by natives of the various regions of the United States and by speakers who have learned English as a second language. This appendix shows the features of a number of dialects and provides a guide to the specific pages covering each of the sounds affected.

APPENDIX E

Appendix E will help you check and correct your pronunciation of a number of words that are frequently mispronounced.

APPENDIX F

Appendix F is a glossary of terms we use with which you may not be familiar. We've tried to minimize the use of technical terms, but there are several we felt we couldn't do without.

APPENDIX G

Appendix G consists of sentences and connected speech passages that contain all the sounds of American English in a variety of phonetic contexts. You and your instructor can use these passages in evaluating your speech for nonstandard sounds.

APPENDIX H

Appendix H provides a number of tear-out Speech Evaluation Checklists. You can use them to evaluate your own speech as well as the speech of others.

FEEDBACK

We've tried to bring you the best book we could that would help you learn the principles of voice and diction and to put those principles into practice as effectively as possible. If you have any suggestions as to how we can improve the book, give us some feedback. Write to us at Pace University, Pace Plaza, New York, NY 10038. We'd like to hear from you.

Chapter Two

The Speech Process

In this chapter, we will examine the speech sounds we make and the ways in which we make them. We will also take a look at the structures we use to produce sound. We believe that a basic understanding of the speech process will help you develop more effective voice production (Chapter 7) and will help you learn and practice the sounds of American English (Chapter 3). In our opinion, if you know how something works, you can use and control it more accurately.

THE NATURE OF SOUND

What Sound Is

When we talk about sound, we're *not* talking about hearing. Hearing is something that happens within your body (outer ear, middle ear, inner ear, nervous system, brain) as a result of sound. Sound is an actual physical event in which acoustic energy is generated. Hearing is the way you receive that acoustic energy from the air and eventually change it to meaningful nerve impulses in your brain.

The physical event that we call sound consists of vibratory energy

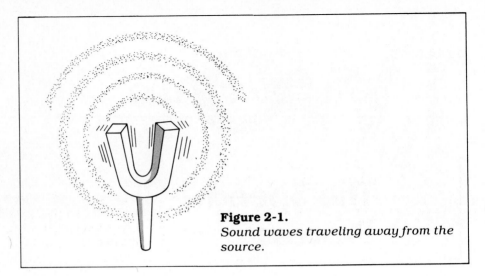

Figure 2-1.
Sound waves traveling away from the source.

that travels through the molecules of the air in ever-widening circles away from the source. To produce sound you need three things: a *force* that sets in motion a *vibrator* that generates vibrations that travel through a *medium*. When the force sets the vibrator in motion, some of the energy of the vibrations is applied to the molecules of air that surround the vibrator. These molecules send along some of their energy to the molecules next to them, and so on. Each molecule transmits some of the energy, and the process continues until there's no energy left. Since the motion of the vibrator is back and forth, waves of energy travel outward in all directions through the air (see Figure 2-1).

Characteristics of Sound

Although we can't see sound, we can observe and measure sound in a number of objective ways, and we do know a great deal about sound. Three of the objective characteristics of sound are important for you to understand. They are *frequency, intensity*, and *spectrum*. Their subjective counterparts are pitch, loudness, and quality.

FREQUENCY AND PITCH

Frequency means the number of vibrations that occur in a given period of time. The frequencies of sounds vary because some vibrating objects vibrate more rapidly than others and, in turn, cause the molecules of air to vibrate at the same rate. Humans can hear sounds that range

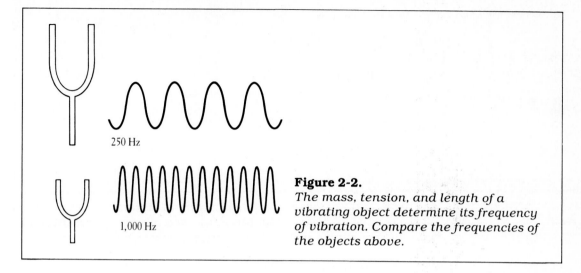

250 Hz

1,000 Hz

Figure 2-2.
The mass, tension, and length of a vibrating object determine its frequency of vibration. Compare the frequencies of the objects above.

from frequencies as low as 20 Hz. (Hz [hertz] means vibrations per second.) The upper limit of hearing is about 20,000 Hz.

How rapidly an object vibrates basically depends on three factors: the object's *mass, tension,* and *length.* In general, small, short, highly tense objects vibrate more rapidly than large, long, low-tension objects (see Figure 2-2).

PITCH

While frequency is an objective (physically measurable) characteristic of sound, pitch is subjective. That is, pitch is determined by the listener's judgment; it occurs within you. Pitch is what we call the highness or lowness of a sound. The relationship is direct: the higher the frequency, the higher the pitch we hear; the lower the frequency, the lower the pitch.

INTENSITY AND LOUDNESS

Intensity is the objective measurement of the amount of energy a sound has. If you apply a greater force to the vibrating object, it will transfer more energy to the air around it. As a result, each molecule of air shoves the next one a little harder, so more energy means higher intensity. A not too pleasant analogy would be a series of chain-reaction collisions in a line of cars at a toll booth. There's much more energy transmitted in a 25 mph collision than in one at 5 mph. And, as with sound, the greater the energy, the farther the sound travels.

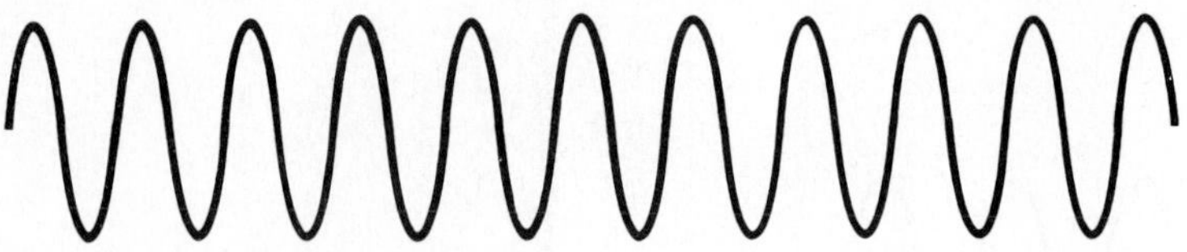

Figure 2-3.
The waveform of a pure-tone produced by a tuning fork (see Figure 2-1).

LOUDNESS

Just as pitch is the subjective interpretation of frequency, loudness is the subjective interpretation of intensity. We perceive high-intensity sounds as being louder than low-intensity sounds.

SPECTRUM AND QUALITY

Figure 2-1 shows the way waves of sound travel away from the source, which in this case is a tuning fork. If we graphically display the movement of one molecule in any one of the waves around the tuning fork, the resulting waveform is the simple sine curve shown in Figure 2-3. That's because a tuning fork is designed and built very precisely to produce a very simple kind of sound that we call a pure-tone. By simple we don't mean easy; we mean that it's not complex. A pure-tone is a very clear, musical tone with the same movement of the molecules repeating over and over again.

Our bodies, as well as most other sound-producing objects, don't produce just one simple pure-tone. Instead, we produce very complex tones that are made up of many pure-tones. The configuration of a complex wave that shows the relative intensities and frequencies of the component pure-tones is called the spectrum. Figure 2-4 shows the spectra of three complex sounds. Compare these with the pure-tone shown in Figure 2-3.

QUALITY

Your subjective interpretation of spectrum is called quality. You're well aware that sounds differ in ways other than loudness and pitch. Each complex sound is unique; there's some intangible *quality* that makes every voice, for example, different. Listen to two singers singing the same note, or the same note played by two different musical instruments. You can hear the differences; there are two distinguishable voices or instruments.

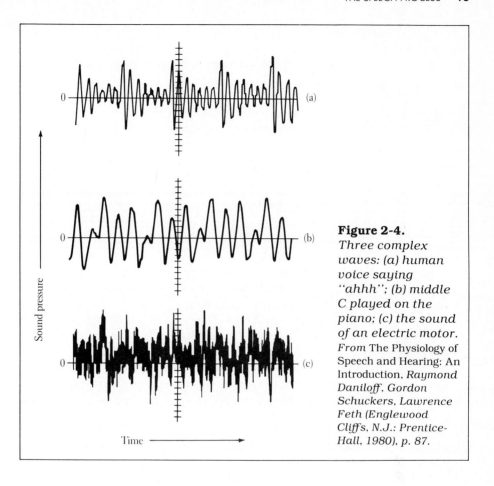

Figure 2-4.
Three complex waves: (a) human voice saying "ahhh"; (b) middle C played on the piano; (c) the sound of an electric motor. From The Physiology of Speech and Hearing: An Introduction, *Raymond Daniloff, Gordon Schuckers, Lawrence Feth (Englewood Cliffs, N.J.: Prentice-Hall, 1980), p. 87.*

THE SPEECH PROCESS

Now we're ready to talk about a particular type of sound: the sound of human speech. First let's look at the body as a sound producer. You'll remember that you need three things to produce sound: a force, a vibrator, and a medium. The human body has the equipment to fill these needs and is an excellent sound producer. There are six distinct processes in producing speech sounds: *audition, innervation, breathing, phonation, resonance, and articulation.*

While it is not within the purview of this text to delve very deeply into two phases of speech production, audition and innervation, we feel that a simple explanation may be in order.

Audition

The auditory process begins with energy, in the form of alternating compressions and rarefactions of the molecules of air, being transmitted through the air as the result of someone speaking. These vibrations are focused by the visible portion of the outer ear, the pinna, and channeled into the external auditory canal. At the end of the canal is the tympanic membrane, or eardrum, which is set into sympathetic vibration. Resting just inside and against the tympanic membrane is the malleus, or hammer, the first of three tiny bones or ossicles. Movement of the tympanic membrane sets the three ossicles, the other two of which are called the incus, or anvil, and stapes, or stirrup, into vibration. The sound energy is thus transformed from molecular energy (or variation in air pressure) into mechanical energy related to the movement of the ossicles.

The end of the ossicular chain (the footplate of the stapes) fits into an opening in the part of the inner ear called the cochlea, which is a snail-shell-like cavity in the temporal bone of the head. The cochlea is filled with fluid and a portion of it is lined with nerve endings. Pressure changes in the fluid caused by an in-and-out movement of the stapes into the opening of the cochlea cause certain of the nerve endings to be stimulated. The nerves attached to these endings gather together to form the auditory nerve, which carries the nerve impulses to the brain where they are perceived as sound, translated into a meaningful message, and stored.

Innervation

There is a highly complex pattern of nervous impulses traveling from the brain to many parts of the body that is necessary to control and coordinate all of the functions which are involved in speech production.

First the central and peripheral nervous systems are involved in controlling the muscles of the abdomen, chest, and diaphragm (the muscular sheath that separates the chest cavity from the stomach) so that the chest cavity is expanded to take air into the lungs, and then compressed to force that air back out again. These actions involve the rather gross movement of large muscle groups.

Next the muscles of the larynx must be controlled and coordinated to bring the vocal folds together and held under the proper tension to produce phonation at the desired pitch and loudness. Most of this control comes from a nerve called the recurrent laryngeal nerve.

In order to resonate the sound that is phonated by the larynx, nerves must control the muscles which vary the size, shape, and tension of the cavities of the head and neck which are responsible for shaping and amplifying the voice in an ever-changing pattern of movement during speech.

Finally, there are many muscles that control movements of the tongue, lips, soft palate, lower jaw, oropharynx, and nasopharynx. The nerves that are responsible for control of the movements of these muscles must exercise control and coordination of movements which are performed with a very high degree of precision, rapidity, and accuracy.

To understand the need for precision and accuracy, let us look at a short sample of speech and examine the articulatory movements just of the tongue. In Lincoln's Gettysburg Address, for example, the first words, "Four score and seven years ago . . ." involve an average of four tongue movements per word. At an average rate of one hundred and twenty words per minute, we would be required to perform four hundred and eighty tongue movements for each minute of speech. In addition, if we were to miss the exact place of articulation for each sound by as little as a fraction of a millimeter, the sound produced would probably come out as a completely different phoneme.

Movements of the articulators are generally controlled by facial and trigeminal nerves, two of the twelve pairs of cranial nerves, on either side of the head.

Movements of the articulators are monitored for accuracy acoustically by the hearing mechanism and kinesthetically through sensory nerves called proprioceptors, located in the muscles themselves, which provide sensory feedback about the movements of the articulators to the brain.

Breathing

We use breathing for our first requirement: a force to move the vibrator. Breathing is the process of bringing air into the lungs and forcing it out again. While the air is on its way out, you can use it to set the vocal folds vibrating and, thereby, produce voice. You can use the mouth to block or impede the breathstream in some way to produce consonant sounds. The way we breathe, that is, actually bring air in and out of the lungs, is quite a simple and uncomplicated process. The way we initiate nerve impulses and muscle contractions to control the process is, as we mentioned, far from simple, so we're not going deeply into that. You should understand, however, how the mechanism for breathing is constructed.

THE MECHANISM

Your breathing mechanism is illustrated in Figure 2-5. It consists of the following elements: the *nasal and oral cavities,* which provide

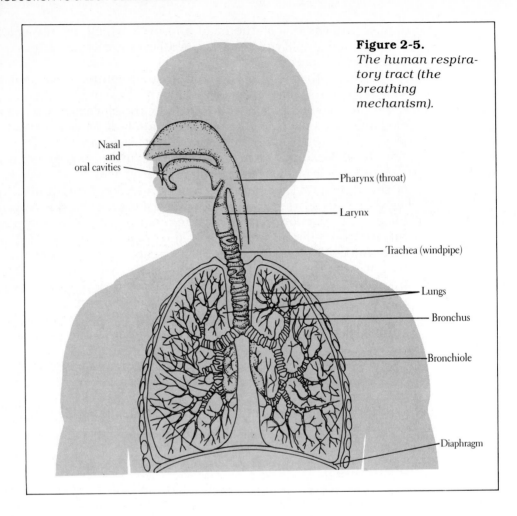

Figure 2-5.
The human respiratory tract (the breathing mechanism).

Nasal and oral cavities

Pharynx (throat)

Larynx

Trachea (windpipe)

Lungs

Bronchus

Bronchiole

Diaphragm

openings in your body that reach to the *pharynx* or throat. The pharynx leads to the *larynx*, which is the uppermost portion of the *trachea* or windpipe. The trachea then divides into smaller and smaller tubes that compose the *lungs.* Surrounding the lungs is a structural framework of bone, cartilage, and muscle (Figure 2-6).

The ultimate objective of breathing is to deliver fresh air to the lungs: to exchange oxygen for waste products (carbon dioxide) and to remove air after it has been used. We do this by increasing and decreasing the size of our lungs, taking advantage of a basic law of physics: air flows from high pressure to low pressure.

The lungs can't increase their size by themselves; they have no muscles. Instead, during inhalation, the muscles of the chest elevate and expand the chest walls, while the *diaphragm* contracts and flat-

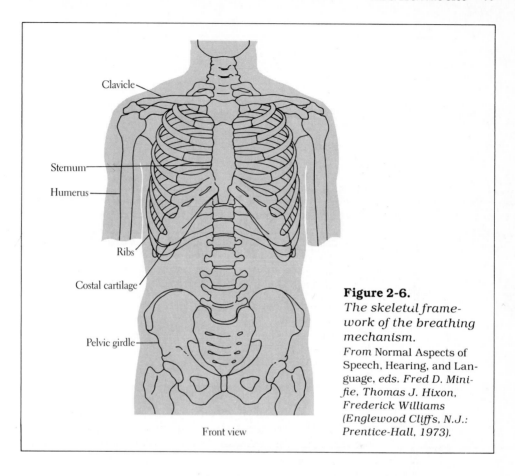

Clavicle

Sternum

Humerus

Ribs

Costal cartilage

Pelvic girdle

Front view

Figure 2-6.
The skeletal frame-work of the breathing mechanism.
From Normal Aspects of Speech, Hearing, and Language, *eds. Fred D. Mini-fie, Thomas J. Hixon, Frederick Williams (Englewood Cliffs, N.J.: Prentice-Hall, 1973).*

tens out. Look at Figure 2-7. This is a schematic diagram of the breathing mechanism during inhalation and exhalation. It shows how the vertical and horizontal dimensions of the chest increase during inhalation. You can verify this yourself. Place one hand lightly on your chest and the other on your abdomen. Breathe deeply in and out. You should feel expansion of both your chest and abdomen as air enters.

Why does the air come into your lungs? The answer is fairly simple. When you increase the dimensions around your lungs, you increase the volume of air the lungs can take; at the same time, you are lowering the air pressure in your lungs to slightly below the pressure of the air outside your body. Because there is an open passageway from your lungs to the outside (through your nose and mouth), air rushes in as a result of the lowered pressure in your lungs. The air will continue to enter the lungs until the pressure inside equals the pressure outside.

A difference in pressure is also the reason air leaves your lungs. When you compress your chest, the air pressure in your lungs becomes

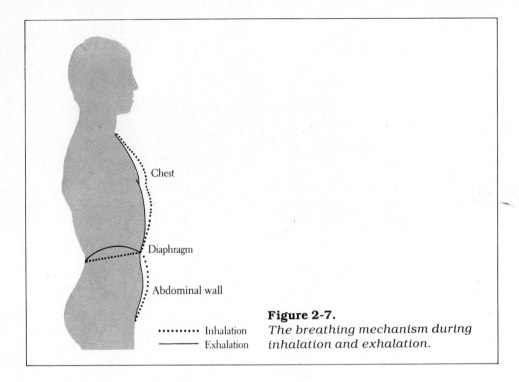

Chest

Diaphragm

Abdominal wall

Figure 2-7.

••••••••• Inhalation
———— Exhalation

The breathing mechanism during inhalation and exhalation.

slightly higher than that outside your body. So once again, air goes from an area of high pressure to an area of low pressure.

Let's review the process. Muscles of the chest lift and expand the chest walls. The diaphragm contracts, lowering the floor of the chest cavity. The lungs expand along with the chest walls, and their volume increases. As volume increases, pressure lowers, and air comes into the lungs. Now the chest walls contract, the diaphragm is pushed back up, and pressure in the lungs increases, causing air to leave. That's one complete cycle of breathing.

BREATHING FOR SPEECH

Quiet–rest breathing is a low-energy process of a regular nature. Few muscles are involved; the diaphragm does most of the work of inhalation, and muscle relaxation helps exhalation. Each cycle of breathing takes roughly as long as the next, and inhalation and exhalation time frames are also equal. Breathing for speech, however, is quite different. For that you take in the amount of air you need for the number of words you plan to say, and you take it in as quickly as possible. Then you try to be a miser with that air, using it as slowly and efficiently as possible, so that you don't run out of air while you're speaking. So

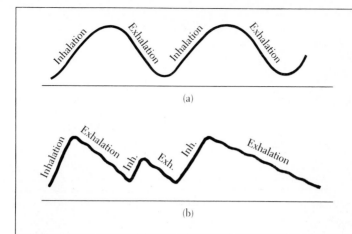

Figure 2-8.
Differences in (a) quiet–rest breathing and (b) breathing for speech. Notice that inhalation and exhalation are about equal in duration for quiet breathing, but that exhalation is much longer for speech breathing.

when you're breathing for speech, you depend on short inhalations and long, controlled exhalations (see Figure 2-8). We use slow, sustained contractions of the abdominal muscles for the major portion of breath control. We'll talk more about speech and breath control in Chapter 7.

We all know that the wind can move things. We also know that its energy can be harnessed to drive mechanical devices such as windmills. Well, that's what we do in speech; we harness the wind, in this case the breathstream, and set it to work in producing voice and speech sounds. We'll see how that happens when we discuss the next two processes.

Phonation

Very simply defined, phonation is the production of sound using the larynx. First, locate the larynx. Figure 2-9 shows the front and back views of the larynx. Now take the thumb and forefinger of one hand, and very gently pinch your "Adam's apple" (thyroid cartilage). With your forefinger, trace the outline of your thyroid cartilage. This cartilage forms the outside wall of the larynx. Look at Figure 2-10. There you see the vocal folds, two bands of tissue located inside the larynx.

The larynx functions very nicely as a valve. By contracting muscles within the larynx, you're able to move the vocal folds so that they come together, entirely closing off the larynx. Why would you want to do this? Primarily to keep food and other substances out of your lungs, but also to build up air pressure for coughing, to hold your breath, to exert strength such as in heavy lifting, and so on. Look at Figure 2-11a. It shows you an overhead view of the vocal folds and a frontal cross-

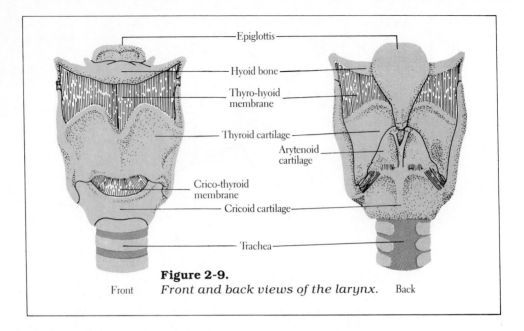

Figure 2-9.

Front   *Front and back views of the larynx.*   Back

section view of the larynx during phonation. Figure 2-11b shows the same views, but during quiet breathing.

SOUND PRODUCTION

We said earlier that a vibrating object and a force are needed to produce sound. Well, we've got both elements here; the breathstream provides

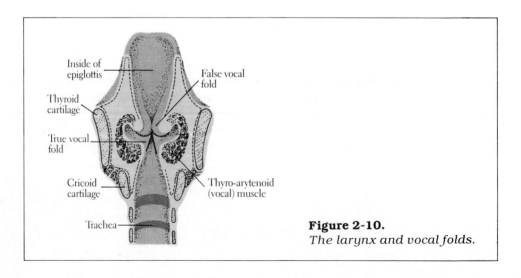

Figure 2-10.
The larynx and vocal folds.

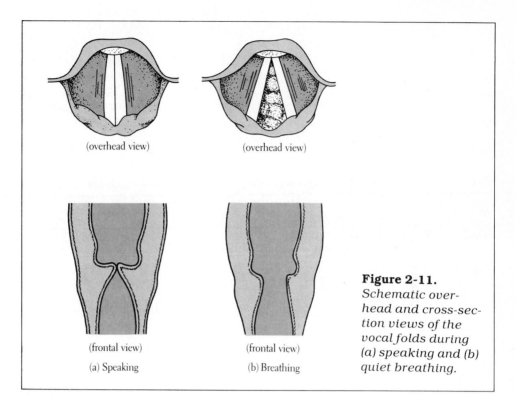

(overhead view)   (overhead view)

(frontal view)   (frontal view)

(a) Speaking   (b) Breathing

Figure 2-11.
Schematic over-head and cross-section views of the vocal folds during (a) speaking and (b) quiet breathing.

the force, and the vocal folds become the vibrating object. Here's how the process works:

1. Air is inhaled.
2. The vocal folds meet, completely closing the larynx and stopping the air flow.
3. The diaphragm and chest muscles relax; the abdominal muscles slowly contract.
4. Air pressure builds up below the vocal folds.
5. Air pressure increases until it overcomes the muscular forces holding the vocal folds closed.
6. Air escapes in very rapid bursts, creating waves of sound in the air above the vocal folds. After each burst, the air pressure decreases and the vocal folds close, causing the pressure to build up again. In this way, the cycle repeats.
7. You continue to hold the vocal folds closed and force air between them for as long as you want to phonate.

You can demonstrate this type of sound production in other ways. Blow up a balloon, then stretch the lips of the balloon tightly by pulling the sides of the tube away from each other. You should be able to produce a high-pitched buzz or whistle. Here's another way. Stick out your tongue, lay it on your lower lip, and hold it down with your upper lip. Now, blow air beneath your tongue! You've created what's known as a ''raspberry.'' Both it and the balloon whistle were created aerodynamically in the same way you create voice.

PITCH

We said earlier that the mass, length, and tension of a vibrating object determine the frequency of vibration. These same factors determine how rapidly your vocal folds vibrate, too.

First, let's consider the normal, usual pitch of your voice. That's determined primarily by the length of your vocal folds; the longer the vocal folds, the lower the pitch of your voice. That, along with the size and shape of the resonating cavities, accounts for people having differently pitched voices. It's also the reason why, in general, women's voices are higher than men's. Since you have no control over how long your vocal folds grow to be or over the basic size of your resonating cavities, you don't have much control over the frequency at which your vocal mechanism resonates most efficiently.

The second thing to consider is how you vary pitch to give speech the intonation patterns so necessary for meaning, as in the rising pitch at the end of many questions. Again, mass, length, and tension are the factors. Using the muscles of the larynx, including the vocal folds themselves, you vary the mass, length, and tension of the folds, and thereby change their frequency of vibration.

Resonance

A third way we vary pitch is through resonance. If you could listen to the sound of your voice *in* your larynx, you wouldn't recognize it as voice at all because, in the larynx, voice is only a buzzing noise. Something else has to happen to make that buzzing noise into recognizable voice. That ''something'' is resonance.

Resonance is the amplification and modification of sound by the cavities of the vocal tract. Those cavities are the larynx, pharynx, sinuses, oral cavity, and nasal cavity (see Figure 2-12). First, we will explain resonance in general, then resonance in the vocal tract. We'll also spend time on resonance in Chapter 7 when we discuss vocal quality.

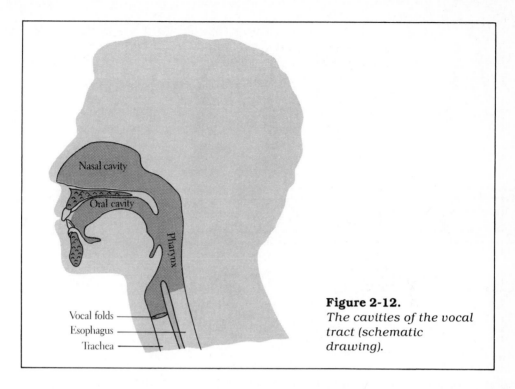

Figure 2-12.
The cavities of the vocal tract (schematic drawing).

Take an empty soda bottle. Blow across and into the neck so as to produce a low-pitched sound like a foghorn. Think for a minute about what happened; you got more sound out of that bottle than you put into it! That's right. All you did was send some air into the bottle (at just the right angle), and you got a deep, rich sound. You actually set the air inside the bottle vibrating, and the foghorn sound was produced, richer and louder than the sound you put in.

Now fill the bottle about a third of the way. Blow into it again. The sound you produce this time should be higher pitched. That's because the water takes up space and reduces the volume of air that can resonate. And, if you'll remember, smaller vibrating bodies usually vibrate more rapidly than larger ones. So the pitch of the sound you hear from the bottle varies with the amount of air in the bottle. Try it. Either add some water or take some out; the pitch of the sound will rise or fall. Incidentally, the shape of the resonator also affects the way it operates. As you change the volume of air in the bottle, you're also changing the shape of the resonating cavity. So the important thing about a resonator is its size and shape.

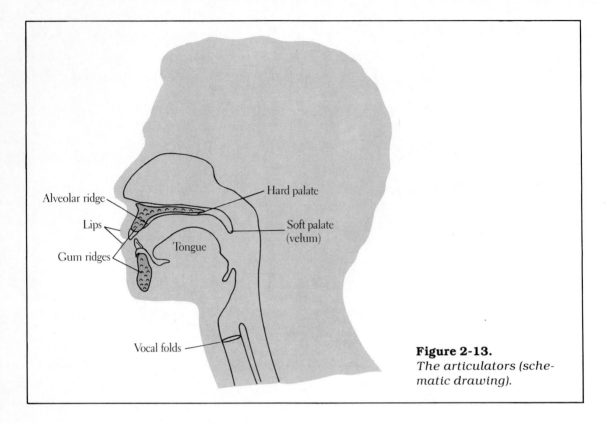

Alveolar ridge

Lips

Gum ridges

Tongue

Hard palate

Soft palate
(velum)

Vocal folds

Figure 2-13.
The articulators (schematic drawing).

RESONANCE IN THE VOCAL TRACT

The cavities in your head and neck are resonators; they're open chambers filled with air. They're actually very sophisticated resonators, for you can change their size and shape and, thereby, change the tones they resonate.

We use the vocal resonators to change the buzz of the vocal folds into voice. The resonators selectively amplify the buzz and not only make your voice louder but also give it its unique quality. You're using your resonators as though they were a series of bottles of various sizes and shapes.

We also use resonance in the production of the different consonant and vowel sounds. Most of that production occurs in the mouth and is called articulation.

Articulation

Articulation is the production of speech sounds as a result of movement of the structures of the vocal tract. Figure 2-13 shows the artic-

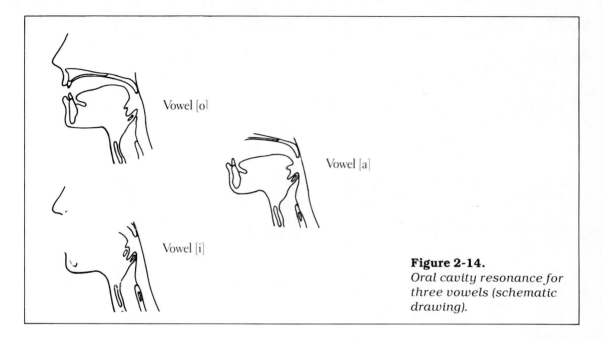

Figure 2-14.
Oral cavity resonance for three vowels (schematic drawing).

ulators. They are the tongue, teeth, lips, gum ridge, hard palate, soft palate, lower jaw, and the glottis (space between the vocal folds). We use the articulators to (1) change the size and shape of the mouth for resonating vowels and (2) produce the consonants by creating sounds. You'll learn more about consonants and vowels in Chapters 5 and 6, so we'll discuss their production only briefly here.

When you produce vowels, you take the vocal buzz and put it into a different sized and shaped "bottle" for each vowel. Try this: say *hee-haw*. You should be able to feel your mouth, which was almost closed for *hee*, opening wide for *haw*. By opening wider, you changed from a small resonating cavity to a large one. Look at Figure 2-14. Note that you vary your mouth's size and shape to produce different vowel sounds.

Consonants are an entirely different matter. Say the word *kick*. At the beginning and the end, you should feel your tongue pressing up to the soft palate, then exploding air. Try the word *pup*. With this word, you create the explosion with your lips. When producing consonants, then, the articulators are actually involved in sound production (see Figure 2-15), whereas they are not involved in producing vowel sounds.

Articulation is an amazing process. You make an incredible number of complicated movements just to produce a simple sentence. And what's more amazing, you're able to duplicate movements, returning time and time again to exactly the right spot.

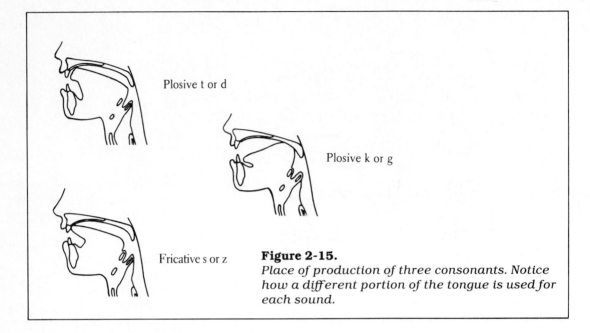

Plosive t or d

Plosive k or g

Fricative s or z

Figure 2-15.
Place of production of three consonants. Notice how a different portion of the tongue is used for each sound.

SUMMARY

We use six processes in producing speech sounds: audition, innervation, breathing, phonation, resonance, and articulation. Audition is the process of hearing (see Chapter 4). Innervation is the neural control of the speech and breathing mechanism. Breathing is the inhalation and exhalation of air and provides the force for sound production. Phonation is the production of vocal sound by the vocal folds. Resonance is the amplification and modification of sound using the cavities of the vocal tract. Articulation is the movement of the vocal tract structures to produce speech sounds.

SUGGESTED READINGS

Daniloff, R., Schuckers, G., and Feth, L. *The Physiology of Speech and Hearing: An Introduction.* Englewood Cliffs, N.J.: Prentice-Hall, Inc., 1980.

Minifie, F., Hixon, T., and Williams, F. (Eds.). *Normal Aspects of Speech, Hearing, and Language.* Englewood Cliffs, N.J.: Prentice-Hall, Inc., 1973.

Zemlin, W. *Speech and Hearing Science: Anatomy and Physiology,* 3d ed. Englewood Cliffs, N.J.: Prentice-Hall, Inc., 1988.

Chapter Three

The Sounds of American English

SPEECH COMES FIRST

Each of you now reading this book has been given a great and wondrous gift. It's a gift that has been given to only a very small fraction of all the people who have ever lived on this planet. In fact, only two-thirds of the people alive today have it. What is this gift? Literacy—the ability to read and write.

Literate people are fortunate in many ways; but when they begin to study speech, they are often placed at a disadvantage. They have been given, as Marshall McCluhan said, "an eye for an ear." In other words, literate people frequently confuse speech with writing. Illiterate people, on the other hand, know something that few literate people are aware of: *language is speech, and writing is only its reflection.*

Writing attempts to do what the tape recorder does, to capture and make available something that has been said (or thought) in another place and at another time. Of course, the tape recorder does a much better job.

Imagine that instead of reading the sentences on this page, you were listening to a tape recording of the authors speaking these sentences. You would hear many "things" that can't be put in print, things that make up the total spoken content of our words. You would hear qualities of voice as well as rate and emphasis. You could make fairly accurate guesses as to the age of the authors and their emotional states at the time. Certainly you would know whether the voice belonged to a male or female. But what do you know about the authors as a result of *reading* the words? Unless it is a description of him or her, what can you know of an author's age or sex from reading? Nothing! Because we strip speech of its qualities when we reduce talk to the medium of writing. Communication that began as something designed for our ears is, finally, transmitted to our eyes.

Sounds, Not Letters

There's a lot of confusion about writing and speech. Most people don't seem to be aware that letters and sounds are different in fundamental and important ways.

SPEECH AND WRITING CONFUSION

Most of us are unable to deal with words other than in writing, and it's hard to understand why. You probably wouldn't say that you had heard a picture or that you had seen music. Nor would you claim to smell a flavor or taste an aroma. But this confusion of the senses—*synesthesia*, it's called—affects most people in their beliefs about language. Somehow, they find it hard to grasp the fact that *speech consists of sounds that come out of your face* and *writing is marks you make with your hand.* It's because of this mix-up between visual and auditory reflections of language that many people believe speech consists of "saying letters." For example, if you say *thinkin'* or *goin'* in place of *thinking* or *going,* you are said to be "dropping the g." But you also know that the *l* of *almond,* the *t* of *listen,* and the *ch* of *yacht* are all "silent letters," so although you're not producing them, you're not dropping them, either. Or perhaps you've heard a person pronounce his name and later saw it spelled and wondered, "Why would he pronounce it *that* way when he spells it *this* way?" We really do depend on our eyes to translate what we hear with our ears.

Why do we have these mix-ups between the auditory and the visual? Mainly because the system that educated us supports the belief that talking is subordinate to writing. The reason for that belief is inherent in the long, arduous, and formal process by which we learn to write as compared to the casual, easy, and seemingly automatic way we learn to speak. Think about it. Someone had to teach you how to write; years and years of study, great feats of memorization, hours upon hours of practice, and most of this occurring within the atmosphere of the classroom. Did anyone teach you how to speak your native language? Or did your speech develop without the classroom, without books, without exams, without conscious learning? That's why you use the written word as the point of reference for the spoken; you have been taught to depend on letters instead of sounds.

THE PROBLEM WITH LETTERS

The difference between sounds and letters is a fundamental one and is really indispensable to you if you want to understand spoken language. Writing is a passive medium. It reflects what we say in a subtle and mysterious way. The written word *cat* is a good example of this, It is composed of a series of marks—*c*, *a*, and *t*—that allow us to recapture the utterance *cat*. But the marks are not the same as the utterance. When we say aloud the word *cat*, we produce speech sounds by movements of structures within the head, throat, and chest. Our spelling of the word *cat* cannot reflect those movements with any great degree of direct correspondence.

ENGLISH SPELLING AND ENGLISH SPEECH

The alphabet we use today was first used about 1,300 years ago. When it was new, it accurately reflected the patterns of speech because it adhered to the underlying principle of all alphabets. This principle has two conditions: (1) each written symbol will represent one spoken sound; (2) no spoken sound shall be represented by more than one symbol. In other words, there should be one, and only one, symbol for every sound in the language.

Today the situation is, to put it mildly, not quite what it was. English spelling no longer accurately reflects English speech sounds. The reason is, speech is dynamic, personal, and transitory while writing is static, institutionalized, and permanent. Language changes over time, but writing is frozen. The written language you learned was going out of date 1,000 years ago!

How many English languages are there? If you're talking about *written* languages, the answer is one. (With the exception of a few minor spelling differences—color/colour, for example—every English writer uses exactly the same symbols in exactly the same way.) If you're talking about spoken English languages, the answer is thousands! Does an English speaker from Boston speak the same way as someone from New York City? Does someone from Atlanta sound the same as someone from San Francisco? On hearing them, would you mistake the words of a native of Trinidad for the words of someone born and raised in Quebec? Speakers all over the world write English in essentially the same way, but their letters would give you no clue as to the way they sound.

At this point in time, English has strayed so far from the alphabetic principle that it's a miracle we can pronounce from spelling at all. For example, George Bernard Shaw's often quoted spelling of "fish" as *ghoti*, with the *f* from enou*gh*, the *i* from w*o*men, and the *sh* from na*ti*on. Or how about this: take the *mn* from autu*mn*, the *ai* from pl*ai*d, and the *c* from *c*ello and you can write *mnaic* for "match." Try another. Take the *k* of *k*iss, the a-sound of m*e*ringue, and the t-sound of de*bt* for an unusual spelling of "cat": *kibt*.

We could give you lots more examples, but we've made our point: there is enough duplication and overlap in our spelling to allow any word to have more than one "logical" pronunciation. And that gives us, in this speech class, a problem.

You're going to be spending a lot of time talking about speech sounds. But because of the inadequacies of English spelling, you don't have any accurate means of taking notes in such a way that your notes can tell you about sounds. Here's an example: The vowel sound in the word *do* is also in all the following spellings: *ewe, beauty, crew, shoe, cool, group, rude, fruit, true, rheumatism,* and *Sioux!* At the same time, the letter "e" has all of the following pronunciations: *pet, few, sew, eye, women, mete, serve, sergeant,* and *Jones!* You may know what you mean at the time you write your notes, but what about hours later? Do you think you'll remember which sound you meant when you wrote, "Work on 'e' tonight"?

I.P.A.

Fortunately, we do have a tool that will help us out of our dilemma: the International Phonetic Alphabet (I.P.A.). This alphabet (*not* a language) was designed about one hundred years ago for the purpose of writing down the sounds of a language. I.P.A. is international, meaning it can be applied to any language; it is phonetic, meaning it is based on observed speech sounds; it is an alphabet, meaning it adheres without exception to the alphabetic principle of one sound per symbol. Although you may not have heard of I.P.A. until now, it is in widespread use today by people who wish to accurately record spoken language. In addition to linguists, I.P.A. is used extensively by actors, radio and TV announcers, speech pathologists, teachers, and anthropologists.

I.P.A. can be very useful to you as you learn more about speech. First, by learning the I.P.A. symbols, you will be learning to distinguish all the sounds of spoken English. In other words, we'll use I.P.A. as an ear training tool. Second, as you become familiar with I.P.A., you'll begin to associate the symbols with actual movements of the speech mechanism, which will reinforce the sounds as you learn them. Third, I.P.A. solves the problems created by English spelling; it provides us with a common framework for understanding speech sound variations.

I.P.A. Transcription

When you write something in I.P.A. you have *transcribed* it. If you are new to I.P.A. you may be tempted to regard transcription as merely being a weird version of English spelling, and you may spend your time trying to find equivalents between written English spelling and this new, unfamiliar alphabet. If you do that, you're trying to move from one written form to another without the intervening awareness of the *sounds* of speech. This practice will only slow down your learning of I.P.A. Remember, you only use I.P.A. symbols to record speech; it is not for writing.

To help distinguish between I.P.A. transcription and traditional English spelling, I.P.A. symbols are always enclosed in brackets. For example, *k* is the eleventh letter of the English alphabet, but [k] is the I.P.A. symbol used in transcribing the first sound in the English words *king, queen, cool,* and *choir* and the last sound in *rock* and *antique.*

Mostly I.P.A. uses the familiar symbols derived from the Latin-origin alphabets, including English, in use in western European languages. But even if the symbols look familiar to you, don't confuse them with the English letters whose names you've known for years.

The list of symbols shown in Table 3-1, given with key words and dictionary symbols, is completely adequate to transcribe just about any utterance spoken in American English and show accurately the phonetic (sound) content of that utterance. You'll also find practice materials at the end of this chapter that will help you learn phonetic transcription.

The Phoneme

Each of the I.P.A. symbols represents one *phoneme* of American English. A phoneme, though, is not exactly one sound. Instead, it is better described as a *sound family.* Let's look at it this way: the word *dog* refers to a type of animal that includes many different subtypes ranging from Great Danes to Chihuahuas with all sorts of dogs in between. The word *dog,* although it doesn't tell you exactly what kind of dog, fits any type in the dog family. Well, we have sound families, too. Take the phoneme [k], for example. It doesn't sound exactly the same in *cape* as it does in *scrape,* but it's still in the family of [k].

Table 3-1. The Phonemes of American English (I.P.A. Alphabet)

Phonetic Symbol	(I.P.A.) Dictionary Symbol	Key Words	Description
p	p	pat-pen-Paul	voiceless bilabial plosive
b	b	boat-bad-buy	voiced bilabial plosive
t	t	top-tea-ten	voiceless lingua-alveolar plosive
d	d	dog-day-duck	voiced lingua-alveolar plosive
k	k	key-kick-cake	voiceless lingua-velar plosive
g	g	go-game-guess	voiced lingua-velar plosive
f	f	four-feel-phone	voiceless labio-dental fricative
v	v	very-vine-vat	voiced labio-dental fricative
θ	th	thin-thick-thanks	voiceless lingua-dental fricative
ð	th, th, th	the-those-them	voiced lingua-dental fricative
s	s	snake-see-sue	voiceless lingua-alveolar fricative
z	z	zoo-zap-zip	voiced lingua-alveolar fricative
ʃ	sh	she-shoe-shore	voiceless lingua-palatal fricative
ʒ	zh	beige-pleasure	voiced lingua-palatal fricative
h	h	hot-hat-head	voiceless glottal fricative
ʍ	hw	where-which-why	voiceless bilabial glide
w	w	wet-wear-weather	voiced bilabial glide
r	r	red-roses-right	voiced lingua-alveolar glide
j	y	yes-yellow-young	voiced lingua-palatal glide
l	l	left-loose-lick	voiced lingua-alveolar lateral
m	m	man-me-mitt	voiced bilabial nasal
n	n	no-knee-north	voiced lingua-alveolar nasal
ŋ	ng	sing-hang-king	voiced lingua-velar nasal
tʃ	ch	chair-cheat-choke	voiceless lingua-alveolo/palatal affricate
dʒ	j	judge-Jane-jump	voiced lingua-alveolo/palatal affricate
i	ē	see-east-free	high front tense vowel
ɪ	ĭ	sit-in-pit	high front lax vowel
e	ā	ate-pay-able	mid front tense vowel
ɛ	ĕ	bet-bed-end	mid front lax vowel
æ	ă	pat-flat-Adam	low front tense vowel
a	ā	ask (Boston "a")	low front lax vowel
ɑ	a	calm-honest-car	low back lax vowel
ɒ	a	hot (British "a")	low back tense vowel
ɔ	ô	awful-often-all	mid back lax vowel
o	ō	so-open-hotel	mid back tense vowel
ʊ	oo	book-push-wood	high back lax vowel
u	oo	too-pool-food	high back tense vowel

(continued on next page)

Table 3-1.   (Continued)

Phonetic Symbol	(I.P.A.) Dictionary Symbol	Key Words	Description
ʌ	ŭ	up-uncle-usher	low mid stressed vowel
ə	ə	banana-sofa-about	low mid unstressed vowel
ɝ (ɜ)	ur	early-urn-pearl	mid central stressed vowel with retroflexion
ɚ	ər	father-perhaps	low mid unstressed vowel with retroflexion
aɪ	i	ice-light-time	diphthong—low front to high front
aʊ	ou	how-out-ouch	diphthong—low front to high back
ɔɪ	oi	coin-boy-oyster	diphthong—low back to high front
eɪ	ā	game-daze-rain	diphthong—mid front to high front
oʊ	ō	road-home-doze	dipthong—mid back to high back
iɚ-ɪə	ēr	ear-here-peer	diphthong—high front to low mid unstressed with or without retroflexion
ɛɚ-ɛə	âr	air-pare-where	diphthong—mid front to low mid unstressed with or without retroflexion
aɚ-aə	är	are-car-barn	diphthong—low back to low mid unstressed with or without retroflexion
ɔɚ-ɔə	ôr	or-door-shore	diphthong—mid back to low mid unstressed with or without retroflexion
uɚ-ɔə	o͝or	tour-poor-sure	diphthong—high back to low mid unstressed with or without retroflexion

THE ALLOPHONE

Say the following sentence aloud: *I can open a can of beans.* Now say it again, and this time listen to the two utterances of the word *can*. The vowel seems to change slightly, doesn't it? Now reverse the *cans*, saying the noun as if it were the verb. It may sound strange to you, but it doesn't change the meaning. That's because both those sounds are *allophones* of the phoneme [æ]. An allophone is a *variation of a phoneme.* You can hear that it's slightly different, but not different enough that you would call it another phoneme. So remember, even though we say we're using one sound per symbol, each I.P.A. symbol really represents a family of sounds that are so similar, it's hard to hear the differences among them.

Phonetics and Phonemics

The difference between phonetics and phonemics is like the difference between a musical performance and its underlying musical score. A composition may be played by a string quartet, or played by a sixty-piece orchestra, or whistled by one person. Take the case of one composition performed in two ways: first played by the Beatles, and second, delivered to your captive ears as elevator music. You know that these performances share a specific and precise pattern (the melody), but you also know that they are very different as physical events.

Similarly, with speech, the sounds we utter (phonetics) are realizations of underlying sound categories (phonemics) that exist in the minds of speakers and listeners who share a common language.

We use a modified phonemic approach in this text. That is, we emphasize phonemic distinctions, and look at phonetic differences wherever we think a closer examination of articulatory events would be helpful.

Dialects and Standard Speech

Up to now we've been talking as though there were but one spoken American English. But you know from your own experience that there are varieties, or *dialects*, spoken across the nation.

DIALECTS

A dialect is a variation of a language; it is spoken by a subgroup of speakers. This subgroup differs geographically or socially or ethnically, and so on, from the rest of the speakers of the language. The dialect can differ in pronunciation, vocabulary, and grammar. For example, how do you say *Florida?* Do you use the vowel in *oar* or the vowel in *are?* Do you call the paper container you use for groceries a *sack* or a *bag?* Do you say "I be going" or "I am going"? These are just a few examples of dialectical differences.

REGIONAL DIALECTS

Linguists generally identify four large geographical areas within the United States that have definable regional dialects. These regional dialects are *Eastern, New England, Southern,* and *General American.* In addition, many linguists recognize a major dialect within the Eastern region: *New York Metropolitan.*

STANDARD SPEECH

Is there any one standard way to speak American English? Any one standard dialect that doesn't vary across the country? Is any one regional dialect preferable to another? We don't think so. When the authors speak of "standard," we refer to the speech of one of the major regional dialects that we listed above. Within that region, we view the standard as the following: *Standard speech describes the language of the majority of the educated people in the region.* You can find a listing of the significant phonetic features of the major regional dialects in Appendix D.

NONSTANDARD

If you live in Massachusetts and say the word *greasy* so that it rhymes with *fleecy,* your production would be considered standard. Should you use the same pronunciation in North Carolina, your production would be *non*standard. Why? Because in North Carolina, most people say *greasy* so that it rhymes with *breezy.* So what's standard in one place may not be standard in another. And what's standard for one social subgroup may be nonstandard in another.

Notice that when we say "nonstandard," we simply mean "different." We don't believe that any region has a "better" dialect than another region. Is there any advantage to speaking "standard" for an area? We think so. It has to do with the way listeners may judge you simply by the way you speak. The standard of an area usually carries more prestige for the speaker simply because it reflects the way the well-educated speak. It also provides a more formal way of speaking that is probably more versatile than the way you speak with your family and friends.

FOREIGN ACCENTS

If you've learned a second language, chances are you learned to speak it not like a native but, rather, with an accent that reflected your first language. For example, if your first language is American English, you learned to speak Spanish, say, with an American accent. Conversely, if your first language is Spanish, you probably speak English in a way that indicates that fact to your listeners. Why do these accents exist? They come about as a result of the phonemic differences between languages. Let's use English and Spanish as examples. In English, the words *seat* and *sit* are pronounced with two very distinct phonemes, [i] and [ɪ]. Very distinct, that is, to someone whose native language contains those sounds. Since Spanish does *not* have the [ɪ] of sit, the native

Spanish speaker doesn't hear that there are two separate sounds produced, and he says, "I will seat down on the seat." *Sit* and *seat* probably sound the same to him; the difference must be taught.

CLASSIFICATION OF SOUNDS

Take a look at Table 3-1. You'll see that the phonemes of our language have been placed in three general categories: *consonants, vowels,* and *diphthongs.* Each category differs from the others in the way its sounds are produced, particularly in the way the articulators modify the breathstream. Let's examine them individually.

Consonants

The consonant sounds are produced when the articulators obstruct the breathstream either completely or partially. Make the first sound in the word *kiss.* You produce it by holding the back of the tongue firmly against the soft palate, which shuts off the breathstream completely. Then you build up air pressure and suddenly explode the air past the point of obstruction. The last sound in *kiss,* though, only needs a partial obstruction. You force the breathstream through the narrow opening between your tongue and teeth, making a hissing sound.

Classification of Consonants

We classify the consonant sounds according to three factors: *voicing, place of articulation,* and *method of articulation* (see Table 3-2).

VOICING

If you produce voice at the same time that you produce a consonant sound, the consonant is said to be *voiced.* If there is no voice with the consonant, it is *voiceless.* The difference is usually fairly easy to hear, but if you have trouble telling if a consonant is voiced or voiceless, try this: gently rest your fingers on either side of your thyroid cartilage (Adam's apple) and hum. You should be able to feel vibrations with your fingertips. Now say the first sound in the word *vat.* Again, there should be vibrations. Now say the first sound in the word *fat.* You shouldn't feel vibrations because the word *fat* begins with a voiceless sound.

Table 3-2. Consonants: Method of Articulation

Place of Articulation	Plosives		Fricatives		Nasals		Glides		Lateral		Affricates	
	vs	*v*	*vs*	*v*	*vs*	*v*	*vs*	*v*	*vs*	*v*	*vs*	*v*
Bilabial (both lips)	p	b				m	ʍ	w				
Labio-dental (lip-teeth)			f	v								
Lingua-dental (tongue-teeth)			θ	ð								
Lingua-alveolar (tongue-gum ridge)	t	d	s	z		n		r		l		
Lingua-alveolo/palatal (tongue-gum ridge/palate)											tʃ	dʒ
Lingua-palatal (tongue-palate)			ʃ	ʒ				j				
Lingua-velar (tongue-soft palate)	k	g				ŋ						
Glottal (vocal folds)			h									

Look at Table 3-2. You'll see that a number of the consonant sounds are in pairs on the chart. We call these pairs *cognates.* Cognate sounds are sounds produced in the same place, in the same way, using the same articulators: the only difference is one sound is voiced, the other is voiceless.

PLACE OF ARTICULATION

The point at which we obstruct the breathstream is an important factor in consonant classification. To identify the physical place of articulation, we use the names of the articulators involved. Look again at Table 3-2. The places of articulation of the various consonants are listed down the left side of the chart. The listings are (1) bilabial (both lips); (2) labio–dental (lip–teeth); (3) lingua–dental (tongue–teeth); (4) lingua–alveolar (tongue–gum ridge); (5) lingua-alveolo/palatal (tongue-gum ridge/palate); (6) lingua–palatal (tongue–palate); (7) lingua–velar (tongue–soft palate); (8) glottal (the space between the vocal folds). The first sound in the word *pet,* for example, is a bilabial sound—you make it with both lips.

METHOD OF ARTICULATION

Method of articulation means the physical process used to produce the sound. The various methods of articulation are listed from left to right in Table 3-2. Let's take the time now to explain each method briefly.

1. *Plosives* are sounds you make by blocking off the breathstream entirely for a very short period of time, just long enough to build up some air pressure behind your articulators. You then suddenly "explode" this air to produce the sound. The first sound in *pet* is plosive.
2. *Fricatives* differ from plosives in that you don't have to block off the breathstream as completely. All you need is a very narrow opening through which you can squeeze some air. The first sound in the word *see* is a fricative.
3. *Glides* are consonant sounds you make while you're moving your articulators from one position to another. You can hear and feel the motion. The first sound in the word *yes* is a glide. Say it slowly to feel the gliding motion.
4. *Nasals* are just as the name suggests. You produce the nasals by lowering the soft palate and blocking the oral cavity with the lips or the tongue. You then let the air go out the nostrils. The first and last sounds in the word *man* are nasals.
5. *Lateral* sounds (English has only one) are produced by dropping the sides of the tongue and allowing the air to leave by the sides of the mouth. The first and last sounds in the word *lull* are laterals.
6. *Affricates* are really consonant combinations. The two English affricates are formed by joining together a voiceless plosive with a voiceless fricative, and a voiced plosive with a voiced fricative. The first and last sounds in the word *charge* are affricates.

You'll learn the method of articulation in more detail when you read Chapters 5 and 6 on consonants and vowels.

Vowels

What are the vowels of spoken English? Your first impulse is probably to say that the vowels are "a, e, i, o, u, and sometimes y." Wrong! Those are, unfortunately, the vowels of *written* English. We don't name the vowels of spoken English to separate them from the consonants; instead, we define them by how they are produced. *The vowels of spoken English are speech sounds produced without obstruction of the breathstream by the articulators.* Here's an example: open wide and say *ahhh*. You'll notice that the breathstream is not blocked at all.

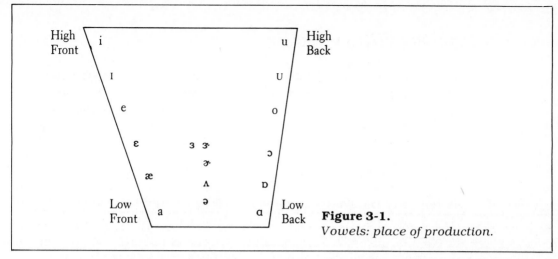

Figure 3-1.
Vowels: place of production.

*WORDS FOR PHONETIC TRANSCRIPTION PRACTICE   See the text reference on page
42. Transcribe the following words in I.P.A. The answers are on page 43.*

Level 1		*Level 2*		*Level 3*	
1 pat	[_____]	26 judge	[_____]	51 machines	[_____]
2 boat	[_____]	27 bother	[_____]	52 shouted	[_____]
3 flat	[_____]	28 wheel	[_____]	53 relative	[_____]
4 rope	[_____]	29 embassy	[_____]	54 Chicago	[_____]
5 two	[_____]	30 yellow	[_____]	55 oyster	[_____]
6 east	[_____]	31 tire	[_____]	56 boiler	[_____]
7 room	[_____]	32 laughing	[_____]	57 English	[_____]
8 dog *	[_____]	33 friend	[_____]	58 laundry*	[_____]
9 fed	[_____]	34 thumb	[_____]	59 downtown	[_____]
10 snake	[_____]	35 pens	[_____]	60 calm	[_____]
11 grass	[_____]	36 cage	[_____]	61 burgers	[_____]
12 phone	[_____]	37 vision	[_____]	62 early	[_____]
13 thought*	[_____]	38 beige	[_____]	63 arrive	[_____]
14 this	[_____]	39 cruise	[_____]	64 rather	[_____]
15 think	[_____]	40 prank	[_____]	65 under	[_____]
16 awful*	[_____]	41 shops	[_____]	66 church	[_____]
17 raise	[_____]	42 street	[_____]	67 jumbo jet	[_____]
18 book	[_____]	43 pains	[_____]	68 exit	[_____]
19 cheap	[_____]	44 cute	[_____]	69 Olympics	[_____]
20 lunch	[_____]	45 broad*	[_____]	70 crime	[_____]
21 sell	[_____]	46 track	[_____]	71 prizes	[_____]
22 plane	[_____]	47 painting	[_____]	72 computer	[_____]
23 roll	[_____]	48 fools	[_____]	73 magazines	[_____]
24 easy	[_____]	49 desks	[_____]	74 carwax	[_____]
25 table	[_____]	50 strong*	[_____]	75 flounders	[_____]

*See notes on regional occurence of [ɔ], page 216.

Classification of Vowels

We'll also use three factors to classify the vowels. They are *height of the tongue, the place of production,* and *muscle tension.* Let's briefly explain each one, and you can look at the vowel chart (Figure 3-1) as we go along.

HEIGHT OF THE TONGUE

You raise your tongue to different heights to create different vowel sounds. Say the words *see* and *saw.* You should be able to feel your mouth opening for the word *saw.* That's because *saw* has a lower tongue position than *see.*

PLACE OF PRODUCTION

''Place'' really refers to the part of the tongue primarily responsible for producing a particular vowel—the front, middle, or back. The vowel in *see* is made with the front of the tongue; the vowel in *saw* is produced with the back of the tongue.

MUSCLE TENSION

The tension of the tongue muscles also affects vowel production. Try this: place the thumb and forefinger of one hand lightly on your neck above the larynx. Swallow. You should be able to feel muscle contractions. Keeping your fingers in the same place, say the words *see* and *sit.* The vowel in *see* is tense, so you can probably feel the tongue muscles contracting. The vowel in *sit* is lax (no tension) so you won't feel the muscles contracting as much.

DIPHTHONGS

A diphthong is a *vowel blend;* two vowels are blended together and said in such a way that the sound begins with one vowel and ends with the other. You use a smooth, gliding motion, and although two vowels are used, the resulting diphthong is perceived as one sound. The sound that follows the initial consonant in the word *time* is an example of a diphthong.

Phonetic Transcription

Now it's time for you to begin practicing phonetic transcription. At the beginning you'll frequently feel frustrated; it will take a while for you

ANSWERS FOR PRACTICE TRANSCRIPTION The I.P.A. transcription that follows represents STANDARD pronounciations. Check with your instructor for regional variations.*

Level 1

1 pat	[pæt]
2 boat	[bot]
3 flat	[flæt]
4 rope	[rop]
5 two	[tu]
6 east	[ist]
7 room	[rum]
8 dog*	[dɔg]
9 fed	[fɛd]
10 snake	[snek]
11 grass	[græs]
12 phone	[fon]
13 thought*	[θɔt]
14 this	[ðɪs]
15 think	[θɪŋk]
16 awful*	[ɔful]
17 raise	[rez]
18 book	[buk]
19 cheap	[tʃip]
20 lunch	[lʌntʃ]
21 sell	[sɛl]
22 plane	[plen]
23 roll	[rol]
24 easy	[izi]
25 table	[tebl]

Level 2

26 judge	[dʒʌdʒ]
27 bother	[baðɚ]
28 wheel	[ʍil]
29 embassy	[ɛmbəsi]
30 yellow	[jɛlo]
31 tire	[taɪɚ]
32 laughing	[læfɪŋ]
33 friend	[frɛnd]
34 thumb	[θʌm]
35 pens	[pɛnz]
36 cage	[keɪdʒ]
37 vision	[vɪʒn]
38 beige	[beɪʒ]
39 cruise	[kruz]
40 prank	[præŋk]
41 shops	[ʃaps]
42 street	[strit]
43 pains	[peɪnz]
44 cute	[kjut]
45 broad*	[brɔd]
46 track	[træk]
47 painting	[pentɪŋ]
48 fools	[fulz]
49 desks	[dɛsks]
50 strong*	[strɔŋ]

Level 3

51 machines	[məʃinz]
52 shouted	[ʃautəd]
53 relative	[rɛlətɪv]
54 Chicago	[ʃɪkago]
55 oyster	[ɔɪstɚ]
56 boiler	[bɔɪlɚ]
57 English	[ɪŋglɪʃ]
58 laundry*	[lɔndri]
59 downtown	[dauntaun]
60 calm	[kam]
61 burgers	[bɝgɚz]
62 early	[ɝli]
63 arrive	[əraɪv]
64 rather	[ræðɚ]
65 under	[ʌndɚ]
66 church	[tʃɝtʃ]
67 jumbo jet	[dʒʌmbodʒɛt]
68 exit	[ɛksɪt]
69 Olympics	[əlɪmpəkʃ]
70 crime	[kraɪm]
71 prizes	[praɪzəz]
72 computer	[kəmpjutɚ]
73 magazines	[mægəzinz]
74 carwax	[kaaɚwæks]
75 flounders	[flaundɚz]

*See notes on regional occurence of [ɔ], page 216.

to train yourself to hear the fine differences between sounds and to stop thinking of sounds as being letters. After all, you never had to do it before. Start with the basic transcription list on page 41. Have someone read the words aloud to you, or listen to a tape recording. Transcribe what you actually hear, not what you think *should* be said. Don't write what you hear in English spelling; you'll only confuse the visual and auditory inputs. When you're ready, move on to short phrases and simple sentences and, finally, complex sentences and longer utterances.

Part Two

DICTION

IMPROVING VOICE AND DICTION

We'd like to say a few things that are meant to help you get the most out of this part of the book. In this extremely important section, you get a chance to put theory into practical application in your own speech.

Chapter 4 is the shortest chapter in the book, but it might just be one of the most important. It covers material that will save you time and effort as well as increase your chances of success. The first part of the chapter outlines a routine to follow. The second part will help you distinguish between accurate and inaccurate productions of sounds. The third part gives you a set of warm-up exercises to follow before you practice. You'll make faster progress if you take the time to read this chapter and try the warm-ups before working on any of the sounds in Chapters 5 and 6.

Chapters 5 and 6 present the individual sounds of American English using a systematic approach to improving diction. You'll find specific instructions on how to use these chapters in the how-to section of Chapter 4.

Chapter Four

Improving Voice and Diction: The Basics

We've all seen televised competitions where world-class skaters, gymnasts, or divers perform incredibly complicated and dangerous routines. Have you ever wondered how they are able to perform the same exact sequence of moves, time after time, with almost no variation? Sure, they make mistakes, but few and far between. Have you also ever wondered what goes into perfecting such routines? One thing is certain; athletes don't start with the finished product. They build their routines move by move, starting with the simplest. After they master simple moves, they add more complex and difficult moves, while still practicing the first. By the time athletes are ready for serious competition, their routines are second-nature to them.

To a certain extent, improving diction is a little like learning a complicated gymnastic routine. When you are successful, you have mastered a complicated routine, one that requires fine auditory discrimination and precise muscular control, and you perform it spontaneously. You achieve success in much the same way as the gymnast. First you master the simplest moves, and then you increase the level of difficulty and complexity until you have mastered your target sound.

That's the way, too, that we present exercises on the individual sounds of American English in Chapters 5 and 6: by level of difficulty. Each section starts with a sample sentence, typical spellings, a description of the sound, and, in many cases, drills to help you to produce the sound accurately. Then come drills on single words under headings that indicate where in the word the target sound is located. The word level is followed by the phrase, the sentence, and longer connected speech levels. Level 1 drills contain the target sound in contexts that are fairly easy to produce. Level 2 drills present the sound in slightly more difficult sound contexts. Don't start Level 2 drills until you are sure you have mastered Level 1. Level 3 drills are more difficult, usually dealing with troublesome sound combinations and contrasts. You absolutely should not try Level 3 until you have mastered Level 2. The most difficult level we call the "Challenge" level. At this level, exercises contain the target sounds in quantities and combinations that may be extremely troublesome. The Challenge sections are the only places you'll find "tongue-twisters." We've minimized the use of tongue-twisters because we believe that they cause more people to fail than to succeed.

How to Do It

Unless your instructor specifies a different procedure, we recommend that you use the following routine for working on sounds you may have difficulty articulating correctly.

1. FOLLOW THE EAR TRAINING GUIDE PRESENTED ON PAGE 49.You'll find that having a clear, accurate auditory perception of the sound is an essential first step in mastering the production of that sound.
2. TRY PRODUCING THE SOUND BY ITSELF. Have someone check your production. Once you are able to produce the sound consistently correctly, go on to the drill words.
3. TRY THE SOUND IN SINGLE WORDS. Take your time with each word. Listen carefully, and don't go on until you're satisfied that you've said the word correctly.
4. TRY THE SOUND IN PHRASES AND SENTENCES. Again, take your time. You're not trying to be perfectly accurate the first time around. And, it's okay to exaggerate the sound in practice; not all of what you do in practice will come out in conversational speech.
5. BECOME AWARE OF THE POSITION AND MOVEMENTS OF YOUR ARTICULATORS. As you are working on Step 2, try to experience the feeling of what is happening to your tongue, your lips, your hard and soft palates. This can be helpful in stabilizing the correct production of the sound.

    You'll probably find it helpful to monitor yourself visually with the aid of a mirror, particularly when you're working on the sounds produced at the front of the mouth. You may want to buy a small compact or shaving mirror to use in practice and to take to class with you.

6. DON'T BE DISCOURAGED. Remember, you may be trying to change habit patterns of long standing, so there's a good chance that your first efforts won't be immediately successful. Frequent practice is often necessary to achieve the results you're after.

7. PRACTICE FOR A SHORT PERIOD EVERY DAY. Twenty minutes a day, *every day.* You won't tire as easily, and you won't forget as much between practice sessions.

8. GATHER YOUR OWN PRACTICE MATERIALS. Make word lists from the words *you* use every day. Read articles from newspapers and magazines or dialogues from plays. The idea is to become proficient in contexts that are usable to you.

9. USE APPENDIX B FOR ADDITIONAL HELP. In Appendix B you'll find procedures outlining more ways to correct misarticulations of some of the more difficult sounds. If you are working on any of those, be sure to refer to these procedures. They will probably help you work more efficiently and effectively.

Ear Training

Speech pathologists tell the apocryphal story of the mother who was trying to correct her child's pronunciation of the word *soap.* It seems that the child was saying, *thoap.* The mother said to the child, "The word is *soap,* not *thoap.* Now say, *ssss.*" And the child did. "Say it again," said the mother, "say *ssss - ssss - ssss.*" Of course the child said it, perfectly. "Now say, *soap.*" And the child said, *"thoap."*

Like that child, you and I have an auditory image of how each word we say should sound. And when you customarily say a word and misarticulate a sound or sounds in that word, you hear your own pronunciation as being correct. The way you pronounce your words and articulate your sounds becomes the comfortable, familiar, and "right" way. You may not notice that your production of a sound is different from the way others pronounce that sound.

When you change the way you articulate a sound from an incorrect to a correct production, it is important to monitor the way you make that sound until you are able to make it correctly without consciously trying. It is therefore important that you learn to discriminate, auditorially, between your accurate and inaccurate productions of that sound. We call the process of learning to discriminate accurately *speech discrimination* or *ear training.*

Here are a few simple rules to follow that will make the process of ear training as effective and worthwhile as possible:

1. **Work with someone,** possibly a partner from your speech class, who pronounces your sounds correctly.
2. Your partner should use normal voice, but also **your partner should always keep his or her mouth covered in some way.** That's so you won't be getting visual cues.
3. **Always go from an easier performance task to a more difficult task.** Ear training performance tasks range from easy to difficult in the following categories:

RECOGNITION

1. Train your ear to recognize whether the target sound occurs in a word spoken by the partner.
2. Train your ear to recognize *where* the target sound is in a word (beginning, middle, end) when spoken by the partner.

DISCRIMINATION

1. Train your ear to distinguish between correct and incorrect productions of the target sound as produced by your partner in random order, and be able to point out and distinguish the correct from the incorrect version.
2. Train your ear to distinguish between correct and incorrect productions, but with the target sound at the beginning, then the end, then the middle of nonsense syllables.
3. Train your ear to distinguish between correct and incorrect productions, but with the target sound occurring at the beginning, end, and then middle of actual words.
   Example A: Your partner says, "I'm going to say a word two times. Tell me whether I say it the same way or differently: *soap - thoap.*" **Answer:** "Differently."
   Example B: Your partner says, "I'm going to say the same word twice, but the [s] sound will be correct in one and incorrect in the other. Tell me which is correct, the first word or the second word: *soap - thoap.*" **Answer:** "The first word."
4. Train your ear to distinguish between correct and incorrect productions, but with the target sound in words, phrases, then sentences.

Perform tasks 1 through 4 using a tape recorder to record your sound production. Then listen to the tape with your partner and identify your own correct and incorrect productions of the target sound. Then repeat tasks 1 through 4 without the tape recorder.

When you practice ear training, you'll do better if you make sure you're performing each task at a satisfactory level before you advance to the next. If you follow this procedure, by the time you've repeated the tasks, you probably will be able to accurately monitor your own productions of the target sound. Then you should repeat the tasks each time you practice your target sound or sounds.

Warm-ups

Now you're almost ready to start working on the sounds of American English. To help you progress more rapidly, we suggest you try some warm-up exercises before each practice session (even though you may feel slightly ridiculous).

Sensitizing Exercise

This exercise should help you become more aware of your articulators and how you use them in speaking.

1. Place the tip of your tongue between your upper lip and the upper tooth farthest back in your mouth on the right side. Now, slowly slide your tongue tip forward to the front teeth, then all the way back on the left side. Now, reverse the movement; first forward to the front teeth, then back to the teeth on the right side. Repeat, placing the tongue tip between the lower lip and the lower teeth.

2. Touch the inside of the upper front teeth with the tongue tip. Slowly slide the tip upward. The first soft tissue you feel is the gum. Next, you will feel a bump extending backward inside your mouth. This is the gum ridge or alveolar ridge. Several consonant sounds are produced with the tongue tip touching this ridge.

    Now, drop the tip of the tongue to the floor of your mouth, open your mouth, and alternately raise the tongue tip, touch the alveolar ridge, and drop the tongue again.

3. Starting with the tip of your tongue at the gum ridge, slowly curl the tip upward and backward along the roof of your mouth. You should encounter a concave area. This is the hard palate. In case you have difficulty locating it, it's the place where peanut butter always gets stuck.

    Now drop your tongue. Raise it so that the front third is touching the hard palate. With your mouth open, alternately raise the tongue to the hard palate and lower it. Do this a few times as rapidly as you can.

4. Hold a mirror in front of your mouth so that you can see the back of your mouth. With your mouth wide open, say *ga-ga-ga*. You should be able to see the back of your tongue rising up and the back part of the roof of your mouth dropping down to meet it. This part of the roof is called the soft palate or velum. Alternate raising and lowering the tongue and soft palate, first by repeating *ga-ga-ga*, then by performing the sound movement but without making any sound.

Now you're ready to start on the sounds of American English.

Chapter Five

Diction:
The Consonants

All the exercises you need to work on the consonant sounds are in this chapter. Each consonant is listed below along with the page at which coverage begins:

[p]
[b]

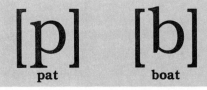

Sample: **[p] PAT WAS VERY HAPPY.**
           [b] THE BOY WAS IN THE RUBBER BOAT.
Spellings: **p** as in **pat**   **b** as in **boat**
           pp as in **happy**   **bb** as in **rubber**
           gh as in **hiccough**   **pb** as in **cupboard**

Description

[p] and [b] are cognate sounds; [p] is a voiceless bilabial plosive, [b] is voiced. You produce them by stopping the airstream with your lips, building up pressure, and suddenly releasing the air.

 Production: [p]

1. Put your lips together; press them fairly firmly closed.
2. Build up air pressure in your mouth; don't let any air escape through your nose. Keep your teeth slightly apart.
3. Allow the air pressure to force your lips apart making an audible explosion of air.

Production: [b]

1. Follow all the steps for [p], but start to produce voice at the same time that your lips close.
2. Don't press the lips as firmly or hold them together as long as you did for [p].

Problems

[p] and [b] are sounds you learned to produce with very little difficulty. The problems that exist with these sounds are usually minor and are corrected quite easily.

PROBLEM 1. CONFUSION OF [p] AND [b]

People whose first language is Arabic or Chinese (or another Asian language) frequently find it difficult to distinguish between voiced and voiceless plosives. They may voice the voiceless sound, and vice versa, which turns the [p] into a [b] and the [b] into a [p]. Speakers of Romance languages (French, Italian, Spanish) sometimes weaken the articulation of voiceless plosives so that plosives such as [p] sound voiced. Check your production by trying the following contrast drill.

Contrast Drill for [p] and [b]

Say the words in the following lists aloud. First read down the list of [p] words, making sure you don't feel or hear voice. Then read down the list of [b] words, this time listening and feeling for voice. For the last step, read across, contrasting pairs of words—the first word voiceless, the second voiced.

[p]		[b]	[p]		[b]
pat	—	bat	lap	—	lab
pet	—	bet	rope	—	robe
pie	—	by	rip	—	rib
pen	—	Ben	staple	—	stable
pond	—	bond	rapid	—	rabid
cap	—	cab	napped	—	nabbed

PROBLEM 2. FRICATIVE [p]

If you don't press your lips together firmly enough, [p] loses its explosive quality and sounds rather like an [f]. To avoid this, make sure your lips touch each other firmly and completely, leaving no gaps that can let air escape. Also, don't let the air out until you've built up sufficient pressure to make a strong, sudden sound. As you read the Level 1 drills, feel for lip pressure and closure.

PROBLEM 3. FRICATIVE [b]

This problem occurs most often with people whose first language is Spanish. Their pronunciation of *berry* may sound like *very*. This is because one Spanish phoneme is a bilabial fricative that sounds rather like [v] to English speakers. If you make this substitution, maintain firm lip pressure when you read the practice words.

PROBLEM 4. STRESS

When [p] and [b] are followed by stressed vowels, as in *apart* and *above*, you must make a strong plosive sound. You should feel the air on your hand if you hold it about two inches in front of your mouth and say *pie*. But when an unstressed vowel follows, the [p] and [b] won't be as strong. They are also weaker when they are followed by [l], [r], [s], and [t]. The Level 2 and 3 practice words will give you some of these combinations to work on.

LEVEL 1 DRILLS FOR [p]

 Level 1 Practice Words for [p]

Say the words in the following lists slowly and clearly. Listen carefully, and also feel for the right degree of lip pressure. Don't voice the [p]; there are no [b] words in this list. The words in the *Middle* list all have a stressed [p]. Don't overdo the final [p].

Beginning	End	Middle
pea	seep	Japan
peak	keep	append
piece	leap	unpaid
peck	jeep	upon
pin	tip	Muppet
pig	cheap	mopping
pick	dip	napkin
picnic	deep	happy
pen	teacup	teapot
pie	ape	tepee
penny	cape	apply
pendant	gape	uphill

Beginning	End	Middle
pay	tap	caper
pain	step	opposed
page	stop	apology
pace	gap	upper
pod	cup	taping
pan	hope	suppose
pack	top	impact
put	mop	appoint
pawn	hoop	opponent
poke	hope	opinion

[p]
[b]

▼ Level 1 Practice Phrases for [p]

Say the following phrases slowly.

stew pot	pay day	paint pail
step up	tea cup	pick up
passing parade	Ping-Pong	push and pull
pink poodle	cup cake	pencil point

▼ Level 1 Practice Sentences for [p]

Say the following sentences slowly but easily. Don't overdo it. Read them a number of times, and, if you can, have someone listen to you.

1. They were like two peas in a pod.
2. I hope you'd like a piece of pie.
3. The pencil point shattered on impact.
4. Stop taping after the first page.
5. Step up the pace on the way to the peak.
6. My opponent apologized for pushing me.
7. Do you keep the penny-saver coupons?
8. The jeep drove uphill through the pit.
9. Pat knocked over the paint pail after the picnic.
10. I put my money in the pick-up truck on pay day.
11. She found a penny under the napkin near the cupcake.
12. The Ping-Pong match had a happy ending.
13. Pay the pawn ticket for the Japanese teapot.
14. They pushed and pulled until the pig was pinned.
15. Opinion was divided over the unpaid appointment.

[p]
[b]

LEVEL 2 DRILLS FOR [p]

The words at this level are slightly more difficult to say because of the other consonants appearing in them. Say the words slowly and clearly. Listen carefully, and feel for the right degree of lip pressure. There are no [b] words in the list, so as in Level 1, try not to voice the [p].

Level 2 Practice Words for [p]

Beginning	*End*	*Middle*
pearl	creep	apart
Peter	reap	repay
peal	sleep	appear
pushed	slope	repair
pooled	strip	vapor
peach	skip	superior
parlor	chip	repel
pelt	gripe	dripping
pelvis	clap	space
person	grape	special
parole	strap	responsible
pension	chop	slipper
punch	shop	zipper
pier	scoop	compel
paddle	snip	hopping

Level 2 Practice Phrases for [p]

Say the following phrases slowly.

stop sign	slipping zipper	grape pop
repair shop	superior straps	responsible person
sip of punch	paddle in the pool	slipper strap

Level 2 Practice Sentences for [p]

Read the following sentences slowly and clearly. Don't overemphasize. Read them a number of times. If you can, have someone listen to you.

1. In my opinion, pearls come from superior oysters.
2. Vapor curled up from the ship's swimming pool.
3. Responsible persons repair their own paddles.
4. They were compelled to push the grapes up the slope.
5. We pooled our personal funds to pay for repairs.

6. The stop sign appeared to be sloping.
7. The pealing chimes rang from the shipping pier.
8. The grape pop really packed a punch.
9. A scoop of peach ice cream melted in the parlor.
10. I was hopping mad when they pelted me with wood chips.

LEVEL 3 DRILLS FOR [p]

At this level you'll find words that are slightly more difficult to say, usually because they are blends of [pl], [pr], or [pt]. Make sure to produce the [p], but be aware that the stress will vary; emphasize the [p] only slightly in [pl] and [pr], and don't give any emphasis to the [p] in [pt]. Notice that when *ed* follows *p*, it's pronounced [pt]. For example, *wrapped* is pronounced the same as *rapt*.

 Level 3 Practice Words

Try saying the words in the following lists slowly and clearly.

[pl] *All Positions*	[pr] *Beginning and Middle*	[pt] *Middle and End*
please	priest	crept
place	praise	except
pleasant	press	slept
plastic	prank	rapt
plow	proud	˙wrapped
hopeless	progress	concept
explicit	repressed	hoped
staple	represent	popped
apply	appropriate	leaped
ample	opera	topped
plume	prince	soaped
applause	prize	optical
aplomb	probe	cryptic
plum	prune	mapped
plank	appraise	septic
pliers	pretty	peptic

[p]
[b]

Level 3 Practice Phrases for [p]

plastic wrapper	explicit promise
prune plums	pleasant place
cryptic concept	slept at the opera
accept applause	hopelessly repressed
proud priest	

Level 3 Practice Sentences for [p]

Follow the directions given for Level 2 sentences.

1. I was pleased to represent the opera company.
2. We planted plastic tulips in the spring.
3. You must display your pool pass.
4. There was an ample supply of press cards.
5. He plowed the pea patch under this spring.
6. It was hopeless to try to repair the stapler.
7. Practical jokes are not appropriate in this place.
8. The patient dropped his toothpaste in the water pitcher.
9. The zookeepers opposed the sheepshearing.
10. He unwrapped all the presents except Paul's.

LEVEL 1 DRILLS FOR [b]

Level 1 Practice Words for [b]

Say the words in the following lists slowly and carefully. Listen closely and correct your production until you are sure you have a clear and correct sound. Remember that the [b] should have slightly less pressure than the [p]. Remember, too, that [b] is a voiced sound.

Beginning	End	Middle
beam	fib	about
bean	jib	abound
beet	cab	above
beef	tab	abeam
bed	nab	abbey
bend	ebb	hobby

Beginning	End	Middle
bake	lab	maybe
book	hub	nobody
because	dub	hobo
bait	tub	cabinet
bucket	tube	Cuba
bad	job	fibbing
back	fob	webbing
biology	mob	obey
bond	stab	fabulous
boat	web	ebony
Boston	swab	abacus
banana	scab	obedient
bank	snob	ebbing

Level 1 Practice Phrases for [b]

Say the following phrases slowly.

bunch of bananas	bean bag	big hot tub
bank book	bio lab	fabulous backhand
bad back	bait bucket	ebony cabinet

Level 1 Practice Sentences for [b]

Read the following sentences slowly and clearly. Don't overdo it. Read them a number of times, and if you can, have someone listen to you.

1. The hobo left the train in Boston.
2. Bob rented a cabin with a beamed ceiling.
3. The bait was sold by the bucket.
4. She stayed in bed due to a bad back.
5. The ebony cabinet was full of Cuban cigars.
6. I wouldn't give that bag of books to anybody.
7. There is a bundle of beanbags above the tub.
8. Maybe we left the abacus in the bio lab.
9. The banana boat was abeam when the tide was ebbing.
10. The cookbook showed a tub full of bacon and beef.

[p]
[b]

LEVEL 2 DRILLS FOR [b]

 Level 2 Practice Words for [b]

The words in the following lists are slightly more difficult to produce because of the other consonants present. Say the words slowly and distinctly.

Beginning	End	Middle
beach	glib	abyss
bear	slab	caboose
Bill	slob	saber
best	rib	Robert
bell	rob	ribbon
Bette	rub	labor
bird	lobe	October
birch	strobe	harbor
bail	scribe	subway
bizarre	globe	ruby
buzzer	tribe	rabbit
burned	grab	urban
bull	club	auburn
bashful	crab	eyeball
bias	drab	throbbing

 Level 2 Practice Phrases for [b]

Say the following phrases slowly.

throbbing earlobe	bashful bull	urban subway robber
best rubies	labor in October	birds in the birches
burning ribbons	global tribes	bell and buzzer

 Level 2 Practice Sentences for [b]

Read the following sentences slowly and clearly. Read them a number of times. If you can, have someone listen to you.

1. Bette was too bashful to join the club.
2. After Bill planted a birch tree, he baled hay.
3. The ruby-red hummingbird flew near the harbor.
4. Robert's bull was judged best in the October show.
5. They tried to grab the bear near the caboose.
6. You can get an urban sunburn on Tar Beach.
7. The bells and buzzers gave me a throbbing headache.
8. The rabbit tried to rub his rib like a bird.
9. He labored to inscribe his name on the globe.
10. The tribe threw the saber into the abyss.

[p]
[b]

LEVEL 3 DRILLS FOR [b]

Level 3 Practice Words for [b]

The [b] words in the following lists contain various blends and combinations. Also, some of the words will have [p] for contrast. Try the words, saying them slowly and clearly.

[bl]	[br]	[bd]
bleed	breathe	mobbed
blip	bridge	rubbed
blade	abrade	blabbed
blend	bread	knobbed
black	brand	stubbed
block	brown	fibbed
Casablanca	cobra	barbed
blimp	umbrella	probed
oblong	abroad	abdicate
able	abracadabra	snubbed

Level 3 Practice Phrases for [b]

Say the following phrases slowly and clearly.

scrub the curb	collectible blimps
Casablanca bridge	bland probes
brand-new broom	raspberry pablum
billion pebbles	brown icecubes
combat drumbeat	

[p]
[b]

Level 3 Practice Sentences for [b]

Now you can try sentences that combine difficult blends and also offer [p] and [b] for contrast.

1. They made a billion balloons in December and November.
2. The view from the bridge was pretty bleak.
3. The party at Pebble Beach disturbed the neighbors.
4. We had crabcakes and boiled lobster at the clambake.
5. The parrot would only say, ''Pretty boy, pretty boy.''
6. Overall, the Labor party asked probing questions.
7. They probably had icecubes in the cooler at the curb.
8. In September, I saw Bogart in *Casablanca.*
9. I fed raspberry pablum to my baby brother.
10. The brand-new lightbulbs burned out.

Challenge Sentences for [p] and [b]

The following sentences contain [p] and [b] in difficult blends and combinations; scan them silently before you read them out loud.

1. The puppy bumped his paws and stopped abruptly.
2. The purple bubble burst its bonds and popped up.
3. The bouncy baby bubbled and babbled happily after its bottle.
4. Barbary pirates were a positive threat to the prosperity of European companies before the growth of large populations.
5. Do people prefer bright baubles or pretty peonies and poppies?
6. Special spirits inspired Spencer not to do his job in dribs and drabs.
7. The proper production of breakwaters can prevent broad-beamed boats from broaching.
8. The blushing bride breathed happily after the priest blessed the bridal breakfast.
9. The imbibing of Burgundy and Beaujolais was practiced during every bountiful repast.
10. Every prospective producer should practice punctuating pages of prompt books before buying scripts.

Challenge Materials for [p] and [b]

A facile play-by-play announcer can generally find abundant work in local markets, although this work will generally be on a part-time basis. In small and medium markets, newspeople, staff announcers, and even sales personnel add to their income by broadcasting local sports. This is a difficult assignment, however, requiring good on-air skills and an extensive knowledge of the sport. . . .

Baseball games have many periods of little or no activity, so the play-by-play person must be able to fill with talk of interest to the audience. This ability will become particularly apparent in rain-delay situations.

Baseball play-by-play also entails the ability to follow action quite a distance away. Good vision, or the ability to compensate for poor vision by an in-depth knowledge of the game is essential.

Football is a technically oriented game, and the play-by-play announcer has to be up on the plays and able to follow them. In-depth analysis is often provided by a color commentator. In addition, there are many statistics to be followed, including downs, yardage on previous carries, and so on. . . .

Lewis B. O'Donnell, Carl Hausman, Philip Benoit, *ANNOUNCING: Broadcast Communicating Today*

[t] [d]
top   dog

Sample: **[t] THOMAS LIKED TO WALK TWO TIGHT ROPES.**
[d] THE DOG DIGS FOR BONES IN THE YARD.

Spellings: **t** as in **two**   **d** as in **dog**
tw as in **two**   **dd** as in **ladder**
th as in **Thomas**   **pt** as in **ptomaine**
ed as in **liked**   **bt** as in **doubt**
ght as in **tight**   **ed** as in **poured**
tt as in **tattoo**

[t]
[d]

Description

[t] and [d] are cognate sounds. [t] is a voiceless lingua-alveolar plosive. You produce it by blocking the airstream with the tongue and upper gum ridge, building up air pressure and suddenly releasing it. [d] is produced in the same way. Just add voice as you produce it.

Production: [t]

1. Narrow the tongue and place it against your upper gum ridge. Make sure the sides of the tongue touch the sides of the upper molars. Lower your jaw slightly, keeping your teeth apart.
2. Hold your tongue firmly in place against the gum ridge. Force some air from your lungs and allow pressure to build up behind your tongue.
3. Let the air pressure overcome your tongue and force it away from the gum ridge. This way, the air escapes quickly and goes over the dropped tongue and between the teeth.

Production: [d]

Follow Steps 1 and 2, and start Step 3. As the air pressure begins to force your tongue away from the gum ridge, add voice. Try to time your voicing so that it begins at exactly the same time that your tongue starts to leave the gum ridge.

Contrast Drill for [t] and [d]

Slowly read the following pairs of words aloud. Remember, [t] is voiceless and [d] is voiced. Try to feel and hear the difference.

[t]		[d]	[t]		[d]	[t]		[d]
tea	—	dee	kitty	—	kiddy	feet	—	feed
tip	—	dip	rated	—	raided	hit	—	hid
ten	—	den	writing	—	riding	let	—	led
tan	—	dan	butted	—	budded	sat	—	sad
tie	—	die	knotted	—	nodded	right	—	ride
tuck	—	duck	matter	—	madder	cot	—	cod
toe	—	doe	otter	—	odder	shoot	—	shooed

Problems

PROBLEM 1. DENTALIZATION

[t] and [d] are tongue–gum ridge sounds. Some people, including those whose first language is Spanish or Italian, tend to dentalize the sounds, that is, they make the sounds on the back of the upper front teeth. Look closely at your mouth in the mirror while you say the word *tea*. If you can see the sides of your tongue peeking around your upper incisors, you're probably dentalizing. You can hear a difference, too. A dentalized [t] sounds hissy and slightly ''wet.''

Place the tip of your tongue lightly on the upper gum ridge. (The exact spot is where you burn yourself when you bite into a piece of steaming hot pizza.) Don't press too hard; if you do, the tongue spreads out and overlaps onto the teeth. Now say the following words aloud, reading *across* the page. Alternate saying the words, first dentally and then nondentally. (Say the words in parentheses dentally.)

(tea)	tea	(tea)	tea	(tea)	tea	(tea)	tea	(tea)	tea
(tap)	tap	(tap)	tap	(tap)	tap	(tap)	tap	(tap)	tap
(top)	top	(top)	top	(top)	top	(top)	top	(top)	top
(toe)	toe	(toe)	toe	(toe)	toe	(toe)	toe	(toe)	toe
(too)	too	(too)	too	(too)	too	(too)	too	(too)	too
(die)	die	(die)	die	(die)	die	(die)	die	(die)	die
(day)	day	(day)	day	(day)	day	(day)	day	(day)	day
(do)	do	(do)	do	(do)	do	(do)	do	(do)	do
(dog)	dog	(dog)	dog	(dog)	dog	(dog)	dog	(dog)	dog

Use a light touch with your tongue, and return it precisely to the same place each time. Listen carefully as you say the words. Try to eliminate the ''wetness.''

PROBLEM 2. OMISSION OF [d] AND [t] IN THE MIDDLE AND END OF WORDS

Sometimes it's easier to simply skip [d] and [t] than to take the extra effort to produce them. This usually happens when [d] and [t] are preceded by other consonants, such as in the words *perfect, west,* and *sounds.* Correcting this problem is not quite as easy as you would think, so don't start on it until you have progressed to Level 2 drills.

PROBLEM 3. AFFRICATED [t]

When you make the [t], don't press your tongue too tightly against the gum ridge. Sometimes this may result in the normally plosive [t] sound-

[t]
[d]

ing like a fricative or, more accurately, like a combination plosive and fricative. For example, the word *too* [tu] might sound like [tsu]. So when you make the sound [t], make sure there is a clean, sharp break that you can feel as your tongue leaves the gum ridge.

The same problem occurs when [t] and [d] are blended with [r], as in *drew* and *true.* We'll cover that in the Level 3 drills.

PROBLEM 4. SUBSTITUTION OF [d] FOR [t]

This substitution occurs most often in words like *city, butter, metal,* in which the [t] receives secondary stress. It's very easy, in words like those, to simply carry over your voicing from the vowel that precedes [t] to the vowel that follows. This is one of the most pervasive nonstandard substitutions in our language. We'll cover it in Level 3.

LEVEL 1 DRILLS FOR [t]

 Level 1 Practice Words for [t]

Say the words in the following lists slowly and distinctly, reading down each column. Start with the *Beginning* words. These have short, precise sounds; don't hold them longer than necessary. Listen carefully, and adjust your production until you are satisfied that the sound is clear and correct.

Beginning	End	Middle
tea	eat	attack
team	meet	until
teen	neat	autumn
tip	pit	atone
Tim	mitt	intend
tin	knit	voted
take	fate	vitamin
tape	bait	eaten
Ted	bet	enter
ten	net	guitar
tag	at	entire
tan	fat	banter
time	cat	center
Tom	cot	attire
top	pot	cuter
tub	but	computer
talk	caught	outer

Beginning	End	Middle
toss	fought	item
toe	coat	fighter
tone	note	data
took	put	attend
too	cute	meter

Now read the *End* column again, and try not to *over*correct the [t]. When this sound is the last sound in a word, it usually is not aspirated; that is, you should not make it with a puff of air.

 Level 1 Practice Phrases for [t]

Say the following phrases slowly.

top ten	two-tone	tea time
tag team	fat cat	cute note
toe tapping	tan boot	tomtom
computer center	after autumn	took vitamins
tank full of bait	took his coat	meet the voters
enter data	attend the fight	toss in the pot

 Level 1 Practice Sentences for [t]

Say the following sentences slowly but naturally. Don't overdo it. Read them a number of times and, if you can, have someone listen to you.

1. A <u>tan</u> <u>cat</u> was asleep on his <u>coat</u>.
2. <u>It</u> was <u>fate</u> that we <u>met</u>.
3. <u>Enter</u> the <u>data</u> <u>into</u> the <u>computer</u>.
4. <u>Ten</u> cars were <u>towed</u> from the parking <u>meter</u>.
5. He was <u>caught</u> only <u>ten</u> miles from the <u>attack</u>.
6. <u>Take</u> the <u>note</u> from under the <u>tea</u> <u>pot</u>.
7. <u>Tim</u> saw the <u>team</u> <u>taking</u> <u>vitamins</u>.
8. Was <u>Tom</u> fixing the <u>motor</u> <u>until</u> <u>ten</u>?
9. She <u>bought</u> a <u>tank-top</u> <u>swimsuit</u>.
10. He <u>put</u> the <u>tape</u> across the <u>gate</u> of the <u>tomb</u>.
11. <u>Tom</u> is the <u>tall</u> boy who plays the <u>guitar</u>.
12. <u>Night</u> is a good <u>time</u> <u>to</u> <u>meet</u> in <u>autumn</u>.
13. <u>It</u> was <u>too</u> <u>cute</u> <u>to</u> <u>put</u> on <u>top</u>.
14. The <u>attack</u> was <u>fought</u> near the mine <u>pit</u>.
15. I <u>put</u> the <u>tip</u> of my <u>toe</u> in the <u>center</u> of the <u>tub</u>.

[t]
[d]

LEVEL 2 DRILLS FOR [t]

PROBLEM 1. OMISSION OF [t] IN THE MIDDLE AND END OF WORDS

This problem is most common when you must produce another consonant immediately before [t]. For example, the word *past* [pæst] becomes *pass* [pæs]. This generally occurs simply because you *under-articulate;* that is, you don't raise your tongue up quite high enough to product the [t]. Your mind, however, fills in the missing [t] because of context *(He went pass the end of the street)* and so you don't notice the omission. The following contrast drill will help you listen for the omission.

▼ **Contrast Drill for Omission of [t]**

Read the following pairs of words slowly and carefully. Take extra effort to produce the [t]. You should be able to hear it clearly in the second word of each pair.

pass	—	past	lease	—	least
guess	—	guest	roof	—	roofed
chess	—	chest	miss	—	mist
stay	—	state	ten	—	tent
row	—	wrote	star	—	start
mass	—	mast	tess	—	test

PROBLEM 2. CONFUSION OF [t] AND [d] IN THE END OF WORDS

Words that end in *ed* such as *raced, banned,* and *feasted* can sometimes cause confusion as to whether the last sound should be a [t] or a [d] and whether it should be part of a separate syllable or just added to the previous one. Here are some general rules that may help:

- If the sound preceding *ed* is voiceless, pronounce the *d* as a [t]. **Example:** *wrapped* [ræpt]
- If the sound preceding *ed* is voiced, pronounce the *d* as [d]. **Example:** *banned* [bænd]
- If the sound preceding *ed* is a [d] or a [t], the *ed* is pronounced as a separate syllable, [əd]. **Example:** *patted* [pætəd]

Level 2 Practice Words for [t]

Say the words in the following columns slowly and clearly, reading down the columns starting with *Beginning.* These words have slightly more difficult combinations to produce; also, you'll have to remember the rules about "ed."

Beginning	End	Middle
teach	feast	feasted
tease	greased	cheated
teeth	leased	eastern
till	grit	sister
tiller	slit	misty
table	slate	later
tale	debate	visitor
telephone	blessed	invested
terrain	west	lettuce
tax	flat	faster
tally	passed	pastor
touch	just	router
tunnel	dust	rusted
tardy	smart	charted
taco	forest	lasting
toddler	thought	loiter
torch	lost	daughter
toil	brought	oyster
told	wrote	hotel
toad	scout	rotor
Toledo	ghost	poster
tooth	roofed	sooty
tour	goofed	rooster

Beginning and End	Beginning and Middle	Middle and End
tint	telltale	rotate
taunt	tested	extort
toast	toasted	intent
taste	tasting	state
toot	tooted	attest
tent	talented	start
tensed	tilted	stunt
tilt	titanic	attempt

[t]
[d]

Level 2 Practice Phrases for [t]

attempted to start	western forest	late visitors
telephone table	greased lightning	great debate
state taxes	brought the note	visitor's tent
toddler teaser	pastor's daughter	smart thoughts
talented sister	telephone talk	tasted lettuce

Level 2 Practice Sentences for [t]

Say the following sentences slowly and distinctly, but don't exaggerate the [t].

1. Sometimes the tongue is faster than the eye.
2. Which is the most expensive hotel in Toledo?
3. The pastor arrived ten minutes later than his sister.
4. The tangle of wires rested against the telephone pole.
5. The stunt car brushed against the sides of the tunnel.
6. The rooster was faster than greased lightning.
7. I saw "The Best of the West" last night.
8. The forester passed through the dusty terrain.
9. I can attest to the quality of the teaching.
10. Her daughter lost the slate-colored poster on the tour.
11. He leased the torch to the tardy visitors.
12. The scout faced ten wagons to the east at sunset.
13. The best man's toast to the newlyweds was outstanding.
14. They attempted to extort ten dollars each from the teachers.
15. The smart patient sought help from the first doctor.

LEVEL 3 DRILLS FOR [t]

Sometimes the combination of [t] plus [s] or the [sts] combination can be difficult. If you have problems with these, see [s], Level 3, page 129.

PROBLEM 1. SUBSTITUTION OF [d] FOR [t]

The most common problem with [t] is the tendency for people to voice it when it is not in the syllable receiving the primary stress, as in the words *batter, butter, bitter, sitting,* and *party.* The result is a substitution of [d] for [t]. To avoid this, use a light touch of your tongue on the gum ridge, and be sure to stop voicing for the brief instant that it takes for you to produce the [t]. Try the following:

Production Drill

Read the words in the following lists, reading across the page. Gradually shorten the pause between the syllables, and reduce the amount of [h].

bat . . . her	bat . . her	bat . her	bat her	batter
but . . . her	but . . her	but . her	but her	butter
bit . . . her	bit . . her	bit . her	bit her	bitter
kit . . . he	kit . . he	kit . he	kit he	kitty
let . . . her	let . . her	let . her	let her	letter

Contrast Drill for [d] and [t]

Say the following pairs of words slowly. Try to feel and hear the difference between the [d] and [t].

[d]		[t]	[d]		[t]
badder	—	batter	bidder	—	bitter
leader	—	liter	padding	—	patting
seeding	—	seating	pudding	—	putting
wading	—	waiting	faded	—	fated
riding	—	writing	wedding	—	wetting
raiding	—	rating	heading	—	heating
shudder	—	shutter	ladder	—	latter

Practice Words for [d] for [t] Substitution

batter	bitter	butter
writing	rating	wetting
shutter	latter	heating
sitting	pretty	city
letter	suited	pity
twenty	thirty	forty
fifty	sixty	seventy
patted	petting	kitty
sooty	smarter	litter

[t]

[d]

Now take the words above and others you can find to practice with, and make up short, simple sentences. Ask your instructor or a member of your class to listen to you and to be especially aware if you are overcorrecting.

PROBLEM 2. [t] FOLLOWED BY [n] OR [l]

This is an especially difficult combination of sounds to deal with because it occurs so frequently. There's no mystery about it, though, and it's not hard to correct. Typical words are *little, bottle, kitten.*

The trick is this: don't let your tongue move away from the gum ridge after making the [t]. When it's followed by an [l], you simply hold up the tip and let the sides drop, exploding the air laterally. When it's followed by an [n], drop the soft palate and let the air come out the nose. Be careful not to substitute [d] for [t]. Here are some practice words:

[tl]	[tn]
little	button
battle	mountain
petal	cotton
glottal	bitten
bottle	certain
total	kitten
metal	fountain
cattle	mitten
settle	mutton
accidental	rotten
oriental	au gratin
parental	forgotten
continental	batten

Make sure you're not producing a *glottal stop* instead of a [t]. A glottal stop is not really a sound at all. You make it simply by stopping the air flow momentarily with the vocal folds. Try it with the word *little.* Leave out the [t] in the middle and say ''li/le.'' That's a glottal stop. It's not a [t] but our minds perceive it as one.

PROBLEM 3. [tθ] OR [tð] COMBINATIONS

There is a time when the standard way to produce the [t] is on the teeth instead of the gum ridge. That's when it's followed by [θ] or [ð], as in *hit the ball* or *at the game.* You anticipate the placement of the tongue on the teeth for the [t], and you get it there a little early. It requires a little extra effort to produce the [ð] or [θ] after the [t]. Try these phrases:

hit the ball	at the game	at third
bright thought	put out the light	sent that
went through	eight-thirty	sit there

PROBLEM 4. [kt] COMBINATION

When the [kt] combination occurs at the end of a word, we sometimes tend to omit the [t]. Try the following words. Make sure to say the [t].

act	fact	tact	duct
knocked	peeked	faked	locked
checked	rocked	soaked	trucked
impact	exact	infect	obstruct
correct	precinct	suspect	respect

PROBLEM 5. [tr] BLEND

We mentioned the [tr] blend in Problem 3. Affricated [t] (p. 67). If you let your tongue slide back off the gum ridge on its way to making the [r], it sounds as though you're adding [tʃ], and making the plosive [t] into a fricative. Say the following words slowly and carefully. Do you hear a [tr] or a [tʃ]?

treat	trip	true	trap	train
trust	trout	trial	truck	trawl

▼ **Production Drill**

Read the words in the following lists aloud, from left to right. Gradually close the gap between the syllables as you go.

tuh . . . rue	tuh . . rue	tuh . rue	tuhrue	true
tuh . . . rip	tuh . . rip	tuh . rip	tuhrip	trip
tuh . . . rap	tuh . . rap	tuh . rap	tuhrap	trap

[t]
[d]

 Practice Words for [tr]

Beginning	Middle	Beginning	Middle
true	entrust	transistor	theatrical
trip	detract	tractor	partridge
trap	entrap	trial	Patrick
treat	entreat	truce	contrived
troop	entropy	trowel	Amtrak
track	actress	trouble	attribute
train	electric		

 Practice Sentences for [tr]

1. The electric train went off the track.
2. Patricia was a true actress.
3. It was a treat to make the trip on Amtrak.
4. We had nothing but trouble with the new tractor.
5. He contrived to trick the contractor.

 Level 3 Practice Sentences for [t]

1. The lieutenant tried to calm the victim.
2. The troop train tripped the electronic switches.
3. It's a fact that cattle stay away from electric fences.
4. Take the trail to the right, then turn left.
5. Gilbert was the most treacherous tropical storm of this century.
6. The call went to the precinct at eight-thirty.
7. The little kitten liked to drink milk from the bottle.
8. The tea kettle was made of bright metal.
9. I thought I saw a fountain in the courtyard.
10. The first baseman tossed the ball to the shortstop.
11. The satellite tracking system operated infrequently.
12. The crates of buttons were incorrectly packed.
13. Frequent typhoons twisted the trees on the mountains.
14. His shorts were made from fifty percent cotton twill.
15. I asked him to close the shutters and put out the lights.

Challenge Sentences for [t]

1. Twenty teachers of Latin trusted their students not to start trouble.
2. Tommy Tune tapped his way to stardom with twinkle toes.
3. The detective was tricked into betraying his secret to the beautiful temptress.
4. The dentist dropped his button into the fountain and bit his metal fountain pen abruptly.
5. If Patrick trusts his mother's sister mistakenly in a distracted instant, is he liable to be sued for "Auntie trust?"

Challenge Materials for [t]

> Betty Botter bought some butter,
> But, she said, the butter's bitter
> If I put it in my batter,
> It will make my batter bitter.
> But a bit of better butter
> Will make my batter better.
> So she bought a bit of butter
> And put it in her batter.
> And it made her batter worse.

LEVEL 1 DRILLS FOR [d]

Almost all the misarticulations that can happen with [t] can also happen with [d]. This might be a good time to reread Problems 1 through 4 on pages 67–68. Do the contrast drill and the drill for dentalization.

Here are Level 1 practice words. Take your time with them; say them slowly and clearly. Listen carefully and correct your production until you are satisfied that you are producing the correct sound. These are short, precise sounds; don't hold them too long.

 Level 1 Practice Words for [d]

Beginning	End	Middle
deep	seed	seeding
deem	bead	feeding
dip	kid	India
dim	bid	bidding

[t]
[d]

Beginning	End	Middle
day	aid	wading
date	made	shady
den	fed	shedding
Debbie	said	bedding
Dan	add	candy
dash	sad	handy
Don	odd	body
dock	nod	fodder
dive	wide	shoddy
duck	bud	cider
dust	mud	muddy
dog	sawed	under
dawn	pawed	undo
dough	mowed	odor
doze	code	soda
dew	hood	pudding
duke	food	moody

Level 1 Practice Phrases for [d]

dusty dog	wedding day	dive under
made in the shade	feeding at dawn	sad kid
odd candy	in debt to Don	dashing Don

Level 1 Practice Sentences for [d]

1. The grass was <u>damp</u> with <u>dew</u> at <u>dawn</u>.
2. They <u>had soda</u> on their <u>wedding day</u>.
3. Her hair was <u>damp under</u> her <u>hood</u>.
4. It was <u>dumb</u> to <u>dive under</u> the <u>dock</u>.
5. They broke the <u>code</u> by <u>adding</u> the <u>dates</u>.
6. <u>Cider</u> from <u>India</u> has an <u>odd odor</u>.
7. <u>Don</u> feels <u>moody</u> in <u>bad</u> weather.
8. The furious <u>bidding</u> was <u>led</u> by the <u>doctor</u>.
9. We went <u>wading</u> in the <u>deep shady</u> pool.
10. He <u>sawed</u> logs and <u>mowed</u> the lawn in the <u>dim</u> light.

LEVEL 2 DRILLS FOR [d]

It's very easy to omit [d] when it follows another consonant or comes at the end of a word. When you read the following list of words aloud, make sure you put a [d] every place it should be. Be especially careful at the end of words; make an extra effort to voice the sound so you don't substitute [t] for it, but at the same time, don't overcorrect it.

Some of the words in the following list have [t] in them, and in some [d] occurs more than once. There are also other consonants in the words that may make the accurate production of [d] more difficult.

Level 2 Practice Words for [d]

Beginning	End	All Positions
diesel	plead	heeded
deer	reared	speeded
ditto	filmed	building
discreet	skilled	did
data	famed	raided
dateline	skated	razed
desk	ranged	amazed
dentist	hemmed	added
desert	sled	decided
Dallas	clad	divided
dunk	blood	detained
dirty	word	dented
dot	bird	doubled
doll	plod	darted
dart	guard	dandy
dory	toward	dangled
doily	void	dirtied
doting	sewed	padded
duty	brood	bedded
duel	stewed	deducted

Level 2 Practice Phrases for [d]

dangled in the void   amazed the guard   padded sled
dirty doilies   dented the desk   double dunked
hemmed and hawed   decided to divide   doting dentist

Level 2 Practice Sentences for [d]

1. He avoided the dirty extra duty.
2. The datelines ranged from Dallas to Desert City.
3. I decided to find some diesel fuel after daybreak.
4. Dawn poured oil in the dirty old pan.
5. We plodded toward the dentist's building.
6. The guard was detained after the building was razed.
7. He dunked the ball discreetly.
8. The deer reared up and ran around the sled.
9. Did you drop the dividers from the bill?
10. The padded doilies were soiled.

LEVEL 3 DRILLS FOR [d]

The difficulties at this level occur primarily with the [dr] blend, [d] followed by [n] and [l], and omitting [d] before [z] as in *hands*. Let's take the omission problem first.

 Level 3 Practice Words for [dz]

Say the words below carefully. Try to produce one sound that combines [d] and [z] together.

hands	bands	stands	sands
reeds	heeds	beads	weeds

Notice that these words all end in [z]. Make sure you're saying the [d] firmly and pronouncing the [z]. Let's try some more.

seeds	feeds	leads	needs
bids	kids	lids	rids
raids	maids	fades	shades
lends	bends	sends	tends
lands	strands	grands	brands
binds	finds	grinds	blinds
pounds	sounds	mounds	grounds

 Level 3 Production Drill for [dr]

Use the same technique you used for the [tr] blend. Read the words below aloud, from left to right. Make a clean break between the tongue and the gum ridge. Don't slide the tongue along the palate. As you read, gradually close the gap between the syllables.

duh . . . rue	duh . . rue	duh . rue	duhrue	drew
duh . . . rip	duh . . rip	duh . rip	duhrip	drip
duh . . . raw	duh . . raw	duh . raw	duhraw	draw

Level 3 Practice Words for [dr]

dream	adrift	draw	hundred
drip	adroit	drain	droop
drape	hydrant	drop	drag
overdrawn	adrenaline	hydrogen	cathedral
drink	dressing	driver	Padre Island

Level 3 Practice Words for [dn] and [dl]

Another problem occurs frequently when [n] follows [d]. Use the same technique you used for [tn], and leave your tongue tip touching the gum ridge for [n]. This technique also works for [d] followed by [l].

hidden	student	rodent	redness
sudden	sadden	shouldn't	couldn't
ridden	widen	hadn't	wouldn't
riddle	middle	paddle	padlock
dwindle	idle	poodle	redlight

Level 3 Practice Sentences for [d]

1. The students chase rodents in the dorms.
2. It saddens me to see dwindling woods.
3. One hundred paddles were hidden in the woods.
4. The hydrant drained into the middle of the road.
5. Feed the birds sunflower seeds.
6. The dory was suddenly set adrift.
7. You shouldn't let your hands be idle.
8. I drew a cash advance for five hundred dollars.
9. I hadn't ridden since I was a kid.
10. He lends me dozens of books of riddles.

[k]
[g]

Challenge Sentences for [d] and [t]

1. It's difficult to detect defective transistors.
2. Stetson's wrist festered after he treated the rust with fast-acting detergent.
3. Dierdre didn't deserve the treatment she received at the hands of the dirty dozen.
4. I'd bet dollars to doughnuts that the director didn't traumatize the actress directly.
5. Discreet diplomats don't state matters categorically under duress in difficult situations.

Challenge Materials for [d] and [t]

Following the trail with the sureness of a bloodhound came General Zaroff. Nothing escaped those searching black eyes, no crushed blade of grass, no bent twig, no mark, no matter how faint, in the moss. So intent was the Cossack on his stalking that he was upon the thing Rainsford had made before he saw it. His feet touched the protruding bough that was the trigger. Even as he touched it, the general sensed his danger and leaped back with the agility of an ape. But he was not quite quick enough; the dead tree, delicately adjusted to rest on the cut living one, crashed down and struck the general a glancing blow on the shoulder as it fell; but for his alertness, he must have been smashed beneath it. He staggered, but he did not fall; nor did he drop his revolver. He stood there, hugging his injured shoulder, and Rainsford, with fear again gripping his heart, heard the general's mocking laugh ring through the jungle.

Richard Connell, *The Most Dangerous Game*

Sample: [k] THE QUIET LOCKSMITH WAS THE PLAY'S KEY CHARACTER.
[g] YOUR GRADES GO DOWN WITH VAGUE GUESSES ON EXAMS.

Spellings: **k** as in **key**   **g** as in **go**
               c as in **cat**   **gg** as in **egg**
               ck as in **lock**   **gu** as in **guess**
               cc as in **occur**   **gue** as in **plague**
               ch as in **echo**   **x** as in **exam** (with [**z**])
               qu as in **queen**   **gh** as in **ghost**
               que as in **plaque**
               cqu as in **lacquer**
               kh as in **khan**
               x as in **lax** (with [**s**])

[k]

[g]

Description

[k] and [g] are cognate lingua-velar sounds; [k] is voiceless, but [g] is voiced. They are plosives that you produce by blocking the breath-stream with the back of the tongue and soft palate, building up the pressure, and suddenly releasing it.

▼ Production: [k]

1. Open your mouth slightly.
2. Raise the back of your tongue and press it against the soft palate.
3. Build up air pressure behind the tongue. Don't let any air escape through your nose.
4. Let the air pressure force your tongue away from the palate. Make sure the release is sudden—an explosion.

▼ Production: [g]

Follow the same steps as for [k]. Produce voice as the tongue begins to block the airstream.

Problems

PROBLEM 1. CONFUSION OF [k] AND [g]

This is really a problem in voicing. It usually occurs as a simple error of pronunciation, or it could be due to failure to voice the [g]. The following contrast drill should help you distinguish between the two sounds.

Contrast Drill for [k] and [g]

First read down the column of [k] words. Then read down the column of [g] words. The last step is to read pairs of words across. Read slowly and carefully, and make sure to hear and feel the difference between voiceless [k] and voiced [g].

[k]		[g]	[k]		[g]
Kate	—	gate	sacking	—	sagging
came	—	game	lacking	—	lagging
cape	—	gape	lock	—	log
cap	—	gap	tuck	—	tug
cash	—	gash	pick	—	pig
cut	—	gut	duck	—	dug
coast	—	ghost	rick	—	rig
coat	—	goat	chuck	—	chug

PROBLEM 2. WEAK OR FRICATIVE [k] AND [g]

These two sounds require a firm and complete closure between the back of the tongue and the soft palate. If you don't have complete closure, you produce a weak or almost fricative sound. In a similar problem, people sometimes allow air to enter the nasal passages, nasalizing the sound. If you have either of these problems, try the drill below.

Production Drill

[k] and [g] need strong, active articulation. Say the following sounds, reading across. Say them forcefully. Try to get as much air out on [k] and [g] as you do on [b] and [t].

[p . . . t . . . k . . . g]
[p . . . t . . . k . . . g]
[p . . . t . . . k . . . g]

Now try the following. Say [k] three times as strongly as you can, then say the word that follows.

[k k k] cat [k k k] cat [k k k] cat
[k k k] cap [k k k] cap [k k k] cap

Now try the same thing with [g].

[g g g] gap [g g g] gap [g g g] gap
[g g g] gab [g g g] gab [g g g] gab

PROBLEM 3. PRONUNCIATION OF THE LETTER [x]

Many people become confused about how to pronounce *x;* whether it's a [ks] or a [gz]. Usually they fail to voice the [gz]. This won't happen if you know a couple of simple rules:

- When *x* is followed by a stressed vowel, it's pronounced [gz]. **Example:** *exam* [ɛgzæm]. (The word *exit* is pronounced [ɛksit].)
- When *x* is followed by a pronounced consonant or an unstressed vowel, it's pronounced [ks]. **Example:** *extra* [ɛkstrə] and *exit.*
- When the word ends in *x,* it's pronounced [ks]. **Example:** *wax* [wæks].

In other words, the only time you pronounce *x* as [gz] is when it's followed by a stressed vowel. Here are some words in which the *x* is a [gz]:

exact	examine	example	exhibit
exist	exert	exempt	exotic
executive	exuberant	exhaust	exaggerate

Here are some words in which the *x* is a [ks]:

ax	exit	except	excuse
mix	experiment	explain	Dixie
box	exciting	excellent	exposed

PROBLEM 4. OMISSION OF [k] IN THE cc AND ex SPELLING

Don't omit [k] in words such as *accept.* Although *cc* can be pronounced [k], as in *occur,* in words like *accept* the *cc* indicates a [k] followed by an [s]. Try these words:

accept	accident	access	vaccination
accessory	accent	accelerate	successive
except	excited	expect	expose
excavate	expose	experiment	experience

LEVEL 1 DRILLS FOR [k]

Level 1 Practice Words for [k]

Say the words in the following lists slowly and carefully. Correct your production until you are satisfied that you are producing a firm, clear sound. Start with the *Beginning* words.

[k]
[g]

Beginning	End	Middle
key	beak	because
keep	peek	peeking
kit	pick	picking
kid	stick	sticking
cape	fake	aching
cane	bake	making
chemistry	neck	beckon
Kevin	check	echo
can	pack	backhand
cab	tack	sacking
cup	buck	duckpins
come	stuck	lacquer
common	stock	backhoe
calm	dock	doctor
cause	chalk	walking
cough	walk	hockey
coat	joke	backer
comb	smoke	checkup
cushion	took	joker
cookie	book	picky
coop	spook	okay

 Level 1 Practice Phrases for [k]

common cause	back ache	Cape Cod
echo echo echo	a buck a book	neck check
cup of cookies	cabin cushions	hockey stick

 Level 1 Practice Sentences for [k]

1. Put on your backpack and take a walk to the dock.
2. I bought duck decoys on Cape Cod.
3. He had a back ache from playing hockey.
4. I left my hiking stick in the back of the pickup.
5. Kevin wrote the book on backhand returns.
6. The key to the chemistry cabinet is in the lock.
7. The engine's knock was caused by low octane fuel.
8. Doctors advise making time for checkups.
9. The backhoe stuck in the chalky soil.
10. Cookies commonly find their way under cushions.

LEVEL 2 DRILLS FOR [k]

 Level 2 Practice Words for [k]

The words at this level generally have slightly more difficult sound combinations. In addition, some words have more than one [k] and may have [g] for contrast. Say the following words carefully and slowly. Make sure you don't omit the [k] at the end position, but don't over-emphasize it.

Beginning	*End*	*Middle*
keel	streak	working
kilowatt	bleak	liquor
king	trick	locker
cute	drink	flicker
cumulus	shrink	looking
curious	flicker	turkey
cable	milk	raccoon
keg	desk	silky
kelp	drank	lucky
catch	thank	Alaska
kangaroo	task	tracking
carry	park	drinking
courtesy	work	shrinking
culprit	jerk	parking
curb	hulk	sticking
cargo	fork	anchor
cold	historic	gasket
course	prank	flunking
cool	blank	thanking

	All Positions	
skunk	kicking	chemical
Antarctic	practical	casket
electric	backpack	kink

 Level 2 Practice Phrases for [k]

drink of milk	bleak streak	historic prank
kangaroo court	curious looking	sticking anchor
cute king	catch a skunk	practical work

[k]

[g]

 Level 2 Practice Sentences for [k]

1. The kangaroo is a curious kind of animal.
2. It was hard work catching King Kong.
3. He went to Alaska tracking the culprits.
4. The anchor went into the locker with a loud clank.
5. He was elected Kilowatt King by the electric company.
6. The cashier shook with fear after he caught the raccoon.
7. We had a continental breakfast in the park before work.
8. There's a lot of work for marketing consultants.
9. It wasn't practical to be carrying cargo.
10. I had a lucky streak at the casino.

LEVEL 3 DRILLS FOR [k]

Many people have problems with [k] when it is blended with certain other consonants such as [l], [r], [s], and [w]. When you read the following words, try to produce the [k] blends as one sound; mesh them together, don't separate them.

 Level 3 Practice Words for [k]

[kl]	[kr]	[ks]	[kw]
claim	crisp	hoax	quiet
clasp	crew	Cokes	quit
clash	crush	jokes	quilt
cloth	cross	fix	queen
incline	concrete	Bronx	quest
enclose	recruit	excellent	quack
inclement	Democrat	fixture	qualify
buckle	sacrifice	mixture	inquest
sickle	incredible	expand	conquest
ankle	increase	express	acquaint
circle	microfilm	axiom	acquit
icicle	incriminate	excuse	inquire
bicycle	accrue	exercise	acquire

Level 3 Practice Sentences for [k]

1. Excuse me, is this the express train to the Bronx?
2. He broke his bike when it didn't clear the curb.
3. His insurance rates increased after he filed his claims.
4. A cycle of breathing consists of one inhalation and one exhalation.
5. He hid the incriminating microfilm in the camera.
6. I couldn't close the clasp on the buckle.
7. Biking is an excellent form of exercise.
8. The new recruits made incredible sacrifices.
9. They cleared a circle on the incline.
10. The mixture expanded and spilled on the cloth.
11. I couldn't break through the crowd to the box seats.
12. He fixed the clock so that it worked fairly accurately.
13. He flexed his muscles as he picked up the ax.
14. He quit so quietly I thought it was a hoax.
15. The quilt was acquired by the queen.

Challenge Sentences for [k]

1. Chris couldn't skate or ski until he fixed the broken clasp on his exercise jacket.
2. Clarence declared that Clarissa should quit her quest and become quiet.
3. Speak succinctly and quickly, or the wicked queen will lock up your Cokes.
4. Buckle the package to your bicycle to decrease the constant destruction of its cordage.
5. Clancy declaimed ''Casey at the Bat'' at the Coroner's Convention across the causeway from Connecticut.
6. I bought a box of biscuits, a box of mixed biscuits, and a biscuit mixer.
7. I requested a cup of proper coffee in a copper coffee cup.

[k]

[g]

▼ **Challenge Materials for [k]**

The Curriculum is a large creature but little understood. It is so long that it stretches almost from one end of the Catalog to the other, leaving room only for the Calendar, the Faculty and Administration, and the Index, which are squeezed in before and after the lengthy and complicated Curriculum.

The size of the Curriculum is accounted for by its being full of Fields, Disciplines, Departments, Requirements, Concentrations, and Prerequisites. At the heart of the Curriculum are the Courses, which are themselves full of esoteric little symbols, meaningful only to Academians, such as 112a,b, MWF, and TTH. There may also be such cryptic words and expressions as "arranged," "half-course," and "May be repeated for credit."

Richard Armour, *The Academic Bestiary*

LEVEL 1 DRILLS FOR [g]

▼ **Level 1 Practice Words for [g]**

Say the words in the following lists slowly and distinctly. Listen closely and adjust your production until you are satisfied that the sound is clear and strong enough, but don't overdo it. Start with the *Beginning* words.

Beginning	*End*	*Middle*
geese	fatigue	ego
give	big	agony
gift	wig	began
gate	vague	dignify
gave	egg	misguided
game	beg	again
get	nutmeg	engage
guess	peg	ignite
gab	sag	wagon
gadget	bag	navigate
gun	bug	magnet
gum	Doug	agate
gush	tug	disgust
gown	jug	bagpipe

Beginning	End	Middle
guide	bog	dogma
gone	jog	yoga
gaudy	fog	toga
go	dog	dugout
gopher	vogue	Uganda
good	dug	megaton
gooey	hug	foghorn
goof	mug	negotiate

[k]

[g]

Level 1 Practice Phrases for [g]

begin again	dog days	get a guide
engagement gift	gaudy wagon	gooey gum
big foghorn	gushing jug	jog in the bog

Level 1 Practice Sentences for [g]

1. The fog made it hard to navigate the big tug.
2. The goat began to butt against the gate.
3. I had to beg Doug to go to the game.
4. The guide used magnetic gadgets to find the geese.
5. I guess I left the bag of nutmeg in the station wagon.
6. It's good for your ego to jog with your dog.
7. He gave toy bagpipes as gifts again.
8. The gophers dug big tunnels in the peat bog.
9. The dog days of August are disgustingly hot.
10. We negotiated with the dignified man from Uganda.

LEVEL 2 DRILLS FOR [g]

Level 2 Practice Words for [g]

Words at this level have sound combinations that make it more difficult to produce a distinct [g]. In addition, the [g] may appear more than once in a word, and some words may have [k] for contrast.

Say the words in the following lists carefully and slowly. Make sure to produce the [g] in each word. Be careful not to overemphasize the [g] in the end position.

[k]
[g]

Beginning	End	Middle
gear	league	beguile
guilt	intrigue	figure
guild	twig	forget
gaze	plague	elongate
gainful	leg	nugget
gale	flag	smoggy
gallon	snag	trigger
gamble	brag	buggy
gang	cog	hugging
gasket	clog	luggage
garden	frog	organ
garage	analog	regard
garlic	dialogue	regular
gull	plug	sugar
girth	rug	signature
girl	bulldog	cigarette
gall	slug	vigorous
gauze	monologue	elegant
going	colleague	fragment
gold	rag	foggy

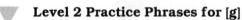

▼ Level 2 Practice Phrases for [g]

forget dialogue	gold nuggets	gauze fragment
elegant luggage	hugging the rug	gang of girls
intriguing bulldog	going, going, gone	regular sugar

▼ Level 2 Practice Sentences for [g]

1. The vague statement of guilt had no legal standing.
2. He gambled that he wouldn't hit the trigger guard.
3. The garden was full of elegant forget-me-nots.
4. The fragments of garlic were covered with gauze.
5. The luggage and baggage carts were guarded closely.
6. It was going to be difficult to shift gears.
7. It was too buggy and foggy to go frog hunting.
8. Regular coffee is served with milk and sugar.
9. I felt guilty after forgetting the monologue.
10. The girl's signature was vague and elongated.

LEVEL 3 DRILLS FOR [g]

[k]
[g]

Here are practice words for the blends [gl], [gr], and [gz]. Say them slowly as blends, not separating consonants. There are also practice words for the combination [gd]. Say them distinctly, listening for both consonants.

Level 3 Practice Words for [gl], [gr], and [gz]

[gl]	[gr]	[gz]
gleam	grease	eggs
glitter	green	pigs
glimpse	grip	twigs
glare	grin	begs
glad	graduate	tugs
glance	grant	rigs
glass	grass	clogs
glottis	gross	bugs
gloves	grunt	bags
glucose	groom	wags
aglow	agree	exact
angler	aground	exist
igloo	angry	example
wiggly	congress	exhausted
neglect	hunger	exempt
angle	regret	exonerate
single	telegram	executive
legal	vagrant	exuberant
snuggle	monogram	exotic

Level 3 Practice Words for [gd]

bagged	tagged	flagged	snagged
fatigued	shrugged	begged	bogged
wagged	bugged	rigged	zigged
lagged	logged	tugged	lugged
gagged	zagged	hugged	mugged

Level 3 Practice Sentences for [g]

1. From this angle it was hard to see the gleam of light from the igloo.
2. You need fertile ground to grow grass.
3. I was exhausted from hunting for exact examples.

[k]

[g]

4. He shrugged even though his shirt was snagged.

5. The engraving glittered under the glass.

6. I begged her not to put all her eggs in one basket.

7. They asked the guard to show them the executive quarters.

8. The angry captain let the boat go aground.

9. The rig was controlled by a single gear.

10. I asked for the exact name of the gracious angler.

11. I jogged from the Bureau of Engraving to the Department of Agriculture.

12. Are you going to the groundbreaking ceremony?

13. A clove of garlic goes a long way.

14. The greasy telegram was regrettably costly.

Challenge Sentences for [g]

1. Vicky was dragged, kicking and screaming, from the grungy guardroom because of her flagrant neglect.

2. The sluggish English bulldog gave Greg an exuberant kiss with his wiggly tongue.

3. The legal eagle was exhausted from trying to guess the going rate for gumballs.

4. The gregarious gambler gave a good tug on his gloves, glanced at the gas gauge, and gunned his engine.

5. The existence of the angry telegram was guaranteed by the hungry graduate.

Challenge Sentences for [g] and [k]

1. The regular caretaker took his gardening with a grain of salt.

2. Be careful to calculate the correct gradations when giving gratis recipes.

3. The groom agreed to create a croquet court that his acquaintances would elect to call classic.

4. The bag lady haggled with the ticket taker over the cost of enclosing her luggage in concrete.

5. Could Captain Queeg have predicted he would end up the subject of an inquest in the excellent book by Herman Wouk, *The Caine Mutiny?*

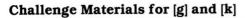

Challenge Materials for [g] and [k]

[k]
[g]

1. The road goes west out of the village, past open pine woods and gallberry flats. An eagle's nest is a ragged cluster of sticks in a tall tree, and one of the eagles is usually black and silver against the sky. The other perches near the nest, hunched and proud, like a griffon. There is no magic here except the eagles. Yet the four miles to the Creek and stirring, like the bleak, portentous beginning of a good tale. The road curves sharply, the vegetation thickens, and around the bend masses into dense hammock. The hammock breaks, is pushed back on either side of the road, and set down in its brooding heart is the orange grove.

Cross Creek, Marjorie Kinnan Rawlings

2. Making Pickles That Keep Their Crunch

Forget building a better mouse trap. The Agriculture Dept. has a patent on a better pickle—one that doesn't lose its crunchiness. Carbon dioxide causes pickles to go limp, and Agriculture researchers have come up with a mutant strain of a bacteria that does not produce the gas during the fermentation process. That difference could simplify matters for the $400 million-a-year fermented pickle business.

Carbon dioxide creates gas pockets inside the cucumbers that destroy their desirable crunchiness and eventually leave them fit only for the relish heap. Pickle producers' current damage-control program involves a whole series of steps: They bubble nitrogen through the fermentation tanks to dissipate carbon dioxide. That means that tanks must be kept open, leaving them susceptible to mold growth. So pickle-makers keep their tanks outdoors, where the sun's ultraviolet rays can kill off mold. But rainwater and other contaminants can get in, so the pickle industry adds liberal doses of salt.

With the new bacteria, picklemakers can move their tanks indoors and cut down on salt and nitrogen. Researchers at North Carolina State University and Mt. Olive Pickle Co. in Mount Olive, N.C., are giving Agriculture's bacteria a try.

"Developments to Watch," *Insight*

[f]
four

[v]
very

Sample: [f] <u>F</u>OUR <u>PH</u>ONE CALLS ARE ENO<u>UGH</u>.
[v] IT WAS <u>V</u>ERY HOT, O<u>F</u> COURSE.

Spellings: **f** as in **four**   **v** as in **very**
ff as in **affair**   **f** (only in the word **of**)
gh as in **enough**   **ph** (only in **Stephen**)
ph as in **phone**   **vv** as in **savvy**
lf as in **half**

Description

[f] and [v] are cognate labio-dental sounds. [f] is voiceless, but [v] is voiced. They are fricative sounds that you produce by forcing the breathstream between your upper teeth and lower lip.

Production: [f]

1. Very lightly, rest the cutting edge of your upper front teeth against your lower lip.
2. Let your tongue rest against the floor of your mouth.
3. Start the breathstream moving, and force it between your lower lip and upper teeth. Don't allow any air to escape through your nose. Make sure you use a light touch. If you press too hard, not enough air comes through.

Production: [v]

Follow the same steps you used for [f]. As soon as you feel your teeth and lip touch, add voice.

Problems

PROBLEM 1. CONFUSION OF [f] AND [v]

Native-born speakers of American English usually don't have many production problems with [f] and [v]. Some nonnative speakers, especially native German speakers, may frequently confuse [f] and [v] or substitute [w] for [v]. The contrast drills below will help you eliminate such confusion.

[f]

[v]

Contrast Drill for [f] and [v]

Say the following words aloud. First read down the list of [f] words, making sure you don't hear or feel voice. Then read down the list of [v] words, this time listening and feeling for voice. For the last step, read across, contrasting pairs of words—the first word voiceless, the second voiced.

[f]	[v]	[f]	[v]
feel — veal		proof — prove	
fine — vine		half — have	
fast — vast		leaf — leave	
fail — veil		surface — service	
fan — van		rifle — rival	
fat — vat		shuffle — shovel	

Contrast Drill for [v] and [w]

Say the following words aloud. First read down the list of [w] words, making sure that you can feel the pursing movements of the lips; you shouldn't make lip-teeth contact. Then read down the list of [v] words, making sure that you feel the contact between your upper teeth and lower lip. For the last step, read across, contrasting pairs of words.

[w]	[v]	[w]	[v]
west — vest		went — vent	
wet — vet		wile — vile	
wine — vine		wane — vane	
wail — veil		worse — verse	
waltz — vaults		wend — vend	

PROBLEM 2. SUBSTITUTION OF [b] FOR [v]

This occurs most often with native Spanish speakers. For example, the word *very* would become *berry*. Try the contrast drill below if you have this substitution.

Contrast Drill for [b] and [v]

Say the following words aloud. First read down the list of [b] words, feeling the plosive quality of the sound. Next, read down the list of [v]

[f]
[v]

words, making sure to feel that there is not a buildup of air resulting in a plosive sound. You should feel your teeth touching your lip, not both lips touching each other. For the last step, read across, contrasting pairs of words.

[b]		[v]	[b]		[v]
ban	—	van	bend	—	vend
berry	—	very	saber	—	saver
beer	—	veer	dub	—	dove
bile	—	vile	robe	—	rove
best	—	vest	curb	—	curve
bow	—	vow	curbing	—	curving
boat	—	vote	bane	—	vane

PROBLEM 3. OMISSION OF [v]

This is a problem shared by many native speakers. There is a tendency to omit the [v] in the word *of* or to assimilate it into the next word. There is also a tendency to omit the [v] when it's followed by a word beginning with a consonant. You'll work on this problem in the Level 2 Phrases.

LEVEL 1 DRILLS FOR [f]

Level 1 Practice Words for [f]

Say the words in the following lists slowly and clearly. Listen carefully and correct your production until you're satisfied that the sound is clear. Remember, [f] is voiceless. Start with the *Beginning* words.

Beginning	*End*	*Middle*
fee	beef	effect
feed	chief	infect
fit	thief	affect
fin	if	benefit
fate	miff	confident
fake	waif	headphone
fed	deaf	café
fend	chef	infant
fan	tough	magnify

Beginning	End	Middle
fat	half	jiffy
fact	chaff	muffin
funny	puff	offend
fine	huff	offhand
fight	wife	taffy
fog	off	topography
foe	cough	defend
photo	knife	coffee
phone	enough	confide
foot	goof	confound
food	cuff	affinity

[f]
[v]

▼ **Level 1 Practice Phrases for [f]**

fine beef	funny photo	off the cuff
safe by a foot	face the fact	deaf chef
enough affinity	tough muffin	defend the fans

▼ **Level 1 Practice Sentences for [f]**

1. The chef was five feet tall.
2. The funny-tasting coffee was the chief complaint.
3. They charged the photo fee over the telephone.
4. The singer was offended by coughing at the benefit.
5. "Where's the beef?" has become a fact of life.
6. It was fate that confined us to the café.
7. He ate half the muffin but drank all the coffee.
8. The infant's infection confounded the physician.
9. He confidently paid the farmer with fake bills.
10. The headphones magnified the effect of the music.

LEVEL 2 DRILLS FOR [f]

Words at this level have slightly more difficult combinations of sounds, and some have [v] for contrast. Say them slowly and distinctly, making sure that the [f] doesn't pick up any voicing from adjoining voiced sounds.

[f]
[v]

 Level 2 Practice Words for [f]

Beginning	End	Middle
fear	aloof	before
fever	giraffe	afford
female	playoff	befall
field	bluff	refuse
finish	belief	snowfall
finger	relief	effort
Philip	loaf	breakfast
Phyllis	cliff	wishful
face	housewife	satisfy
favor	Joseph	terrify
fair	shelf	glorify
fell	strafe	cupful
ferry	strife	mouthful
fallacy	leaf	steadfast
first	brief	offend
furry	safe	prefect
furnace	proof	rectify
fire	grief	perfect
file	self	kingfisher
five	stiff	rarefy
forest	staff	parfait
four	whiff	default
full	gruff	defer

 Level 2 Practice Phrases for [f]

fifty-five	famous females	foolish faults
brief whiff	perfect parfait	furnace fire
steadfast effort	breakfast loaf	four fallacies
save face	before the ferry	gruff staff

 Level 2 Practice Sentences for [f]

1. The first fall came in fifteen minutes.
2. I was satisfied with a mouthful of breakfast.
3. He could afford to make an effort to be brief.
4. She picked fifty perfect daffodils.
5. The forest was full of rough roads.

6. Joseph saw four terrifying movies.
7. I took a fast ferry to Martha's Vineyard.
8. Phyllis was famous for her vanilla parfait.
9. I was relieved to finish finals before vacation.
10. The field crew removed the snowfall after the playoff.

[f]
[v]

LEVEL 3 DRILLS FOR [f]

Here are practice words for four blends that can cause difficulty. They are [fl], [fr], [fs], and [ft]. Say them carefully, as one sound. Don't let any vowel sound creep in between the consonants in the blends.

▼ **Level 3 Practice Words for [f]**

[fl]	[fr]	[fs]	[ft]
flake	free	beliefs	raft
floor	frog	skiffs	reefed
flunk	friend	reefs	laughed
flame	frost	graphs	beefed
flush	frenzy	laughs	left
inflexible	infringe	safes	staffed
cauliflower	afraid	chefs	after
sniffle	Afro	chafes	shafted
raffle	refreshment	calf's	rafted
scuffle	grapefruit	handcuffs	laughter
waffle	antifreeze	takeoffs	safety

▼ **Level 3 Practice Sentences for [f]**

1. His face grew flushed when he won the raffle.
2. I'm afraid I infringed on my friend.
3. He laughs at others' beliefs.
4. We reefed the sail on the raft in complete safety.
5. I left the snowflakes on the frosty shelf.
6. Everyone enjoyed the free refreshments.
7. I found the cauliflower on the floor.
8. He jumped safely from the flaming rafters.
9. Some chefs are inflexible about flush-fitting covers.
10. We beefed up the skiff's frames after it fell.

[f]
[v]

Challenge Sentences for [f]

1. Florence fried fifty fat cauliflowers for five of her finest friends.
2. Please inform Fred if any funny references are made before breakfast is finished.
3. The chef fixed the food for the afternoon on a flame that was four-fifths safe.
4. The officer fortified his position with an official effort that found favor with the infantry.
5. Finish the furniture with a different polish than that you found for us on Friday.

LEVEL 1 DRILLS FOR [v]

Level 1 Practice Words for [v]

Say the words in the following lists slowly and clearly. Listen carefully and correct your production until you feel sure that the sound is clear and accurate. Try to start your voicing at the same time that your teeth touch your lip. Start with the *Beginning* words.

Beginning	*End*	*Middle*
veto	weave	even
vee	eve	event
victor	give	given
vintage	native	divide
view	connective	evict
vacate	wave	invent
vague	gave	devote
vain	pave	pivot
vend	concave	heaven
vet	have	devoted
vent	five	paving
van	I've	having
vast	dive	avoid
vow	of	convent
vouch	dove	advance
vitamin	above	nova
vine	wove	avid
voice	cove	advent
void	jove	cave-in
vote	move	moving

Level 1 Practice Phrases for [v]

heaven above	had a view	voice vote
concave paving	have in advance	moving van
vitamin invention	avoid a cave-in	vowed to veto

Level 1 Practice Phrases for [v]

1. The <u>veto</u> was <u>given</u> an <u>advantage</u>.
2. I <u>vowed</u> to take a <u>vitamin</u> in <u>advance</u>.
3. The <u>native</u> <u>dove</u> into the <u>wave</u> in the <u>cove</u>.
4. There was a <u>cave-in</u> in the <u>pavement</u> near the <u>convent</u>.
5. The <u>vent</u> blocked my <u>view</u> so I had to <u>move</u>.
6. The <u>nova</u> exploded in the <u>vast</u> <u>void</u>.
7. <u>Even</u> during the <u>eviction</u>, the apartment was <u>vacant</u>.
8. He <u>divided</u> the <u>van</u> <u>evenly</u>.
9. Number <u>five</u> grape <u>vine</u> has produced <u>vintage</u> wines.
10. Out <u>of</u> <u>devotion</u>, she <u>wove</u> the sign <u>of</u> the <u>dove</u>.

LEVEL 2 DRILLS FOR [v]

Level 2 Practice Words for [v]

The words at this level contain consonants that are more difficult to produce, and may have [f] for contrast. Say the following words slowly and clearly, and listen for a distinct [v].

Beginning	*End*	*Middle*	*All Positions*
veal	leave	fever	divisive
veer	pave	believing	vivid
village	believe	invisible	evolve
vessel	relative	river	vivacious
very	passive	silver	valve
vase	brave	prevent	Vancouver
vapor	enclave	gravy	velvet
valentine	save	shaving	survive
value	arrive	favor	preventive
vulture	glove	cavity	survivor
verse	serve	starving	vivisection
verbal	observe	service	convivial
virtue	stove	device	Vivian
volume	clove	clover	verve
volley	drove	nonverbal	vindictive

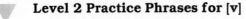

Level 2 Practice Phrases for [v]

The preposition *of* contains the sound [v], but people often omit it or assimilate it into the following word. Say the following phrases, making sure to put the voiced sound [v] in the word *of*. Don't overdo it, though, especially when the consonant that follows is voiceless. In that instance, it's normal to "devoice" the [v] slightly.

loaf of bread	can of worms	nick of time
pair of shoes	one of hers	best of it
two of them	ace of spades	one of the boys
barrels of fun	hill of beans	glass of water
cup of coffee	jug of wine	some of us

Many people tend to omit the [v] when it comes at the end of a word. They also omit it or assimilate it into the next word if that word begins with a consonant. Say the following phrases, making sure to produce a moderately strong [v].

five dollars	five times	five more
five hundred	five million	five months
five thousand	have many	live wire
have one on me	I've done it	give me
give them	save me	leave me
love me	have some	save some

Level 2 Practice Sentences for [v]

1. I tried to save five dollars.
2. Give me the vial with the vaccine.
3. I have one of them at the office.
4. I was able to observe the driver arriving five minutes late.
5. Love me, love my dog.
6. Varsity football is regarded positively by most universities.
7. Please leave the gloves for Valerie.
8. The entire village savored the aroma of the clover.

9. The silver river runs through the valley.
10. Many people shiver with a strange fever on Valentine's Day.

[f]
[v]

LEVEL 3 DRILLS FOR [v]

Level 3 Practice Words for [v]

Here are some practice words for three blends that can be troublesome: [vl], [vz], and [vd]. Say them carefully, as one sound. Don't let any vowel sound creep in between the consonants of the blend.

[vl]	[vz]	[vd]
evil	halves	saved
shovel	shelves	loved
marvel	leaves	received
rival	loves	proved
snivel	hooves	lived
grovel	heaves	revolved
gravel	curves	curved
gavel	shoves	shoved
oval	moves	moved
level	carves	carved
hovel	deceives	deceived
weevil	slaves	slaved
survival	grooves	grooved

Level 3 Practice Sentences for [v] and [f]

1. Vivian was a vivacious vixen, variously proving herself vindictive and benevolent.
2. The oven from Harvey's hovel was moved over to the bottom level of the valley house.
3. Heaven help the evil villain who deceives his virtuous wife with visions of vicarious living!
4. Vincent viewed the bevy of lovelies and vowed he would forever be moved.
5. Did you receive a Valentine from your lover in view of your lively division?

[f]

[v]

Challenge Sentences for [f] and [v]

1. They proved that the levels were uneven.
2. He deceived us in the way he moved on the curves.
3. It's the best work of fiction I've read in five years.
4. Speaking for myself, I've never been happier.
5. I was positive there was a live wire on the pavement.
6. I've told you at least five thousand times never to do it.
7. Half of the shelf was overflowing.
8. I haven't received the load of concrete yet.
9. Make sure to leave some of it for me to give away.
10. I lost the chance for victory in only seven moves.

Challenge Materials for [f] and [v]

1. The inventor of the fluorescent light probably thought he was doing mankind a favor. After all, fluorescent lighting is cheaper, brighter and cooler that other forms. He didn't realize that his invention would forever bedevil photographers.

Fluorescent lights don't emit the full color spectrum. That's why color pictures taken under them have a sickly green cast. Our eye automatically compensates for the imbalance in fluorescent light, so we don't notice it, but cameras and film record the real color.

Bob Krist, "Traveling Photographer," *Travel and Leisure*

2. Several years ago, Johnny Carson made a joke on his television show that there was a toilet paper shortage in this country. He then went on to describe what some of the more dire consequences of this shortage might be. The implication of this joke was that the viewers had better go out and stock up on toilet paper right away or else they would have to face these consequences. The subject made for a good laugh, but there was in fact no toilet paper shortage at all. Within several days, however, a real shortage did develop. Because people thought there was a shortage, they went out and bought up all of the toilet paper they could find, and, as a result, they disrupted the normal flow of toilet paper distribution.

This serves as a good example of the self-fulfilling prophecy. This is the phenomenon whereby a person believes something to be true which is not, acts on that belief, and by his action causes the belief to become true. As you can see, the self-fulfilling prophecy is a case where the world of thought overlaps with the world of action. And it happens in all avenues of life.

Roger von Oech, A Whack on the Side of the Head

[f]

[v]

3. The scroll work along the edge of the porch was wet with the fog. The fog dripped from the Monterey cypresses that shadowed off into nothing towards the cliff above the ocean. You could see a scant dozen feet in any direction. I went down the porch steps and drifted off through the trees, following an indistinct path until I could hear the wash of the surf licking at the fog, low down at the bottom of the cliff. There wasn't a gleam of light anywhere. I could see a dozen trees clearly at one time, another dozen dimly, then nothing at all but the fog. I circled to the left and drifted back towards the gravel path that went around to the stables where they parked the cars. When I could make out the outlines of the house I stopped. A little in front of me I had heard a man cough.

My steps hadn't made any sound on the soft moist turf. The man coughed again, then stifled the cough with a handkerchief or a sleeve. While he was still doing that I moved forward closer to him. I made him out, a vague shadow close to the path. Something made me step behind a tree and crouch down. The man turned his head. His face should have been a white blur when he did that. It wasn't. It remained dark. There was a mask over it.

I waited, behind the tree.

Raymond Chandler, The Big Sleep

[θ]
[ð]

Sample: [θ] I <u>TH</u>OUGHT IT WAS A <u>TH</u>IN SLICE.
              [ð] MY MO<u>TH</u>ER SAID <u>TH</u>EY WERE <u>TH</u>E BEST.
Spellings: **th** as in **ba<u>th</u>**   **th** as in **wi<u>th</u>**
               tth only in **Ma<u>tth</u>ew**   **the** as in **ba<u>the</u>**

Description

[θ] and [ð] are cognate lingua-dental sounds. They are fricatives that you produce by squeezing the breathstream between your tongue and teeth.

 ## Production: [θ]

1. Open your mouth until your teeth are slightly apart.
2. Round the tip of your tongue; don't try to point it too sharply.
3. Place your tongue so that it protrudes very slightly between your upper and lower front teeth.
4. Force the breathstream to come out between your tongue and teeth. Don't press too tightly; you'll end up forcing the sound. Don't let any air escape through the nose.

 ## Production: [ð]

Follow the steps for [θ]. Add voice as soon as you feel your tongue touch your teeth.

Problems

[θ] and [ð] are sounds that cause trouble for both native and nonnative speakers. They're very weak sounds (hard to hear) and are two of the last sounds children acquire. Since these sounds exist in only a few languages, most nonnative speakers have difficulty with them.

PROBLEM 1. TONGUE PLACEMENT

Most misarticulations of [θ] and [ð] result in sounds that are similar to [t] and [d]. That's because you are placing your tongue too close to the gum ridge behind your upper front teeth or because you're putting your tongue too firmly on the teeth to produce a fricative. Instead, you produce a plosive. If you are misarticulating these sounds, try this:

[θ]
[ð]

▼ **Production Drill**

1. Review the production notes on [θ] and [ð].
2. Look in a mirror and say the [θ] sound.
3. Make sure you can see the edge of your tongue protruding between the teeth. Say [θ] again. It may feel unusual and uncomfortable, but don't let that bother you.
4. Say the [θ] sound over and over again. Don't move your tongue between sounds. Try the following:

    [θ] . . . [θ] . . . [θ] . . . [θ] . . . thin

    [θ] . . . [θ] . . . [θ] . . . [θ] . . . thanks

    [θ] . . . [θ] . . . [θ] . . . [θ] . . . thought

    Monitor your production visually with the mirror and by listening carefully. If you're unsure, ask your instructor to help.
5. Once you're satisfied with [θ], try the same exercise with [ð].

    [ð] . . . [ð] . . . [ð] . . . [ð] . . . the

    [ð] . . . [ð] . . . [ð] . . . [ð] . . . those

    [ð] . . . [ð] . . . [ð] . . . [ð] . . . them

▼ **Contrast Drill for [θ] AND [t]**

If you're satisfied that you can produce the [θ] sound correctly in the previous drill, you can go on. In the following drill, contrast the words in the first column, which contain [t], with the [θ] words in the second column.

[t]	[θ]	[t]	[θ]
tin	— thin	tread	— thread
tick	— thick	true	— through
tanks	— thanks	boat	— both
taught	— thought	bat	— bath
tie	— thigh	oat	— oath
tinker	— thinker	bet	— Beth

[θ]
[ð]

Now try contrasting [d] words with [ð] words.

[d]		[ð]	[d]		[ð]
day	—	they	ladder	—	lather
doze	—	those	wordy	—	worthy
dough	—	though	load	—	loathe
den	—	then	laid	—	lathe
dine	—	thine	seed	—	seethe
dare	—	there	breed	—	breathe
udder	—	other	ride	—	writhe
mudder	—	mother	fodder	—	father

PROBLEM 2. [θ] AND [ð] CONFUSION

Since both [θ] and [ð] sounds are spelled in exactly the same way, many times people don't know which sound to use. Even if English is your native language and you know instinctively, most of the time, how a word is pronounced, you can still become confused. Maybe these general rules (which have exceptions) can help:

- Use the voiced sound [ð] when the word ends in *ther*. **Example:** bother [baðɚ]
- Use the voiced sound [ð] when the word ends in *the*. **Example:** breathe [brið]
- Use the voiceless sound [θ] when the *th* follows a pronounced consonant. **Example:** month [mʌnθ]

So *rather* uses [ð], *lathe* uses [ð], and *fifth* uses [θ].

PROBLEM 3. SUBSTITUTION OF [f] FOR [θ]

Sometimes people attempt to make the [θ] and [ð] without protruding their tongue. If the lower jaw comes forward and up at the same time, a fricative sound is produced with your lip and teeth instead of with your tongue and teeth. Try the following Contrast Drill.

Contrast Drill for [θ] and [f]

First read down the column of [f] words. Then read down the column of [θ] words. Finally read across, contrasting pairs of words. Feel for contact between your tongue and teeth on the [θ] words. You shouldn't feel any contact between your lip and teeth on those words. Complete the drill and then do it again, this time using a mirror to control your lip movement.

[f]		[θ]		[f]		[θ]	
fin	—	thin		froze	—	throws	
fink	—	think		free	—	three	
fought	—	thought		miff	—	myth	
first	—	thirst		sheaf	—	sheath	
Fred	—	thread		reef	—	wreath	

[θ]
[ð]

PROBLEM 4. SUBSTITUTION OF [s] FOR [θ] AND [z] FOR [ð]

These substitutions are commonly made by nonnative speakers. If you make this substitution, try the following.

▼ **Contrast Drill for [θ] and [s]**

Read down the list of [s] words first. Use a mirror, and make sure your tongue stays behind your teeth. Next read down the list of [θ] words. Use the mirror again, and this time, make sure your tongue protrudes slightly between your teeth. For the last step, read across, contrasting pairs of words.

[s]		[θ]		[s]		[θ]	
sink	—	think		miss	—	myth	
sought	—	thought		pass	—	path	
sick	—	thick		mouse	—	mouth	
seem	—	theme		moss	—	moth	
sin	—	thin		mass	—	math	
saw	—	thaw		worse	—	worth	
sing	—	thing		face	—	faith	
sigh	—	thigh		truce	—	truth	
sank	—	thank					

▼ **Contrast Drill for [ð] and [z]**

Read the list of [z] words first. Use the mirror, and keep your tongue behind your teeth. Then read down the list of [ð] words, saying each word carefully. Use the mirror again, and this time make sure your tongue protrudes slightly between your teeth for the [ð] words.

[z]		[ð]		[z]		[ð]	
Zen	—	then		breezing	—	breathing	
zee	—	thee		close	—	clothe	
razzer	—	rather		seize	—	seethe	
teasing	—	teething		tease	—	teethe	
closing	—	clothing		laze	—	lathe	

[θ]
[ð]

LEVEL 1 DRILLS FOR [θ]

▼ **Level 1 Practice Words for** [θ]

Say the words in the following lists slowly and clearly. Listen carefully, and correct your production until you are satisfied that it is accurate and clear. You may want to use a mirror so that you can see if your tongue is far enough between your teeth. Remember, [θ] is a voiceless sound. Start with the *Beginning* words.

Beginning	*End*	*Middle*
theme	beneath	ether
thief	heath	anything
thin	myth	nothing
thicken	Judith	ethnic
thing	faith	pathetic
think	Beth	pathway
theta	death	Matthew
theft	math	bathmat
thank	bath	methane
thud	path	toothpick
thug	mammoth	Kathy
thumb	Kenneth	pathos
thump	mouth	motheaten
thong	moth	Nathan
thigh	oath	python
thaw	both	anthem
thought	tooth	bathtub
thousand	youth	youthful

▼ **Level 1 Practice Phrases for** [θ]

thick thumb	thought nothing	give thanks
think thin	motheaten python	mammoth theft
pathetic thug	beneath the ether	youthful theme

▼ **Level 1 Practice Sentences for** [θ]

1. Math is not my thing.
2. I had faith in a spring thaw.
3. Kathy was headed on a path to tooth decay.
4. He had both a thug and a thief under his thumb.

5. Matthew found methane gas beneath a high heath.

[θ]
[ð]

6. According to a popular myth, a toothache you think about won't go away.
7. It was a pathetic, motheaten bathmat.
8. I thought Beth said "Thank you."
9. A mammoth had an incredibly thick thighbone.
10. Judith didn't think of bathtub accidents.

LEVEL 2 DRILLS FOR [θ]

Level 2 Practice Words for [θ]

The words at this level contain certain other consonants that make [θ] more difficult to produce accurately. These include [r], [l], [m], and [p]. Say each word slowly, and distinctly. Make sure you don't add any voice to the [θ]. You may find it helpful to overemphasize the [θ] on the first two or three readings. Start with the *Beginning* column, and don't move on until you are fairly confident that your production is accurate.

Beginning	*End*	*Middle*
theory	wreath	atheist
thistle	fifth	birthday
therapy	wealth	bathtowel
thirst	health	earthy
third	breath	healthy
thermometer	warmth	Southport
Thursday	worth	pathfinder
thorough	earth	something
three	cloth	everything
thrifty	fourth	lethargic
threat	north	stethoscope
thread	south	toothpaste
thirteen	growth	withheld
thrush	truth	truthful
thrive	tablecloth	stealthy
throng	girth	breathy
thrash	zenith	bathrobe
throat	stealth	athlete
threw	fortieth	withhold
thwart	fiftieth	Parthenon

[θ]
[ð]

Level 2 Practice Phrases for [θ]

third Thursday   withheld the truth
threw something   three bathrobes
thrifty thread   fourth birthday
fifth time   thirsty throng
sore throat

Level 2 Practice Sentences for [θ]

1. Truthfully, I'm thrifty about birthday cakes.
2. Southport is a thoughtlessly wealthy town.
3. A person of girth needs a lot of earth for growth.
4. Thrushes thrive in the north.
5. A fourth share was nothing to throw away.
6. Withholding taxes take a fifth of everything I earn.
7. He started therapy for his sore throat on Thursday.
8. We withdrew stealthily under cover of camouflage cloth.
9. A tablecloth is composed of thousands of threads.
10. His breathy voice resulted from unhealthy toothpaste.

LEVEL 3 DRILLS FOR [θ]

Level 3 Practice Words for [θ]

When [θ] is surrounded by other consonants in a cluster, the result is a "tongue twister." Such clusters are [θs] as in *myths*, [ksθ] as in *sixth*, [pθ] as in *depth*, [nθ] as in *ninth*, [θl] as in *ethyl*, and [dθ] as in *width*. Take these words slowly; they can be very difficult to produce accurately. When [θ] is followed by [s], combine the two into one sound. Don't stop production between the two; keep the breathstream going while you are moving your tongue back. Remember, these words have the voiceless [θ].

[nθ]	[θl]	[dθ]	[θs]	[ksθ]
seventh	ethyl	width	myths	sixth
ninth	faithless	breadth	fifths	six-thirty
tenth	Kathleen	hundredth	tenths	
menthol	lethal	thousandth	sevenths	
synthetic	ruthless		months	

[nθ]	[θl]	[dθ]	[θs]	[ksθ]
labyrinth	athlete		ninths	
anthology			paths	
Anthony			baths	
month			moths	

[θ]
[ð]

Level 3 Practice Sentences for [θ]

1. I bought a sixth can of synthetic oil.
2. Two fifths equals four tenths.
3. Old myths and old athletes can stretch beyond truth.
4. Kathleen was a ruthless depth-editor.
5. Length times width equals area.
6. It was a lethal dose of methyl alcohol.
7. It sunk only three-thousandths of an inch.
8. His seventh breath was longer than his eleventh.
9. It was his third faithless love affair.
10. Surfers set healthy records on ninth waves.

Challenge Sentences for [θ]

1. Theoretical mathematics involves mythical thinking in the third and fourth dimensions.
2. Thirty-three theologians thrust their thirsty tongues through their teeth.
3. Three threadbare travelers threaded their way through isothermal pathways to reach their zenith.
4. The other thermometer has a plethora of mercury at its pith.
5. Thanks for thinking of both of us; it was thoroughly thoughtful of you.

LEVEL 1 DRILLS FOR [ð]

Level 1 Practice Words for [ð]

Say the words in the following lists slowly and clearly. Listen carefully and adjust your production until you are satisfied with it. You may want to use a mirror so that you can check your tongue to make sure it

[θ]
[ð]

is far enough out between your teeth. We've saved words that end in [ð] for Level 2 since they are fairly difficult to pronounce smoothly. In Level 1, we suggest that you start with the *Middle* words first. It's easier to produce [ð] when it's preceded by a vowel. Remember to start your voicing of [ð] early enough.

Middle	*Beginning*	*Middle*	*Beginning*
either	thee	wither	they
within	them	without	then
neither	their	bathing	that
whether	though	together	thou
feather	than	gather	the
father	thy	mother	thine

 Level 1 Practice Phrases for [ð]

either one	feather bed	their mother
gather together	father is there	other feather
within and without	that bather	thee and thou

Level 1 Practice Sentences for [ð]

Note: the word *the* is one of the most frequently used in the English language. Yet many people are confused as to how to pronounce it, especially when they see it in print. Here are rules you can use to help you when you read aloud:

- The word *the* is pronounced [ðə] when it's followed by a consonant.
- The word *the* is pronounced [ði] when it's followed by a vowel.

So it's [ðə] *beginning* and [ði] *end.*

1. The feather bed was very soft.
2. My mother said that it was the end.
3. We can move the furniture together.
4. The critic made a scathing attack after the opening.
5. We were gathering cotton before the hot weather.
6. I like bathing in cool, soothing waters.
7. Neither one cared about the weather.
8. I knew without a doubt that it was the other one.

9. They were within the boundaries.
10. Therein lies the tale of Wuthering Heights.

LEVEL 2 DRILLS FOR [ð]

 Level 2 Practice Words for [ð]

The words at this level have consonant combinations in which the [ð] may be hard to produce clearly, and words that end in [ð]. Listen carefully for the [ð]; make sure you voice it when it's preceded or followed by voiceless consonants. Some of the words at this level may also have [θ] for contrast. Start with the *Beginning* words and then do the *Middle*. Save the *End* for last.

Beginning	*Middle*	*End*
these	although	with
those	rather	bathe
therefore	soothing	soothe
this	smoothly	lathe
thus	teething	tithe
thereafter	breathing	seethe
theirs	clothing	writhe
thence	writhing	breathe
thusly	leather	clothe
therein	rhythms	teethe
themselves	Mothers Day	smooth
that's	southern	scathe

Level 2 Practice Sentences for [ð]

1. Descartes said "I think, therefore I am."
2. I threw a blanket over the leather couch.
3. Either one is okay with me.
4. Teething rings can soothe a baby's teeth.
5. I have three exams this Thursday, then no more.
6. They attempted to bathe in their clothing.
7. I knew without a doubt the train would run smoothly.
8. The pit was seething with writhing reptiles.
9. Nevertheless, the theater was the oldest.
10. That's the way it is with my father.

[θ]
[ð]

LEVEL 3 DRILLS FOR [ð]

Level 3 Practice Words for [ð]

There are three [ð] blends that are difficult: [ðd], [ðz], and [rð]. In practice, you may have to draw the [ð] out slightly and overemphasize it. Try the following words, and listen closely for the [ð].

[ðd]	[ðz]	[rð]
breathed	breathes	farther
bathed	bathes	further
clothed	clothes	northern
seethed	seethes	worthy
smoothed	smoothes	worthiness
soothed	soothes	earthen
writhed	writhes	farthermost
loathed	loathes	swarthy

Level 3 Practice Sentences for [ð]

The following sentences contain the blends you've just practiced, as well as [ð] words from Levels 1 and 2. In addition, you'll find some [θ] words for contrast. Read the sentences a few times. Start off very slowly and carefully, but in subsequent readings, try to imitate normal speech rate and patterns.

1. My mother loathes snakes.
2. The Northern Lights are brighter the farther north you travel.
3. I washed my clothes as I bathed in the river.
4. The seaworthy vessel sailed south by southeast.
5. She was clothed in cotton that breathed.
6. Give him either the Novocaine or the ether.
7. Father's brow smoothed, and he breathed easier.
8. Don't bother me with unworthy questions.
9. My brother furthered his career with clear thinking.
10. That is the time that we'll be through.

Challenge Sentences for [ð] and [θ]

1. "Lather that leather thong," said the other feather merchant thoughtlessly.

2. "Bother your other brother," the author's father declared, wordily.
3. Smooth sailing, thought the sailor, thinking how seaworthy was his sloop from Boothbay.
4. Neither his father nor his mother bothered to clothe him, though they thought he was thoughtless about his appearance.
5. Nothing was further from her mind than the idea of furthering the expedition to the north.
6. As the throng gathered together, they withered at the sight of the thing's clothing.
7. There abide these three: faith, hope and charity. . .
8. "Breathes there a man with soul so dead, who never to himself hath said, this is my own, my native land." (Edward Barett Hale)
9. Brother against brother—that was the theme of the theatrical *Pathfinder.*
10. "Other times, other thoughts," breathed my brother through the thick ether.

[s] [z]

Sample: [s] THE DOG LOST THE SCENT OF THE SNAKE IN THE GRASS.
[z] THEY HOSED OUT THE CAGES AT THE ZOO.

Spellings: s as in **snake**   z as in **zoo**
ss as in **grass**   x as in **Xerox**
sc as in **scent**   se as in **hose**
c as in **cent**   zz as in **blizzard**
ps as in **psychology**   ss as in **scissors**
tz as in **waltz**   s as in **music**
sch as in **schism**
x as in **exit**
(with [**k**])

[s]
[z]

Description

[s] and [z] are cognate lingua-alveolar sounds. They are fricatives that you produce by forcing air between your tongue and the upper or lower front teeth.

Production: [s]

1. Place your tongue in the position to say [t], but don't say it.
2. Drop the tip of your tongue down and slightly back, but keep the sides lightly pressed against the middle and back upper teeth. Your tongue should now be pointing at the cutting edges of your front teeth or toward the gum ridge.
3. Make a shallow groove lengthwise along the midline of your tongue. Keep the sides up.
4. Blow the breathstream at the cutting edge of the teeth; create a "hissing" sound. [s] is voiceless.

Production: [z]

Follow the steps for [s]. Start voicing as soon as the air begins to move.

Problems

[s] and [z] are sounds that can cause you a lot of trouble. They are difficult sounds to produce—they require precision actions by the articulators, especially accurate movements, and fine auditory discrimination to produce just the right amount of "hiss." And, if you don't get it exactly right, people notice.

Although you can correct minor distortions fairly easily, major distortions, such as a frontal or lateral lisp, take more time and usually require trained guidance. If you have a frontal or lateral lisp, your instructor will probably refer you to Appendix B.

PROBLEM 1. "WHISTLING" [s] OR [z]

If the sound you make is too sharp or too high in pitch, you're probably holding your tongue tip too high and too close to the teeth. Gradually lower the tongue tip a millimeter at a time, and, at the same time, draw it back ever so slightly. Listen carefully as you produce an [s] with each adjustment. You'll probably notice that the pitch of the sound drops. Ask your instructor or another student to tell you when you've reached the right pitch. Keep practicing the sound until you're sure you can remember it. See Appendix B for more help.

PROBLEM 2. EXCESSIVE SIBILANCE

This is a high-pitched hissiness that seems to pervade a person's entire speech pattern. It usually results from overemphasizing and prolonging the [s]. Many times it's coupled with a whistling [s] and [z]. Try to make the [s] and [z] as short as you can, without actually omitting them when you practice the word lists. See Appendix B for more help.

PROBLEM 3. "BROAD" [s] AND [z]

In this problem, the sounds are too low in pitch or too broad. This happens when you let the air go out to one side of the mouth instead of down the central groove or when you fail to make a groove at all. See Appendix B for additional help.

PROBLEM 4. UNVOICING OF [z]

This problem is common in the speech of native speakers as well as those with Spanish and German language backgrounds. It happens when you start voicing halfway through the production of [z], and occurs most frequently at the end of words, often when forming plurals. Although for most English nouns, the addition of *s* forms a plural, the pronunciation can vary. Here are some general rules that may make it easier for you.

Forming English Plurals

- If the noun ends with a voiceless consonant, the *s* becomes the voiceless sound [s]. **Examples:** books–[buks], pants–[pænts]
- If the noun ends in a voiced consonant, the *s* becomes the voiced sound [z]. **Examples:** legs–[lɛgz], cans–[kænz]
- If the noun ends with [s], [z] [ʃ], [ʒ], [tʃ], or [dʒ], then the *s* becomes the syllable [ɪz]. **Examples:**

roses	— [rozɪz]	masses	— [mæsɪz]
prizes	— [praɪzɪz]	causes	— [kɔzɪz]
bushes	— [buʃɪz]	flashes	— [flæʃɪz]
garages	— [gəraʒɪz]	mirages	— [mɪraʃɪz]
witches	— [wɪtʃɪz]	catches	— [kætʃɪz]
judges	— [dʒʌdʒɪz]	hedges	— [hɛdʒɪz]

[s]

[z]

- The same rules hold true for verbs, too. Here are some examples:

kicks	— [kɪks]	stops	— [staps]
hugs	— [hʌgz]	runs	— [rʌnz]
hisses	— [hɪsɪz]	passes	— [pæsɪz]
fizzes	— [fɪzɪz]	raises	— [rezɪz]
washes	— [waʃɪz]	rushes	— [rʌʃɪz]
hitches	— [hɪtʃɪz]	watches	— [watʃɪz]
urges	— [ɝdʒɪz]	wedges	— [wɛdʒɪz]

Now try the following contrast drill for [s] and [z].

Contrast Drill for [s] AND [z]

Read down the list of [s] words first. Notice the absence of voice. Then read down the list of [z] words, feeling for voice. Make sure to start voicing at the start of the sound. The last step is to read across, contrasting pairs of words.

[s]	[z]	[s]	[z]
sue	— zoo	busing	— buzzing
sap	— zap	loose	— lose
sip	— zip	fuss	— fuzz
racer	— razor	spice	— spies
lacer	— laser	device	— devise

LEVEL 1 DRILLS FOR [s]

Level 1 Practice Words for [s]

Say the words in the following lists slowly and clearly. Listen carefully, and adjust your tongue to produce the clearest, strongest [s]. Don't overdo it. Use moderate air pressure. Start with the *Beginning* words.

Beginning	*End*	*Middle*
see	bets	acid
seam	pets	aside
sit	bats	basic
sift	cats	cassette
sin	pats	decent
sing	rats	decide
safe	plates	essay
sane	rates	icing

Beginning	End	Middle
saint	oats	kerosene
set	pass	Tennessee
send	place	medicine
sack	pace	baseball
sag	bless	guessing
sand	mass	passing
Sam	kiss	racing
sign	bus	busing
sight	miss	fantasy
soon	mess	foster
suit	hiss	pester
soup	grass	rooster
soak	juice	east
soar	menace	west
soft	purchase	also
sauna	priced	mist
soot	goodness	racer
sound	cactus	priced
sun	caps	bossy
supper	tips	blossom
Sunday	tops	presser
someday	pups	messy

[s]

[z]

Level 1 Practice Phrases for [s]

sad sack	soft soap	cats and rats
cactus flower	purchase price	new suit
set aside	sing song	pass the soup
kiss me	safe and sound	out of sight

Level 1 Practice Sentences for [s]

1. It's hard to see cats in the grass.
2. The heavy safe made the floor sag.
3. I sent the package last week.
4. He didn't pass the salt.
5. I'm going to sign the lease on the house.
6. He bought the suit at a low price.
7. The sand made a mess on the seat.
8. It's the tip of the iceberg.
9. That's your basic racing car.
10. Set aside a bottle of battery acid.

[s]

[z]

LEVEL 2 DRILLS FOR [s]

The words at this level are more difficult to produce accurately because of the sounds that precede and follow the [s]. Start with the *Beginning* words, go next to the *End* column, then to the *Middle* column. Make sure the [s] has enough force to be easily heard.

 Level 2 Practice Words for [s]

Beginning	End	Middle
sell	actress	assemble
sail	address	worrisome
salt	blouse	assign
search	endless	icicle
certain	release	saucy
circle	press	sissy
central	furnace	sister
sorry	nauseous	policy
soil	depress	proceed
solve	lettuce	taste
cycle	breathless	jealousy
solar	thoughtless	essential
spite	police	courtesy
sold	worse	classic
Sarah	hearse	bicycle
ceiling	verse	deceive
sulk	curse	blister
solemn	nurse	recent
soccer	face	thermostat

 Level 2 Practice Sentences for [s]

1. Sarah lowered the thermostat on the furnace.
2. The soccer game proceeded in spite of the rain.
3. They sent the blouse to the wrong address.
4. The police found the stolen classic car.
5. The actress had to rehearse the role of the nurse.
6. That's the worst lettuce I ever tasted.

7. They searched in an endless circle.
8. Send me a press release.
9. My sister sold her new bicycle at a loss.
10. Problem solving is an endless cycle.

Level 3 Problems and Drills

[s] is most difficult to produce when it occurs in *blends* with other consonants. Some blends that can be troublesome are [sw], [sp], [str], [skr],
and [sts].

PROBLEM 1. [sw] AND [ʃ] CONFUSION

Sometimes people may substitute [ʃ] as in *shoe* for [s] as in *sue.* Try it.
See what happens when the [ʃ] is substituted for the first sound in the
word *swim.* This substitution happens when you drop your tongue tip
too soon before the [w].

▼ Production Drill

1. Produce a long [s], stop completely, then say the rest of the word.
2. Read across each line. Gradually shorten the [s] and bring the parts
    together.

sss . . . weet	ss . . weet	s . weet	sweet
sss . . . wing	ss . . wing	s . wing	swing
sss . . . way	ss . . way	s . way	sway
sss . . . well	ss . . well	s . well	swell
sss . . . wine	ss . . wine	s . wine	swine

▼ Practice Words for [sw] (Beginning Position Only)

sweet	sweat	swan	swab
sweep	swept	swallow	swelter
Sweden	swell	swarm	Swiss
swim	swear	swollen	switch
swill	suede	swoosh	swatch
swift	swam	swoon	swindle
sway	swag	swamp	swinger
swing	swine	swum	swale

PROBLEM 2. [sp] AND [ʃ] CONFUSION

The same thing that happens with [sw] can happen with [sp] if you lower your tongue too soon.

Production Drill

1. Produce a long [s], stop completely, then say the rest of the word.
2. Read each line across. Gradually shorten the [s] and bring the parts together.

sss . . . peak	ss . . peak	s . peak	speak
sss . . . pit	ss . . pit	s . pit	spit
sss . . . pare	ss . . pare	s . pare	spare
sss . . . pool	ss . . pool	s . pool	spool
sss . . . pry	ss . . pry	s . pry	spry
sss . . . print	ss . . print	s . print	sprint

Practice Words for [sp]

Beginning	*End*	*Middle*
speak	lisp	respect
speed	hasp	teaspoon
spit	clasp	desperate
spin	grasp	despair
spill	cusp	perspire
Spain	rasp	respond
spare	wisp	Mr. Spock
spat	crisp	respite
span	gasp	inspire
spackle	wasp	desperation
spot		respiration
spawn		cuspidor
spore		rasping
spoke		hospital
spool		conspiracy
spoon		trespass
spunky		conspicuous
sponge		Hispanic
spry		
spurt		
spring		

PROBLEM 3. TONGUE SHAPING

With [str], the trouble occurs when you prematurely flatten your tongue to make the [t]. This results in [ʃt], so that the word *street* might sound like *shtreet*. This distortion is very common in New York City and other Eastern, urban areas.

Production Drill

1. Produce a long [s], stop completely, then say the rest of the word.
2. Read across each line. Gradually bring the two parts together, shortening the [s] at the same time.

sss . . . treet	ss . . treet	s . treet	street
sss . . . trip	ss . . trip	s . trip	strip
sss . . . tray	ss . . tray	s . tray	stray
sss . . . trap	ss . . trap	s . trap	strap
sss . . . truck	ss . . truck	s . truck	struck
sss . . . tripe	ss . . tripe	s . tripe	stripe

3. Read the following pairs of words very slowly, extending the first sound of each word slightly longer than you usually would. Listen carefully; avoid using [ʃ] in the second word.

steam	—	stream	sting	— string
stay	—	stray	state	— strait
stain	—	strain	stand	— strand
stoke	—	stroke	stole	— stroll
stove	—	strove	stuck	— struck
stop	—	strop	stew	— strew

Practice Words for [str]

For this set of words, we'll group *Beginning* and *Middle* separately. There is no *End* group for this set.

Beginning

straddle	street	stream
streak	strip	string
strict	stray	straight
strain	stranger	stretch
stress	strap	strand
strangle	strontium	strop
structure	struck	struggle
strung	straw	strong
stripe	strike	stride

[s]
[z]

Middle

instrument	construction	frustrate
instruct	restrict	restrain
downstream	Main Street	constrict
destroy	distress	distract
abstract	airstrip	bloodstream
astronaut	mistreat	obstruct

PROBLEM 4. ANTICIPATION OF [k]

Problems with [skr] are usually the result of anticipating the [k]. You raise the back of the tongue too early, and, as a result, the tip lowers. You then substitute [ʃkr] for [skr]. If you do this, the word scrape might sound like *shcrape*.

 Production Drill

1. Produce a long [s], stop completely, then say the rest of the word.
2. Read each line across. Gradually shorten the [s] and bring the parts together.

sss . . . creen	ss . . creen	s . creen	screen
sss . . . cript	ss . . cript	s . cript	script
sss . . . crape	ss . . crape	s . crape	scrape
sss . . . cratch	ss . . cratch	s . cratch	scratch
sss . . . crew	ss . . crew	s . crew	screw
sss . . . crub	ss . . crub	s . crub	scrub

 Practice Words for [skr]

For this set, too, we've grouped *Beginning* and *Middle* separately. There's no *End* list for this sound.

Beginning

screen	scream	screech
script	scribble	scrimmage
scrape	scratch	scrap
scrabble	scramble	scrub
scruffy	scrunch	screw

Middle

describe	discreet	discretion
discrimination	unscrupulous	unscrew
inscribe	postscript	corkscrew
prescription	transcribe	subscribe

PROBLEM 5. OMISSION OF [t]

The most common problem with this blend is omitting the [t]. This omission probably occurs because of the precise tongue movements required and because the sounds involved are weak, high-frequency sounds that are hard to hear.

▼ **Production Drill**

Think of the [sts] blend as being *two* sounds, not three. It's composed of [s] followed by a [ts] blend. The [ts] is the same sound as the last sound in the word *cats.*

Make a long [s], stop completely, then make a [ts] sound:

sss . . . ts   sss . . . ts   sss . . . ts   sss . . . ts

Read across

beas . . . ts	beas . . ts	beas . ts	beasts
wris . . . ts	wris . . ts	wris . ts	wrists
gues . . . ts	gues . . ts	gues . ts	guests
cas . . . ts	cas . . ts	cas . ts	casts
rus . . . ts	rus . . ts	rus . ts	rusts
coas . . . ts	coas . . ts	coas . ts	coasts

▼ **Practice Words for [sts] (End Position Only)**

beasts	feasts	priests	Baptists
fists	wrists	mists	insists
bastes	pastes	pests	nests
bests	rests	guests	tests
casts	masts	blasts	lasts
rusts	busts	dusts	gusts
firsts	bursts	costs	thrusts
rousts	posts	roasts	coasts
boasts	hosts	boosts	roosts
hoists	foists	joists	jests
jousts	frosts	wastes	tastes

[s]

[z]

PROBLEM 6. INVERSION OF [k] AND [s]

This inversion is one of the pet peeves of many a speech teacher. It occurs primarily in the word *ask.* If you invert the two consonant sounds, ask [æsk] becomes ax [æks]. Generally, all it takes to correct this problem is a few practice sessions in which you slowly repeat the correct word over and over again. At first it may seem to be a tongue twister, but with a little practice it becomes much easier.

Contrast Drill for [ks] and [sk]

Say the following pairs of words slowly and carefully. Make the vowel sound in each word longer than usual, and be certain that you hear a [s] before the [k] in the second word of each pair.

axe	—	ask	backs	—	bask
max	—	mask	decks	—	desk
ducks	—	dusk	tacks	—	task

Level 3 Practice Words for [sk]

Say the following words slowly and distinctly. Emphasize the [sk] a little more than you usually would.

cask	husk	tusk	grotesque
disk	picturesque	risk	asterisk
brisk	musk	brusque	mosque
ask	mask	dusk	bask
frisk	desk	arabesque	task

Level 3 Practice Sentences for [s]

1. The screaming guests had been frightened by the snakes.
2. The spilled bleach left a white streak in the blouse.
3. The instructor spoke respectfully to the students.
4. She asked him if he could swim to Sweden.
5. The streets were clogged with construction machinery.
6. She soaked her swollen arm discreetly.
7. "It's the last straw," he said with restraint.
8. The Spanish moss swayed in the swampy mists.
9. The mosquito is a pest that makes you scratch.
10. The Orient Express stops twice before leaving France.

▼ **Challenge Sentences for [s]**

1. Amidst the mists and coldest frosts,
   With barest wrists and stoutest boasts,
   He thrusts his fists against the posts,
   And still insists he sees the ghosts.
2. He straddled the stream, rather than destroy the structure of the abstract sculpture.
3. Describe the scrambled inscriptions for your unscrupulous instructor.
4. "Subscribe to the *Main Street Sun*," whispered the sweet young, though strict, Miss.
5. The master's assistant will register your instrument or instruct you in its use.

▼ **Challenge Materials for [s]**

1. A skunk sat on a stump.
   The stump thunk the skunk stunk.
   The skunk thunk the stump stunk.
   I think they both stunk.

   Anonymous

2. Each of us, from the very beginning of our lives, has had unique and individual experiences. Scientists tell us that every sensory experience—that is, everything we have ever felt, tasted, heard, seen and so forth—is recorded in the memory banks of our brain. From the very beginning of our lives, we experience things that no other person has experienced in exactly the same way. Each new sensory message received is interpreted in terms of things that we have experienced in the past. The past events color and shade our interpretation of present events.

   Functional Business Presentations, Paul R. Timm

3. Consider how we adapt to stress. Stress can be one of the most damaging influences on the biological makeup of the body, to say nothing of its effect on our ability to communicate interpersonally. Stress is a stimulus just like hitting your head on an apple tree. And any stimulus causes one or more reactions. We may have a headache under extreme stress. We may sweat under extreme stress. All of

[s]

[z]

these are biological reactions our bodies are making to signal us that we are overloading our sensory systems.

How do we adapt to stress? By adapting biologically, we may decide to overeat. Yet overeating may produce just the opposite effect we desire, especially if a stress-prone digestive system can't handle that much food. We may decide to overdrink, but find the consequences of the local pub worse than the cure. We may also lie awake with a case of insomnia while trying to solve a stressful problem and pay for that wakefulness the next day. As we can see, these negative biological adaptations cause more stress, not less.

Each Other: An Introduction to Interpersonal
Communication, John R. Bittner

4. To Some in Desert, Torpor Means Survival

As many creatures prepare to shut down operations for the winter and hide out underground, a few animals are still deep in slumber and will not awake until winter is in full force. These opposite-season slumberers, or estivators, have received little study but are believed to live underground for extended periods during the hottest, driest weather in the desert.

Estivators, which include the Mohave ground squirrel and several species of mice, are forced underground not by the extreme heat but by the need to conserve what little body water they have, says Bruce Wunder, professor and chairman of Colorado State University's biology department, where several experiments on dormancy are being conducted. Estivators vary considerably in their slumber periods, with the Mohave ground squirrel spending about nine months underground and the mice often reemerging after a few days.

"Science Briefing," *Insight*

5. The best material for ties is silk. You can get away with a polyester that looks like silk, or a polyester and silk combination, which can be excellent, but you are safer if you stick with one hundred percent silk. If you have to skimp on your wardrobe, skimp on your suits or shirts before you try to save money on your ties. There is nothing that will destroy a businessman's image as certainly as a cheap tie.

John T. Molloy's New Dress for Success, John T. Molloy

LEVEL 1 DRILLS FOR [z]

Level 1 Practice Words for [z]

Say the following words slowly and distinctly. Listen carefully, and adjust your tongue for the clearest [z] possible. Start with the *Beginning* words, and then go on to the *Middle* words.

Beginning	*Middle*	*End*
zenith	easy	bees
zip	amazing	ease
zipper	busy	is
zinc	daisy	his
zinnia	fuzzy	gaze
Zen	amusement	days
zany	teasing	as
zephyr	music	because
zombie	noisy	was
zodiac	choosing	buzz
zone	Tuesday	wise
zoom	design	noise
zucchini	using	choose
zygote	hazy	news
zoo	grazing	nose

Level 1 Practice Phrases for [z]

zigzag	zodiac zone	was his
buzzing bees	noisy music	busy Tuesday
using his nose	is it a zoo	hazy days
was it his	as is	amazing design

Level 1 Practice Sentences for [z]

1. She was gazing at a fuzzy wool sweater.
2. Does the amusement park close early on Tuesdays?
3. I was zigzagging through the zinnias.
4. The zany music was noisy.
5. She was always teasing.
6. Is that the right Zip Code zone?
7. I didn't choose that zodiac design.
8. I love the buzzing of the bees in the daisies.
9. He was using his nose to find news.
10. San Diego has an amazing zoo.

[s]

[z]

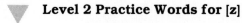

Level 2 Practice Words for [z]

The words at this level are more difficult to produce accurately because of different combinations of consonants, and because they may have [s] for contrast. Start with the *Beginning* words, go next to the *Middle* column, and when you say the *End* words make sure to voice the [z] long enough.

Beginning	*Middle*	*End*
zeal	freezing	sees
zero	blizzard	dries
zebra	crazy	prize
zesty	buzzer	refuse
Xerox	disaster	rise
zillion	blazer	trapeze
zilch	rising	bruise
zircon	example	draws
Zurich	causing	lies
zoology	clumsy	falls
xylophone	result	sells
zealous	Brazil	cars

Level 2 Practice Sentences for [z]

1. She was refusing to wear the violet blazer.
2. The bruise was due to my clumsy move.
3. There are a zillion cars in Brazil.
4. Sometimes its a disaster when the stock market falls.
5. The river flows zestfully over the sandbars.
6. A trapeze is an example of the height of craziness.
7. The city of Zurich lies next to a river.
8. He was awarded a prize for braving the freezing blizzard.
9. I was sure a rising tide would cause the warning buzzer to sound.
10. She was studying zebras in zoology.

LEVEL 3 DRILLS FOR [z]

Sometimes people have a tendency to unvoice [z] and turn it into an [s] when [z] is blended with other consonants. Say the following words, making sure to voice the [z]. Also, make sure that the two consonants blend into one sound.

[dz]	[nz]	[vz]
reeds	beans	believes
bids	bins	gives
fades	rains	waves
reds	tens	shelves
dads	cans	halves
rods	barns	gloves
cords	lawns	stoves
codes	loans	loves
woods	groans	wolves
foods	spoons	grooves
floods	buns	shoves
rides	lines	hives

Level 3 Practice Sentences for [s] and [z]

1. He really shovels in the junk foods.
2. She paints green lawns and red barns.
3. As the saying goes, the race is to the swift.
4. He goes with the flow and rides with the tides.
5. Wood stoves are my answer to the energy crisis.
6. I can't stand long bus lines in the mornings.
7. Deposit cans are worth five cents apiece.
8. She fought her way through the wolves standing outside.
9. My sister groans when she lends me money for school.
10. Sometimes this is an exercise in patience.

Challenge Sentences for [s] and [z]

1. Suzie was busy as a bee while Ezra lazed around noisily.
2. Cereal with raisins cause frenzy when dizzy services confuse their orders for those containing pecans.
3. Franz Schubert composed a series of musical interludes.
4. No one believes that cruising packs of wolves bruise herds of cows.
5. Xerox earns zillions of dollars by setting examples for other rising companies.

[ʃ]
[ʒ]

[ʃ] [ʒ]

she   beige

Sample: [ʃ] SHE DREAMED THAT HE LIVED IN A MANSION MADE OF SUGAR NEAR CHICAGO'S RUSSIAN EMBASSY.
[ʒ] SHE WAS A VISION IN BEIGE AND AZURE AT THE GARAGE.

Spellings: **sh** as in **she**   **s** as in **measure**
             c as in **ocean**   **ge** as in **beige**
             s as in **tension**   **z** as in **azure**
             ss as in **fissure**   **j** as in **bijou**
             ch as in **Chicago**
             t as in **nation**
             sch as in **schnapps**
             chs as in **fuchsia**
             sc as in **fascist**

Description

[ʃ] and [ʒ] are cognate sounds. They are lingua-palatal fricatives. You produce them very much like the [s] and [z], except the tongue is farther back.

Production: [ʃ]

1. Open your mouth slightly so that your teeth are apart and your lips are separated.
2. Round your tongue slightly, and raise the sides so that they are against the upper molars.
3. Raise the front of the tongue so that it points to the area just behind the gum ridge.
4. Keep the sides of the tongue up and start the breathstream flowing. Force the air against the front teeth, but make sure to keep the front of the tongue elevated. [ʃ] is voiceless.

Production: [ʒ]

Follow the same steps as for [ʃ]. This time add voice at the same instant that the air starts to move.

Problems

[ʃ] and [ʒ] are fairly easy to articulate, and most people don't have many problems with them. The most frequent problems are confusion of [ʃ] and [ʒ], lateral emission, and substitution of [tʃ] as in *chip* and [dʒ] as in *huge.*

PROBLEM 1. CONFUSION OF [ʃ] AND [ʒ]

Contrast Drill for [ʃ] and [ʒ]

First read aloud the column of [ʃ] words. You shouldn't feel voice. Then read the column of [ʒ] words. This time feel and listen for voice. The last step is to read across, contrasting pairs of words.

[ʃ]		[ʒ]
glacier	—	glazier
Aleutian	—	illusion
shock	—	Jacques
shallow	—	jabot
assure	—	azure
pressure	—	pleasure
fission	—	vision

PROBLEM 2. LATERAL EMISSION

If you don't press your tongue firmly against the upper side teeth, the air can escape from the sides of your mouth. Hold your hands with the forefingers touching the corners of your mouth, as though you were making a megaphone with your hands. Say the sound [ʃ] very force-fully. Do you feel any air on your fingers? If you do, you're emitting the

[ʃ]
[ʒ]

air laterally. Make the sound again, and make sure the sides of your tongue are up and touching the teeth. Hold two fingers about one inch in front of your mouth. Try to direct the stream of air at your fingers. If you have great difficulty directing the air out the front of the mouth, you should read Appendix B.

PROBLEM 3. CONFUSION OF [tʃ] AND [ʃ]

The following contrast drill should help you with this problem, which is common among those whose first language is Spanish.

Contrast Drill for [ʃ] and [tʃ]

Read the words in the following lists aloud, slowly and clearly. First read down the list of [ʃ] words, then read the list of [tʃ] words. You should not feel any plosive characteristics when you read the [ʃ] words. The last step is to read the words across, contrasting the pairs.

[ʃ]	[tʃ]	[ʃ]	[tʃ]
sheet	— cheat	share	— chair
sheep	— cheap	marsh	— march
ship	— chip	hash	— hatch
shin	— chin	wash	— watch
shoe	— chew	cash	— catch

LEVEL 1 DRILLS FOR [ʃ]

Level 1 Practice Words for [ʃ]

Say the words in the following lists slowly and clearly. Listen carefully, and correct your production until you are sure you're producing the right sound. If you're not certain, ask your instructor or another member of the class to help. Start with the *Beginning* words.

Beginning	*End*	*Middle*
she	dish	option
sheep	fish	action
ship	finish	addition
Chicago	diminish	condition
shin	Danish	education
shed	wish	temptation
chef	vanquish	notion

Beginning	End	Middle
champagne	mesh	mention
shabby	mustache	fashion
shack	hash	cushion
shut	ash	punishment
shun	cash	machine
shock	hush	usher
shop	toothbrush	washing
shine	wash	tension
chauffeur	push	tissue
shook	bush	ocean
sugar	posh	pressure
shoe	smash	fissure
shove	mush	insure

▼ **Level 1 Phrases for** [ʃ]

machine shop	push and shove	wash the dish
shook sugar	fashion shoe	shabby chef
shine a shoe	pressure cushion	fish dish

▼ **Level 1 Practice Sentences for** [ʃ]

1. She shouted an additional complaint.
2. The usher was shut out of the show.
3. I mentioned that I had shipped the machine.
4. What's your position on voice and diction in education?
5. He mistakenly shook sugar on his corned beef hash.
6. The chef baked Danish pastries in the coffee shop.
7. The sub was shaken by the pressure at the ocean floor.
8. The sheep were shipped to the stockyard in Chicago.
9. The chauffeur stopped at the barber shop for a shave.
10. A shoeshine was always a temptation for me.

LEVEL 2 DRILLS FOR [ʃ]

Words at this level contain some consonant combinations and blends that may be difficult to produce, such as [ʃl] as in *facial* and [ʃr] as in *shrink*. When you say these combinations, try not to make them separate sounds; instead, blend them together, without letting the [ʃ] become hidden or too broad. There are no "Level 3 Drills for [ʃ]."

[ʃ]
[ʒ]

Level 2 Practice Words for [ʃ]

Beginning	End	Middle
shield	leash	facial
shale	English	partial
shell	fresh	racial
shelf	plush	special
shallow	smash	commercial
chandelier	varnish	martial
shore	Irish	foolishly
short	Welsh	glacier
sheer	harsh	crushed
shower	mustache	crashed
shovel	trash	brushed
schnapps	clash	insurance
sure	foolish	crochet
charades	relish	direction
schwa	establish	discussion
shrink	Polish	wishes
shrank	flush	inflection
shrug	flash	relaxation
shriek	lush	resurrection
shrewd	rush	nationally
shrill	rash	spatial
shrimp	Spanish	vicious
shrub	sash	Russian
shrine	slash	Martian

Level 2 Practice Phrases for [ʃ]

spatial relations	Polish nation	short shower
crashed on shore	fresh relish	Spanish sash
shrill shriek	foolish charades	brushed varnish

Level 2 Practice Sentences for [ʃ]

1. I relished the thought of looking for shells at the shore.
2. He shrank back from the sheer face of the glacier.
3. The flashlight was crushed when the shelter collapsed.
4. She is a commercial insurance underwriter.

[ʃ]
[ʒ]

5. It's hard to establish a mustache and not seem foolish.
6. Don't brush against the fresh varnish.
7. Are you sure you gave the schwa the right inflection?
8. The boat shook as waves crashed against the shore.
9. She used her shawl as a shield against the showers.
10. The commercials really are what pushed the shovels.

LEVEL 1 DRILLS FOR [ʒ]

Level 1 Practice Words for [ʒ]

Say the following words slowly and clearly. Make sure you are voicing the [ʒ]. Correct your production until you're satisfied with the sound. If you're not certain, ask your instructor or a classmate to help. There are no English words that begin with this sound.

End	*Middle*	*Middle*
beige	lesion	decision
garage	leisure	occasion
barrage	casual	conclusion
sabotage	abrasion	vision
massage	illusion	incision
prestige	collision	Asia
rouge	confusion	precision
corsage	evasion	explosion
camouflage	visual	erosion
mirage	pleasure	version
entourage	measure	corsages
collage	treasure	garages

Level 1 Practice Phrases for [ʒ]

measure for measure   camouflage rouge
precision explosion   Asian vision
pleasurable leisure   visual mirage
casual decision   beige garage
prestige occasion

Level 1 Practice Sentences for [ʒ]

1. He took <u>pleasure</u> in pointing out the <u>collage</u>.
2. She could always find a <u>treasure</u> in a used <u>corsage</u>.
3. The <u>explosion</u> occurred after the <u>collision</u>.
4. He always draws a <u>conclusion</u> with <u>precision</u> thinking.
5. Your <u>version</u> adds to the <u>occasion</u>.
6. It gave the <u>illusion</u> of a <u>casual decision</u>.
7. The art of <u>visual evasion</u> is called <u>camouflage</u>.
8. The <u>beige garage</u> was destroyed in an act of <u>sabotage</u>.
9. The singer's <u>entourage</u> milled about in <u>confusion</u>.
10. He <u>measured</u> the distance of the <u>incision</u> from the <u>abrasion</u>.

LEVEL 2 DRILLS FOR [ʒ]

Practice Sentences for [ʒ] and [ʃ]

Each of the following sentences contains both [ʒ] and [ʃ]. Listen closely, and don't voice the wrong sound.

1. Always shower after a pleasurable massage.
2. They're casual about relaxation in Chicago.
3. I was assured that the ocean would be azure in color.
4. We measured the beach erosion while on our vacation.
5. Teaching is still a prestige occupation.
6. The dog could be vicious on occasion.
7. The sheep were shaken by the explosions.
8. He shouldn't wear that brushed denim leisure suit.
9. Shoveling sand can be pleasurable.
10. She can't make a decision about shoes.

Challenge Sentences for [ʃ] and [ʒ]

1. Charlotte shoved the brazier aside with pleasure in an unusual display of vicious satisfaction.
2. Fresh fish are an unusually delicious dish when served with Polish sausage and relish.
3. The occasional decision required by the shipping supervisor was foolishly sabotaging the entire entourage.

4. He shaved and showered before brushing his teeth but neglected to massage some polish into his shoes.
5. The mirage showed the result of the camouflaged garage in the process of explosion.

[h]

Challenge Materials for [ʃ]

"First impressions are lasting impressions." You probably heard that saying before, but have you ever given it serious thought? Have you ever contemplated the ramifications of your first impressions on other people? Your first impression is the initial impact you make on another person. In this regard, it covers the areas of dress, voice, grooming, handshake, eye contact, and body posture. The way you choose to manipulate each of these various factors has a profound effect on how other people will perceive you initially. Positive first impressions make initial and subsequent communications with other people much easier and more comfortable. Negative initial impressions can cut off a relationship before it ever gets started. Some people can overcome poor initial first impressions, but it is not easy. Many people give up rather than trying to reverse another person's negative first impression.

Philip L. Hunsaker and Anthony J. Allesandra,
The Art of Managing People

[h]
hot

Sample: **HELEN HEATED THE WHOLE HOUSE UNTIL IT WAS TOO HOT.**
Spellings: **h** as in **hot**
wh as in **whole**

Description

[h] is a voiceless glottal fricative. It is simply a stream of air from the larynx directed through the open mouth.

[h]

 Production: [h]

1. There's no special position or movement for [h]. Start with your tongue resting on the bottom of your mouth.
2. Open your mouth, constrict your vocal cords as though you were going to whisper.
3. Force the air out of your mouth. Don't produce voice, and don't let any air out of your nose.

Problems

Very rarely does anyone have a problem producing [h]. It's an easy sound to make, and it's one of the first sounds we learn. The only real problem occurs when people *don't* make the sound, as sometimes happens with English speakers from the Caribbean, and those whose first language is French. These speakers may omit the [h] when it is in the beginning position of a word. If you've been told that you omit [h], try the following drill.

 Production Drill

The following words begin with [h]. Say the [h] three times, then say the word. Make sure you hear the [h] at the beginning of the word.

> [h . . h . . h . .] home
> [h . . h . . h . .] him
> [h . . h . . h . .] hum
> [h . . h . . h . .] ham

Now try the same drill with the Practice Words below.

 Practice Words for [h]

There are only a few words that contain the letter [h] in which it isn't pronounced, for example, *hour, heir, honest, honorary,* and *herb,* so you're usually safe pronouncing it. Incidentally, there are no English words that end with the [h] sound. Because you can produce this sound so easily, we've only provided Level 1 words and sentences.

Beginning	*Middle*	*Beginning*	*Middle*
heat	unheated	heed	behind
hat	ahead	happy	behave
head	cowhide	hurt	anyhow

Beginning	Middle	Beginning	Middle
humid	Ohio	hungry	rehearse
human	perhaps	who	lighthouse
humor	somehow	house	overhaul
huge	unharmed	health	White House
help	exhale	here	coherent

[h]

Practice Sentences for [h]

1. It isn't the heat that bothers me, it's the humanity.
2. Somehow, I think that lighthouse is beyond help.
3. They were happy, but hungry, after the rehearsal.
4. Perhaps it's not as humid in the western half of Ohio.
5. Too huge a helping can be hazardous to your health.
6. Harry wrote the play *Humor in the White House.*
7. Who ate the other half of the hamburger?
8. He took a huge inhalation at the end of the hallway.
9. The passengers were unharmed in the hijacking.
10. Incoherent sentences are hard to handle.

Challenge Materials for [h]

1. To a small band of determined advocates, the idea of a "hydrogen economy" has been a dream. After all, hydrogen is one of the most abundant chemical elements in the world. And as a fuel, it is completely nonpolluting: Burn it and all you get is lots of energy and a little bit of steam. There's one big problem, though. Most of the world's hydrogen is tied up with oxygen in the form of water. Splitting those molecules to obtain hydrogen takes as much energy as it releases as a fuel.

So only a handful of researchers have led the search for economical ways to produce hydrogen. But that was before warnings that carbon dioxide produced from burning fossil fuels was probably responsible for the greenhouse effect, a devastating global warming. The hydrogen economy could beat that problem by using nonfossil energy, such as solar, to extract a pollutionfree, transportable fuel from water. Suddenly, eager scientists are betting on hydrogen.

"The Fuel of the Future Is Making a Comeback," *Businessweek,*
November 28, 1988

[ʍ]
[w]

2. The bat should be held diagonally (neither too vertically nor too horizontally). It should be held completely still,
away from the body and as high as is comfortably possible
in readiness to lash out instantly at the pitch. There are
both advantages and disadvantages to holding the bat either
horizontally or vertically. Babe Ruth held his bat in a vertical position, and for that reason was a low-ball hitter. The
average batter couldn't possibly hit a high pitch with his bat
pointed toward the heavens. Tris Speaker held his bat very
flat at shoulder level and looked at the pitcher from over his
elbow. As a result he was a good high-ball hitter.

Dell Bethel, Inside Baseball

[ʍ] whine   **[w]** wine

Sample: [ʍ] THE <u>WH</u>EEL OF THE <u>WH</u>ETSTONE <u>WH</u>IRRED.
[w] <u>W</u>ANDA DROPPED <u>O</u>NE OF THE <u>W</u>ATCHES IN THE
LIQ<u>U</u>ID.

Spellings: **wh** as in **where**   **w** as in **wet**
w after **t** in **twelve**   **o** as in **one**
u after **k** in **quit**   **u** as in **liquid**

Description

[ʍ] and [w] are bilabial glides you make by moving your lips while you're
producing the sound. The air is emitted between the lips. They are cognate sounds; the [ʍ] is voiceless, while the [w] is voiced.

Production: [ʍ]

1. Round your lips and purse them. Raise the back of your tongue
toward the soft palate, but don't let it touch. Keep your mouth
slightly open.
2. Blow air out of your mouth with enough force to make an audible
rush of air.

3. As you create the sound, open your mouth slightly. Keep this sound very short, and don't add voice.

Production: [w]

Follow the same steps used for [ʍ]. This time add voice as soon as you purse your lips. Continue to voice it as your lips open slightly.

Problems

PROBLEM 1. THE DISAPPEARANCE OF [ʍ]

Chances are you don't know very many people who use the [ʍ] sound consistently. As a matter of fact, the [ʍ] sound seems to be going out of our language fairly rapidly. Listen to your pronunciation of these words: *what, why, when, where, anywhere.* Do you use [ʍ] or [w]? How about other people around you? What do they say? Do they contrast *witch* and *which?*

So the question is, what's the standard way to pronounce those words? Should you use [ʍ] or [w]? Well, community standards where you live may dictate whether you make the distinction between [ʍ] and [w] or not. Your instructor can offer you the guidance you'll need to decide on your own pronunciation.

Contrast Drill for [ʍ] and [w]

Say the words in the following lists aloud, reading across. Contrast the word pairs. The left column should contain the sound [ʍ] and the right column, the sound [w].

[ʍ]		[w]	[ʍ]		[w]
where	—	wear	whirred	—	word
which	—	witch	whetstone	—	wet stone
whether	—	weather	while	—	wile
whale	—	wail	whey	—	way
whine	—	wine	when	—	wen

This contrast drill is the only one we've included for the [ʍ]. Since the decision to use that sound is a matter of choice, we'll avoid using that sound in the drills that follow for [w]. That way there will be less confusion.

[ʍ]
[w]

Problems

PROBLEM 1. SUBSTITUTION OF [v] FOR [w]

Nonnative speakers sometimes have this problem. Try the Production Drill first, then try the Contrast Drill.

▼ Production Drill

This drill is designed to help you learn to produce the [w] sound. First say the sound [u] (as in cool), then say the word that follows. Read across, and gradually shorten the spacing between [u] and the word.

[u] . . . air	[u] . . air	[u] . air	wear
[u] . . . itch	[u] . . itch	[u] . itch	witch
[u] . . . end	[u] . . end	[u] . end	wend
[u] . . . ache	[u] . . ache	[u] . ache	wake
[u] . . . aid	[u] . . aid	[u] . aid	wade

You can try this same production drill with other [w] words, too.

▼ Contrast Drill for [w] and [v]

Once you can produce the [w] correctly, you're ready to try contrasting [w] and [v]. Say the following words aloud. First read down the list of [w] words. Use a mirror, and check to see that there is no lip-teeth contact. Then read the list of [v] words. Finally, read the pairs across. Try to feel and hear the difference between the [w] and the [v].

[w]		[v]	[w]		[v]
wine	—	vine	we	—	vee
wet	—	vet	wane	—	vane
wail	—	veil	waltz	—	vaults
west	—	vest	wiser	—	visor
wend	—	vend	wiper	—	viper
worse	—	verse	wow	—	vow
went	—	vent	weal	—	veal

LEVEL 1 DRILLS FOR [w]

Since the [w] is so easy to produce, all the practice exercises are at Level 1.

[ʍ]

[w]

Level 1 Practice Words for [w]

Say the words in the following lists slowly and clearly. Note that there are no words in English that end with the [w] sound.

Beginning	Middle	Beginning	Middle
we	awake	woman	quack
wake	byway	woods	reward
witty	cobwebs	weird	unwise
wave	midweek	waffle	backward
weak	thruway	wash	dwarf
wife	highway	welcome	dwindle
wide	everyone	weld	seaweed
window	quick	walk	quiz
with	quiet	wedding	required

Level 1 Practice Sentences for [w]

1. The thruway was closed for one hour due to high winds.
2. I was late for the quiz because I woke up at twelve.
3. The supply of wood had dwindled by Wednesday.
4. Grapes are really wine on the vine.
5. Young men in the West frequently wear vests.
6. It was the last waltz at the wedding.
7. It takes me until midweek to brush away the cobwebs.
8. I rewarded the dog with a sandwich.
9. The weather has been wetter than usual.
10. We walked through the seaweed in the backwash.

Challenge Sentences for [ʍ] and [w]

1. We awoke while the wives of the highway workers wondered whether the weather would worsen.
2. The quiet woman squeezed water out of the seaweed without a backward glance seaward.
3. "A quick quiz," quoted the professor, quieting the qualms of the quivering students.
4. "Which witch is the one working weirdly in Ipswich on Wednesdays?" queried the quack.
5. It is unwise to reward widows of White House workers who wickedly wield weapons to bushwhack their spouses.

[r]

I keep six honest serving men
(They taught me all I knew);
Their names are What and Why and When
And How and Where and Who.

Rudyard Kipling, "The Elephant's Child"

red

Sample: **THE RED FERRY WENT IN THE WRONG DIRECTION.**
Spellings: **r** as in **red**
           rr as in **ferry**
           rh as in **rhythm**
           wr as in **wrong**

Description

[r] is a voiced lingua-alveolar sound that can be produced in two ways.
The first way, usually at the beginning of words, you produce it rather
like a fricative by curling the tip of the tongue up and back. In the second way, usually after a vowel or at the end of a word, you produce it
as a glide that sounds like a vowel. Both ways produce a glide because
the articulators are in motion.

 ## Production—Method 1

1. Open your mouth slightly. Protrude your lips just a bit.
2. Raise the tip of your tongue to a point slightly behind the gum ridge,
    but don't make contact. At the same time, spread the sides of your
    tongue so that they touch the upper side teeth. You don't want air
    to escape from the sides of your mouth.
3. Produce voice.

Production—Method 2

This time keep the tongue tip down and slightly in back of the lower front teeth while you raise the center portion. This position is not used as much as Position 1.

Problems

[r] is one of the most troublesome sounds in our language and for a variety of reasons. Normally, it's one of the last sounds children master, and many times certain nonstandard productions, such as substituting [w] for [r], as in *wed* for *red,* can be continued into adult speech patterns. Many nonnative speakers have difficulty producing [r] due to the fact that it may not exist in their language at all or is very similar to another sound. The use of [r] varies from region to region in American speech, so it's confusing even to native speakers. We'll cover the problems in production first and then go over regional usage.

PROBLEM 1. TRILLED [r]

The sound of a trilled [r] is almost that of a [t] or [d]. It's produced by tapping the tongue very lightly and quickly against the gum ridge. Try this: say the word *car.* If you've trilled the [r], you'll feel the tongue tip touch.

 ### Production Drill

Say the word *are* very slowly, almost separating it into vowel-consonant. Say it a few times. Monitor your production carefully. Try to keep the tip of your tongue from touching anything. Now try the following drill: say the word *are,* stop completely, but don't move your tongue at all. Then add the [r] word that follows. As you read across, make your pause shorter and, finally, drop the *are.*

are . . . red	are . . red	are . red	are red	red
are . . . ripe	are . . ripe	are . ripe	are ripe	ripe
are . . . rode	are . . rode	are . rode	are rode	rode

Here's another way. Say the vowel [ɝ] as in the word *turn.* Hold it for a moderately long time, then add the [r] word that follows. Read across.

[r]

er . . . red	er . . red	er . red	er red	red
er . . . rose	er . . rose	er . rose	er rose	rose
er . . . rye	er . . rye	er . rye	er rye	rye
er . . . rain	er . . rain	er . rain	er rain	rain
er . . . raw	er . . raw	er . raw	er raw	raw

PROBLEM 2. OVERLABIALIZATION AND [w] FOR [r]

One of the most common problems is an [r] that sounds rather like a [w]. This happens if you purse your lips too much or if your tongue is inactive while the [r] is produced. Try the following:

Contrast Drill for [w] and [r]

Say the following words aloud. Use a mirror and note the position of your lips. Try to minimize lip movement for the [r] words. First read the list of [w] words, then the list of [r] words. Then read across, contrasting the pairs of words. Repeat the words and watch your lips in the mirror.

[w]	[r]	[w]	[r]
weep	— reap	wage	— rage
weed	— reed	wise	— rise
wed	— red	twice	— trice
wing	— ring	twain	— train
wipe	— ripe	twist	— tryst
west	— rest	twill	— trill
wait	— rate	tweeze	— trees
won	— run	tweet	— treat
woe	— row	away	— array

PROBLEM 3. SUBSTITUTION OF [l] FOR [r]

If English is your second language, your [r] may sound like an [l], so that *red* becomes *led.* This is especially true of people whose first language was an Oriental one. Native speakers of Oriental languages tend to produce the [r] with the tongue tip touching the gum ridge, which is an unacceptable practice in English.

Contrast Drill for [r] and [l]

Say the words in the following list aloud. First, read the list of [l] words. Notice the contact between your tongue and the gum ridge. Then read the list of [r] words. Try to keep your tongue tip from touching anything as you produce the [r]. Purse your lips slightly. Finally read across, contrasting the pairs of words.

[l]		[r]	[l]		[r]
leaf	—	reef	blew	—	brew
leap	—	reap	blight	—	bright
lid	—	rid	bland	—	brand
lip	—	rip	bled	—	bread
late	—	rate	class	—	crass
lend	—	rend	clew	—	crew
lag	—	rag	cloud	—	crowd
law	—	raw	glass	—	grass
lot	—	rot	flesh	—	fresh
lug	—	rug	flank	—	frank
light	—	right	flay	—	fray
play	—	pray	fly	—	fry

PROBLEM 4. INTRUSIVE [r]

When a word that ends with a vowel is followed by a word that begins with a vowel, some people will bridge the gap between the words with an [r]. We call this type of [r] *intrusive.* This is widespread in New England and New York City.

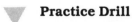

Practice Drill

Say the following phrases carefully making sure you don't add an [r].

law and order
saw a man
vanilla ice cream
drama and speech

Alaska and Alabama
go to Africa on vacation
Havana is the capital of Cuba.
Your idea is okay.

PROBLEM 5. SUBSTITUTION OF [v] FOR [r]

[r] is very difficult to articulate accurately. So, some speakers replace it with [v] in initial position and between vowels by using a light lip-teeth contact instead of the more precise adjustments required by the [r] glide. The result is that *berry* may sound like *bevy.* If you have this problem, try the following practice drills.

[r]

 Contrast Drill for [v] and [r]

Say the following words aloud. Use a mirror to note the position of your lips when you say [v]. Avoid any contact between your lower lip and upper front teeth while you say the [r] words. During the actual moment when you are saying the [r], you should not feel contact between your articulators.

[v]		[r]	[v]		[r]
vain	—	rain	avail	—	a rail
veal	—	reel	avid	—	arid
vice	—	rice	heaven	—	heron
vote	—	wrote	divide	—	deride
vat	—	rat	moving	—	mooring
van	—	ran	cleaver	—	clearer
vest	—	rest	bevy	—	berry

 Practice Drill

The [v] for [r] substitution occurs also in the [br] and [pr] blends. This is due to giving the [b] and [p] a fricative quality by not pressing the lips together tightly enough. Try the following phrases, making sure to articulate distinctly and precisely.

Brooklyn Bridge	his brother's bride	Great Britain
broken promises	bring back	brain drain
broad protection	bright eyes	Bryn Mawr

Special Problems

It's possible that you still are having difficulty in producing an acceptable [r] sound even after trying all the drills. If so, talk to your instructor about this. Perhaps you should read Appendix B (Special Speech Problems) or check with a local speech and hearing center to see if you can get (or need) additional help.

LEVEL 1 DRILLS FOR [r]

How [r] is pronounced varies with the regions of the country. Pronunciations of [r] preceding a consonant in middle position (as in *tired*) and in final position (as in *care*) are seldom heard in the South and New England, and can be considered to be optional in many other areas.

[r]

Ask your instructor, and listen to the way educated people in your area talk before you decide on the correct pronunciation.

Level 1 Practice Words for [r]

Say the words in the following lists slowly and clearly. Listen carefully and adjust your production until you are satisfied you have produced the desired sound. Start with the *Beginning* words. Even though the final [r] may be optional, say the [r] in the *End* words so that you can get an auditory and tactile feeling for it. Don't overdo it by curling your tongue too far back. The final [r] is just a small amount of [r] added to a vowel or diphthong.

Remember that in many areas of the South pronunciation of *Middle* words, such as *Mary, Carolina,* and *very,* may or may not include [r]. Your instructor is the best guide to the acceptable pronunciation in your locality.

Beginning	*End*	*Middle*
reap	peer	marry
reed	dear	carry
rim	mere	Harry
rig	near	arrow
ring	wear	narrow
ray	there	merit
rake	care	berry
rate	tear	hurry
rain	bear	array
red	affair	carrot
wreck	hair	around
ran	pair	orange
rap	air	terrific
rub	chair	wearing
run	war	caring
write	chore	direct
ride	door	very
rock	cure	tomorrow
rob	tire	furrow
round	tour	tearing
roam	tar	worry
wrote	car	borrow
room	far	turkey
root	or	pouring

[r]

Level 1 Practice Phrases for [r]

red hair	worry tomorrow	very direct
hurry around	wreck the car	terrified bear
narrow room	orange carrot	near here
marriage rite	pouring rain	write to Harry

Level 1 Practice Sentences for [r]

1. I roamed around the room looking for the rake.
2. I put the rock near the rim of the tire.
3. He hurried to borrow the carfare.
4. The pirate told a terrific tale of raiding the port.
5. The wedding ring was neither here nor there.
6. Harry wanted to tour Arizona by car.
7. The rain poured down at a rate of one inch per hour.
8. She rang the bells without very much care.
9. He worried that the tar would ruin the rug.
10. I wrote to Karen asking her to fly here tomorrow.

LEVEL 2 DRILLS FOR [r]

The [r] words at this level are more difficult to produce because of the presence of other sounds such as [l]. In addition, the *Middle* words contain [r] preceding a consonant, so you may have doubts as to local pronunciation. We suggest that you pronounce the [r] (even if others in your area don't) simply to get experience. Take your time with these words. Say them slowly and clearly. If you have doubts as to the accuracy of your production, ask your instructor or another member of the class.

Level 2 Practice Words for [r]

Beginning	*End*	*Middle*	*Combination*
reel	leer	barrel	rather
rile	peer	florist	burger
race	velour	warm	farther
rail	clear	alarm	armory
roll	implore	spiral	roar
royal	lair	Lawrence	rare
rasp	pear	fork	rural

Beginning	End	Middle	Combination
Ralph	father	storm	barrier
rules	mother	burn	carrier
ruffle	sister	birthday	purser
raffle	elsewhere	girl	farmer
rubble	welfare	Cheryl	dormitory
rectangle	liar	choral	runner
reassure	square	glory	racer
riddle	stare	parallel	writer
rusty	flair	pearl	career
roost	lure	flowered	reader

[r]

▼ **Level 2 Practice Sentences for [r]**

1. It's rare to find a real pearl.
2. The carrier was on a rural route.
3. Ralph has the list of rules for the raffle.
4. I burned the burgers on the barbecue fork.
5. My mother said I'd be a millionaire.
6. The weather was clear after the storm.
7. The florist climbed the spiral staircase.
8. I implore you not to bother my sister.
9. The purser threw the roll over the rail.
10. The bear chased my father with a roar.

LEVEL 3 DRILLS FOR [r]

This level has some difficult blends you might want to practice.

▼ **Level 3 Practice Words for [pr]**

If you purse your lips too much, the [pr] blend may sound like [pw]. Use a mirror and try these words:

preach	priest	pretty	preserve
prince	price	prank	prepare
prime	prize	pray	pronounce
appraise	approve	apricot	appropriate
appreciate	improve	April	impress
waterproof	depress	interpret	enterprise
oppress	express	shipwreck	surprise

[r]

 ### Level 3 Practice Words for [br]

This blend can be misarticulated the same way as [pr].

breed	bred	broad	briefcase
bring	brown	bread	Brooklyn
breeze	broom	bride	Libra
brought	abrasive	abrupt	upbringing
abridge	abroad	Hebrew	celebrate

 ### Level 3 Practice Words for [gr] and [kr]

Make sure to produce these as true blends. Don't let a vowel creep in between the two consonants.

[gr]	[kr]	[gr]	[kr]
gracious	crouch	diagram	secret
granddad	crude	congress	concrete
grillwork	crumb	telegraph	cockroach
groggy	cry	kilogram	aircraft
grinder	crash	pedigree	democrat

 ### Level 3 Practice Words for [fr]

Don't let a consonant separation occur here, either.

friend	fried	French	fraction
freedom	fragile	freeze	deepfry
front	frown	frame	girl friend
affront	African	afraid	bullfrog
defraud	belfry	defrost	waterfront

 ### Level 3 Practice Words for [tr]

If you press your tongue too firmly against the gum ridge when you make the [t] and then slide your tongue back, the sound produced is somewhat like [tʃr]. To avoid this, press the tongue lightly against the palate and make a clean break on the way back to making the [r].

trim	tree	troop	triple
true	trash	train	neutral
tribe	trend	track	mattress
trunk	trigger	try	metric
entreat	oak tree	attractive	patriotic
entrance	trestle	atrium	electricity

Level 3 Practice Words for [dr]

Produce these the same way as [tr]. Just add voice early enough.

dream	drink	drew	gumdrop
drip	drape	drive	withdrawn
drum	dragon	drain	hundred
address	Andrew	undress	raindrop
children	Mildred	quadrant	foundry

Level 3 Practice Sentences for [r]

1. The prime rate rose three points this year.
2. April gives us freedom from the trials of winter.
3. I put the French vanilla ice cream in the freezer.
4. I'll have a burger, rare, and an order of fries.
5. When you're angry, a frown spreads across your face.
6. He broke the bottle of apricot brandy.
7. She prided herself on her freeze-frame photography.
8. That's where the schooner ran aground.
9. I purchased an unabridged dictionary.
10. It was a plot to defraud the African prince.
11. He was a firm believer in law and order.
12. The bumpy drive aggravated my injuries.
13. The fragile crystal broke in the crate.
14. I brought red roses home for our anniversary.
15. She won the blue ribbon for her brown bread.

[r]

Challenge Sentences for [r]

1. The crooked criminal cried gratingly around the grimy court.

2. Friday afternoon traffic across the Brooklyn Bridge increases abruptly at approximately three thirty.

3. Fred affronted his friend who was reading an African tome regarding the approved way to cross the Nile River.

4. Borrowing a brush before entering a store in order to purchase one is purely breeding trouble.

5. Prince Andrew prayed with his priest to produce a present for his pretty princess.

6. Transit authority trains travel on thoroughly straight rails.

7. The dreary day was characterized by a drenching drizzle of no paltry proportions.

8. The gray grizzly grunted and grimaced as he grasped the great round beehive in the tree.

9. The brown rock was rubbed with vigor by the gray-bearded old prospector.

10. Fame and fortune follow forth from earning a richly deserved reward.

Challenge Materials for [r]

Talking on the radio does not require a permit—anyone can do that. But the operator of broadcasting equipment must have one, just as the operator of a motor vehicle must have a license. If you control technical functions of a station, by turning on the transmitter or regulating the volume of sound that will be broadcast, the Federal Communications Commission says that you must hold the proper license or permit. Recently the FCC had modified its requirements for broadcast operators. Under the new regulations, all that is required is a *Restricted Radiotelephone Operator Permit,* which can be obtained by any United States citizen simply by filing an application.

John Hasling, *Fundamentals of Radio Broadcasting*

[j]
yes

[j]

Sample: **YES. IN MY OPINION THAT VIEW IS FAMILIAR.**
Spellings: **y** as in **yes**
           io as in **opinion**
           ie as in **view**
           u as in **use**
           e as in **few**
           ia as in **familiar**
           j as in **hallelujah**

Description

[j] is a voiced lingua-palatal glide. You produce it by raising the tongue toward the palate and gliding it toward the position of the next sound. [j] is voiced.

Production: [j]

1. Open your mouth slightly.
2. Place the tip of your tongue behind your lower front teeth.
3. Raise the front of your tongue toward the hard palate. Keep the tip in place behind your lower front teeth, and pull your lips slightly back.
4. Produce voice and let your tongue and lips glide to the position of the next sound. Don't let any air out your nose.

Problems

Because of its vowel-like qualities, most people don't have much trouble producing [j] accurately. Most of the problems involve regional usage or result from learning English as a second language, but are not misarticulations.

PROBLEM 1. SUBSTITUTION OF [dʒ] FOR [j]

If your native language doesn't have this sound, you will probably substitute the sound associated with the letter *j*. In other words, *yet* would become *jet.* The opposite can occur, too. That is, if the letter *j* is pronounced as a *y* in another language, speakers new to English might pronounce *jam* as if it were *yam.* Use the Contrast Drill below to reinforce the difference between the two sounds.

Contrast Drill for [j] and [dʒ]

Say the words in the following lists aloud. Read the list of [dʒ] words first. Feel the way the tongue tip touches the gum ridge. Then read the list of [j] words. As you say the first sound of each word, be sure to keep your tongue tip down behind the front teeth. Finally, read across, contrasting the pairs of words.

[dʒ]		[j]	[dʒ]		[j]
jet	—	yet	Jack	—	yak
jam	—	yam	jeer	—	year
juice	—	use	jail	—	Yale
Jell-O	—	yellow	jowl	—	yowl
Jess	—	yes	jarred	—	yard
joke	—	yoke	jot	—	yacht

PROBLEM 2. OMISSION OF [j]

Even native English speakers become confused as to whether to pronounce [j] when it's represented by a letter other than *y.* The general rule is that you use [j] after consonants such as [k, b, f, v, h, p] with such spelling as:

> *cu* as in *cupid*
>
> *eau* as in *beauty*
>
> *ew* as in *few*
>
> *ue* as in *hue*
>
> *ie* as in *view*
>
> *pu* as in *putrid*

Pronounce the [j] when it is followed by [n] as in *union.* It almost doesn't make sense to state rules such as these when they have a great many exceptions. Perhaps the best solution is to simply observe usage.

LEVEL 1 DRILLS FOR [j]

Since there are few production problems with [j], the drills are all at Level 1. Note that there are no words ending with [j]. The pronunciation

[j]

of [j] is optional in those words that are starred, and occurs much more in the South than in the West and Northeast.

 Level 1 Practice Words for [j]

([j] is optional in starred words.)

Beginning	Middle	Beginning	Middle
year	onion	universe	figure
yes	senior	U.S.	employer
use	communicate	eurythmics	regular
you	beyond	Utah	student*
Yankee	usual	uranium	Malaysia
yawn	cue	Jung	popular
yard	Tuesday*	yield	distributor
youth	reduce*	Uganda	triangular
unit	institute*	university	royalty
Europe	cute	Johannes	J. R. Ewing
yellow	duke*	yogurt	New York

 Level 1 Practice Sentences for [j]

1. <u>Yes</u>, <u>you</u> can have the <u>yacht</u> tonight.
2. The <u>Institute</u> sent Jeff to <u>Europe</u> last <u>year</u>.
3. They sold <u>millions</u> of lemon <u>yellow</u> <u>units</u>.
4. Bakers <u>use</u> egg <u>yolks</u> by the <u>yard</u>.
5. I tried to <u>communicate</u> with that <u>cute</u> <u>senior</u>.
6. The problem of <u>uranium</u> disposal has become <u>universal</u>.
7. The <u>Eurythmics</u> <u>used</u> to be a popular group on <u>U.S.</u> campuses.
8. <u>Johannes</u> was a transfer <u>student</u> from the <u>University</u> of <u>Uganda</u>.
9. High-<u>yield</u> <u>onion</u> seeds are grown in <u>Malaysia</u>.
10. Many New <u>Yorkers</u> think J. R. <u>Ewing</u> comes from a <u>royal</u> <u>oil</u> family.

left

Sample: **LAURA LEFT THE YELLOW PILLOW IN THE HALL.**
Spellings: **l** as in **left**
  ll as in **pillow**
  ln as in **kiln**

Description

[l] is a voiced lingua-alveolar lateral. You produce it by dropping the sides of the tongue and allowing air to escape around the sides.

Production: [l]

1. Place the tip of your tongue against your upper gum ridge.
2. Open your mouth wide enough to slip the tip of your finger between your teeth.
3. Keep the sides of the tongue down.
4. Produce voice. Don't let any air through your nose.

Problems

PROBLEM 1. DISTINGUISHING BETWEEN "DARK" [l] AND "CLEAR" [l]

The [l] we described above is called the "clear" [l]. It's the [l] that occurs in the beginning of a word or immediately after a beginning consonant. Try the word *let*. You should feel as though you're making the sound entirely with the front of your tongue. The tongue tip remains touching the gum ridge throughout the [l] and the back stays down.

The "dark" [l] is called dark because it is produced, to a great extent, by the back of the tongue and is slightly muffled. Say the word *ball*. You should feel your tongue tip still touching the gum ridge, but the back of your tongue lifts slightly. Now say the word *lull* slowly a few times; the difference between the two [l] sounds should become more apparent. Some people, however, may even drop the tongue tip from the gum ridge and produce the [l] entirely with the back portion near the palate. If you produce the [l] this way, you probably won't feel the tip of the tongue.

Many foreign languages do not make use of the "dark" [l] at all. It does, however, exist in all dialects of English, usually at the end of words and sometimes in the middle. Some people, especially in the

[l]

West and Midwest, use the "dark" [l] in beginning position. Try the Contrast Drill below to see how you produce the [l].

▼ **Contrast Drill for "Clear" [l] and "Dark" [l]**

Read the following pairs of words aloud. Make sure your tongue tip is touching the gum ridge each time you produce the sound [l]. Use the "clear" [l] in the first word of each pair and the "dark" [l] in the second.

"clear" [l]		"dark" [l]	"clear" [l]		"dark" [l]
let	—	tell	lap	—	pal
lip	—	pill	lean	—	kneel
lead	—	deal	lick	—	kill
late	—	tail	led	—	dell
load	—	dole	Luke	—	cool
lost	—	stall	light	—	tile

If you are having difficulty producing the "clear" [l], we suggest that you refer to Appendix B, Special Speech Problems.

PROBLEM 2. SUBSTITUTING [r] FOR [l]

If your first language was one of the Oriental languages, you may have difficulty with the [l]. Chances are you produce this sound with your tongue tip *behind* the gum ridge. The result is a sound similar to the [r]. Try the following Contrast Drill.

▼ **Contrast Drill for [r] and [l]**

Read the words in the following lists aloud. Read them across, in pairs. The first word of each pair will start with [r], the second with [l]. Notice how the tongue is back farther in the mouth for [r], and it's more in the front for [l]. Make sure the part of the gum ridge you're touching for [l] is just behind the upper teeth.

[r]		[l]	[r]		[l]
red	—	led	brew	—	blue
reed	—	lead	pray	—	play
right	—	light	frame	—	flame
rode	—	load	fry	—	fly
rate	—	late	grow	—	glow
rush	—	lush	graze	—	glaze
rise	—	lies	prod	—	plod

Practice these words a few times, concentrating on the differences between [l] and [r]. Ask your instructor or a classmate to listen to you. When you're satisfied, try the Level 1 Practice Words.

[l]

PROBLEM 3. OMISSION OF [l]

This happens usually when [l] either precedes or follows another consonant such as in the word *already*. When you're trying the practice
words, make sure you pronounce the [l] in each word.

PROBLEM 4. SUBSTITUTION OF [w] FOR [l]

You are making this substitution if you pronounce the word *late* so
that it sounds like *wait*. Read Appendix B and do the drills for [l] there
before you start on the Level 1 drills in this chapter.

PROBLEM 5. UVULAR PRODUCTION OF [l]

The uvula is a small fleshy structure that hangs in the rear of the
mouth from the center of the soft palate (velum). English speakers
don't ordinarily use this structure in speech, but some speakers may
make it into an articulation point by excessive "darkening" of the [l]
by raising the back of the tongue rather than the tip. Try the drills for
[l] in Appendix B, which will help you firmly establish the alveolar ridge
as the contact point for [l].

LEVEL 1 DRILLS FOR [l]

 Level 1 Practice Words for [l]

Say the words in the following lists slowly and clearly. Make sure the
tip of your tongue touches the gum ridge behind your upper front teeth:
not on the teeth, and not behind the gum ridge, but squarely on the
gum. Listen carefully and monitor your production until you're sure
that you are producing the "clear" and "dark" [l] accurately and that
you're using the "dark" [l] only where it's appropriate. Start with the
Beginning words.

Beginning	*Middle*	*End*
lean	allow	kneel
lid	alike	deal
late	daylight	bail
let	pillow	fell
led	yellow	mill
laugh	eleven	bell
lot	always	tall
lawn	follow	ball
long	dolly	pill
like	telling	style
look	along	pile
lunch	believe	motel

[l]

Beginning	Middle	End
loud	balloon	pool
leave	fill-up	cruel
law	belong	hotel
love	only	feel
low	valley	will
lip	fellow	fool

 Level 1 Practice Phrases for [l]

late lunch	look alike	laugh a lot
always believing	follow a balloon	daylight yellow
motel pool	tall pile	fell in the pool

Level 1 Practice Sentences for [l]

1. I <u>let</u> <u>lunch</u> go on too <u>long</u>.
2. <u>Eleven</u> <u>always</u> <u>follows</u> ten.
3. That <u>motel</u> <u>pool</u> has <u>style</u>.
4. I don't <u>believe</u> how <u>loud</u> that <u>laugh</u> was.
5. I was <u>kneeling</u> on the railing over the <u>mill</u>.
6. She was <u>telling</u> me about the ''<u>look alike</u>'' contest.
7. Take the <u>yellow</u> <u>pillow</u> <u>along</u>.
8. They're <u>always</u> too <u>late</u> to make a <u>deal</u>.
9. <u>While</u> I waited for you, I <u>located</u> a <u>dollar</u> <u>bill</u>.
10. <u>Larry</u> tried to <u>call</u> <u>collect</u> from <u>Long</u> <u>Island</u>.

LEVEL 2 DRILLS FOR [l]

The words on this level are generally more difficult to produce because the sounds in them may require a wider range of movement by the articulators and because of the [pl], [bl], and [lp] blends. If you say each word carefully and make sure that your tongue tip touches your gum ridge, you should be ready to try these blends.

One additional difficulty results with production of the syllabic [l]. You produce the syllabic [l] when it is in an unstressed syllable following [t], [d], or [n], as in the words *petal*, *pedal*, and *channel*. To produce the syllabic [l], you leave your tongue touching the gum ridge; you don't remove it after producing the sound before the [l]. The [l] is made by simply dropping the sides of the tongue. Here are some words to try:

 Production Drill

Read down each column. Don't remove your tongue from the gum ridge before making the [l].

[l]

[tl]	[dl]	[nl]
petal	pedal	channel
bottle	paddle	panel
little	muddle	funnel
settle	middle	kennel
rattle	candle	arsenal

Listen carefully and try the words again. If you are producing the syllabic [l] correctly, you won't hear a vowel between the [l] and the sounds that go before.

Level 2 Practice Words for [l]

Read the words in the following lists slowly and carefully. Take special time with the words that contain [pl], [bl], [lp], [fl], and syllabic [l]. Don't let a vowel creep in between the two consonants of the blend.

Beginning	*End*	*Middle*
lure	apple	plank
leaves	bobble	blue
lapse	quarrel	raffle
leases	schedule	weld
lustrous	quail	railing
lair	help	pearl
link	curl	twelve
liar	dimple	garlic
leer	triple	belt
laws	shrill	ugly

Level 2 Practice Sentences for [l]

1. I love the smell of garlic.
2. I heard the shrill call of the owl.
3. A liar is a person with a lot of memory lapses.
4. You don't find cultured pearls in clams.
5. He had a triple black belt.
6. Lorraine tried to weld the broken railing together.
7. I like long gold necklaces.
8. The plank started to curl in the moist climate.
9. The falling leaves were red and yellow.
10. The apple rolled along the trail.

[l]

LEVEL 3 DRILLS FOR [l]

The following drills are more difficult than the ones you've done so far. The words combine the blends you practiced in Level 2, and we've added others, such as [lz], along with words containing more than one [l]. Remember, if a word starts and ends with [l], the first [l] will be "clear," sometimes the second will be "dark."

 Level 3 Practice Words for [l]

lonely	fields	lull	wrinkle
bells	lulls	lilt	boggle
lately	jails	literally	legal
rolls	lollipop	collegial	eclectic
helpless	scheduled	swelter	exclaim
eagle	likely	glue	lethal
liability	faultless	exclaim	clavicle

 Level 3 Practice Sentences for [l]

1. She's not likely to be lonely.
2. The sweltering heat leaves me feeling helpless.
3. I'm planning for limited liability.
4. I was wallowing in the glow of collegial smiles.
5. The lock was literally welded closed.
6. The colors blended together beautifully.
7. He scheduled the hearing for his helpless client.
8. She liked to be awakened by little bells, not alarms.
9. There will likely be hail or sleet late tonight.
10. Fields of clover and alfalfa dotted the landscape.

 Challenge Sentences for [l]

1. Lilly slowly ladled little Letty's lentil soup into the lemon-yellow bowl.
2. Lawrence flew to the Italian Alps to listen to the local yokels yodel.
3. "Will you lift the ladder later?" lisped Lester as he looked longingly at a cold cola.
4. "No man who has once heartily and wholly laughed can be altogether irreclaimably bad." (Thomas Carlyle)
5. Laura laughed as she sang, "Merrily we roll along, roll along, roll along, o'er the bright blue sea."

▼ **Challenge Materials for [l]**

It is hard for a North American to conceive of cultures that do not place a high premium on friendliness. Politicians and salesmen, corporate managers and artists, teachers and policemen, along with members of most occupations and professions learn early in life the value of friendliness. The concept itself is considered part and parcel of popularity, which is a prime ingredient of success in democracies. From their early years in the United States, children are taught to believe in friendliness.

Faith S. Yousef, in Larry A. Samovar and Richard E. Porter,
Intercultural Communication: A Reader

Sample: **THE MAN WAS CALM AFTER HE HIT HIS THUMB
WITH THE HAMMER.**
Spellings: m as in **man**
mm as in **hammer**
mb as in **thumb**
lm as in **calm**
mn as in **column**
gm as in **diaphragm**

Description

[m] is a voiced bilabial nasal. It is a vowel-like consonant for which you continuously emit the breathstream through your nose.

Production: [m]

1. Close your lips but keep your teeth very slightly apart.
2. Lower your soft palate, and rest your tongue on the floor of the mouth.
3. Produce voice, allowing the air to come out through your nose.

[m]

Problems

There are very few problems with the production of [m]. This is one of the first and easiest sounds that children learn. When problems do exist, they are usually errors of omission or of assimilating [m] into the next sound. All the drills for [m] are at Level 1.

LEVEL 1 DRILLS FOR [m]

Level 1 Practice Words for [m]

Say the words in the following lists slowly and clearly. Make sure your lips are closed, and seal off the mouth entirely. Pronounce each [m] distinctly. Don't allow it to become part of the next consonant. Start with the *Beginning* words.

Beginning	*End*	*Middle*
me	thumb	hammer
mitt	team	coming
mate	paradigm	gleaming
metal	fame	demand
mask	time	clamp
moving	name	tomcat
mister	bomb	summer
middle	broom	semester
mistake	column	camera
milk	term	woman
minnow	groom	family
mine	psalm	omen
Mike	autumn	remember
mouse	synonym	fireman
month	crumb	somewhere

[m]

Level 1 Practice Phrases for [m]

room full	summer time
I'm going	term paper
some fun	time out
tempt me	time bomb
come true	fame game
remember me	team name

Level 1 Practice Sentences for [m]

1. I'm going to school for one summer semester.
2. It was a mistake to wear the metal mask.
3. It's time to make an effort to complete my term paper.
4. He's the only man I know who isn't coming with the team.
5. Don't tempt me with a room full of cameras.
6. The fireman clamped his thumb on the gleaming bomb.
7. You can call me mister, if you can't remember my name.
8. The Romans certainly made mammoth columns.

Challenge Materials for [m]

To be filed under B, for either bizarre, which the following conversation was, or for the Block Drugstore, where the exchange took place.

Waiting for a prescription to be filled at the drugstore, which is on Third Avenue near 21st Street, Mike Marks became aware of the lovely music on the pharmacist's radio.

Mike Marks: That's terrific music. What is it? Wagner?

Pharmacist, busily working on the prescription: No, Mahler.

Mike Marks: Mahler? I don't believe it.

Pharmacist: What did you ask me?

Mike Marks: I asked you who wrote that music.

Pharmacist: Oh, I thought you asked me what *my* name was.

Ron Alexander, "Metropolitan Diary," *The New York Times*, October 12, 1988

[n]
no

Sample: **DUE TO PNEUMONIA HE COULD NOT PICK UP PENNIES WITH A KNIFE.**

Spellings: **n** as in **no**
nn as in **penny**
kn as in **knife**
gn as in **gnat**
pn as in **pneumonia**
mn as in **mnemonic**

Description

[n] is a voiced lingua-alveolar nasal. It's a vowel-like consonant you produce by blocking the airstream at the gum ridge with your tongue and emitting it nasally, in a continuous release.

Production: [n]

1. Open your mouth slightly. Place the tip of your tongue on the upper gum ridge. At the same time, place the sides of your tongue along the upper inside surface of the molars.
2. Lower the soft palate so that air can leave via your nostrils.
3. Produce voice.

Problems

There are very few problems with [n]. We learn this sound very early in life, so misarticulations are seldom serious. The most common problems are omission of [n] and assimilating it into the sounds surrounding it. [n] is most often assimilated when it is followed by another consonant. It then takes on the characteristics of that consonant. For example, in the phrase *in cold water*, [ɪn kold wɔtɚ], the [n] changes to [ŋ] and the word becomes *ink*. Here are some phrases and words in which this happens. Try them slowly, making sure to produce the [n].

[n]

income tax	in cold water	concrete
in capitals	in front	unpopular
infrequent	unbiased	in back
in fact	tin whistle	incomplete

LEVEL 1 DRILLS FOR [n]

Since [n] is a relatively easy sound to produce, all the drills are at Level 1.

Level 1 Practice Words for [n]

Say the following words slowly and clearly. Listen to your production, and feel it as well. Make sure you use only the tip of your tongue for the [n]. Don't omit it, and don't assimilate it.

Beginning	*End*	*Middle*
knee	keen	penny
knit	tin	peanut
name	mane	cannot
nap	pan	many
north	mine	honey
nose	began	finish
next	token	cleaner
nation	satin	lightning
nail	alone	flint
needle	spoon	opener
knowledge	mitten	bench
gnarled	brown	tunnel
pneumatic	burn	blend
number	drawn	blond
know	scorn	concert
nearing	mention	incomplete
nil	barn	inquire

Level 1 Practice Sentences for [n]

1. She began knitting the cap in November.
2. The flint knife was found in the abandoned tin mine.
3. I inquired about the tenpenny nails.
4. He used satin-finish varnish on the table.
5. The price of peanuts is nearing a penny a pound.

6. The old brown barn burned last night.
7. Nancy didn't have any subway tokens.
8. With all our knowledge, thunder and lightning still frighten many of us.
9. Some students get incomplete grades because they procrastinate.
10. He put his sore hand in cold water for an hour.

[ŋ]
sing

Sample: **I THI**N**K THAT SI**NG**I**NG **IS GOOD EXERCISE FOR YOUR TO**NG**UE.**
Spellings: **ng** as in **sing**
n as in **think**
nc as in **anchor**
n as in **anxious**
ngue as in **tongue**

Description

[ŋ] is a voiced lingua-velar nasal. It is a vowel-like consonant you produce by blocking off the breathstream with the tongue and soft palate and letting the air out through the nostrils, in a continuous stream.

Production: [ŋ]

1. Open your mouth fairly wide.
2. Place the back of your tongue against your soft palate, as though you were going to say the first sound of the word *go*.
3. Lower your soft palate, produce voice, and let the air and sound leave through your nose.

[ŋ]

Problems

PROBLEM 1. DECIDING WHETHER TO USE [ŋ] OR [n]

This is a sound we learn very easily as children, and it's easy to produce. Almost no one has problems with accurate production, as long as they produce it. But a good many people have difficulty deciding *when* to use [ŋ], and many inadvertently substitute [n] for [ŋ].

This substitution is commonly called "dropping the *g*." From a phonetic point of view there is no "g" to be dropped, but people are inclined to describe pronunciations such as *goin'*, *thinkin'*, *askin'*, and *workin'* with such a phrase. Actually, these pronunciations result from the substitution of [n] for [ŋ]. It is very common and very ancient in English speech, but it may be viewed as too informal in many situations. Your instructor can tell you about the social standing of [n] for [ŋ] in your area.

Try the following drills.

Production Drill

Let's borrow a word from baseball—*inning*. This word contains the sound [n] in the middle, and the sound [ŋ] at the end. Say the word slowly, and feel the way the tongue moves. Maintain the same pause in the middle as you read across the page.

> in . . . ning in . . . ning in . . . ning in . . . ning in . . . ning

Repeat this line another five or six times. Make sure you feel the back of your tongue touching the soft palate in the second syllable.

Now say the following, slowly and distinctly, reading across. Again, make sure to make contact between your tongue and soft palate.

> sing . . . sing . . . sing . . . sing . . . sing . . . sing . . . sing . . . sing
>
> sing . . . ing sing . . . ing sing . . . ing sing . . . ing
>
> singing . . . singing . . . singing . . . singing . . . singing . . . singing
>
> kink . . . kink . . . kink . . . kink . . . kink . . . kink . . . kink . . . kink
>
> kink . . . ing kink . . . ing kink . . . ing kink . . . ing
>
> kinking . . . kinking . . . kinking . . . kinking . . . kinking . . . kinking

Now try the following words. Say them slowly.

sing	king	ring
sting	wing	bring
long	strong	wrong
hang	gang	rang

If you're satisfied with your production of [ŋ], you can go on to the Contrast Drill below.

Contrast Drill for [n] and [ŋ]

Read across the page, contrasting the pairs of words. Notice the difference between [n] in the first word and [ŋ] in the second. You should be able to feel and hear the difference. Read slowly and distinctly. If you're not sure of your production, ask your instructor or a member of the class to help.

[n]		[ŋ]	[n]		[ŋ]
thin	—	thing	lawn	—	long
sin	—	sing	ton	—	tongue
win	—	wing	stun	—	stung
ban	—	bang	run	—	rung
fan	—	fang	gone	—	gong
pan	—	pang	sun	—	sung

PROBLEM 2. [ŋ] SPELLING CONFUSION

A great many people, especially nonnative speakers, become confused by English spelling and don't know when to use [ŋ] alone and when to follow it with [g]. For example, *finger* is pronounced [fɪŋgɚ], with [g] following the [ŋ]. But the word *singer* has no [g]. It's pronounced [sɪŋɚ]. Here are some simple rules that should clear up some of the confusion:

- Use [ŋ] when the word ends in *ng*. **Example:** *sing* [sɪŋ]
- Use [ŋ] when *ng* or another suffix is added to a root word ending in *ng*. **Example:** *singing* [sɪŋɪŋ]
- Use [ŋ] + [g] when the *ng* is in the middle of the original word. **Example:** *finger* [fɪŋgɚ]
- Exceptions: Use [ŋ] + [g] in the superlative and comparative forms of certain words such as *long, longer, longest; strong, stronger, strongest; young, younger, youngest.*

[ŋ]

Here are more examples:

[ŋ] + [g]

longer	stronger	linger
finger	hunger	language

[ŋ] alone

singing	ringing	banging
hanging	prolonging	bringing
hangar	belonging	flinging
singer	swinger	ringer

Note: *nge* is *not* pronounced [ŋ], but [ndʒ] as in *lunge*. For example, *stranger, arrange, hinge, orange, sponge,* and *change* do not contain the sound [ŋ].

PROBLEM 3. INTRUSION OF [k] AND [g]

Even if you do know the rules, you may be adding these sounds and not be aware of it. For example, adding [k] to *thing* turns it into *think*. If this is a problem for you, try this:

Contrast Drill for [ŋ] and [ŋk]

Say the following pairs of words. The first word in each pair ends in [ŋ]; the second ends in [ŋk].

[ŋ]	[ŋk]	[ŋ]	[ŋk]
thing	— think	hang	— hank
sing	— sink	bang	— bank
ring	— rink	rang	— rank
wing	— wink	tang	— tank
sting	— stink	sung	— sunk
clang	— clank	bung	— bunk

Production Drill

Now say the words below very slowly. Don't remove your tongue from your soft palate until you have completed the [ŋ]. Listen for any telltale "clicking" sound.

sing . . . . . . sing . . . . . . sing . . . . . . sing . . . . . . sing
. . . . . . sing

sing . . . ing sing . . . ing sing . . . ing sing . . . ing sing
. . . ing

[ŋ]

Now try the same thing with the words in the Contrast Drill above.

LEVEL 1 DRILLS FOR [ŋ]

▼ **Level 1 Practice Words for** [ŋ]

At this level, you won't have to worry about the rules of usage. All the words in the Level 1 drills have [ŋ] alone, not followed by [g].

Say the words in the following lists slowly and clearly. Make sure you feel contact between the back of your tongue and your soft palate. Monitor your production carefully. If you have doubts, ask your instructor or a member of the class to help. There are no words in English that begin with the [ŋ] sound.

Middle	*End*	*Middle*	*End*
bangs	herring	hangman	amazing
ringer	icing	wings	among
singer	king	tongs	jogging
length	tongue	youngster	racing
strength	gang	stingers	nursing
gangster	strong	things	dancing
thronged	asking	gongs	staying
ringed	wrong		

▼ **Level 1 Practice Phrases for** [ŋ]

staying among	amazing throng	doing wrong
racing and jogging	strong hanger	amazing wings
gongs and things	asking the singer	buying rings

▼ **Level 1 Practice Sentences for** [ŋ]

1. I'm always asking the wrong questions.
2. Those are amazing racing shoes.
3. Nursing is one of the helping professions.
4. The king was staying in the middle of things.
5. We stopped jogging and started dancing.
6. Running and jumping conflict with eating and relaxing.
7. Insulting words can be damaging to youngsters.
8. The gangster wore a sterling silver ring on his pinkie.
9. "Hangman" is a good game for playing on long trips.
10. Singing in the rain can be dampening to your spirits.

[ŋ]

LEVEL 2 DRILLS FOR [ŋ]

Level 2 Practice Words for [ŋ]

The words at this level have been divided into two lists: words containing [ŋk] and words with [ŋg]. Read them slowly and carefully. Be sure you have them right before you go on to the sentences.

[ŋk]	[ŋg]	[ŋk]	[ŋg]
bank	finger	junk	England
anchor	longer	donkey	angle
drinker	stronger	larynx	penguin
thinker	hunger	thanks	younger
jinx	hungry	planks	tangle
ink	angry	bankrupt	mingle

Level 2 Practice Sentences for [ŋ]

These sentences contain the [ŋk] and [ŋg] blends as well as words from Level 1.

1. Thanks for taking my change to the bank.
2. I'm still hungry after I eat junk food.
3. The tongue is located above the larynx.
4. I don't have the strength for jogging.
5. English vowels are longer than Spanish vowels.
6. Two triangles make one rectangle, I think.
7. The song they were singing so strongly was annoying.
8. She's staying later for the dancing.
9. Donkeys have an amazing amount of strength.
10. Thanks to you I didn't get a single one wrong.

Challenge Sentences for [ŋ]

1. The singer fulfilled his secret longing by learning a song while clinging to a cliff.
2. Nothing is as fine as finding a single perfect wedding ring.
3. The winning goal was banked into the netting by the smiling right wing of the English hockey team.

4. "Your Anchor Banker understands" is the advertising slogan of a leading savings bank.
5. The angry child was wringing wet when he hung his wrinkled swimming trunks from the swinging shingle.

[ŋ]

Challenge Materials for [ŋ]

1. If you stopped to think about how much time you spend communicating, you would probably be surprised. Responding to sounds from alarms, turning on radios, reading morning papers, answering phones, stopping at traffic lights, buying gas from local dealers, getting messages and giving instructions to assistants, writing memos, ordering coffee, and so on—within a few hours you have sent and received thousands of communication messages.

Lyman K. Steil, Larry L. Barker, Kittie W. Watson, *Effective Listening: Key to Your Success*

2. Imagine the largest shopping mall you've ever seen. Then double it. Then triple that. Because it's so large, divide it in two—why not with a scenic harbor. Shopping makes one hungry, so dot the mall with some of the world's great restaurants. Shopping leads to fatigue, so throw in a few of the world's greatest hotels. Shopping produces lots of money, so you'll need several banks. Put this shopping mall in a location that will make it one of the world's commercial centers. *Viola!* Hong Kong.

Elizabeth Devine and Nancy L. Braganti, *The Travelers' Guide to Asian Customs and Manners*

[tʃ]
[dʒ]

[tʃ] chair   [dʒ] judge

Sample: **[tʃ] THE KITCHEN CHAIR HAD A NATURAL WOOD
          COLOR.**
          **[dʒ] THE JUDGE SAT ON THE EDGE OF HIS SEAT AS
          HE HEARD THE SOLDIER ACCUSE THE GYPSY.**

Spellings: **ch** as in **chair**   **j** as in **judge**
           tch as in **kitchen**   **g** as in **gypsy**
           tu as in **natural**   **dg** as in **edge**
           ti as in **question**   **dj** as in **adjective**
           c as in **cello**   **d** as in **soldier**
           te as in **righteous**   **gg** as in **exaggerate**
                                            di as in **cordial**
                                            du as in **gradual**
                                            ge as in **George**

Description

[tʃ] and [dʒ] are cognate sounds. [tʃ] is voiceless, and [dʒ] is voiced. They
are affricate sounds, which you produce by blocking off the breathstream between the tongue and gum ridge, partially for a plosive and
partially for a fricative. The [tʃ] is a blend combined of [t] and [ʃ]. The
[dʒ] is a blend of [d] and [ʒ].

Production: [tʃ]

1. Open your mouth slightly.
2. Place the tip of your tongue against the gum ridge, and lift the sides
    to touch the teeth, as though you were going to make the sound [t].
3. Build up air pressure.
4. Release the air pressure very suddenly, but only allow a very small
    portion of your tongue tip to leave the gum ridge. Although you
    started with [t], you'll finish with [ʃ].

Production: [dʒ]

Follow the same steps used for [tʃ]. The only difference is voice. Produce voice as soon as you feel your tongue touch the gum ridge.

Problems

If you have difficulty producing any of the sounds that make up [tʃ] and [dʒ], read the sections of this chapter that apply to those sounds. Once you or your instructor are satisfied with your production of the component sounds, you can go ahead and work on [dʒ] and [tʃ].

PROBLEM 1. FAILURE TO VOICE [dʒ]

If you don't produce enough voice, you make the sound [tʃ] instead of [dʒ]. This turns the word *joke* into *choke*. To avoid this, you must start voicing at the very beginning of the [dʒ] and hold it all the way through the [dʒ]. Try the following Contrast Drill.

 Contrast Drill for [tʃ] and [dʒ]

Read the words in the following lists aloud, slowly and carefully. First read down the column of [tʃ] words. Notice how your voicing begins in the middle of the words after the [ʃ] is complete. Then read down the list of [dʒ] words. You should feel voicing right at the start. Then read across the page, contrasting pairs of words, listening and feeling for the differences between the voiceless and voiced sounds. Read the lists a few times until you're sure you can distinguish the two sounds.

[tʃ]		[dʒ]	[tʃ]		[dʒ]
choke	—	joke	lunch	—	lunge
cheer	—	jeer	etch	—	edge
chest	—	jest	britches	—	bridges
cheap	—	Jeep	searches	—	surges
chew	—	Jew	riches	—	ridges
chin	—	gin	batches	—	badges
chip	—	gyp	cinches	—	singes
chump	—	jump	perches	—	purges

PROBLEM 2. SUBSTITUTION OF [ʃ] FOR [tʃ]

Nonnative speakers often make this substitution. Here is a Contrast Drill that may help.

[tʃ]
[dʒ]

Contrast Drill for [tʃ] and [ʃ]

Say the following words aloud. First read down the list of [ʃ] words. Then read the list of [tʃ] words, making sure you say the [t] portion of the blend. Finally read across, contrasting pairs of words. Feel for the hard contact between the tongue and alveolar ridge for [tʃ]. Notice how there isn't any hard contact for [ʃ].

[ʃ]		[tʃ]	[ʃ]		[tʃ]
sheet	—	cheat	wash	—	watch
ship	—	chip	dish	—	ditch
share	—	chair	marsh	—	march
shanty	—	chanty	lashing	—	latching
shop	—	chop	washed	—	watched
shore	—	chore	mashing	—	matching
shoe	—	chew	wishing	—	witching
cash	—	catch	busher	—	butcher

PROBLEM 3. SUBSTITUTION OF [j] FOR [dʒ]

This substitution usually results from confusion between the letter *j* and the sound [j]. This is due to the fact that the letter *j* is pronounced as [j], as in *yes*, in some other languages, and this problem is usually experienced only by nonnative speakers. To correct this problem, you must replace one association pattern with another. Here's a Contrast Drill that will help.

Contrast Drill for [j] and [dʒ]

Read the following words aloud. Read across the page, contrasting the pairs of words. The first word contains the sound [j], and so shouldn't have the tongue tip touching at all. Feel for tongue–gum ridge contact in the second word. Read the lists a few times until you're satisfied that you're pronouncing the words correctly. Then go on to Level 1 words.

[j]		[dʒ]	[j]		[dʒ]
yoke	—	joke	year	—	jeer
use	—	juice	yell	—	gel
yule	—	jewel	yard	—	jarred
yellow	—	Jell-O	yaw	—	jaw
yam	—	jam	paying	—	paging
yet	—	jet	Yale	—	jail

LEVEL 1 DRILLS FOR [tʃ]

[tʃ]
[dʒ]

▼ **Level 1 Practice Words for [tʃ]**

Say the words in the following lists slowly and clearly. Listen carefully and correct your production until you are sure it is accurate. Make sure to produce the full blend, and not just a [ʃ]. Start with the *Beginning* words.

Beginning	*End*	*Middle*
chief	beach	kitchen
chin	each	butcher
chain	peach	hatchet
champion	winch	hitchhike
chat	inch	patching
chime	catch	coaching
chowder	match	bunching
choose	patch	munching
chew	watch	watching
China	coach	teaching
chop	ouch	enchant
chow	hitch	matching
chug	itch	hatching
chunky	much	penchant

▼ **Level 1 Practice Phrases for [tʃ]**

cheap chalk	chitchat	chief coach
kitchen match	catch much	teach a child
watching China	inch of ketchup	Chowder Beach

▼ **Level 1 Practice Sentences for [tʃ]**

1. The clam <u>chowder</u> was <u>much</u> too <u>chewy</u>.
2. He <u>chose</u> to <u>question</u> the <u>teacher</u>.
3. He was the <u>champion</u> <u>catcher</u> and <u>pitcher</u>.
4. <u>Peach</u> fuzz will make you <u>itch</u> if you <u>touch</u> it.
5. The <u>coach</u> ate <u>lunch</u> in the <u>kitchen</u>.
6. Plant <u>bunches</u> of <u>beech</u> trees in <u>chalky</u> soil.
7. The <u>matching</u> <u>China</u> plates <u>chipped</u> easily.
8. <u>Hitchhikers</u> are always <u>watching</u> for <u>cheap</u> rides.
9. The <u>butcher</u> used a <u>hatchet</u> to open the <u>ketchup</u>.
10. A <u>winch</u> pulls <u>inch</u> by <u>inch</u> by <u>inch</u> . . .

[tʃ]

[dʒ]

LEVEL 2 DRILLS FOR [tʃ]

 Level 2 Practice Words for [tʃ]

Say the words in the following lists slowly and distinctly. Make sure you produce the full [tʃ] blend, even though it appears with other sounds that may be difficult to make.

Beginning	*End*	*All Positions*
chair	bleach	achieved
cheer	reach	fracture
chill	rich	church
charm	scorch	ritual
chest	mulch	ratchet
chicken	porch	chinchilla
chili	leach	researching
chocolate	clutch	cha-cha
choice	breech	bachelor
chuckle	crouch	preaches
chance	grouch	choo-choo
chirp	French	watched
cello	wrench	actual
children	ranch	sculpture
Charley	branch	satchel

 Level 2 Practice Phrases for [tʃ]

chocolate chips	French chili	actual choice
choice chinchilla	grouchy bachelor	cheery children
chirping cello	church sculpture	charming ranch

 Level 2 Practice Sentences for [tʃ]

1. I gave a bowl of chili to each child.
2. Charley actually led the marching.
3. The mulch pile reached almost to the porch.
4. We bleached the stain out of the birch chair.
5. I drew a sketch of the preacher at the church.
6. Do you want to purchase that Chinese chest?
7. Do French restaurants serve chocolate chip cookies?
8. The branch fractured under the weight of the chicken.
9. I chuckle every time I watch them dance the cha-cha.
10. Bachelor-watching is a ritual at dude ranches.

▼ **Challenge Materials for** [tʃ]

"The windchill factor" is a fitting phrase for our time. People like to use it because it sounds good, but it doesn't mean much. There's simply no way to put a number on how cold we feel.

It's typical of our penchant for overstating things. I kept hearing weather reporters say, "The temperature in Chicago is minus nineteen degrees but the windchill factor makes it feel like minus sixty-five degrees, so bundle up."

It's as though nineteen below zero didn't sound cold enough. We have to find some way to make it sound even worse than it was. That's twentieth-century hype. You can't just say what something is. The plain and simple facts of the matter don't sound good enough or bad enough. To produce the desired effect, we exaggerate.

Why in the world would anyone have to exaggerate a temperature of nineteen degrees below zero?

Andy Rooney, *Word for Word*

LEVEL 1 DRILLS FOR [dʒ]

▼ **Level 1 Practice Words for [dʒ]**

Say the following words slowly and carefully. Listen closely. Make sure to voice the entire consonant blend. Start with *Beginning* words.

Beginning	*End*	*Middle*
jeep	age	imagine
gee	bandage	enjoy
gyp	cabbage	budget
gin	damage	agent
Jane	vintage	gadget
gem	teenage	digit
gent	fudge	object
gender	wedge	pigeon
Jack	hedge	magic
John	cage	edgy
job	package	major
junk	wage	manager
jump	badge	budging
jaw	budge	paging
joy	baggage	damaging
join	page	aging
joke	nudge	fidget

[tʃ]
[dʒ]

Level 1 Practice Phrases for [dʒ]

jump for joy	magic pigeon	paging Jack
join the pageant	baggage agent	vintage cabbage
aging major	jab at the jaw	gypped John

Level 1 Practice Sentences for [dʒ]

1. John ripped the gem from the guard's cage.
2. In the package was a gadget.
3. Jane enjoyed the wedge of fudge.
4. The major lost his badge in the jeep.
5. The managing agent would not pay a high wage.
6. Don't damage the hedge.
7. The magician used an imaginary pigeon.
8. There was a joke written on the edge of every page.
9. Jack's new job is balancing the budget.
10. Jack's old job was jumping on baggage.

Level 2 Drills for [dʒ]

Level 2 Practice Words for [dʒ]

These words combine sounds with more difficult articulatory movements. Say the words slowly and distinctly. Make sure to voice the [dʒ]. Start with the *Beginning* words.

Beginning	*End*	*All Positions*
genius	garbage	ginger
jeans	courage	judge
George	large	dodged
Jill	message	exaggerate
geranium	strange	agile
gelatin	village	bulges
jelly	pledge	fragile
jealous	college	registrar
genial	foliage	suggest
journalism	wreckage	grudge
gentle	grudge	Georgia
jarred	barge	lounging
gerbil	bridge	region

Level 2 Practice Phrases for [dʒ]

ginger jar	strange village	gentle judge
college registrar	dodged wreckage	large barge
regional foliage	fragile genius	agile gerbil

Level 2 Practice Sentences for [dʒ]

1. Attending college is a privilege.
2. The judge was gentle as well as genial.
3. Sausage and ginger don't mix.
4. I was jarred by the wreckage of the garage.
5. George was jealous of my beautiful geraniums.
6. The registrar let me take psychology at another college.
7. The garbage can was wedged rigidly against the wall.

Challenge Sentences for [dʒ] AND [tʃ]

1. He majored in lunch at college.
2. That was a strange choice to make.
3. I almost choked when I saw the damage to my jeans.
4. I suggested that the children chew more quietly.
5. Charley was known to exaggerate about his courage.
6. He actually worked his way through college selling gadgets.
7. Jeff caught a big striped bass in the channel near the beach.
8. He was teaching seamanship as we watched.
9. Jane lost her gold chains and engagement ring.
10. She wrote about range wars and prairie justice.

Chapter Six

Diction: The Vowels and Diphthongs

On the following pages you'll find drills for working on vowels and diphthongs. Because of regional dialects, some of the words we use as examples for particular vowels may be pronounced differently in your area of the country. For example, in upstate New York the word *Florida* generally is pronounced with the vowel [ɑ] as in *top,* while in Orlando it is generally pronounced with vowel [ɔ] as in *tall.* When you come across such words, either skip the examples that don't match the pronunciation in your region, or say them in the way that is standard for your area.

Don't, however, assume that a different pronunciation is always regional; it could be nonstandard for your area. Check with your instructor or someone else who is knowledgeable about pronunciation in your region. We don't advocate any particular regional dialect as being preferable over another. We do, however, advocate "standard for your area" as being preferable over nonstandard.

We've arranged the vowels in the following order:

Back Vowels

[ɑ] as in *calm*   p. 214

[ɔ] as in *awful*   p. 216

[o] as in *rope*   p. 220

[ʊ] as in *book*   p. 222

[u] as in *too*   p. 224

Mid Vowels

[ʌ] as in *up*   p. 227

[ə] as in *banana*   p. 229

[ɝ] as in *early*   p. 232

[ɚ] as in *father*   p. 235

Diphthongs

[aɪ] as in *ice*   p. 237

[aʊ] as in *how*   p. 242

[ɔɪ] as in *coin*   p. 244

[eɪ] as in *raid*   p. 200*

[oʊ] as in *robe*   p. 220*

Minor Diphthongs

[ɪɚ] as in *gear*   p. 197*

[ɛɚ] as in *pair*   p. 205*

[ɑɚ] as in *car*   p. 214*

[ʊɚ] as in *poor*   p. 223*

[ɔɚ] as in *pore*   p. 218*

*Included under vowels

[i]

[i]

see

Sample: **SHE COULD SEE THE REAPING MACHINES IN THE FIELD.**

Spellings:
e as in **he**	**ee** as in **see**
ea as in **eat**	**ie** as in **field**
eo as in **people**	**ei** as in **receipt**
ey as in **key**	**is** as in **debris**
i as in **marine**	**ae** as in **Caesar**
ay as in **quay**	**oe** as in **Phoenix**
ey as in **money**	**y** as in **easy**

Description

[i] is a high, front, tense vowel.

Production: [i]

1. Open your mouth very slightly. Spread your lips just a little and pull the corners back slightly, as though you were going to smile. Your teeth should be almost touching.
2. Touch the back molars with the sides of the back of the tongue.
3. Put the tip of the tongue behind the lower teeth and arch the tongue up and forward. Continue to touch the rear upper teeth. Keep the soft palate tensed so that there's no nasal emission of air.
4. Produce voice.

Problems

[i] is not a difficult sound to produce. Probably the most frequently occurring problem is the addition of the schwa ([ə]) after [i] when it is followed by [l], as in *feel*. This is very common, but not standard, in the Southern United States. Try the following drill.

Production Drill

If you add [ə] to [i], you should feel your jaw drop slightly as you say it. If there is no extra sound, your jaw will remain steady. Say the words

[i]

in the following list slowly and carefully, reading across the page. First you'll break a word into two parts. Then you'll join the parts together. As you say the words, place the back of your hand so that it is touching the underside of your jaw to feel if your jaw drops. You can also use a mirror for this.

fee . . . l	fee . . l	fee . l	feel
mee . . . l	mee . . l	mee . l	meal
dee . . . l	dee . . l	dee . l	deal
whee . . . l	whee . . l	whee . l	wheel
ree . . . l	ree . . l	ree . l	reel
hee . . . l	hee . . l	hee . l	heel
stee . . . l	stee . . l	stee . l	steel

LEVEL 1 DRILLS FOR [i]

▼ **Level 1 Practice Words for [i]**

Say the words in the following lists slowly and clearly. Alter your production until you are sure you are saying the sound acceptably. If you're not sure of the standard sound, ask your instructor to identify a word that you do say correctly. Use that word as your comparison word when you're in doubt.

Beginning	*End*	*Middle*
eat	be	mean
evening	he	need
each	knee	Pete
eager	pea	team
Eden	we	teach
even	fee	keep
Egypt	tea	heat
eke	me	week
eating	gee	weep
Eve	vee	deep
equip	handy	feet
ego	gooey	beat

▼ **Level 1 Practice Phrases for [i]**

each week	tea for me	even heat
Pete and Eve	need to eat	keep the team
deep vee	equip to teach	be mean

[i]

Level 1 Practice Sentences for [i]

1. He paid the fee for the new key.
2. Teach me how to heat the tea.
3. We were eager to bring the equipment for the team.
4. Keep heading toward me.
5. Each week we had a new teacher.
6. Eve eked out a living selling beehives.
7. We were eating marshmallows that were gooey.
8. Pete was a handyman who was quick on his feet.
9. We even had to feed ourselves on the trip to Egypt.
10. He hurt his knee when he fell into the deep hole.

LEVEL 2 DRILLS FOR [i]

The following drills contain [i] in more difficult contexts, including words in which [l] follows [i].

Level 2 Practice Words for [i]

Say the following words slowly. Start with *Beginning words.*

Beginning	*End*	*Middle*
ear	see	steel
eel	she	heel
eagle	agree	receive
easy	glee	speed
east	plea	increase
either	flee	cheese
eerie	three	please
equal	free	deal
evil	speech	believe
easel	speed	sleet

Level 2 Practice Phrases for [i]

agree to flee	cheesy meal	either easel
steel heel	speech speed	easy to believe
receive three	eerie eagle	see no evil

Level 2 Practice Sentences for [i]

1. That's easy for me to equal.
2. We agreed that my dog really has fleas.

3. The guilty plea was part of the deal.
4. See no evil, hear no evil, speak no evil.
5. The three greeting cards were free.
6. She didn't hear you speak last evening.
7. The early eagle catches the eel.
8. Sleet came from the eastern sky like drops of steel.
9. These readings are in a book called *Speaking Clearly.*
10. The cheese spread made a greasy meal.

$$[\text{I}]$$
sit

Sample: **THE RICH SYRUP SPILLED ON THE ENGLISH BOOK.**
Spellings: **i** as in **it**   **y** as in **syrup**   **o** as in **women**
         e as in **English**   **u** as in **busy**   **ei** as in **forfeit**
         ui as in **build**   **ee** as in **been**   **ie** as in **sieve**
Note: [I] does not normally occur at the ends of words, except when the letter y occurs in unstressed position, as in the word pretty. Speakers in the South and New England will frequently use [I] instead of [i] at the ends of such words.

Description

[I] is a high, front, lax vowel. It is very much like [i], being made in almost the same place and the same way. The difference is that [I] is lax, and [i] is tense, so [I] is a shorter, slightly lower pitched sound.

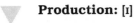

Production: [I]

1. Open your mouth very slightly. Your upper and lower teeth should be close together, but not quite as close as for [i]. Spread your lips slightly, but don't smile for this vowel.
2. Touch the back sides of your tongue to the upper molars. Place the tip behind the lower front teeth. The back of the tongue will be slightly lower than it was for [i].
3. Produce voice.

[ɪ]

Problems

PROBLEM 1. DISTINGUISHING BETWEEN [ɪ] and [i]

[ɪ] is actually not a difficult vowel to produce for native English speakers. Some people who have learned English as a second language, however, may have difficulty if the sound [ɪ] does not appear in their native language. Such languages are the Romance languages—Spanish, French, Italian, and other languages developed from Latin. If you have difficulty distinguishing between [ɪ] and [i], try the following Contrast Drill.

Contrast Drill for [ɪ] and [i]

Read the words in the following lists aloud slowly and carefully. First read down the columns, then read across. When you read across, contrast the pairs of words, listening for the differences between the [i] in the first word, and the [ɪ] in the second.

[i]		[ɪ]	[i]		[ɪ]
eat	—	it	jeep	—	gyp
seat	—	sit	bean	—	been
heat	—	hit	peak	—	pick
meat	—	mitt	cheek	—	chick
cheap	—	chip	bead	—	bid
Jean	—	gin	deep	—	dip
reach	—	rich	beat	—	bit
peel	—	pill	steal	—	still

PROBLEM 2. ELONGATION OF [ɪ]

If you hold on to [ɪ] too long, as many speakers do in the South, you may add an extra sound, the schwa ([ə]), to it. For example, the word *pill* becomes [pɪəl] instead of [pɪl]. [ɪ] is a shorter sound than [i]. Read the words presented in the Contrast Drill above to feel the difference in length. When you read the words in the drills that follow, make sure to cut the [ɪ] off without adding [ə].

LEVEL 1 DRILLS FOR [ɪ]

Level 1 Practice Words for [ɪ]

Read the words in the following lists slowly and carefully. Monitor your production until you're sure it's correct. Ask your instructor to identify a word that you say correctly. Use that word for comparisons. Start with the *Beginning* words.

[ɪ]

Beginning	*End (y)*	*Middle*
it	any	bit
in	funny	big
if	baby	wind
imply	heavy	dinner
infer	candy	fit
ignite	handy	committee
into	tiny	hit
impact	honey	wit
inborn	money	knit
invent	dandy	king

Level 1 Practice Phrases for [ɪ]

funny baby	into money	whipped honey
big committee	heavy dinner	invented candy

Level 1 Practice Sentences for [ɪ]

1. The <u>dinner</u> was <u>fit</u> for a <u>king</u>.
2. <u>Many</u> people confuse the words <u>infer</u> and <u>imply</u>.
3. <u>Did</u> you <u>invent</u> that <u>funny</u>-flavored <u>candy</u>?
4. We felt the <u>impact</u> of the <u>big wind</u>.
5. The <u>committee</u> spent all the <u>money</u>.
6. <u>Many</u> a <u>tiny baby</u> likes a <u>bit</u> of <u>honey</u>.
7. <u>It</u> felt like a <u>bit</u> of rain.
8. One car <u>hit</u> hard <u>into</u> the other.
9. <u>Did</u> you enjoy the <u>funny</u> movie?
10. Rags can <u>ignite</u> <u>if</u> left under the <u>sink</u>.

LEVEL 2 DRILLS FOR [ɪ]

Level 2 Practice Words for [ɪ] and [ɪɚ]

The vowel [ɪ] is frequently combined with [ɚ] to produce a minor diphthong, [ɪɚ]. It's not a difficult diphthong to produce, but whether or not you produce it with "r-shading," that is, use the [ɚ] or the [ə], can cause heated criticism and arguments between speakers of the same regional dialect. Here's an example: Many people in New York, and much of New

[ɪ]

England (as well as other parts of the country) pronounce the word *Korea* in such a way that others might confuse it with *career*. Our advice is to determine which pronunciation is standard for your region, and then try to be consistent.

Try the following practice words. They all contain [ɪɚ] in different sound contexts. Listen to hear if you pronounce the words with [ɚ] or [ə].

ear	steers	bier	fears
eerie	weird	clear	cheers
fear	shears	career	gears
appear	jeers	hear	smears
we're	tear	near	beard

In the lists below, we've included some words that have the letter *i* in an unstressed position, such as in the word *Africa*. The alternate standard pronunciation of these words is with a schwa [ə], instead of [ɪ]: [æfrəkə].

Make sure that you are cutting off the [ɪ] and not adding a schwa to it.

Beginning	*End (y)*	*All Positions*
ill	busy	pretty
irritate	foamy	silly
igloo	tally	chilly
isn't	rally	script
Illinois	Sally	wilt
Indiana	slimy	flinch
itch	rainy	English
its	briny	printing
is	shiny	city
ingenious	seedy	written

Level 2 Phrases for [ɪ]

chilly igloo	it's written	English script
irritating itch	pretty shiny	busy city

Level 2 Sentences for [ɪ]

1. Chicago is a big city in Illinois.
2. Read it as it's written in the script.
3. My English teacher irritates me immensely.

4. The Indy 500 rally is run even if it's rainy.
5. I'm itching from sitting in poison ivy.
6. Is he too ill to pitch this spring?
7. Isn't that printer's ink a pretty color?
8. The fire extinguisher made a slimy, foamy mess.
9. The wilted flowers were on the window sill.
10. It wasn't a silly idea, it was ingenious.

▼ **Challenge Sentences for [i] and [ɪ]**

1. Sitting in the rear seat, he cleaned the windows in minutes.
2. Rip Van Winkle reaped the winter wheat in ripped denim jeans.
3. The slim slipper seemed simple when seen in brilliant sunlight.
4. "The difference between the reason of man and the instinct of the beast is this, that the beast does not know, but the man knows that he knows." (John Donne)
5. "If a man sits down to think, he is immediately asked if he has the headache." (Ralph Waldo Emerson)

▼ **Challenge Materials for [i] and [ɪ]**

1. On first hearing, the computer term *wysiwyg* (pronounced wizzy-wig) sounds like a general gee-whiz description for computer wonders. In fact, it's an acronym for "What You See Is What You Get"; *wysiwyg* is applied to a system that can display on a computer screen an exact facsimile of what will be printed on paper.

Jack Rosenthal, "On Language," *The New York Times Magazine,*
August 28, 1988

2. Around every activity there develops a unique language, a special jargon or list of terms, the use of which saves time and trouble and prevents confusion. Import-export is no exception. There is a set of standard *shipping terms* to specify who makes the arrangements for each step in international shipping and who pays the charges. Most important, these terms indicate where the transfer of title

takes place. Who has title determines who bears the risk for loss or damage to the cargo at each point in its voyage.

Kenneth D. Weiss, Building an Import Export Business

    3. Water had become fascinating. It was fascinating to water the lawn. It was fascinating to direct a fine mist at a flowerpot. It was fascinating to take a bucket and measure the flow of water that filled the tank that watered my cows. It was fascinating to watch the saddle horses dip their muzzles in a spring. Suddenly other things in the landscape were not interesting. Wind generators were not interesting. Electricity was not interesting. Power lines were not interesting. Telephones were not interesting, and all the wires and relays over the prairie that laced this largely empty region to the fervid nation were not so very interesting anymore. Water had become the only interesting thing. It has rained one-quarter of an inch in three months. I had watched water-laden clouds go overhead at terrific speed without losing a drop. Montana was getting less rain than the Mojave Desert. The little clouds that look like the clouds on a baby's crib were the sort of thing you wanted to shout at. Wind beat the ground on the rumor of water. Cowmen hauled water to battered, unusable pastures to feed cows and calves. Forest springs remembered by generations suddenly went away.

Thomas McGuane, "Fishing the Big Hole," Condé Nast Traveler,
March 1989

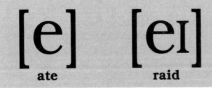

[e] [eɪ]
ate   raid

Sample: **THE LADY SAID THE TRAIN WAS DELAYED EIGHT HOURS.**

Spellings: **a** as in **ate**   **ei** as in **eight**
               ea as in **break**   **ay** as in **delay**
               ai as in **train**   **ee** as in **matinee**
               au as in **gauge**   **et** as in **sachet**
               ey as in **prey**

Description

[e]
[eɪ]

[e] is a mid, front, tense vowel. In stressed syllables, especially those in final position, and when the vowel is followed by a voiced consonant, we tend to use a diphthong, [eɪ], which is longer than [e] and drops in pitch. Using the diphthong instead of the vowel (or vice-versa) doesn't change the meaning of a word.

Production: [e]

1. Lower your tongue to a point just a bit lower than the position for [ɪ]. Open your mouth slightly. Just the rear of your tongue should touch the upper back teeth, and the tip should be behind the lower front teeth.
2. Produce voice. As you do, pull the corners of your lips back very slightly.

Problems

PROBLEM 1. ADDITION OF [ə]

When [e] is followed by [l], we sometimes add the schwa ([ə]) between the [e] and the [l]. If you do this, try the following:

Production Drill

Say the following words, reading across the page. The words will be broken at first, but you'll join the parts together as you go across. Make sure to stop producing voice entirely during the breaks, which will become shorter and shorter.

may . . . l	may . . l	may . l	mail
say . . . l	say . . l	say . l	sail
pay . . . l	pay . . l	pay . l	pail
ray . . . l	ray . . l	ray . l	rail
fay . . . l	fay . . l	fay . l	fail
tray . . . l	tray . . l	tray . l	trail

PROBLEM 2. CLIPPED [e]

Many languages don't use the diphthong [eɪ] at all. When speakers of those languages learn American English, they frequently use only the vowel [e]. As a result, their speech may have a characteristically clipped sound. Is this true of the way you speak? You can find out by trying the following contrast drill.

[e]

[eɪ]

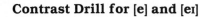

Contrast Drill for [e] and [eɪ]

Read slowly across the columns. The first word in each pair should have a shorter [e] than the second. The second word should use the noticeably longer diphthong [eɪ].

If the vowel sounds seem to be the same length, try dropping your pitch as you extend the vowel.

[e]		[eɪ]	[e]		[eɪ]	[e]		[eɪ]
rate	—	raid	face	—	faze	lace	—	laze
mate	—	maid	race	—	raze	mace	—	maze
state	—	stayed	grace	—	graze	safe	—	save
plate	—	played	wait	—	wade	fate	—	fade
grate	—	grade	eight	—	aid	trait	—	trade

PROBLEM 3. LOWERED [e]

In the metropolitan New York area, speakers tend to lower [e] when it comes before [l]. The result is to replace [e] with [ɛ] so that *fail* [fel] sounds like *fell* [fɛl]. Try the drills in the section on [ɛ] (p. 204), and the following Contrast Drill.

Contrast Drill for [ɛ] and [e]

Read the words in the following lists aloud slowly and carefully. First read down the columns, then read across. When you read across, contrast the pairs of words, listening for the difference between the [ɛ] in the first word and the [e] in the second.

[ɛ]		[e]	[ɛ]		[e]
fell	—	fail	jell	—	jail
shell	—	shale	hell	—	hail
weld	—	wailed	sell	—	sale
meld	—	mailed	tell	—	tale
bell	—	bail	dell	—	dale

Level 1 Drills for [e]

Say the words in the following lists slowly. Listen carefully as you say them, and try to make the vowel [e] the correct length. Avoid adding the schwa or lowering [e] before [l]. Since [e] is a sound of relatively few problems, all the drills are at Level 1.

[e]
[eɪ]

Beginning	End	Middle
able	delay	break
eight	matinee	train
age	away	label
ace	gray	great
ache	repay	place
April	pray	flake
angel	replay	scrape
aim	relay	slate
ape	weigh	relation
acorn	stay	belated
acre	sleigh	chaotic
aid	stray	aggravate

Level 1 Phrases for [e]

great place	break the label	matinee day
able to repay	relay race	weigh acorns

Level 1 Sentences for [e]

1. It would be great to take the day off.
2. I'll pay you back on Thursday.
3. We'll be able to meet you at the train by eight.
4. Show the instant replay of the relay race.
5. Wednesday and Saturday are matinee days.
6. Scrape the snowflakes off the slate.
7. This backache won't go away today.
8. They won't take it if you break the label.
9. They attacked the ape on the Empire State Building.
10. Did you enjoy your April vacation in Asia?
11. They don't serve ale in jail.
12. It was great to awaken to that view of the bay.
13. The sleigh can't stay on the frozen lake.
14. The acorns caused chaos when they rolled in the way.
15. Aim the bug spray away from your face.

[ɛ]

bet

Sample: **I DIDN'T USE MY HEAD WHEN I MADE A BET WITH MY FRIEND.**

Spellings: **e** as in **bet**   **ea** as in **head**   **ai** as in **again**
a as in **any**   **ie** as in **friend**   **ei** as in **heifer**
eo as in **leopard**   **ae** as in **aesthete**
u as in **burial**

Description

[ɛ] is a mid, front, lax vowel. It is shorter than [e] and lower pitched.

Production: [ɛ]

1.   Open your mouth slightly wider than for [e].
2.   The very back of the tongue is touching the upper molars, and the tip is behind the lower front teeth.
3.   Produce voice.

Contrast Drill for [ɛ] and [e]

Contrast the following pairs of words:

[e]		[ɛ]	[e]		[ɛ]	[e]		[ɛ]
late	—	let	mail	—	Mel	freight	—	fret
bait	—	bet	rake	—	wreck	wait	—	wet
fade	—	fed	rain	—	wren	trade	—	tread
pain	—	pen	braid	—	bread	flayed	—	fled
paste	—	pest	saint	—	scent	stayed	—	instead

Problems

This sound is one of the most often used in the English language. There are few real difficulties in producing the sound. There are some substitutions of other sounds for [ɛ], however. A common substitution, especially in the South, is [ɪ] for [ɛ] as in *pin* for *pen.* Try the following Contrast Drill.

[ɛ]

▼ **Contrast Drill for [ɛ] and [ɪ]**

Say the words in the following lists slowly, reading across the page. The first word of each pair contains the sound [ɪ] and the second contains the sound [ɛ]. Ask your instructor or a fellow student to listen to you and to correct your pronunciation.

[ɪ]		[ɛ]	[ɪ]		[ɛ]	[ɪ]		[ɛ]
pin	—	pen	sit	—	set	bit	—	bet
tin	—	ten	wrist	—	rest	lid	—	led
him	—	hem	lint	—	lent	been	—	Ben
mint	—	meant	hid	—	head	rid	—	red
since	—	cents	sinned	—	send	will	—	well

▼ **Practice Words for [ɛɚ]**

The vowel [ɛ] is frequently combined with [ɚ] to produce a minor diphthong, [ɛɚ]. It's a simple diphthong to produce, but whether or not you produce it with "r-shading" will be noticed quickly by speakers of your regional dialect. Our advice is to determine which pronunciation is standard for your region, and then try to be consistent.

Try the following practice words. They all contain [ɛɚ] in different sound contexts. Listen to hear if you pronounce the words with [ɚ] or [ə].

bear	scares	cares
scare	wears	dares
aware	snares	fairs
share	fared	stared

LEVEL 1 DRILLS FOR [ɛ]

[ɛ] is a relatively easy sound to produce accurately, so we've provided only Level 1 Drills. Just make sure you're producing [ɛ] and not another vowel in these drills.

▼ **Level 1 Practice Words for [ɛ]**

Say the words in the following lists slowly. Monitor your production to make sure you are producing the desired sound. Ask your instructor or

[ɛ]

a classmate to listen to you if you're not sure of your pronunciation. Start with the *Beginning* words. Note: [ɛ] does not occur in end position in English.

Beginning	*Middle*	*Beginning*	*Middle*
end	pen	any	rent
edge	pledge	echo	center
eggs	again	elderly	pledge
extra	gentle	engineer	forget
every	tent	exit	energy
enter	sent	elbow	said
ever	heaven	educate	mess

 Level 1 Practice Phrases for [ɛ]

heaven sent   extra echo
forget the rent   any exit
every edge   a mess again
gentlemen's pledge   center entrance
bent elbow

Level 1 Practice Sentences for [ɛ]

1. Eggs again?
2. I sent the rent on Wednesday.
3. I pledged my help to the Center for the Elderly.
4. The squeak of Fred's pen set my teeth on edge.
5. I need every bit of extra energy I can get.
6. I missed the exit because of the mess.
7. The sunset tinted the tent a pale yellow.
8. The engineers couldn't get rid of the extra echoes.
9. Don't forget to give me the fifty cents.
10. He got his education sitting in front of the TV set.

 Challenge Materials for [ɛ]

1. "Good morning."
"Today we will take up the broken chair. The thing to

[ɛ]

do with a broken chair is this. First, carefully carry the chair to the driveway and put it in the back of the car. Next, get in the car and take the broken chair to someone who knows how to fix it. Ask how long it will take. On the day it's supposed to be finished, return with a great deal of money. The chair will not be finished that day. Keep returning until finally the chair is fixed. This is how to repair a broken chair. Broken chairs may also be taken to the dump.''

Andy Rooney, Word for Word

2.   There are several good reasons for making your own bread. Anyone who has ever taken a golden loaf fresh from the oven knows that special joy of eating the first warm slice, and breathing its heady fragrance.

Beyond the earthy pleasures of savoring the flavor, aroma and texture of homemade bread, the best reason for doing your own baking is knowing that the produce is thoroughly edible, comprising purely nutritious ingredients with names a child could understand. Children can smell a fresh loaf down the block. If you want company, leave the kitchen door open and a pot of jam on the table.

The American Heart Association Cookbook

3.   Hear the sledges with the bells—
    Silver bells!
What a world of merriment their melody foretells!
    How they tinkle, tinkle, tinkle,
      In the icy air of night!
    While the stars that oversprinkle
      All the heavens, seem to twinkle
      With a crystalline delight;
    Keeping time, time, time,
    In a sort of Runic rhyme,
To the tintinnabulation that so musically wells
    From the bells, bells, bells, bells,
      Bells, bells, bells,—
From the jingling and the tinkling of the bells.

Edgar Allan Poe

[æ]

pat

Sample: **A FLAT TIRE IS NO LAUGHING MATTER.**
Spellings: **a** as in **pat**   **au** as in **laugh**
                ai as in **plaid**

Description

[æ] is a low, front, slightly tense vowel. It is a longer sound than [ɛ] and lower pitched.

Production: [æ]

1. Drop your lower jaw noticeably from the position for [ɛ].
2. Place your tongue tip behind the lower front teeth. Flatten the entire tongue slightly, and raise the middle and back slightly.
3. Produce voice. Make sure to keep the soft palate energized to prevent nasal emission of air.

   Note: There is another vowel that frequently takes the place of [æ], and is used mostly in New England. This is a low, front vowel, [a], as in the words *ask, half, park*, that is commonly called the "Boston 'a.'" It is produced in a position somewhere between [æ] as in *hat* and [ɑ] as in *father*. This is simply a regional pronunciation, and there is nothing "nonstandard" about it.

Problems

PROBLEM 1. DISTINGUISHING BETWEEN [ɛ] AND [æ]

If you raise the back and sides of the tongue just a little too much, you change an [æ] word to an [ɛ] word. For example, *bat* becomes *bet*. There are some regional differences, too. Say the words, *merry, marry, Mary*. If you live in the Northeast, you probably say each word with a different vowel. Elsewhere you may be saying them the same, with the vowel [ɛ].

For words in which there's an [r], then, we would consider the use of [ɛ] to be regional. Substituting [ɛ] for [æ], as in *bet* and *bat,* is common in the Great Lakes region. Try the following Contrast Drill:

Contrast Drill for [ɛ] and [æ]

Say the words in the following list slowly, reading across the page, contrasting the pairs of words. The first word of each pair will contain the vowel [ɛ], the second word will contain [æ]. Listen carefully to hear the difference between the two. Ask your instructor to check your pronunciation.

[ɛ]	[æ]	[ɛ]	[æ]
bet —	bat	fed —	fad
ten —	tan	led —	lad
end —	and	head —	had
Ed —	add	set —	sat
Ken —	can	lend —	land
send —	sand	bed —	bad
said —	sad	pest —	past
left —	laughed	leg —	lag

PROBLEM 2. DISTINGUISHING BETWEEN [ɒ] AND [æ]

Sometimes people have difficulty distinguishing [ɒ] as in *hot* from [æ] as in *hat.* This is common in New England and may be considered standard there. Try the following Contrast Drill.

Contrast Drill for [ɒ] and [æ]

Say the words in the following list slowly, reading across the page. Contrast the pairs of words. Ask your instructor to check your pronunciation if you're not sure. The first word of each pair will have the sound [æ], the second word will have [ɒ].

[æ]	[ɒ]	[æ]	[ɒ]
hat —	hot	cat —	cot
map —	mop	shack —	shock
pat —	pot	cap —	cop
jab —	job	tap —	top
sack —	sock	Dan —	Don

PROBLEM 3. DIPHTHONGIZATION

You may be in the habit of producing [æ] with your jaw too high, near the position for [ɛ]. This will result in a diphthong, [ɛæ], instead of the pure vowel [æ]. This most often happens before voiced consonants, especially the nasals. To prevent this, you must move the articulators quickly. The following Transfer Exercises will help. (The exercises are adapted from Hilda B. Fisher, *Improving Voice and Articulation*, Second Edition [Boston: Houghton Mifflin, 1975].)

▼ Transfer Exercises

The beginning word of each line below is one in which [æ] is not as likely to change to a diphthong as in some of the words following on that line. Avoiding diphthongization is likely to be more difficult in later words on the same line. Listen carefully to your production of [æ] in the first word of a line. Then, in producing every other word in the line, try to copy the same pure [æ] vowel you produced in the first word. Circle the words you find most difficult and practice them repeatedly, transferring the vowel sound from a "safe" word in that line to your troublesome word.

1. at add ant aunt act actor actual
2. bat bad bath bass bash batch balance back bag bang bank
3. fat fad fan fast fact fang fashion
4. sat sad sand sash sack sang sank
5. hat had half hand hash hatch hack hang hank
6. pat pad pan path pass patch pack pang
7. cat cad can cash catch can't
8. mat mad matter mass man mash match mangle
9. lad laugh lass lash latch lap lab lamb lamp lank
10. dad Dan dash dab dam damp dank
11. tat tan tap tab tam tack tag tang tank
12. rat radish rather raft wrap rash ran ram rang
13. gap gaff gander gallon gash gag gang
14. gnat nab nap nasty gnash knack nag
15. chat chatter chap chastise champion chant

16. plait plaid plan plant plaque
17. blab bland blast black blank
18. glad glass gland glance
19. grad grab grand grass gramp
20. trap tramp trash track
21. stab stamp stand staff stash stack stank
22. slap slab slash slant slam slack slang
23. snap snack snatch snag
24. flat flap flab flash flask flack flag flank
25. exact example examine examination

[æ]

LEVEL 1 DRILLS FOR [æ]

 Level 1 Practice Words for [æ]

Say the words in the following lists slowly. Listen carefully as you say them. If you're not sure of your production, ask your instructor or a classmate to listen to you and identify a word you say correctly to use for comparison. Start with the *Beginning* words. Do not go on to the phrases or sentences until you have had enough practice on single words. There are no English words ending with the [æ] sound.

Beginning	*Middle*	*Beginning*	*Middle*
at	bat	add	pat
actor	fat	annex	canned
after	habit	attic	fact
act	Jack	atom	have
ant	ham	adding	handy
Anthony	had	apt	band
anchor	banner	Andy	happy
and	hat	aim	cat

 Level 1 Practice Phrases for [æ]

after the fact	at bat	handy map
bad habit	added an act	canned ham
happy band	fat cat	have a hat

[æ]

Level 1 Practice Sentences for [æ]

1. Anthony packed his bag.
2. Can I have a hand with this anchor?
3. The fact is, he was acting.
4. Jack bought a canned ham.
5. The handyman cleaned the attic.
6. He had three turns at bat.
7. Happiness can get to be a habit.
8. The banner was at the head of the band.
9. The fat cat ate a whole can of sardines.
10. Andy and Pat can't ride in the back.

LEVEL 2 DRILLS FOR [æ]

Level 2 Practice Words for [æ]

Say the words in the following lists slowly and carefully. Make sure you don't nasalize the vowel when there's a nasal consonant in the word. Also, many of the words at this level are easily diphthongized. Listen carefully. If you're not sure of your production, ask your instructor or a classmate to listen to you.

Beginning	*Middle*	*Middle*	*Middle*
angle	fast	class	plant
amplify	bland	grant	grand
ankle	sandwich	brand	placid
angry	fans	grass	pants
asking	lands	stranded	pangs
Alice	sank	strap	standing
ample	wax	flapping	California
antler	clash	slant	fragment
answer	crash	slang	plank
as	hassle	clang	shrank

Level 2 Phrases for [æ]

bland sandwich	plank shrank	ample antlers
ask the class	fast flapping	angry answer

Level 2 Sentences for [æ]

1. I can't stand an unwaxed car.
2. I'll have a stab at it after exams.

[æ]

3. The fans were standing while the band played the National Anthem.
4. He gets angry when we ask too many questions in class.
5. They were stranded on the grass strip after the crash.
6. The ham sandwiches in the snack bar are pretty bland.
7. Sandy is never ready with a pat answer.
8. Alice felt hassled on the last trip to Lake Placid.
9. No matter how fast I flap my wings, I can't fly.
10. There's an ample planting season in Southern California.

▼ **Challenge Materials for** [æ]

Dear Diary:

The other day my friend Natalie Minewski of New Paltz, N.Y., dialed the Highland (N.Y.) Diner.

"I ate lunch at your diner on Wednesday," she said. "Now I realize that I left my black hat there. Please look to see if it's still there."

"I'll look," the man at the diner said. He sounded wary.

Many minutes later he was back on the line.

"No, lady. I asked everybody."

"Don't you have a lost and found?"

"Oh, wait a minute."

Returning again, he said, "No, lady. I looked."

"It's a soft hat, a black beret," Ms. Minewski said, becoming insistent.

"Beret? Hat? I thought you said cat."

Ms. Minewski picked up her hat that afternoon.

Rosalie M. Franklin, in "Metropolitan Diary," *The New York Times,* March 16, 1988

[ɑ]
([ɒ])

[ɑ] ([ɒ])

calm

Sample: **IT DIDN'T BOTHER HIM AS HE CALMLY LOCKED THE CAR.**

Spellings: **a** as in **calm**   **o** as in **lock**
          ea as in **heart**   **ow** as in **knowledge**
          e as in **sergeant**   **aa** as in **bazaar**

Description

[ɑ] is a low, back, lax vowel. The mouth position is the widest open of all the vowels. The tongue has only the very back part slightly raised; the rest of it is relaxed. An alternate form, [ɒ], is very close in placement (slightly higher and more tense) and is a regional variant in some American dialects, notably in New England.

 Production: [ɑ]

Open wide, and say *ahhh.*

Problems

Very few. There are a couple of substitutions, but they are regional. For example, New Englanders tend to say *park* with the vowel [a], and along with certain New Yorkers and West Indians might say the word *hot* with the vowel [ɒ]. It probably doesn't matter which you say as long as you are consistent.

Before [r] many New Yorkers raise and round [ɑ], resulting in a nonstandard vowel resembling [ɔ]. *Card* then may sound like *cord*, *star* sounds like *store*, and *far* sounds like *four*. Listen for this when you do the practice words, and check for lip-rounding with a mirror. Opening the mouth a little bit wider and relaxing the lips will change *tore* back to *tar*.

LEVEL 1 DRILLS FOR [ɑ]

 Level 1 Practice Words for [ɑ] and [ɑɚ]

Listen carefully as you say each word. Some of the words contain the minor diphthong [ɑɚ]. It doesn't matter if you pronounce it with r-shad-

[ɑ]

([ɒ])

ing, that is with [ə] as opposed to [ɚ]. Just be consistent with your regional pronunciation.

Say the words in the following lists slowly. All the drills for [ɑ] are at Level 1. There are no English words that end in [ɑ].

Beginning	Middle	Beginning	Middle
ah	calm	on	top
are	frog	arms	father
honest	bomb	alarm	stars
obvious	locker	occupy	guard
art	spot	onset	response
argue	palms	arson	stopping
arch	smart	army	follow
article	hot	operation	modern
olive	knowledge	almonds	heart

▼ **Level 1 Practice Phrases for** [ɑ]

obvious response	calm frog	card shark
argue about art	smart bomb	farmyard barn
on top of	spot the guard	Charlie's cart

▼ **Level 1 Practice Sentences for** [ɑ]

1. They had an honest argument with their father.
2. Stopping is the obvious response when the guard is armed.
3. The fog crept into the harbor on little frog's feet.
4. Sighing "ahh" can be calming.
5. Watch them stop the cars at the top of the yard.
6. Star-gazing is a pleasurable occupation on some nights.
7. The pool shark spotted the ball on the mark.
8. The palm trees arched into the sky over the dark oasis.
9. Sorry, this locker room is occupied.
10. The arson squad turned the bomb over to the army.

awful

Sample: **I THOUGHT THE LAUNDRY DID AN AWFUL JOB IN A SHORT TIME.**
Spellings: **aw** as in **awful**   **au** as in **laundry**   **oo** as in **door**
o as in **wrong**   **ough** as in **thought**   **augh** as in **taught**

Description

[ɔ] is a mid, back, lax vowel. The lips are usually rounded.

 Production: [ɔ]

1. Close the mouth very slightly from the position of [ɑ], and slightly round your lips. Elevate the back of your tongue a bit, but don't touch your upper teeth.
2. Produce voice. Make sure there's no nasal emission.

Problems

Use of [ɔ] varies almost from word to word, region to region. Words that are pronounced with [ɔ] in one region may be pronounced with [ɑ] or [ɒ] in others. For example, the word *water* may be pronounced with [ɑ] in upstate New York and with [ɔ] in downstate New York. Floridians usually say *Florida* with [ɔ], but northerners say it with [ɑ]. How do *you* say such words as *fog, wash, caught, coffee,* and *auto?*

    In the drills that follow, we've used words that are pronounced with [ɔ] in at least one regional dialect. You'll have to determine the usage in your area by consulting your instructor and others knowledgeable on the subject.

PROBLEM 1. NONSTANDARD [ɔ]

Although use of [ɔ] varies greatly around the country, there is a nonstandard production. It occurs when you round your lips too much and close your mouth slightly. It frequently is associated with the dental and gum ridge consonants because they require a slight closing of the mouth. Look at your mouth in a mirror as you say *awful.* Do your lips suddenly round before you make the sound? Is your mouth almost closed? If so, you are probably producing the nonstandard sound. Here's another test: put the back of your hand lightly against the

[ɔ]

underside of your chin and say *all*. Did your jaw drop? It should, but only very slightly.

If your jaw drops a great deal, you're probably producing a nonstandard diphthong that sounds close to [ɔə]. This sound is produced for two reasons: you're saying the [ɔ] with too much lip-rounding, and the [ə] results because you're dropping your jaw *before* you stop producing the [ɔ]. This nonstandard production is very common in the New York metropolitan area. Ask your instructor to listen to you, and if you produce the nonstandard diphthong, try the following drill.

▼ **Production Drill**

Say the following pairs of words. The first word of each pair contains the sound [ɑ]. The second has the sound [ɔ]. Hold your chin and look in a mirror while you say the words. Don't let your jaw rise or your lips round—go from the position for [ɑ] to the position for [ɔ] without moving anything except your tongue. Ask your instructor to listen.

[ɑ]	[ɔ]	[ɑ]	[ɔ]	[ɑ]	[ɔ]
cot	— caught	hock	— hawk	la	— law
on	— awning	wok	— walk	tot	— taught
lot	— lawn	knot	— gnawed	don	— dawn

LEVEL 1 DRILLS FOR [ɔ]

▼ **Level 1 Practice Words for** [ɔ]

Say the following words slowly and carefully. If a particular word is not pronounced with [ɔ] in your area, eliminate it. (Check with your instructor first.) Find a word you consistently pronounce correctly, and use that word for comparison.

Beginning	*End*	*Middle*
awful	draw	tall
often	law	stall
August	straw	thought
auction	jaw	wrong
autumn	saw	chalk
also	flaw	hawk
author	craw	fought
audio	claw	caught
awesome	maw	yawn
awkward	gnaw	song
awning	paw	long
offer	raw	dawn
auburn	slaw	ball
always	thaw	fawn

[ɔ]

 Level 1 Practice Phrases for [ɔ]

| raw coleslaw | also an author | August auction |
| gnaw its paw | awesome audio | long song |

 Level 1 Practice Sentences for [ɔ]

1. I always thought he would break the law.
2. August can be awfully long.
3. We saw her last autumn at the auction.
4. That dog always offers its paw.
5. I bought the wrong kind of coleslaw.
6. We all like to draw with chalk.
7. The straw baskets hung from the awning in the stall.
8. He fought to cross the ice during the thaw.
9. Authors don't always admit their flaws.
10. Dawn often colors her hair auburn.

LEVEL 2 DRILLS FOR [ɔ]

Level 2 Practice Words for [ɔ] **and** [ɔɚ]

Many words couple the [ɔ] and [ɚ] sounds in the minor diphthong [ɔɚ]. Make an extra effort to stop your jaw from rising and your lips from rounding too much. If you don't, the first part of the diphthong, mostly the sound [ɔ], will become distorted, and the diphthong seems to separate into two distinct sounds as your jaw drops again. Say each of the practice words slowly, comparing it with a word you know you say correctly. If you're not sure, ask your instructor or a classmate to listen.

Beginning	Middle	Middle	Middle
oar	born	morning	sports
orchid	store	drawn	thorn
organ	four	cork	north
ornate	corn	horn	born
orchestra	north	fourth	storm
Orient	core	cord	ward
orphan	score	more	door
ornament	bore	war	tore
Orlando	floor	lore	forty
ordeal	fortune	shore	spore

Beginning	Middle	Middle	Middle
order	snore	fourteen	dormant
orator	dorm	warm	swarm
oral	dorsal	dory	story
oracle	glory	forceps	force
orbit	horse	course	forbid

[ɔ]

Level 2 Practice Phrases for [ɔ]

ornate store	fourteen stories	warm floor
morning course	north forty	more corn
dormant spore	north shore	born in a storm

Level 2 Practice Sentences for [ɔ]

1. I bought a totally awesome audio system.
2. The storm washed an oar up on the shore.
3. He steered a broad course by the North Star.
4. I had an awful cough all morning.
5. I ordered it all at the store.
6. Have you ever stored corn in straw?
7. The orator spoke of law and order.
8. It was an ordeal listening to the snoring in the dorm.
9. The score was fourteen to four.
10. The horse forced its way through the door.

Challenge Sentences for [ɔ]

1. Norton ordered audio equipment from a store in the north ward of Boston.
2. The mortician often saw long cordons of autos swarming along the boardwalk.
3. Orlando, Florida, has long been called a city of the fourth glory.
4. The law office was warm despite the strong autumn storm of the morning.
5. The haughty horseman was ordered off the course because of his unsportsmanlike oratory.

[ou]
[o]

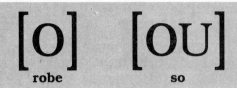

[o] [ou]
robe   so

Sample: **SO, I ASKED HIM TO ROW THE BOAT HOME.**
Spellings: **o** as in **so**   **oa** as in **boat**
          ow as in **row**   **oe** as in **toe**
          ough as in **dough**   **oo** as in **brooch**
          eo as in **yeoman**   **eau** as in **beau**

Description

[o] is a mid, back, tense vowel. The jaw is up slightly higher than for
[ɔ], and the lips are rounded. In stressed syllables, especially those in
final position, and when the vowel [o] is followed by a voiced consonant, we tend to use a diphthong, [ou], which is longer than [o] and
drops in pitch. Using the diphthong instead of the vowel (or vice-versa)
doesn't change the meaning of a word.

Production: [o]

1. Open your mouth about halfway. Round your lips and slightly
    purse them. Touch the tip of your tongue to the back of your lower
    teeth, but do it lightly.
2. Raise the back of your tongue as you purse the lips. Produce voice.
    Make sure there's no nasal emission.

Problems

[o] is fairly easy to produce accurately. Actually, most native speakers
produce the diphthong [ou] more than the pure vowel [o], especially in
stressed syllables and before voiced consonants. People living in the
upper Midwest tend to use the pure vowel [o] consistently, as do nonnative speakers who have only the pure vowel [o] in their languages. It
doesn't really matter which one you use for meaning.

See if you can hear a difference in length in the following pairs of
sounds. The second word should use the noticeably longer diphthong [ou].

[o]	[ou]	[o]	[ou]	[o]	[ou]
rope	— robe	coat	— code	post	— posed
lope	— lobe	boat	— bowed	host	— hosed
dose	— doze	rote	— rowed	gross	— grows

[ou]

[o]

LEVEL 1 DRILLS FOR [o]

Level 1 Practice Words for [o]

Say the words in the following lists slowly. Listen for length: do you use the vowel [o] or the diphthong [ou]?

Beginning	*End*	*Middle*
open	flow	road
over	toe	boat
oh	dough	bowl
oak	throw	sewing
oats	show	pole
ocean	mow	coal
own	grow	grown
omit	follow	stone
odor	glow	whole

Practice Sentences for [o]

1. He owned an ocean-going boat.
2. Put the oatmeal in the bowl next to the stove.
3. We opened the coal stove and began to choke on the smoke.
4. She was sewing closed a hole in the toe.
5. It's hard to follow such a glowing show.
6. I'm told that eating oats lowers cholesterol
7. Only the lonely enjoy flying solo polar flights.
8. I know you would like stone-ground whole wheat toast.

Challenge Materials for [o] and [ou]

When the snow clouds retreated, the gray slopes and jagged cliffs were gone, as were the livestock trails and raw stumps of felled oak. Several inches of fresh snow softened all contours. Hunched against December's cold, I scanned the slope, looking for the snow leopard which was somewhere a thousand feet above near a goat it had killed the previous day. But only cold prowled the slopes. Slowly I climbed upward, kicking steps into the snow and angling toward a spur of rock from which to survey the valley. Soon scree gave way to a chaos of boulders and rocky outcrops, the slopes motionless and silent as if devoid of life.

Then I saw the snow leopard, a hundred and fifty feet away, peering at me from the spur, her body so well molded into the contours of the boulders that she seemed a part of them. Her smoky-gray coat sprinkled with black rosettes perfectly complemented the rocks and snowy wastes, and her pale eyes conveyed an image of immense solitude. As we watched each other the clouds descended once more, entombing us and bringing more snow. Perhaps sensing that I meant her no harm, she sat up. Though snow soon capped her head and shoulders, she remained, silent and still, seemingly impervious to the elements. Wisps of clouds swirled around, transforming her into a ghost creature, part myth and part reality. Balanced precariously on a ledge and bitterly cold, I too stayed, unwilling to disrupt the moment.

George B. Schaller, *Stones of Silence: Journey in the Himalaya*

[ʊ]
book

Sample: **I WISH SHE WOULD PUT THE BOOK IN THE WOODEN BOX.**

Spellings: **oo** as in **book**   **ou** as in **would**
u as in **put**

Description

[ʊ] is a high, back, lax vowel. Your lips are slightly rounded.

Production: [ʊ]

1. Open your mouth to a position slightly higher than for [o]. Round and slightly protrude your lips.
2. Touch your lower front teeth with the tip of your tongue.
3. Produce voice. Make sure there's no nasal emission.

Problems

[ʊ] is a fairly easy vowel to produce. Most of the problems occur when a nonnative speaker isn't sure of how to pronounce a word and substitutes [u] for [ʊ]. For example, *should* becomes *shooed*. Try the contrast drill on page 225 if you're having difficulty distinguishing the two sounds. The drills for [ʊ] are all Level 1. Just be sure you're using [ʊ] and not [u].

LEVEL 1 DRILLS FOR [ʊ]

 Contrast Drill for [ɔɚ] and [ʊɚ]

Some regions don't distinguish between the minor diphthongs [ɔɚ] and [ʊɚ] as in *pore* and *poor*. Sometimes, this can cause confusion and, perhaps, misunderstandings. Another factor to consider is that often times, r-shading on the diphthong varies regionally, too. It doesn't matter if you use the [ɔɚ] or [ʊɚ], just be consistent.

Say the following words slowly and carefully. Make sure you distinguish between [ɔɚ] and [ʊɚ]. Also, listen for the "r-shading" at the end of the diphthong, regardless of which diphthong you use.

[ɔɚ]		[ʊɚ]	[ɔɚ]		[ʊɚ]
pore	—	poor	tore	—	tour
shore	—	sure	lore	—	lure
more	—	moor	yore	—	you're
chore	—	chewer	store	—	stewer

 Level 1 Practice Words for [ʊ]

Say the words in the following lists slowly and carefully. Listen closely, and be sure you are not saying [u] instead of [ʊ]. [ʊ] does not occur in end or beginning positions.

[ʊ]

wood	book	could	put	hoof
stood	should	sugar	pull	push
look	cook	bushel	bully	shook
hook	hood	wooden	couldn't	nook
brook	butcher	wool	bush	rook
wouldn't	cookie	took	good	crook

▼ **Level 1 Practice Sentences for [ʊ]**

1. I couldn't push the wood through the bush.
2. I would do it by hook or by crook.
3. He took the meat off the butcher block.
4. The bully stood still against the pull.
5. The sugar cookies were too good to crumble.
6. The book stood where all could look at it.
7. Wouldn't you like a woolen hood?
8. The horse splashed his hoof in the brook.
9. The cook pushed the saltshaker back in its nook.
10. They lifted the bushel with a wooden pulley.

[u]
too

Sample: **HE WAS TOO LATE TO GO ON THE CRUISE AS A CREW MEMBER.**

Spellings: **o** as in **to**   **oo** as in **too**
ew as in **crew**   **ui** as in **cruise**
ou as in **you**   **u** as in **tuba**
oe as in **shoe**   **ue** as in **true**
                              eau as in **beauty**

Description

[u] is a high, back, tense vowel. It's the highest back vowel, and we make it with our lips considerably rounded.

[u]

Production: [u]

1. Put your jaw in the same place as for [ʊ]. Round your lips so as to leave only a small opening, as for [w].
2. Raise the back of your tongue so that it almost touches your soft palate. The tip should be just touching the gum behind the lower front teeth.
3. Produce voice. Make sure there's no nasal emission.

Problems

[u] is not often misarticulated. It's fairly easy to produce, so only Level 1 Drills are given. Sometimes, though, nonnative speakers may be confused as to which sound to use—[u] or [ʊ]. And there are some regional variations in the pronunciation of words such as *roof* and *root*. Here's a Contrast Drill to help reinforce the differences between [u] and [ʊ].

Contrast Drill for [u] and [ʊ]

Say the words in the following lists slowly, reading across the page. Contrast the pairs of words. The first word of each pair uses a [ʊ] and the second a [u].

[ʊ]	[u]	[ʊ]	[u]
soot	— suit	pull	— pool
look	— Luke	full	— fool
would	— wooed	could	— cooed
stood	— stewed	cookie	— kooky

LEVEL 1 DRILLS FOR [u]

Level 1 Practice Words for [u]

Say the words in the following lists slowly. Make sure you're not saying [ʊ] for [u]. Ask your instructor or a classmate to listen to you if you're not sure. There are only a few words beginning with [u].

Beginning	*End*	*End*	*Middle*	*Middle*
oodles	crew	two	pool	stool
ooze	true	through	fool	coupon
oolong	stew	blue	dues	moon
	shoe	grew	dunes	whose
	flew	glue	tube	soup
	knew	who	food	stoop

[u]

Level 1 Practice Sentences for [u]

1. He jumped in the pool like a fool.
2. Food tubes are the stews of tomorrow.
3. We found a coupon for a soup spoon.
4. Is it true he flew the coop?
5. I carried my shoes while we walked through the dunes.
6. Newton booed while the crooner sang the blues.
7. Louis Armstrong blew a cool trumpet with true enthusiasm.
8. Whose newspaper is due to arrive sooner than Tuesday?
9. Cape Cod has two temperatures: too hot and too cool.
10. U Nu was the premier of Burma many moons ago.

Level 1 Practice Sentences for [ʊ] and [u]

1. They put on a new crew to fly to the moon.
2. Should you pay the dues so soon?
3. I could eat oodles of noodles.
4. Would you please stand on that stool?
5. The crook's shadow grew in the moonlight.

Challenge Materials for [u] and [ʊ]

The best material from which a suit can be made is wool. Wool takes dyes better than any other fabric. It does not snag; it fits well; it does not lose its shape; it is resilient; it lies better on the body; in winter, it's warmer; it outlasts any other fabric. It can also be woven into many different textures and looks.

The second-best suit fabric is a polyester and wool blend. The general rule is the more wool the richer looking the material and the better the suit. Avoid any suit made with less than forty-five percent wool, as well as those made of a blend that has the shiny look of polyester.

John T. Molloy, *John T. Molloy's New Dress for Success*

[ʌ]

up

Sample: **HE WAS LUCKY TO DOUBLE HIS MONEY IN UNDER A MONTH.**

Spellings: **u** as in **up**   **o** as in **month**
ou as in **double**   **oo** as in **blood**
oe as in **does**

Description

[ʌ] is a low, mid, stressed vowel that occurs in stressed syllables and words.

Production: [ʌ]

1. Open your mouth about as wide as for [ɔ] and slightly higher than for [ɑ]. Don't round your lips.
2. Raise the center of your tongue very slightly. Produce voice. Make sure there's no nasal emission.

Problems

[ʌ] is one of the least complicated vowels to produce. But because it doesn't exist in many other languages, nonnative speakers will frequently substitute another sound for [ʌ]. Most often, [ɑ] is substituted, so here's a Contrast Drill to help you distinguish between [ɑ] and [ʌ].

Contrast Drill for [ɑ] and [ʌ]

Read the words in the following lists aloud. First read down the list of [ɑ] words. Then read down the list of [ʌ] words. Finally read across the page, contrasting the pairs of words. The first word of each pair will contain [ɑ], and the second [ʌ].

[ʌ]

[ɑ]		[ʌ]	[ɑ]		[ʌ]	[ɑ]		[ʌ]
hot	—	hut	rob	—	rub	cob	—	cub
cop	—	cup	lock	—	luck	bomb	—	bum
not	—	nut	rot	—	rut	got	—	gut
calm	—	come	mock	—	muck	Don	—	done
cot	—	cut	dock	—	duck	Ron	—	run
gone	—	gun	sob	—	sub	shot	—	shut

Note: [ʌ] occurs *only* in stressed words and syllables. It does not occur at the ends of words. Because it is easy to produce accurately, all the drills for [ʌ] are at Level 1.

LEVEL 1 DRILLS FOR [ʌ]

Level 1 Practice Words for [ʌ]

Say the words in the following lists slowly. Monitor your production to make sure you are producing the sound correctly and not substituting [ɑ] for [ʌ]. If you aren't sure of your production, ask your instructor or a classmate to listen to you. Start with the *Beginning* words.

Beginning	*Middle*	*Beginning*	*Middle*
up	double	under	month
uncle	nothing	other	mother
oven	brother	us	discuss
onion	instructor	ugly	tough
usher	enough	ultimate	bubble

Level 1 Practice Phrases for [ʌ]

nothing under	tough and ugly	the other onion
enough ushers	double up	under discussion

Level 1 Practices Sentences for [ʌ]

1. There's nothing cooking in the oven.
2. We have enough ushers this month.
3. My uncle and my brother have the matter under discussion.
4. My mother doesn't cry when she peels onions.
5. The other instructor is a tougher grader.
6. I blew the ultimate bubble with that ugly looking gum.
7. What's coming up for us next?

▼ **Challenge Materials for** [ʌ]

> If you want to tour Europe at the least expense, and you can arrange your timetable with a certain degree of flexibility, here's what to do: buy a one-way (or roundtrip) ticket to London. When you arrive in London purchase onward tickets from a "bucket-shop."
>
> London is where you'll find the most bucket-shops. The term "bucket-shop" doesn't refer to the product they sell, rather to the fact that unsold tours and airline tickets are sold by this kind of business; sort of like putting the leftovers in a bucket so to speak.
>
> Bucket shops are nothing new, in fact airline tickets and tours have been sold through this kind of outlet for years in London. Only since airline deregulation have bucket-shops come into being in the United States. Typical U.S. "bucket-shops" usually operate as "Discount Travel" clubs. Some require membership (and a yearly fee), others can be used at no cost.
>
> Capt. Richard A. Bodner, *Money Saving Secrets of Smart Airline Travelers*

[ə]
banana

Sample: **THE PRICE OF BANANAS WENT DOWN AGAIN.**
Spellings: a, e, i, o, u, plus virtually any vowel combination, in
          unstressed syllables.

Description

[ə] is a low, unstressed mid vowel. It does not occur in any stressed syllables or in stressed single-syllable words.

[ə]

Production: [ə]

1. [ə] is produced in the same way as [ʌ]. The only difference is in stress (loudness). Open your mouth to a position about the same as for [ɔ]. Rest your tongue in the bottom of your mouth.
2. Produce voice, but not as loud as for [ʌ] or as long.

Notes: [ə] is the vowel we use more than any other in our language. That's because the *other vowels tend to change from their original form to* [ə] *when they are unstressed.* This vowel actually can't be pronounced alone, since it only occurs in unstressed positions, so you may be confused as to what its sound is. For now, let's say that *it sounds just like* [ʌ], *but weaker.* As a matter of fact, the name of this vowel, *schwa,* is from the German word for "weak."

Here are some words that may help explain this. Say the word *above.* It has the stress on the second syllable, so the vowels are [ə] and [ʌ]: [əbʌv]. Say the word a few times to get the feeling of the first sound. Make sure to say the word normally, with the first sound so weak that it's almost not there. Now say *above* with equal stress on both syllables, as you would in a word such as *Ping-Pong.* Sounds strange, doesn't it. When you said *above* that way, you used the vowel [ʌ] twice. Here's another example: the word *the* can be said in two ways. Try these phrases: *the beginning, the end.* Say them a couple of times. You should hear a difference: in phrases in which *the* comes before a consonant sound, we say [ə]; in phrases in which *the* comes before a vowel sound, we say [i]. You have to listen to the stress to decide which vowel was used.

In summary, [ə] is produced in the same way and sounds just like [ʌ], only it is weaker. You use [ə] when other vowels change because they are in unstressed syllables.

Problems

The difficulties with [ə] are really not production difficulties. They are basically difficulties caused by confusing [ʌ] and [ə], omission of [ə], and addition of [ə], such as in the word *athlete.* Here's a Contrast Drill to help you distinguish between [ə] and [ʌ].

Contrast Drill for [ə] **and** [ʌ]

Say the following words and phrases slowly. Each word or phrase contains both the [ə] (marked ‿) and the [ʌ] (marked ⁓).

[ə]

ab̄ove	c̄ome ūp	s̄un up	abrŭpt
cŭt up	cŭt ūp	st̄uck ūp	bŭttercŭp
sev̄en ūp	am̄ong	hŭndred	und̄one

LEVEL 1 DRILLS FOR [ə]

▼ **Level 1 Practice Words for** [ə]

The words in the following lists all contain the vowel [ə]. Because you can spell [ə] so many ways, and the same letter can be pronounced differently in the same word, we've underlined the letters that are to be pronounced [ə]. Say the words slowly and carefully, but make sure to use the conventional stress pattern. Check with your instructor or a classmate if you're not sure.

Beginning	*End*	*Middle*
about	soda	lion
around	Canada	banana
another	sofa	connect
again	tuba	official
agree	vanilla	option
away	Carolina	elephant

LEVEL 2 DRILLS FOR [ə]

▼ **Level 2 Practice Words for** [ə]

Here are more words containing [ə]. This time, though, there's no underlining. Check with your instructor if you're not sure of pronunciation.

Beginning	*End*	*Middle*	*All Positions*
afraid	Roberta	dictionary	apology
amend	area	university	astronomical
aloud	camera	parade	biological
asleep	arena	possible	electrical
across	visa	zoology	culpability
appreciate	panda	professor	agenda

[ɝ]

▼ **Level 2 Practice Sentences for** [ə]

Since you can spell [ə] with any vowel, you may have to double-check the pronunciation of some of the new words in these sentences.

1. Look it up in the dictionary.
2. Did you bring your camera to the parade?
3. Roberta was afraid she would fall asleep in class.
4. I was in that professor's class last semester.
5. I understand that rain is possible later in the day.
6. He walked across the restricted area.
7. I learned about the giant panda in zoology.
8. The elephant charged around the arena.
9. He was an undercover agent.
10. They couldn't agree on an official solution.

early

Sample: **THE EARLY TURTLE IS THE FIRST ONE IN THE HERD.**

Spellings: **er** as in **herd**   **ur** as in **turtle**
ear as in **early**   **ir** as in **first**
our as in **journey**   **or** as in **world**
yr as in **myrtle**   **olo** as in **colonel**
yrrh as in **myrrh**

carly– ɝ|ɪ

Description

[ɝ] is a mid, central, stressed vowel that occurs only in stressed words and syllables. It has an [r] sound to it, but it is different from the consonant in that it is longer and can form a syllable on its own.

The amount of [r] varies in different areas of the country. Less [r] is used in large areas of the South, East, and Northeast. That pronun-

[ɝ]

ciation can be transcribed with another symbol, [ɜ]. We won't use that symbol because we don't think it's important to distinguish between the [ɝ] and [ɜ] symbols.

Production: [ɝ]

1. Open your mouth to the position to say [ɔ], about halfway. Don't round your lips.
2. Raise the middle section of the tongue slightly, and *curl the tip back* until it's pointing to the palate just behind the upper gum ridge. Produce voice. Make sure there's no nasality.

Problems

There is a nonstandard pronunciation that occurs mostly in the East when [ɔɪ] is substituted for [ɝ]. In this substitution, the word *bird* would become something like *boid* because of the addition of the [ɪ] after the [ɜ]. This pronunciation is considered nonstandard in New York City and the Northeast, but is standard in New Orleans and other areas along the Gulf of Mexico.

Here's a contrast drill to help you distinguish [ɔɪ] and [ɝ]. Read each pair of words slowly and carefully, listening for a distinct difference in each word. You can use either [ɝ] or [ɜ] in the second word.

[ɔɪ]		[ɝ]	[ɔɪ]		[ɝ]
boil	—	burl	foist	—	first
foil	—	furl	oil	—	earl
loin	—	learn	boy	—	burr

This substitution is used by only a small number of speakers, so we suggest you check with your instructor or see page 245 for more help.

Only Level 1 Drills are given for [ɝ]. Try not to overpronounce.

LEVEL 1 DRILLS FOR [ɝ]

Level 1 Practice Words for [ɝ]

Say the words in the following lists slowly and carefully, but don't overdo it. Determine the amount of [r] used in your area by checking with your instructor or some other person knowledgeable about your regional dialect.

[ɝ]

Beginning	Middle	Beginning	Middle
early	first	earnest	turtle
earn	nervous	urn	word
irk	attorney	urban	burn
earth	learn	urgent	girl
urge	curve	herb	whirl

Level 1 Practice Sentences for [ɝ]

1. He burned the first dollar he ever earned.
2. She was learning about the curvature of the world.
3. The attorney received an urgent message.
4. Where on Earth did you get that turtle?
5. It was too early for the girl to get a sunburn.
6. He nervously urged me to slow down on the curves.
7. I couldn't read the words on the Grecian urn.
8. He was so earnest, be began to irk me.
9. Herbs are being grown in many urban gardens.
10. Let's give it a whirl.

Challenge Sentences for [ɝ]

1. Her version of the third verse was truly absurd.
2. The bird chirped nervously, reversing an early worm.
3. Herbert observed the curved urn and preferred to earn it.
4. The surly gardener was irked as he turned over the moist earth.
5. Ferdinand was an attorney who heard the good word about Robert Burns.

Challenge Materials for [ɝ]

1. Touch the earth, love the earth, honor the earth, her plains, her valleys, her hills, and her seas; rest your spirit in her solitary places.

Henry Beston, "Orion Rises on the Dunes," *The Outermost House*

2. When we're struggling for words, we often believe that somewhere there exists "the perfect word." Actually, there's no such thing as the perfect word. Rather than wor-

rying about striving for perfection, the practical question for us to ask is, "Which word communicates the best?"

All of us have our favorite words based on our personal taste. And taste in words is about as predictable as taste in ice cream. We also select our words on the basis of experience. Our choice is influenced by the words we heard and used at the dinner table while growing up, the words our community uses, the words that are popular in our region of the country, and the words that are well respected in our business environment.

Sherry Sweetnam, *The Executive Memo*

[ɚ]
father

ample: **HER FATHER'S LETTER GAVE THE GOVERNOR PLEASURE.**

pellings: **Any vowel and *r* combination.**

escription

] is a low, mid, unstressed vowel with an [r] quality. In large areas of
e South, East, and Northeast, the pronunciation is optional, with the
] being used instead. [ɚ] *is used only in unstressed syllables and
words.* It is a shorter, unstressed version of [ɝ], and may be contrasted
with it in the word *murmur* [mɝmɚ].

▼ **Production: [ɚ]**

1. [ɚ] is produced in the same way as [ɝ]. The only difference is in stress (loudness). Open your mouth to the position to say [ɔ], about halfway. Don't round your lips.

2. Curl the tongue tip back until it points just behind the upper gum ridge and raise the center. Produce voice, but not as loud or as long as for [ɝ].

[ɚ]

Problems

[ɚ] is a relatively simple sound to produce. One problem may be that of the "optional" pronunciation. That could occur should you relocate to an area of the country where [ɚ] isn't optional from an area where it is. In that case you may want to consider pronouncing the [ɚ].

Only Level 1 Drills are given for [ɚ].

LEVEL 1 DRILLS FOR [ɚ]

Level 1 Practice Words for [ɚ]

Say the words in the following lists slowly. Although all the drills for [ɚ] are on Level 1, you may have some difficulty deciding when to use [ɚ] and [ɝ]. When both sounds occur in a word or a sentence, we've marked [ɚ] with __. Ask your instructor about the optional pronunciation of [ə] in your area. Remember, [ɚ] is unstressed.

End	*Middle*	*End*	*Middle*
father	eastern	dollar	western
wonder	perhaps	after	cover
bother	answered	caller	sisterly
actor	modern	sailor	government
matter	sisterhood	tire	berserk
buyer	anchorman	tar	counterfeit
bur<u>ger</u>	summertime	turn<u>er</u>	interstate
earn<u>er</u>	lumberyard	runn<u>er</u>	letterhead

Level 1 Practice Sentences for [ɚ]

1. A burger and fries cost a dollar.
2. I'd rather surrender first.
3. Are those American sailors over there?
4. That actor looks like a TV anchorman.
5. The tire goes on the eastern end of the street.
6. Answer the other caller first.
7. My sister ordered a western omelet.
8. Something's bothering my father.
9. Perhaps you'd like more modern furniture?
10. They caught the counterfeiters on Interstate 95.

Challenge Materials for [ɚ]

Culture affects our communication in various ways. It provides us with patterned ways of dealing with information in our environment. It determines what we perceive, how we interpret, and how we respond to messages both verbally and nonverbally. Culture shapes and colors our image of reality and conditions the way we think.

Our communication patterns are often subtle, elusive, and unconscious. It is difficult for even well-informed members of a culture to explain why, in their own culture, the custom is thus-and-so rather than so-and-thus. For example, it would probably be hard for one to explain the "rule" governing the precise time in a relationship when the other person becomes a friend. One simply "feels right." Fortunately, members of the same culture share a great number of such taken-for-granted assumptions about interpersonal relationships and the corresponding "appropriate" behavior.

William B. Gudykunst and Young Yun Kim, *Communicating with Strangers: An Approach to Intercultural Communication*

[aɪ]
ice

Sample: **I WOULD LIKE TO BUY SOME ICE SKATES SOMETIME.**

Spellings: **i** as in **ice** **y** as in **cry** **ye** as in **dye**
ie as in **lie** **uy** as in **buy** **ui** as in **guile**
igh as in **light** **ei** as in **height** **ey** as in **eye**
ais as in **aisle** **ia** as in **diamond**

Description

[aɪ] is a diphthong beginning with a low front vowel and gliding toward a high front vowel.

[aɪ]

Production: [aɪ]

1. Open your mouth to the position for [a]. Your tongue should be flat in the bottom of your mouth, relaxed. Your lips should not be rounded.

2. Produce voice. As you do, lift the back of your tongue toward the position of [ɪ]. Don't close your mouth very much; there should be more tongue movement than jaw movement. Allow your jaw to move only very slightly—straight up, not inward.

Problems

PROBLEM 1. SUBSTITUTION OF [a] FOR [aɪ]

In many areas the [aɪ] is "broadened"; in other words, the first part of the diphthong has its normal value, but the second part is greatly diminished. This happens particularly in the South and Southeast. There is a nonstandard pronunciation, however, in which the second part of the diphthong is entirely missing. The word *time* [taɪm] would become *tahm* [tam]. Check with your instructor to see if you make this substitution. If you do, try the following Production Drill.

Production Drill

Read across the page, saying the "broken" words slowly. Bring the parts together as you read across. Say the first part with the vowel [ɑ] as in *calm*, and say the second part with the vowel [ɪ] as in *sit*.

ta . . . it	ta . . it	ta . it	ta it	tight
la . . . it	la . . it	la . it	la it	light
na . . . it	na . . it	na . it	na it	night
ba . . . it	ba . . it	ba . it	ba it	bite
ka . . . it	ka . . it	ka . it	ka it	kite
ra . . . it	ra . . it	ra . it	ra it	right
sa . . . it	sa . . it	sa . it	sa it	sight

PROBLEM 2. SUBSTITUTION OF [ɔɪ] FOR [aɪ]

If you raise your jaw a little too much, you'll produce a diphthong, [ɔɪ], instead of [aɪ], the same sound you'd get if you substituted *loin* for *line*. The problem seems to occur most often in words in which [aɪ] is followed by a voiced consonant. Do you hear a difference between *right* and *ride?* Between *sight* and *side?* If you make this substitution, try the Problem 1 Drill presented above. Then try the following Contrast Drill:

[aɪ]

Contrast Drill for [aɪ] and Nonstandard [ɔɪ]

Read the words in the following lists slowly. First read down the *vs* (voiceless) column, next down the *v* (voiced) column, and then across the page. When you contrast the pairs of words, try to hold your jaw position constant: don't let it move up.

vs		*v*	*vs*		*v*
right	—	ride	ice	—	eyes
sight	—	side	slights	—	slides
height	—	hide	strife	—	strive
lice	—	lies	ricing	—	rising
rice	—	rise	slighting	—	sliding
light	—	lied	sighting	—	siding
a bite	—	abide	righting	—	riding
tight	—	tide	device	—	devise

If you seem to have difficulty, try using a mirror to look for lip-rounding, which would be associated with lifting your jaw.

LEVEL 1 DRILLS FOR [aɪ]

Level 1 Practice Words for [aɪ]

Say the words in the following lists slowly and carefully. You may want to use a mirror and feel your lower jaw to see if you're closing too much. Start with the *Beginning* words. [aɪ] doesn't occur in unstressed syllables.

Beginning	*End*	*Middle*
ice	tie	sight
item	sigh	kite
eye	shy	rice
ice cream	hi	bite
isotope	thigh	fright
isometric	pie	nice
isolate	pry	dice
icon	sky	price
icing	fry	night

Level 1 Practice Phrases for [aɪ]

an eye for an eye	sky high	out of sight
bite the ice	thigh high	shy sigh

[aɪ]

▼ **Level 1 Practice Sentences for [aɪ]**

1. I read an item about isotopes.
2. The kite was so high it was out of sight.
3. I was too shy to say hi.
4. He spilled rice pudding all over his tie.
5. He wants an ice pack for his mosquito bites.
6. I won it on "The Price is Right."
7. He had a night job as a fry-cook and pie-maker.
8. We became frightened when we were isolated.
9. The right icon would bring a high price.

LEVEL 2 DRILLS FOR [aɪ]

▼ **Level 2 Practice Words for [aɪ]**

These words contain [aɪ] in more difficult sound contexts. Say the words slowly and listen carefully. If you're not sure of your production, ask your instructor or a classmate to listen to you.

Beginning	*End*	*Middle*	*All Positions*
idea	lie	rise	itemize
iron	cry	dime	Irish eyes
island	buy	alive	finite
I've	dry	dried	Mai-tai
I'm	try	tried	typewriter
idle	rely	crime	finalize
I'll	deny	climb	idolize
aisle	fry	pliers	ninety-nine
ideal	guy	hide	jai-alai

▼ **Level 2 Practice Sentences for [aɪ]**

1. He said he didn't find the pliers at the scene of the crime.
2. I tried to buy some dry clothes.
3. I'm sure I dropped the dime in the aisle.
4. He climbed the cliffs on the north side of the island.
5. I try not to rely on ideal solutions.

6. We could see the steam rising from the iron.
7. I tried to time the engine and adjust the idle.
8. Diane started to cry when she realized he was alive.

▼ **Challenge Sentences for [aɪ]**

1. It was five after nine by the time the white-gowned bride sidled down the aisle.
2. The tired pirate tried to hide his eyes with a wide blindfold.
3. Simon sighed with pride as he eyed his island paradise.
4. The ideal crime implies buying iron pliers and shying away from prying eyes.
5. The idle guide fried the spiced rice with dry white wine.

▼ **Challenge Materials for [aɪ]**

1. Our society encourages us to be tense and anxious. Everyday pressures push on us from all directions. "I must get that report done." "When will I ever get to finishing that basement?" "I've got three couples coming for dinner in two hours, and I'm not half ready for them yet." "If there were only more hours in the day." "Sometimes my head feels like it's going to explode, and when I feel like that I'm a real pain for everybody around me." "My butterflies get so bad sometimes that I can hardly function." "When ever I get ready to take a test or make a speech, I get so nervous that I can't think straight and I forget what I'm going to write or say."

These are just a few of the statements people have made to themselves or others because of stress and anxiety. High stress usually keeps us from functioning as we would like. It certainly prevents us from performing as well as we are capable.

Jerry A. Schmidt, *Help Yourself: A Guide to Self-Change*

2. Time is life. It is irreversible and irreplaceable. To waste your time is to waste your life, but to master your time is to master your life and make the most of it.

Alan Lekein, *How to Get Control of Your Time and Your Life*

[aʊ]

[aʊ]
how

Sample: **THE CR<u>OW</u>D SH<u>OU</u>TED AND H<u>OW</u>LED WHEN THE
BALL WENT F<u>OU</u>L.**
Spellings: **ou** as in **shout**   **ow** as in **crowd**   **ough** as in **bough**

Description

[aʊ] is a diphthong beginning with a low, front vowel, and gliding to a
high, back vowel.

Production: [aʊ]

1. Open your mouth for the position of [ɑ]. Your tongue should be
    relaxed and flat in the mouth. Your lips should not be rounded.
2. Produce voice. As you do, close your mouth slightly, and round your
    lips. Your tongue should elevate. Move toward the position for [ʊ].

Problems

PROBLEM 1. SUBSTITUTION OF [ɛaʊ] FOR [aʊ]

This substitution happens if you don't open your mouth enough and if
you draw back the corners of your mouth. If you smile when you say
this diphthong, it will be distorted. This substitution is a frequent nonstandard production. Check with your instructor to see if you produce
[aʊ] in this way. If you do, try the following Production Drill.

Production Drill

Say the following "broken" words, reading across the page. The first
part of each word has the sound [ɑ] as in *calm*. The second has the
sound [ʊ] as in *push*. Gradually join the parts together as you read
across. It may be very helpful to use a mirror to see your lips.

ba . . . u	ba . . u	ba . u	ba u	bow
ka . . . u	ka . . u	ka . u	ka u	cow
na . . . u	na . . u	na . u	na u	now
ha . . . u	ha . . u	ha . u	ha u	how
va . . . u	va . . u	va . u	va u	vow
ta . . . un	ta . . un	ta . un	ta un	town
da . . . un	da . . un	da . un	da un	down

PROBLEM 2. SUBSTITUTION OF [o] FOR [aʊ]

This regional substitution occurs frequently in the Southeast, in the upper Midwest near the Canadian border, and often in areas where people use the pure vowel [o] consistently instead of the diphthong [oʊ]. It results from not lowering the jaw enough at the start of the diphthong, but without the "smile" of the substitution we described in Problem 1. The result is that a word such as *about* sounds something close to "a boat," and can sometimes confuse a listener from another area. Try the following Contrast Drill.

▼ Contrast Drill for [o] and [aʊ]

Read down each column first, then across. When reading across, try to make each pair of words distinctly different.

[o]		[aʊ]	[o]		[aʊ]
know	—	now	a boat	—	about
groaned	—	ground	phoned	—	found
hoe	—	how	oat	—	out
coach	—	couch	moaned	—	mound
bow	—	bough	clone	—	clown
tone	—	town	crowed	—	crowd
honed	—	hound	toll	—	towel

LEVEL 1 DRILLS FOR [aʊ]

▼ Level 1 Practice Words for [aʊ]

All the practice exercises for [aʊ] are on Level 1. Say the following words slowly and carefully. You may want to use a mirror to see lip-rounding and to help prevent the smile. Having someone else watch and listen to you can also help.

[ɔɪ]

Beginning	End	Middle
out	cow	town
ouch	allow	couch
hour	plow	cloud
ours	how	towel
ounce	now	powder
outside	eyebrow	allowance
oust	downtown	growl
outlaw	chow	about

Level 1 Practice Phrases for [aʊ]

our couch	allow an hour	allowance now
how to plow	brown towel	how about

Practice Sentences for [aʊ]

1. It took an hour to get downtown
2. They didn't raise an eyebrow about the cow.
3. Where's the brown towel you took outside?
4. An ounce of prevention is worth a pound of cure.
5. The outlaws growled at the crowd.
6. Some flowers don't open on cloudy days.
7. I said more than ouch when I dropped the couch.
8. Coffee grounds were floating around in my cup.
9. The county raised our mileage allowance.
10. My stomach gave a loud growl in the crowded elevator.

[ɔɪ]
coin

Sample: **ROY TOOK GREAT JOY IN COIN COLLECTING.**
Spellings: **oy** as in **joy**   **oi** as in **coin**

Description

[ɔɪ] is a diphthong beginning with a low, back vowel and gliding to a high, front vowel. Your lips should be slightly rounded.

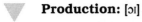

Production: [ɔɪ]

1. Open your mouth almost to the position for [ɔ]. Raise the back of your tongue slightly, and round your lips just a tiny bit.
2. Produce voice. As you do, your jaw should drop slightly. Then, let your tongue lift toward the position for [ɪ], relax your lip rounding, and draw the corners of your mouth back. Make sure there's no nasal emission of air.

Problems

PROBLEM 1. NONSTANDARD [ɔ]

The problems with [ɔɪ] are generally caused by too much lip rounding and not opening the mouth wide enough. If you distort the vowel [ɔ] this way, you will almost certainly distort the diphthong [ɔɪ]. Try the drills for [ɔ] on page 217.

PROBLEM 2. SUBSTITUTION OF [ɝ] FOR [ɔɪ]

If you make this substitution, you would say, for example, *curl* for *coil.* This substitution happens occasionally in the New York area and in some areas of the South. Although it does happen rather infrequently, it's very noticeable to those who don't make the substitution. If you make this substitution, try the following Contrast Drill.

Contrast Drill for [ɔɪ] and [ɝ]

Say the following word pairs slowly and carefully. Read across the page, contrasting [ɔɪ] in the first word with [ɝ] in the second.

[ɔɪ]	[ɝ]	[ɔɪ]	[ɝ]
coil	— curl	loin	— learn
poise	— purrs	foist	— first
poison	— person	oil	— Earl
boys	— burrs	voice	— verse

LEVEL 1 DRILLS FOR [ɔɪ]

Level 1 Practice Words for [ɔɪ]

The drills for [ɔɪ] are all at Level 1. Say the following words slowly and carefully. Listen to your production and make sure you're not substituting [ɝ] or closing your mouth too much.

[ɔɪ]

Beginning	End	Middle
oil	Roy	boil
oyster	employ	join
ointment	destroy	appointment
oily	boy	soy sauce
	enjoy	toys
	annoy	boycott
	coy	coin
	alloy	point
	toy	anoint

▼ Level 1 Practice Sentences for [ɔɪ]

1. They served oysters cooked in soy sauce.
2. Please oil that noisy hinge.
3. I have an appointment for an employment physical.
4. The little boys really enjoyed the toys.
5. I need some ointment for that annoying boil.
6. The coins were made of a copper alloy.
7. The boycott destroyed his profits.

▼ Challenge Sentences for [ɔɪ]

1. The noisily toiling boys coiled the lines boisterously.
2. Burt employed the third toy maker to avoid an employees' boycott.
3. Helen of Troy played it coy with the boys.
4. Always try to avoid poison ivy's annoying, burning oils.
5. The unsoiled ointment was kept in five poison-proof foil containers.

▼ Challenge Materials for [ɔɪ]

Identifying Poison Ivy

Although the appearance of poison ivy, oak and sumac may vary depending on where the plant grows—the leaves may be smooth-edged or scalloped, for example—here are some characteristics to watch for:

- Poison ivy's leaves are usually glossy green in the spring and summer and reddish in the fall.

- Poison ivy and poison oak most commonly grow in three-leaf groupings. Poison sumac, on the other hand, generally has seven to eleven leaves along its stems—one at the tip and others in pairs across the stem.
- Poison-oak leaves often resemble those of the oak tree.
- Poison ivy grows throughout the United States, except in the extreme Southwest. Poison oak is found along the West Coast and from New Jersey to eastern Texas. Poison sumac thrives in moist soil east of the Mississippi River.

"Vital Signs," *McCall's*, July 1988

Part Three

VOICE

Voice *and* diction. You can't separate the two. Think about it; you can't get along with just one. Imagine trying to make yourself understood speaking without consonants and vowels. And what about voice? You could whisper, but most people wouldn't be able to hear you.

Your voice carries a great deal of meaning not only about what you say, but about *you.* Yet most of us don't know very much about voice. As a matter of fact, a great many people have no idea that the voice they hear in their heads isn't the voice that other people hear; they have no idea what their own voices sound like.

Part III is devoted to improving vocal skills, so you'll learn a great deal about your own voice and how you use it. In Chapter 7 you'll learn about voice production; how you control loudness, pitch, and quality. In Chapter 8 you'll learn the factors of vocal expressiveness and get a chance to put them into practice.

Chapter Seven

Voice Production

Who taught you how to produce and use your voice? Not just one person, surely, and probably not in any kind of formal setting. Most of us learn how to use our voices simply by using them. We don't think about voice, we *do* it. Sometimes, though, we don't do it in efficient ways. This can result in voices that may cause physical discomfort, such as a sore throat after loud talking, or voices that others find unusual, unpleasant, or hard to hear.

It's our purpose in this chapter to present the basics of voice production: breathing for speech, loudness, pitch, and quality. By the end of the chapter you should know considerably more about your own voice: how you produce it and how you use it. And, if your voice is one that is not loud enough to hear or calls undue attention to itself, you'll have plenty of exercises to work on. These exercises are listed in Table 7-1, which you can use as a reference after you have completed the work in the chapter.

If you haven't read Chapter 2, we suggest that you do so before you go on with this chapter. In fact, even if you have read it, a review wouldn't hurt. Chapter 2 explains the structures we use for voice production and how we physically make the sound of voice. You should be familiar with that material before you read this chapter.

Table 7-1.   Voice Improvement Exercises

#	Exercise	Page	Breath Control	Loudness	Pitch	Tense Quality	Strident Quality	Metallic Quality	Hoarse Quality	Nasal Quality	Hard Glottal Quality
1	Abdominal Breathing	254	■	■		■			■		■
2	Breath Control—Duration	255	■	■	■						■
3	Breath Control—Breathiness	257	■	■							■
4	Loudness—Force	259	■	■							
5	Loudness—Projection	259		■						■	
6	Loudness—Control	260		■						■	
7	Loudness—Practice	261		■						■	
8	Habitual Pitch	264			■	■	■	■	■		■
9	Relaxation—Progressive	265	■			■	■	■	■		■
10	Relaxation—Fantasy	265	■			■	■	■	■		■
11	Relaxation—Head Rolling	266	■			■	■	■	■		■
12	Relaxation—Sighing	266	■	■		■	■	■	■		■
13	Relaxation—Yawning	267				■	■	■	■		■

Table 7-1.   Voice Improvement Exercises

#	Exercise	Page	Breath Control	Loudness	Pitch	Tense Quality	Strident Quality	Metallic Quality	Hoarse Quality	Nasal Quality	Hard Glottal Quality
14	Nasality—Ear Training	269								■	
15	Nasality—Pulling	271								■	
16	Nasality—Pushing	272								■	
17	Denasality	272								■	
18	Vocal Fry	274	■	■							
19	Hard Glottal Attack	274				■	■		■		■

BREATHING

As we explained in Chapter 2, the breathstream is the powerhouse of voice production. It's difficult to produce effective voice if you don't breathe efficiently; you'll put a strain on the entire vocal mechanism. If you're like most people, you probably don't have any real problems with breathing for speech, but don't stop reading here. If you want to be a more effective oral communicator, you can benefit from an understanding of the hows and whys of breathing for speech.

Breathing for Speech

You breathe differently when you're breathing for speech than you do when you're breathing for purely biological purposes. The difference is not in how much air you take in; you don't have to breathe more deeply for speech. The difference is in how you control your exhalations. In rest breathing, the time taken for inhalation and exhalation is usually about the same. In speech breathing, you take a quick breath in, then gradually let the air out, pacing the exhalation so that it lasts long enough for what you want to say. If you don't control the exhalation efficiently, you may run out of breath, sound strained or breathy, or not be loud enough. So the major difference between speech breathing and biological breathing is breath control.

BREATH CONTROL

You control your rate of exhalation in a couple of fairly simple ways. One form of control is by far the most important—the way you use your abdominal muscles. You could almost consider your abdominal muscles to be the pump that pushes air out of your respiratory system. And, just like a bicycle pump, the harder you push, the faster the air moves. In breathing for speech, the major part of breath control consists of contracting the abdominal muscles, but just the right amount for the level of loudness you want for the sounds you are making. The other form of control is in the use of the vocal folds; here's where they can function as a valve during phonation to help control the rate of air flow.

Not everyone uses the muscles of respiration in exactly the same way, and not everyone uses the abdominal muscles to the same degree in breath control. Most voice and speech experts, however, advocate "abdominal breathing" as the most desirable breathing pattern. What then, if you're not an abdominal breather; should you change your breathing pattern? Before you answer, ask the following questions about your breathing pattern: *Can you breathe comfortably? Can you breathe unobtrusively? Does your breathing pattern allow you to speak effectively?* If you (or a qualified evaluator) answered "no" to any one question, you should attempt to learn the abdominal (also called *central* and *diaphragmatic*) style of breathing. We think it's the most efficient style—the most air for the least work—and the most effective for producing and sustaining loud, clear tones.

Exercise 1. Abdominal Breathing

The following exercise provides a relaxing way to practice abdominal breathing. Try it, even if you are already an abdominal breather; everyone can benefit from a "refresher course."

1. Lie on your back on a comfortable but firm surface.
2. Make sure your knees are supported in a slightly flexed position; your arms should be by your side, with your elbows slightly bent.
3. Place a moderately heavy weight (a book two or three times heavier than this one, for example) on your abdomen near the navel.

4. Begin breathing in and out, through your mouth, so that you push the book up when you breathe in; the book should sink down as you breathe out.

5. Keep one hand on your chest, about three inches below your neck, to make sure you are keeping chest movement to a minimum.

6. Once you are able to move your abdomen in coordination with your breathing in and out, remove the book and put your hand in its place. Continue to move your abdomen up when you inhale and down when you exhale.

7. When you feel you have abdominal breathing under control while lying down, move to a comfortable sitting position. Continue the exercise, keeping one hand on your chest and the other on your abdomen.

8. Take a deep breath with the new breathing pattern. Exhale slowly, sighing the vowel *ahh* with each exhalation. Sustain the vowel for five seconds.

9. Take a deep breath. Exhale slowly, counting from one to five, holding each number for one full second.

10. Take a deep breath, abdominally. Exhale slowly, naming the days of the week at a rate of one per second.

11. Repeat steps 8 through 10 while standing.

Learning to use abdominal breathing comes somewhat slowly. It's important to practice at least once a day for about a week until the process becomes automatic.

Exercise 2. Breath Control—Duration

This exercise is designed to help you develop improved breath control while speaking. It will also help to increase the depth of your breathing.

1. Take three normal rest breaths. Make a mental note as to how much air is going in and out.

2. Take a normal breath in and count to three, holding each number for one second. Do it almost like singing. Make sure to hold each number for one full second and not pause between numbers.

3. Repeat step 2, but this time continue counting until you begin to run out of breath. Do it again, stopping at the same point.

4. Now take a deep breath and count again until you begin to run out of breath; you've counted as high as you can. Repeat this twice, then stop the exercise for a while.

5. Allow at least fifteen minutes after step 4 and start the whole procedure again.

6. Take a deep breath, then say the names of the days of the week, one word per breath. Then do the same saying, first, two words per breath, then three words per breath.

7. Say each of the following phrases on one abdominal breath:
   a. Going home
   b. New moon
   c. Low down
   d. Hard heart
   e. Look sharp

8. Using abdominal breathing, say each of the following phrases using only one breath:
   a. Look at me
   b. Time for lunch
   c. Make my day
   d. Practice makes perfect
   e. Haste makes waste

9. Try breaking up the following poem into short phrases:

Roll on, thou ball, roll on!
Through pathless realms of Space
    Roll on!
What though I'm in a sorry case?
What though I cannot meet my bills?
What though I suffer toothache's ills?
What though I swallow countless pills?
    Never *you* mind!
    Roll on!

Roll on, thou ball, roll on!
Through seas of inky air
    Roll on!
It's true I have no shirts to wear;
It's true my butcher's bill is due;
It's true my prospects all look blue—
But don't let that unsettle you:
    Never *you* mind!
    Roll on!
            ''To the Terrestrial Globe by a Miserable Wretch,'' W. S. Gilbert

The object of these exercises is to gradually increase the length of the phrases you can say until you reach your maximum. Don't push until you feel uncomfortable, and don't do too much deep breathing all at once; you might get dizzy. Try this drill every day, and you'll soon have more efficient breath control.

Exercise 3. Breath Control—Breathiness

Sometimes, people tend so waste so much air that their voices take on a noticeably breathy quality. This breathiness can be deliberate (trying to sound sexy, perhaps) or simply the result of poor breath control due to failure to bring the vocal folds together. In any case, a breathy voice is usually hard to hear, may call considerable attention to itself, and may distract the listener from the speaker's message. You'll need a small hand mirror for this exercise. Make sure it's clean and cold enough so that your breath will condense on the surface.

1. Hold the mirror about an inch away from your mouth. Say *ahh.* Quickly take the mirror away from your mouth and look at it. Check for fogging. Repeat this procedure, and try to see the pattern of fogging on the glass.

2. Hold the mirror in front of your mouth again. Say *ahh* more loudly. Check what's happened to the fogging on the glass. Repeat, and try to reduce the fogging when you say *ahh.*

3. Try the same drill with the other vowels. First, see how much condensation occurs when you say the vowel the way you usually do. Then try to reduce the area of glass that gets covered.

4. Compare the breathy and nonbreathy production. Visually, the breathy production will have a large area of condensation. The nonbreathy production will result in a small area. You should also begin to *hear* the difference.

5. Now go back and do steps 6, 7, and 8 in Exercise 2 again. Make sure to use the nonbreathy voice. (You can monitor your breath flow by placing your fingers about an inch in front of your mouth as you speak.) You will notice a change in the number of words you can comfortably speak on one inhalation.

LOUDNESS

The loudness of your voice says a lot about you. We tend to think of people with weak or soft voices as being shy and timid, perhaps afraid to speak up because they's so unsure of themselves. On the other hand, people with loud, booming voices may be thought of as overbearing, overconfident, and boorish. When a person speaks too loudly, we often pull back—both physically and mentally.

To many people, the person who doesn't talk loudly enough to be easily heard is the more annoying. It's frustrating to have to continually ask a person to speak up or, even worse, to miss much of what that person says.

Loudness problems are usually caused by a person's *inability to produce and sustain* the proper loudness or *failure to monitor* his or her own voice. The result is loudness that is inappropriate for the listeners and the environment as well as the content of the communication. Chapter 8 covers loudness in terms of monitoring your loudness level to produce a voice that fits the content, listeners, and environment. But before you can do those exercises, you must be able to produce a tone of adequate loudness. Let's work on that now.

Controlling Loudness

Have you ever gone to an exciting sporting event such as a hockey match or football game or soccer game? Remember how much you enjoyed yourself? Until the next day, that is, when your throat was so sore you could hardly talk. That sore throat may have lasted for a couple of days or longer. Your sore throat and loss of voice were probably the result of the way you were trying to produce a loud voice.

A loud voice does *not* require a lot of muscular action by the vocal folds and larynx (although that is what hurts). The force behind a loud voice should be supplied primarily by the abdominal muscles.

The vocal folds are set into vibration by the air you force out of the lungs. They don't vibrate due to muscular action of their own. So, to increase the strength of their vibrations, you must increase the force behind the breathstream. You do that by contracting the abdominal muscles.

Try this: place one hand flat against your abdomen just below your breastbone. Say *ahh* and hold it. While you're saying *ahh*, hit the back of your hand with your other fist (not too hard, though). You should have heard a sudden increase in loudness. Now try this: place both hands on your abdomen. At the rate of one number per second, count to four. Start quietly but make each number louder. You should feel your abdominal muscles contract suddenly for each number.

The following exercises should help you develop the proper support for a loud voice. In certain exercises, you'll see series of dots that change in size as shown here: ●●●. Those dots provide a visual guide to help you change loudness levels as specified in the instructions, much in the same way as sheet music shows you a tune. Your voice should grow louder as the dots increase in size and softer as the dots become smaller. Use your loudest voice for the largest dots.

 Exercise 4. Loudness—Force

This exercise is designed to help you increase the force with which your breathstream pushes the vocal folds apart during phonation. Practice abdominal breathing for about five minutes before you do this exercise for the first time.

1. Hold a piece of paper, about the size of this page, lengthwise just under your lower lip. Hold it by the corners closest to you, with the edge of the paper touching your skin.
2. Blow across the surface of the paper, and try to make the paper rise to a horizontal position. Do this five times, feeling for contraction of your abdominal muscles as you blow.
3. Now, use a slightly larger piece of paper. Make the paper rise five times.
4. Repeat step 3 a few times every hour for two or three days. You'll find that it will probably take less effort each day to make the paper rise.
5. Now try saying each of the following phrases and sentences using a very loud voice. Don't strain; use breath energy.
    a. Hello, there. ● ●
    b. Sit still. ● ●
    c. Climb down. ● ●
    d. Speak louder. ● ● ●
    e. Have hope. ● ●
    f. Go away. ● ● ●
    g. I want my ice cream. ● ● ● ● ●
    h. Take that thing away. ● ● ● ● ●
    i. Don't start anything with me. ● ● ● ● ● ● ●
    j. That book is terrible. ● ● ● ● ● ●
    k. Have a happy holiday. ● ● ● ● ● ●

 Exercise 5. Loudness—Projection

This exercise should generate some of the same physical feelings as the previous exercise for force, but this time you'll actually be speaking.

This exercise requires another person to help.

1. Have another person stand facing you, about five feet away. His or her right hand should be at shoulder height, slightly cupped, and facing you.

2. From your position, five feet away, count to five. *Try to speak into the other person's hand.* Yes, you may feel a little silly, but do it anyway. Project your voice, throw it or whatever else you may call it, but speak into the other person's hand.

3. Have the other person take one step backward, and repeat step 2. Continue the procedure until the other person is about forty feet away from you.

4. Now have the other person walk back, one step at a time, reversing the procedure.

5. Now read the following phrases and sentences aloud, again placing them in the other person's hand as he or she moves closer and farther away.

    a. Hello there.
    b. Ship ahoy.
    c. The other way.
    d. Watch out.
    e. On a roll.
    f. I like my new bike.
    g. Color my hair purple.
    h. I don't have a favorite book.
    i. Where are the snows of yesteryear?
    j. Hold the low tone as long as you can.

Exercise 6. Loudness—Control

You don't need anyone to help you with this one. We do suggest, though, that you find a place where you won't bother other people. Again, feel for abdominal muscle contractions.

1. Pick a series of items: numbers, months, letters, and so forth. (Here we'll use numbers to describe the exercise.)

2. Count to five; start with low intensity, and increase intensity with each number. Take a breath between each number and the next. Repeat this twice.

3. Count backward, starting from five. *Start with high intensity, and gradually decrease intensity.* Again, take a breath between productions. Repeat twice.

4. On one breath, count to five. This time you should be loudest at *three*. In other words, gradually increase loudness until you reach *three*, then decrease. Do the entire exercise once a day.

5. Read the following sentences aloud. Start each in a very soft voice, gradually becoming louder until you reach the end.

   a. I'm going home, ●●●●
   b. Look at the time. ●●●●
   c. He's a good man. ●●●●
   d. What are you doing? ●●●●●
   e. Where is my hat? ●●●●

6. Read the following sentences aloud. Begin each sentence softly, and gradually increase the loudness level until you reach the middle of the sentence. Then, decrease the loudness until you reach the end. This may be a bit difficult at first, but stick with it. It will become easier as you go along.

   a. You can come with me, or stay home alone. ●●●●●●●
   b. I tried my hardest, and I finished the puzzle. ●●●●●●●
   c. My soup is too hot, I'll drink it from the saucer. ●●●●●●●
   d. When you get to the top, look around and ski down. ●●●●●●●
   e. My professor is so lazy, he makes us work on our own. ●●●●●●●

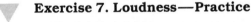

Exercise 7. Loudness—Practice

Read aloud using whatever materials you would like, but we especially recommend the "Letters to the Editor" in your local or school newspaper. The comedian Steve Allen used to include this as a regular feature of his late-night TV show. He would read angry letters to the editor in a loud, angry voice. As he made the writers' points for them, the audience would cheer or otherwise show their approval. Try this yourself. Ask a friend to sit across the room while you read angry letters to him or her. Make sure your voice is adequately loud and that you *project* your voice to your friend.

PITCH

The pitch of your voice—its highness or lowness—is another variable of speech that says a lot about you. As a rule, we apply certain stereotypes to our expectations of what a person's voice should sound like.

For example, we have learned to expect women to generally have higher voices than men. We also expect that there will be an inverse ratio between a person's size and the pitch of his or her voice. In other words, the larger the person, the more low-pitched you expect that person's voice to be. These are just a few examples of common vocal stereotypes and, yes, many times our expectations are incorrect. Were you ever surprised to discover that someone you had only heard speaking over the phone, but had never seen in person, looked quite different from what you had expected?

We all probably know someone who attempts to influence the impression he or she makes on others by speaking in a voice that's too low or high pitched to use comfortably for a long time. By doing so, though, the person puts a strain on the vocal mechanism and also restricts the voice to a narrow pitch range. The vocal mechanism is strained because the person is using his or her vocal folds to produce a pitch they weren't designed to produce for long periods of time.

In Chapter 2 we discussed the factors that determine the frequency of vibration of your vocal folds and the pitch of your voice. You may recall that the main factors in determining the pitch of your voice are the length of your vocal folds and the size of your resonating cavities. The pitch your vocal folds and resonating cavities are naturally suited to produce is called your *optimum pitch*, and you produce it with less effort than other pitches. The pitch you use all the time is called your *habitual pitch*. It is best, for the vocal mechanism, if your habitual pitch is the same as your optimum, because using an habitual pitch that's far from your optimum can result in voice problems. Put it this way: you don't ask a trumpet to do a tuba's job.

Try the following procedure. You can use it to determine your optimum pitch.

Determining Optimum Pitch

For this procedure, you need another person and a piano, electronic keyboard, or other musical instrument capable of playing a musical scale. Don't worry; neither one of you needs to be a musician. The other person is there to help you confirm your judgments.

1. Pick a voice pitch near the middle of your range. Determine the corresponding note on the musical instrument. You do this simply by playing different notes until you decide you've matched the pitch of your voice.
2. Chant "ah" down the scale to the lowest possible pitch your voice can reach. Locate that pitch on the musical instrument. For chant-

ing, which is really a combination of talking and singing, you can use *do, re, me,* and so on or *me, me, me* or any vowel you like.

3. Now, chant up the scale to the highest pitch your voice can reach. Locate that pitch on the piano.

4. Count the number of notes in the range, from the lowest to the highest pitch. Include both the highest and lowest pitches and count both black and white keys.

5. Divide the number of notes by four. Count this number of keys up from the lowest pitch. This should be at (or no more than one key above or below) your optimum pitch.

6. Try phonating at all three of those pitches (one above, optimum, and one below) to determine which is the most comfortable for you. The spread between the lowest and highest notes you can reach is your *pitch range.*

▼ **Determining Habitual Pitch**

Now that you know your optimum pitch, you should see if your habitual and optimum pitches are the same. You'll need the piano and a listener.

1. Read the following passage aloud, at a normal conversational loudness level. Read it three or four times, each time making it more monotonous and more like "machine" talk. Ask your listener to find the note on the piano that's closest to the average pitch of your reading. Here's the passage. It's from a booklet published by the Environmental Protection Agency.

> The decibel is the most commonly used unit to measure sound intensity at its source. The decibel level starts at 0, the hearing threshold, and goes to 180, the level heard when a rocket is launched. Brief exposure to levels over 140 decibels, however, causes pain and can rupture eardrums, resulting in permanent hearing loss. But one can suffer hearing loss or impairment at much lower levels. According to some scientific opinion, continuous exposure for 8 hours to noise levels of approximately 85 decibels can also cause permanent hearing loss.

2. Compare your habitual pitch with your optimum pitch. Are they just about the same? If they're more than two tones away from each other, you should work on changing your habitual pitch.

Changing Habitual Pitch

Changing your habitual pitch to coincide with your optimum pitch is not very complicated. It requires nothing more than ample practice speaking at your optimum pitch using some form of reference point to use when you start, and listening periodically to make sure you haven't strayed off target. For example, when you have determined your optimum pitch you might tape record yourself saying a few phrases at that pitch. Or, you might record the sound of a musical instrument playing a note on that pitch. Listen to that tape recording, and immediately practice saying some phrases or sentences on the same pitch as you hear. *Caution:* If you use a tape recorder for this purpose, be sure to use one that plugs into an AC wall socket; a battery-operated recorder may play back at a different speed from that at which it recorded. This could result in a variation in pitch away from your optimum pitch.

For practice, we suggest that you start with the following drill materials. Then you may go on to use any of the selections in Chapter 8 or other readings from literature, magazines, and so forth. You may want to check your pitch regularly against the standard you are using for your optimum pitch, be it a tape recording, musical instrument, or other sound source. Read your selections aloud at conversational loudness. For best results, and to avoid vocal fatigue, practice twice a day, in the morning and evening. Limit yourself to two readings at each session. Continue your practice session every day until you are satisfied that your optimum and habitual pitch levels are the same.

Exercise 8. Changing Habitual Pitch

Say the following sentences three times each at your optimum pitch. Try not to vary the pitch as you go through each one.

1. Give me a light.
2. Sing us a song.
3. Pick up your litter.
4. Lend him a pencil.
5. Let's take a break.
6. I like to pick flowers in the field.
7. Hand her gloves to her before you go out.
8. Learning the decimal system can be very exciting.
9. The sum of two numbers added together will always be the same regardless of the order in which they are added.
10. Persistence is essential to successful achievement.

Extending Your Pitch Range

Often we use only a small number of the notes available from the total pitch range. We tend to stay more or less in one place on the scale; and when we do move away from that place, we tend to go up rather than down.

RELAXATION

Relaxation is one good way to extend your pitch range. Ever notice that your voice seems lower in the morning after a good night's sleep? That's because you, and your vocal folds, had a chance to relax. Before you deliberately try speaking at a lower pitch, you should be relaxed. Try the relaxation exercises below. They'll make a difference.

Exercise 9. Progressive Relaxation

The purpose of this exercise is to reduce tension. You can do this alone, but it's better if someone reads the directions to you, slowly and in a gentle, soothing voice.

1. Sit with your back touching the back support of your chair. Cross your legs at the ankles. Hold your hands out in front of you at chest level. Shake them energetically for about 5 seconds, then let them fall loosely into your lap. Keep them there.
2. Do the following exercise *in your mind only,* without moving any parts of your body. Concentrate on the toes of your left foot. Let the muscles go loose. Then the sole of your foot, then the ankle. Now, loosen the muscles of your right foot. When your feet have no tension left in them, move on. First to your lower legs, knees, thighs, then buttocks, back, spine, moving very slowly. Then go on to your stomach, chest, shoulders, arms, hands, and fingers, then back up to your neck, jaws, face, and scalp. As you go along, slowly and methodically untie the knots in your muscles until there is no tension left in your body. When you're finished, stand up, stretch, and yawn or take as deep a breath as you can with your mouth wide open, and then release it.

Exercise 10. Fantasy

This is a very pleasant exercise designed to reduce tension. It can also help you fall asleep at night when you're tense and jumpy. The exercise is really quite simple. Find a comfortable position, one that you can hold for a few minutes. Close your eyes and mentally transport yourself to a place that's calm and relaxing. Don't pick a place where you'll get involved in any kind of activity. We recommend that you imagine you're sitting on a deserted beach—just clean, white sand and the ocean waves rolling in with eternal regularity, one after the other. Imagine that you're sitting there listening to the waves breaking against the shore. You'll feel more relaxed after a couple of minutes of this. Just make sure that you concentrate on the waves; block out everything else.

 ### Exercise 11. Head Rolling

This exercise focuses specifically on the neck.

1. Take a comfortable sitting position in a chair with a medium or low back. Holding your body erect, let your head drop forward so that your chin is resting on your chest. Keeping your face pointing forward, roll your head to the right so that your right ear is close to your right shoulder. Make sure not to raise your shoulder. Now, roll your head back and look up at the ceiling. At the same time, let your lower jaw drop. Next, roll your head to the left so that your left ear is near your left shoulder. Don't raise your shoulder. Now, roll your head forward again.
2. Repeat this exercise three times, slowly.
3. If you feel some tightness at the back of your neck during the exercise, try to relax the muscles of your neck and shoulders. The tightness should disappear. If the tightness doesn't ease or if you feel pain, discontinue the exercise. Caution: do not let your head roll all the way back; that sometimes can be painful.
4. Now, roll your head around as before, but this time roll it all the way around in one continuous circle. Repeat the exercise, rolling your head in the opposite direction.

 ### Exercise 12. Sighing

This exercise helps relax the vocal folds and the neck during voice production.

1. Take as deep a breath as possible. Hold it for a count of three. When you release the air, all at once, sigh. That is, say the vowel *ahh* in a very breathy voice. Repeat four or five times, speaking more softly with each sigh.
2. Sigh while you count to three; then try *a, b, c*. In each case, take a deep breath, hold it for a count of three, then sigh. Repeat four or five times.

3. Make sure you monitor the quality of your voice by listening carefully. As you sigh more softly, the amount of air expelled should decrease, and your voice should become less breathy. Even though the breathy quality leaves, it's important to keep production relaxed.

Exercise 13. Yawning

Take a comfortable sitting position in a chair. Open your mouth wide. (Make sure your mouth is wide open. You can't yawn properly with your mouth half shut.) Take as deep a breath as you can. Stretch both arms out to the sides. Now, let the air out in as easy a manner as possible. Repeat this several times, and notice how you begin to feel more and more relaxed. If you have some difficulty in achieving a real yawn the first several times you try this, don't worry: you'll get it. Yawning is very contagious; you can even catch it from yourself. If you are still having difficulty, ask someone else to yawn; you'll probably find yourself yawning in imitation.

SINGING

This is probably one of the best ways to extend your pitch range, especially downward. The only problem is many people think they "can't" sing or are just plain embarrassed to sing in public. That's why we suggest that you do your singing in the shower; it's a great place for it. Here's why: first, a shower's in a room that's usually square or rectangular with walls that are hard and smooth. That makes it a good resonator, so your voice sounds richer and fuller than it does outside. Second, the sound of the running water makes it hard for other people to hear you and affords you some privacy. Finally, the shower relaxes you, and you can reach those low notes more easily.

So try singing in the shower. After a few days you should notice that your range is increasing. Then, it's time to *speak* in the shower. Try such things as Hamlet's soliloquy that begins "To be or not to be . . ." or whatever else you can have fun with.

QUALITY

It has been said of the human voice that it is the best and most accurate indicator of a person's physical and emotional state. Think for a moment of the way people you know sound when they are tired, tense, upset, angry, happy, or sad. It's likely that just by listening to the person's voice you can tell which of those emotions he or she may be feeling. The variations you hear, as well as others, are the reflections of changes in what we call *voice quality.*

Resonance

Let's review the physiological processes affecting voice quality. You may recall that the voice is produced by a series of puffs of air that are emitted between the vocal folds in your larynx. The complex sound created by these puffs is then bounced around (resonated) in several hollow spaces in your neck and head. This process amplifies and modifies some tones of the voice, depending on the sizes and shapes of the cavities in use.

Each person's voice quality is unique. Because no two people have resonating cavities that are exactly the same in size and shape, no two people produce voices with exactly the same acoustic characteristics. That's why it's possible for you to identify people you know when they call you on the phone. In addition, people vary the manner in which they use these resonating cavities according to their physical and emotional states. When you're tense and anxious, you generally hold your vocal folds tense, and the sound you produce has qualities that we have come to recognize as indicating tension. When you are relaxed, your voice reflects that feeling, too.

It's possible for you to assess, by the variations in voice quality, a good deal of meaning over and above what meaning is contained in the context of an utterance. Suppose you detect a note of impatience in your professor's or supervisor's voice. Even though that person's words may be telling you it's okay to be turning your work in late, you know that your next assignment had better be on time or else. Another example might be a person expressing some positive feeling toward you verbally, but there's something in the voice that tells you all is not well in the relationship. It would be difficult, wouldn't it, for a salesperson to sell a group of people on the desirability of an idea, product, or some action if he or she sounded tense or uncertain?

We've all met, at one time or another, people who told us a lot about their personalities just by the kind of voice quality they characteristically used. The person for whom all of life is one terrible catastrophe after another, for whom everything is difficult and unpleasant, will frequently have a voice quality that is petulant and complaining. Who of us has not had our nerves stretched almost to the breaking point while listening to a parent, boss, or teacher whose voice was what we call *strident?* (Stridency is a combination of a very tense quality and high pitch.) Chances are you distinctly remember people with some of these voice qualities, and the memories may not always be pleasant.

To repeat what we said earlier: your voice quality is determined, for the most part, by the size and shape of your resonating cavities. Since you can adjust those cavities and change their sizes and shapes, you can change the quality of your voice. The following sections contain a number of exercises designed to help you work on various voice qualities. We designed these exercises for students in voice and diction classes; they may not suit the purposes of voice coaches and acting teachers whose approach to resonance is planned for a different purpose.

Nasality and Resonance

The way you alter and select the resonating cavities is very important in determining voice quality and in helping to support a loud tone. The following exercises should help you increase and decrease the resonance of different cavities as necessary. We're assuming that the problems in nasality and resonance we describe are not due to any physical problems. If you have physical problems, we advise you to discuss the condition with your instructor.

TYPES OF NASALITY

Nasality problems fall into two types—too much and too little. Let's call "too much" *excessive* and "too little" *denasal.* Sometimes excessive nasality can be characteristic of a person's entire speech pattern with all sounds having a nasal quality, or excessive nasality could occur only when there are nasal sounds in a word. In either case, the cause usually is failure to make firm contact between the soft palate and the pharynx (throat) to prevent nasal emission. Denasality is just the opposite: very close and firm contact is made, not allowing enough nasal emission.

Exercise 14. Nasality—Ear Training

1. Pinch your nostrils closed using your thumb and index finger. Read the following sentence aloud:

   Robert took a good look at the spotted puppy.

   Now, release your nostrils and read the same sentence. Did you hear any difference in voice quality between your first and second readings? If you're not sure, try reading each word two times, alternately pinching and releasing your nostrils.

If there is a difference, chances are your voice tends to be excessively nasal. If your voice has this quality, the likelihood of reducing the nasality depends, in part, on your being able to recognize when you are being excessively nasal and when you are not.

2.   Place a clean, cool mirror directly under your nostrils in a horizontal plane and read the following sentence aloud:

Many people enjoy summer more than winter.

Immediately remove the mirror and look at it. You should notice two cloudy spots on the mirror. Now, wipe the mirror clean again, place it under your nose, and read the following sentence aloud:

The weather report calls for cloudy skies today.

Again, remove the mirror immediately and examine it. Are there any traces of cloudiness this time? If there are, you're probably using excessive nasal resonance. Repeat these two steps until you are sure you can hear when you are using excessive nasal resonance and when you're not.

3.   This part of the exercise consists of contrast drills. Say the following pairs of words, reading down each column from the left. The first word in each pair contains a nasal sound, the second does not.

ban	—	bat	may	—	say	annoy	—	alloy
bin	—	bill	might	—	light	sinning	—	sitting
fin	—	fill	moose	—	loose	hunt	—	hurt
flame	—	flake	now	—	how	glimmer	—	glitter
roam	—	road	nor	—	for	taint	—	taste
seem	—	seep	more	—	tore	under	—	udder
rung	—	rug	nose	—	rose	lent	—	lest
no	—	dough	nap	—	lap	sing	—	sit

Did you hear the difference between the nasal and non-nasal sounds in each pair?

4.   Read the following sentences aloud. There should be no nasal emission during any of the sentences.

a.   Paul was the first of several quarterbacks to try out.

b.   Susie liked school a lot.

c.   Where will you go for your holiday?

d.   I'd like a glass of water, please.

e. It's all right for you to stay.

f. I hope you like the picture.

g. Look for the girls at the beach.

h. Take the key to your father.

i. Write the essay at your desk.

j. Save your cash for the right purchase.

5. The following sentences contain some nasal sounds. As you say each sentence, listen for the nasal sounds. Are you producing any nasal sounds where you should not?

a. Nobody likes to be left in the lurch.

b. Bird in Hand is the name of a town in Pennsylvania.

c. A stitch in time saves an executive headache.

d. Sticks and stones may break my bones.

e. Abraham Lincoln was in error. You *can* fool all the people all the time.

f. Lewis Carroll's other book, *Through the Looking Glass*, is not as popular as *Alice in Wonderland*.

g. "Neither a borrower nor a lender be."

h. Muscle men of the cinema seek fame and fortune by knocking other people's heads.

 Exercise 15. Nasality—Pulling

This exercise is designed to help you energize the area of the soft palate and pharynx.

1. Curl the fingers of both hands toward the palms. Lift your elbows to chest height. Rotate your left hand so that the curled fingers and palm are facing outward, away from you; one thumb should be up, the other down. Hook the fingers of your left hand to the fingers of your right.

2. Begin to count aloud, slowly, from one to ten, and listen carefully to voice quality as you count.

3. At the number five, pull your arms away from each other. Use a strong pull, but make sure to keep your fingers hooked.

4. Did you notice a reduction in the amount of nasality? Did you notice a change in loudness? Most often this exercise produces an energizing effect on the entire body, including the soft palate, and increases the intensity of the voice.

5. Repeat this exercise three times, varying the number at which you begin pulling.

6. Say the names of the days of the week, starting with Sunday; but this time, pull when each day is named. Do you hear a decrease in the amount of nasal emission and/or resonance? Repeat the exercise, saying the months of the year.

7. Now go back and do steps 4 and 5 of Exercise 14.

Exercise 16. Nasality—Pushing

Do this sitting down.

1. Place both hands, palms down, on the front corners of your chair. Count aloud from one to ten. Listen carefully as you count. At the number five, try to push yourself off the seat by pushing down on the chair. Continue to count up to ten. Did you notice any change? What kind of change? Repeat the exercise three times.

2. Repeat the pushing exercise. First, name the days, then the months, pushing downward throughout the entire exercise. You should be able to hear a marked reduction in nasality as you go through the exercise. You can use the same exercise for practice using other words.

3. Now go back and do steps 4 and 5 of Exercise 14.

DENASALITY

Does your voice lack sufficient nasal resonance (the reinforcement of the high frequency vocal overtones that give voice its brilliance and clarity)? Do others believe that you are constantly suffering from a "stuffy nose"? The muffled, dull-sounding voice of a person whose nose is stuffed up is characteristic of the denasal voice quality. Try the following exercise.

Exercise 17. Denasality

1. Vocalize the consonant *m*. Sustain it for ten seconds, repeating it five times.

2. Chant the following group of nonsense syllables five times. Prolong the nasal consonants in the two middle syllables.

ohh—nee—hung—ahh

Repeat this five times.

3. Read aloud the following words, emphasizing and prolonging the nasal sound or sounds in each. Be careful to confine the nasality to just the nasal consonant. Don't let it move into the vowel.

no	on	sing	single
knee	in	ring	finger
my	time	song	monkey
neck	him	hand	spangle
now	hum	along	England
may	name	wing	mangle
kneel	calm	bang	mingle
more	loom	wrong	uncle
mill	moon	sting	dunking
mood	fine	fling	ringer

4. Try the drills for the nasal consonants on page 271. Again, emphasize the nasals, but don't let the nasality spread to the vowels or other consonants.

Tense, Strident, Metallic, and Hoarse Qualities

With the exception of the hoarse voice, these qualities are usually fairly high pitched and seem to be "hard hitting." The quality we call *hoarseness* is a combination of breathiness and harshness resulting in a voice that sounds very rough. Hoarseness can be associated with physical problems of the larynx, so we suggest you see your physician if your voice has been hoarse for a long time.

EXCESS TENSION

The common denominator of these qualities seems to be tension—excess tension in the area of the larynx. Sometimes the tension may be caused by inadequate breath support of loudness. If your instructor feels this is the case, we recommend that you review and practice Exercise 1: Abdominal Breathing (p. 254). If the excess tension is caused by something other than breath support, relaxation exercises (Exercises 9–13 above) can physically relax the laryngeal area. It takes time for the effects of these exercises to be felt, though, so don't expect overnight miracles. Think, instead, in terms of days or a few weeks before you notice significant changes in your voice quality.

VOCAL OR GLOTTAL FRY

This strangely named quality supposedly sounds like bacon frying. That may be stretching the imagination, but the voice does get a rough, bubbly quality, especially at the ends of sentences or thought groups. At these times, the pitch lowers considerably, and the voice weakens.

Many times this quality is indicative of a more serious ailment, so we suggest a visit to your physician. Vocal fry can sometimes be eliminated with the following exercises:

1. Use the sighing technique explained in the Hard Glottal Attack Exercise below.
2. Use the Abdominal Breathing Exercise on p. 254.

 Exercise 18. Vocal Fry

Work on holding your pitch level at the end of the sentence or phrase. A piano can be especially helpful with this. Read phrases and sentences aloud. Find the note on the piano that is close to your pitch at the beginning of the phrase. Play the note again at the end of the phrase, and notice if your pitch has lowered. Try to keep matching your pitch to the note played all the way through your utterance. Repeat often, using various reading material. We suggest that you use the materials for "High Key" on page 300 in your practice.

THROATY

The throaty quality is characterized by the voice that doesn't seem to project at all, staying in the throat with a muffled sound to it. Frequently, the voice is also denasal. Exercises that help eliminate this problem are the Denasality Exercise (p. 272) and the Vocal Fry Exercise above.

HARD GLOTTAL ATTACK

If you have this quality, you seem to hit your vowels hard, especially when the vowel is the first sound in a word. After a long period of using this type of attack, your voice may begin to crack and may become harsh or hoarse. Do the following exercise to try to change your method of attack.

 Exercise 19. Hard Glottal Attack

1. Sigh the vowel *ahh*, beginning it with a slight *h* sound so that it sounds like *hahhh*. Repeat three times.
2. In order, sigh the following: *ohh, aww, eee, aye* five times each, starting with an *h: hohh, haww, hee, haye.*
3. Repeat the previous steps, this time without the beginning *h* sound, but be careful to bring the vocal folds together gently; begin the sound without a hard attack by easing into it. *Think* the "*h*," *but don't say it.*

4. Repeat, this time gently phonating each sound, rather than sighing. Be sure to initiate each sound gently and without a hard attack.

5. Say each of the following words two times. The first time think the *h* before the vowel, but don't say it. The second time, initiate the vowel sound gently and without a hard attack.

I	own	anchor
owe	order	arson
ear	army	evening
owl	awning	over
oar	aisle	open
arm	inn	aiming
up	under	above

6. Say the following phrases and sentences out loud, being careful to initiate each word with a soft attack.
   a. All alone.
   b. In advance.
   c. Eleven o'clock.
   d. Eight hours.
   e. Open ocean.
   f. Enough apples.
   g. I am awake and aware.
   h. All of us are going.
   i. Order your anchors early.
   j. Every army is orderly.
   k. The owl didn't give a hoot about anything.

7. Read the following sentences aloud, again being careful to initiate each word beginning with a vowel using a soft attack.
   a. If we are all looking for answers, what are the questions?
   b. *Annie Hall* is an excellent film.
   c. Is your aunt expecting to get her pen off the table?
   d. "Alexander's Ragtime Band" isn't among my favorite songs.
   e. We were able to observe the evening star through the awning.

Chapter Eight

Vocal Expressiveness

In every school there's at least one teacher who has the nickname of "Mr. Excitement." If you were in one of his classes you'd understand why. He gives his lectures in a dull, dry, and deadly tone, never changing his rate, never varying his pitch, never saying words any louder or softer, speaking in a monotone that puts his students to sleep almost instantly. Faculty members also tend to go to sleep when talking with him in a meeting or conference because his speech pattern is very much like his personality: dull, dry, and deadly.

Perhaps you know or have heard of someone like Mr. Excitement. Maybe you've dozed off in church, in class, or in a meeting. Would you want to get to know someone who speaks in such an expressionless manner? And there are worse things than just falling asleep during a monotonic delivery. We all can probably recall misinterpreting someone's remarks because the right words weren't emphasized.

Vocal expressiveness is what this chapter is all about. We're going to work on how to bring appropriate variety to the way we speak and read aloud. We think that working on vocal expression is important for the following reasons:

- Vocal expressiveness is one of the major factors necessary for gaining and keeping your listener's attention and interest. By the way, that's *your* job. You're the one with the communication purpose to be achieved.

■ Vocal expressiveness can make meanings clear when the actual words leave some doubt.

■ Vocal expressiveness tells your listeners what you think of them, what you think about the words you're saying, and how you feel about yourself. Listeners tend to respect and believe a person who uses vocal expression effectively.

READING ALOUD

Unfortunately, there's a little of Mr. Excitement in most of us. It usually doesn't appear when we're speaking spontaneously, although it can. It generally is noticeable when we read aloud; that's when we "put on" our reading voices. You know what we mean by reading voice; it's an artificial, unemotional, impersonal way of speaking aloud. It's usually very different from the way we speak spontaneously, and it's usually much less effective.

Why Read Aloud?

Even though you may be saying to yourself, "I really don't do much reading aloud," chances are that you will. Most of us do a considerable amount of reading aloud during the normal course of living and working. We read newspaper articles to other people; directions on how to make, build, or cook things; letters and business reports during meetings and conferences; stories and fairy tales to our children, brothers and sisters, nieces and nephews. We could continue to add to the list, but we've made our point: you *do* read aloud. You do it for the same reasons that you speak spontaneously, but you may not be reading effectively.

We'll tell you first what we're *not* going to do: we're not going to teach you to be a professional radio or TV announcer, or a Broadway or film actor, or any such thing. That's beyond the scope of this text. We *do* want to help you become more effective in your everyday speaking and reading. So, we'll teach you how to use the components of vocal expression: *rate, phrasing, intonation,* and *stress.* We'll provide you with some theory and plenty of practice.

COMPONENTS OF VOCAL EXPRESSION

Rate

Can you imagine yourself at Gettysburg listening to Abraham Lincoln deliver the famous Address at the same rate of speech as a stand-up comic in a Las Vegas nightclub act? In all likelihood, the very idea of such a rapid rate of delivery for that somber, serious message would appeal to your sense of the ridiculous rather than the sublime.

There is a classical music program broadcast every morning by radio station WGBH, a venerable and revered public broadcasting station in Boston. This program is carried by many other PBS stations around the country and has a very wide and loyal audience. The disk jockey (if such a title could be conferred on so widely respected a personage as the man who selects the program and delivers the commentary) speaks in a voice very low in pitch, and at a rate of about 60 words per minute. One of the authors, who lives in the area, never dares to listen to that program while driving on the highway, because he almost always falls asleep during the commentary while waiting for the music to start. This author has acquaintances, music lovers all, who make the same complaint. Who would have ever thought that very low pitch and slow rate of delivery could be hazardous to your health?

Rate has a definite effect on our perceptions of people and the relative importance of their messages. Perhaps in your work or school environment, you have come across people who speak at a very rapid rate. Chances are that you tend to place less value on what that person has to say than you would if he or she spoke at a slower rate.

As a rule, we deliver spoken messages at a rate that is appropriate for the content. A rapid rate usually carries the unspoken message, "What I'm saying now is light, frivolous, unimportant, humorous, not meant to be taken too seriously." A slow, deliberate rate, on the other hand, implies, "This message is meant to be considered important and weighty and is to be taken seriously."

The rate of speech also reflects the speaker's physical and emotional states. When you're feeling calm or sad or tired, you'll probably speak relatively slowly. When you are in a state of physical or mental excitement, though, you'll most likely speed things up considerably.

The rate at which you speak affects understanding. The process whereby you take in and interpret messages is a highly complex one. To understand a spoken message, your brain must "hear" all the acoustic elements of the message, then translate them into the concepts or ideas they symbolize, then associate those concepts with the meanings you've attributed to them as a result of all the experiences you've had in your life. You can understand, therefore, that although you can *hear* words just as rapidly as they are spoken, it takes you longer to understand and integrate the message in some meaningful and usable form. When you are presented with a message delivered at a high rate of speed, you have more difficulty dealing with it in a meaningful way. This is especially true if the message is complex or abstract. Then you work particularly hard to understand everything the speaker is saying or you give up trying. In either case, there's a good chance that the speaker's purpose has not been successfully achieved.

If a speaker delivers a relatively unimportant message slowly and deliberately, you may become impatient or bored waiting for the message to be completed because you understood the speaker's intent long before the delivery ended. For communication to be effective, it is important for the rate of delivery to match the meaning the speaker wishes to convey.

Determining Your Own Rate

Before you practice the exercises for rate, you should have an idea of what your average rate actually is. To do this, try the exercise below. You'll need someone to act as your timekeeper and either a stop-watch or a watch with a second hand.

1. Ask your timekeeper to time you to the nearest second and to signal you when it's time to start. At the signal, read through the selection below *silently*. Don't pause to analyze. Don't struggle with the pronunciation of unfamiliar words. When you've completed the silent reading, signal your timekeeper so that you can record the silent reading time in seconds on page 281. The piece you'll be reading is from the Department of Health, Education, and Welfare Publication No. (NIOSH) 75-165.

> The basic idea behind the techniques for limiting a person's exposure to noise is very simple and straightforward. The reference frame dealt with in noise reduction is composed of a sound *source*, the sound wave *path*, and a sound wave *receiver* which, in common circumstances, is an ear or a microphone that is used for measurement.
>
> The best and most satisfying means of reducing noise levels is to reduce the source sound output. This approach may require major modifications to the noisy device. Some of these modifications include better quality control, closer tolerances on moving parts, better balancing of rotating parts, and sometimes even a complete redesign of the technique utilized to perform the job for which this machine is

intended. Since something vibrating causes compression and rarefaction of the air which is observed as sound, the above-mentioned and many other modifications to a sound source are all aimed toward reducing the vibration of any part to the lowest possible level. Normally these modifications are not within the capability of the user and therefore must be left to the equipment manufacturers. Fortunately for those directly affected, manufacturers are beginning to make these changes. There is, however, one set or kind of modification that the user can perform. A particular piece of machinery may be the driving force to produce vibrations but it often is the floor, wall, or other support member that is doing much of the sound radiating. This kind of vibration problem can be effectively reduced by proper use of vibration isolation or vibration damping treatment.

Essentially vibration isolation means that the connection between the driving force and the driven member is such that the vibration is not transmitted through the connection. Any device which behaves as a spring can be utilized for this purpose. Vibration isolators can be made with actual steel springs, or with rubber pads. Vibration isolators are also made out of coils of cable laid on their side or even air can be used when properly contained. The selection of which vibration isolator to use depends on the forces involved, the frequency of the driving force, and the possible natural frequencies of the support member itself. If not properly selected, a vibration isolator can make a problem situation worse.

(380 words)

2. At the timekeeper's signal, read the selection *aloud*. Try to make your listener understand the contents of the passage. If you're doing this outside of class, pretend that you are addressing the entire class. Record your reading time in seconds.

3. Now use a tape recorder and give a brief extemporaneous talk. Talk about your job or your hobbies. Describe a movie you've seen or a book you've read. The subject itself isn't important as long as you can talk about it for at least two minutes. Talk to a real or imagined class. Record the speaking time in seconds. Then replay the tape and count the number of words you said.

4. To find your rate, divide the number of words read or spoken by the

number of seconds. Multiply that number by 60 to find the approximate rate in words per minute (w.p.m.).

$$\frac{\text{words read silently}}{\text{seconds}} \times 60 = \text{w.p.m.} \underline{\hspace{2cm}} \times 60 = \underline{\hspace{1cm}} \text{w.p.m.}$$

$$\frac{\text{words read aloud}}{\text{seconds}} \times 60 = \text{w.p.m.} \underline{\hspace{2cm}} \times 60 = \underline{\hspace{1cm}} \text{w.p.m.}$$

$$\frac{\text{words spoken}}{\text{seconds}} \times 60 = \text{w.p.m.} \underline{\hspace{2cm}} \times 60 = \underline{\hspace{1cm}} \text{w.p.m.}$$

Enter your reading-aloud rate and spoken rate above. Compare these rates with your silent reading rate.

APPROPRIATE RATE

If your oral reading rate falls between 150 w.p.m. and 180 w.p.m. it's within the normal range for this type of material. The middle of the range, 160 w.p.m. to 170 w.p.m., would be considered by most listeners to be the most effective and easiest to understand. Your speaking rate should be slower, probably below 150 w.p.m. In both speaking and reading, of course, the rate will reflect the content of the material, the listener's state of mind, and so forth.

If you've determined that your rate is too fast or too slow, try the following exercises for adjusting rate.

Timed Readings for Rate

Use the following selections for either slow or fast rate. Each selection contains 160 to 170 words and should take exactly one minute for you to read aloud. Continue to read each selection (without looking at your watch) until it takes you one minute.

1. Our shoppers bought a sample of every bicycle lock they could find. Most of the tested locks were cheap, lightweight, and insecure. More than half were rated Not Acceptable because they could be yanked, stomped, or sprung apart without the use of tools. However, we did find several locks that proved quite secure against most common assaults. Those locks were relatively expensive, though, and heavier than many bike riders would want to carry.

Types. Nearly all models tested combine a chain or a

cable with a key lock or a combination lock. The two elements may be separate or attached as an integral unit. We also tested cables meant to be mounted permanently on the bike itself, and oversized shackle locks. The latter, sometimes called horseshoe locks, are essentially padlocks with shackles large enough to fit around a post. The locking devices are listed by type in the ratings.

The oversized shackle locks were generally the most resistant to assault, as the Ratings show.

(Consumer Reports Buying Guide Issue 1981)

2. Motor behavior is basic to the human condition. In an earlier age survival and maintenance often depended upon one's ability to extract a livelihood from nature, construct shelter, and fashion clothing. Today a complex division of labor no longer requires a high degree of self-sufficiency in making provision for ourselves and the members of our immediate family. But modern technology requires a host of new skills, including operating automobiles and jet aircraft. Further, many of our leisure activities, including playing musical instruments and participation in sports like skiing, golf, surfing, and baseball, demand a vast array of motor behaviors.

Within schools, motor skills are interwoven throughout the curriculum at all levels. Using a pencil, writing with chalk, making handwritten letters, drawing pictures, painting objects, employing measuring instruments, and walking from one place to another are all fundamental school activities. Similarly, playground activities and games in physical education involve complex and coordinated movements.

(Educational Psychology Theory and Practice, James Vander Zanden)

3. The manuscript should be typewritten, double-spaced, on white medium-weight paper. The sheets should be of the standard 8½ × 11 size and of good enough quality to permit clear markings in ink. Margins should be about one inch on each side and at the top and bottom. All pages should be numbered consecutively, preferably in the upper right-hand corner, throughout the entire work. Use only one side of the sheet.

A quotation that will run four lines or more is usually set off as a single-spaced, double-indented paragraph.

It is not advantageous to submit the manuscript in any special ornamental binder. If assembled neatly in a folder, envelope, or cardboard box, the manuscript will be more in keeping with the practice of most professional writers and with the preference of most editors. The author should always retain a complete carbon copy of the manuscript, not only to facilitate correspondence between the editor and author, but to serve as insurance against the loss of the original copy.

(The Random House Dictionary, 1978)

4. The mimeograph machine usually produces black copy similar to typing. The master for use on this machine also consists of three layers—the backing sheet, a silk screen coated with a waxy substance, and a clear plastic film which prevents the wax from filling up your typewriter keys. This master is usually typed with the ribbon in the *off* position on your typewriter. As you type, the typewriter keys punch holes (in the shape of your keys) in the coating on the silk screen. When you put the master on the mimeograph machine, the holes allow the ink in the drum to seep out, and the ink is then transferred onto the paper that your machine is feeding. The most commonly used color of ink is black, although there are mimeograph machines that boast of making multiple color copies. Those, however, require that you change an "ink gun" or "drum" and make two or three passes over the paper. You'll seldom encounter them.

(The Least You Should Know about Office Machines, a talk to students, Louise W. Steele)

It's important for you to read these passages a number of times at the rate of 160–170 w.p.m. to get the feeling in your mouth, tongue, and jaw of what that rate is like. You must also get accustomed to that rate in your mind. We'd bet that the first couple of times you read them at the desired rate, it felt awfully strange. After a while the feeling of strangeness will go.

Practice speaking spontaneously at 160–170 w.p.m. Use a tape recorder and count your words afterward, or ask a friend to listen to you and to tell you if you speed up or slow down.

Now we'd like you to try to read a few passages at an average rate of 120–150 w.p.m. This rate is appropriate for serious, somber material, or for material which is difficult for others to grasp (for the authors, such material might be on economic theory). In addition, learning to select various rates will give you a good deal of flexibility in your vocal expressiveness.

The following passages should take from 50 seconds to 1 minute to read.

1. This crisis model of young people caught in a turbulent passage between their late teens and early twenties has come to be equated with the normal process of growing up. We all recognize hallmarks of this sensitive condition: kids who are at once rebellious, listless, and jumpy. Kids who are seized by sudden and riotous swings of mood. When cramped by anxiety, they cannot sleep or work. They may suffer from mysterious maladies and hold to inflexibly high ideals. Often they seem to be gripped by a negative view of themselves and by hostility to the family. They are likely to drop out of school, the job, the romance, or to stay in and be actively resentful.

In short, it's like having flu of the personality.

(*Passages*, Gail Sheehy; 126 words)

2. On Earth, things move in cycles. That is why, after 4.6 billion years of existence, our planet is still young, active, and full of life.

Water runs from the uplands to the sea, quickly as rivers, and seepingly as ground water. It may delay a while and collect in ponds and lakes, but it always ends in the ocean (or, occasionally, in inland seas). It is a natural flow under the pull of gravity.

Why did all the water not end in the sea, leaving the land desert-dry billions of years ago? Because that's only half the cycle.

The other half, powered by the energy of the Sun's radiation, evaporates water from the ocean surface, raises water vapor by the millions of tons a couple of miles into the air, carries it over the land, and drops it as rain.

(*Change!* Isaac Asimov; 141 words)

DURATION

Rate is partly determined by how you produce your vowels. If you sound them very quickly, they become clipped and the words become shorter. Even if you reduce the number of words you say each minute, your speech would still sound rapid. On the other extreme is prolongation. If you hold on to the vowels too long, your speech may be too slow. Use the following drill to vary duration.

Duration Practice

We've found it convenient to use the following system to indicate duration: ˘ for short duration; ¯ for long duration; no marking for average duration.

Exercise 1. Contrast Drill for Duration

Say the following pairs of words aloud. Listen for a difference in how long the vowel sounds in each word are held. Try to exaggerate the difference by making the vowel in the first word of each pair very short, and the vowel in the second word very long.

căp	— cāme	spĕnt	— spānned
slĭp	— slēēve	rĭch	— rīde
grĭp	— grīeve	dŏt	— dūde
pŏut	— pōund	hŏp	— hōme
tŏte	— tōes	flăp	— flāw
rŏtten	— rōses	spăt	— Spāin
păce	— pāys	shŏt	— shāme
frŏnt	— frōnd	brăt	— brāin
păce	— bēige	thĭn	— thīgh
măt	— māde	shĭp	— shy

Exercise 2.

Read the following words aloud, giving the vowels the duration as marked. Remember, ˘ means short duration, ¯ means long duration, no mark means average duration.

hăppy̆	wōnder	sĭck
lōngĭng	shāmefŭl	blŭff
sŭrprīse	ĭnhăbĭtĕd	līkely
sādly	fūtŭre	ăfrāid
pĕppy̆	smīle	sŭppōse

Exercise 3.

Read the following words aloud at an average loudness. First, read the entire list giving the vowel sounds average duration. Then, read the list again, making the vowel sounds as short as possible. Then, give the vowel sounds average duration again. Finally, make the vowel sounds as long as possible.

afraid	inch	clothing	narcotic
backache	snore	rotten	republic
ashamed	pout	total	submerging
prank	browse	creeping	polluted
grieve	doze	speaker	improvement
sleep	grunt	garden	newcomer
glib	swoop	paper	bakery
divide	girl	quarrel	saleable
voodoo	sided	nickname	commitment
fragile	shallow	dynamic	eloping

Now, go back over the above list of words and mark the vowels with the symbols for whatever duration you believe to be appropriate. Pronounce the words in accordance with your duration markings.

Here are more selections for duration. Read them silently first, planning the duration of certain words, perhaps marking them in the text as you did above. Then, read them aloud.

1. Outside the open door
   Of the whitewashed house,
   Framed in its doorway, a chair,
   Vacant, waits in the sunshine.

   A jug of fresh water stands
   Inside the door. In the sunshine
   The chair waits, less and less vacant.
   The host's plan is to offer water, then stand aside.

   ("The Supper after the Last," Galway Kinnell)

2. A poem should be palpable and mute
   As a globed fruit.

   Dumb
   As old medallions to the thumb,

   Silent as the sleeve-worn stone
   Of casement ledges where the moss has grown—

   A poem should be wordless
   As the flight of birds.

   ("Ars Poetica," Archibald Macleish)

Try this same exercise with poetry and literature selections of your own choosing. Continue to be aware of overall rate while you're working on duration.

PAUSING

We can't consider rate without discussing pausing. But the relationship is secondary; we use pausing for much more than simply controlling rate. Often, in fact, rate is subordinate to pausing.

We use pauses for a number of purposes: emphasis, clarity, meaning, attention, reflection, variety, change of ideas, change of mood, and last but not least, for breathing. Without pausing, you tend to lose your listener because pauses act as verbal punctuation marks. Furthermore, we use pausing to regulate the back and forth nature of conversation. If you're a listener, you wait for the speaker to pause before you begin to speak; speaking before you hear the pause is considered an interruption.

Major, or long, pauses are controlled by *thought groups*. A thought group is analogous to the written sentence; it is complete and can stand by itself. Your pause is the verbal punctuation mark. Minor, or short, pauses are used for all the purposes we listed above. Notice that of all the purposes, we listed breathing last. That's right. You should pause for meaning, not just to get air. Pausing should be frequent enough that you don't run out of breath. If you do, it means you're not pausing enough or you're not controlling your breath flow efficiently. Remember, you can only take a quick inhalation during most pauses, so breath control is very important.

▼ **Pausing Exercises**

1. Read the following telephone conversation from *Come Blow Your Horn* by Neil Simon. First read it through silently, then aloud, pretending that you're actually talking on the phone. The pauses were indicated by the author (—), but he didn't indicate their length; that's up to you. Remember, this is a conversation between Alan and Chickie, so the pauses indicate when it's Chickie's turn to talk. When you pause, imagine what Chickie might be saying, and give her enough time to say it.

    Alan: Hello?—Chickie? Don't you know you could be arrested for having such a sexy voice?—Alan—How could I? I just got in from Europe an hour ago—Switzerland—A specialist there told me if I don't see you within a half an hour, I'll die—Yes, tonight—A friend of mine is having a little party—Wonderful guy—hundred laughs — Hey,

Chickie, is your roommate free? The French girl? — Wonderful. Yes. Bring her—No, I can't. I've got to get the pretzels. Can you meet me there? The Hotel Croyden, Room 326, Marty Meltzer—A half hour—Marvelous. I just love you — What? — Yes, Alan *Baker*.

2. Meaningful pauses don't have to be long. Many times we use pauses just for that little extra bit of emphasis; we can set things apart by pausing slightly before or after a word. Mark the following selections for meaningful pauses. Use / to indicate a slight pause and / / to indicate a longer pause, as in the following example:

To be / or not to be. // That / is the question.

Notice how we can change the feeling by changing the pauses:

To be or / not to be.// That is / the question.

Here's one for you to try. First, read it as we've marked it. Then, change the pausing, and mark the second listing to represent the way you'd like to read it.

Tomorrow // and tomorrow // and tomorrow // creeps in this / petty pace / from day / to day. . . .

Tomorrow and tomorrow and tomorrow creeps in this petty pace from day to day. . . .

Here are more practice selections for pausing. Make light marks in pencil so you can change the pauses if they don't seem right when you read the passages aloud. Try each selection a few times, and change the pausing each time.

    a. A hundred feet in the sky he lowered his webbed feet, lifted his beak, and strained to hold a painful hard twisting curve through his wings. The curve meant that he would fly slowly, and now he slowed until the wind was a whisper in his face, until the ocean stood still beneath him. He narrowed his eyes in fierce concentration, held his breath, forced one . . . single . . . more . . . inch . . . of . . . curve . . . Then his feathers ruffled, he stalled and fell.

(*Jonathan Livingston Seagull*, Richard Bach)

b. *Magee:* No kidding—I paint. You'd hate my work though—it's all very abstract—I stand back and splash oil all over everything and then I run all over it with my sneakers and I stick my lunch on it—in fact, my lunch came in second at a showing in Cape Cod.

(*Don't Drink the Water,* Woody Allen)

c. Our ability to design and manufacture home heating and air conditioning equipment that met the exacting performance standards of the manufactured housing industry has made us the number one supplier of these products for many years. While we have been involved to a small degree in the traditional residential housing market for many years, we believed that soaring utility bills would open an entirely new opportunity.

(1979 Annual Report, The Coleman Company)

d. Pace University holds to a philosophy that each student is the center of the institution's responsibilities: that he or she is unique, and that whatever students have in common with each other they have in varying proportions and in different ways. In this view, students can expect the University to provide them with opportunities to realize their full potential and to help them earn respect as mature adults.

(*1980–81 Undergraduate Bulletin,* Pace University)

e. In moving-slow he has no Peer
   You ask him something in his Ear
   He thinks about it for a Year;
   And, then, before he says a Word
   He will assume that you have Heard—

   A most Ex-as-per-at-ing Lug.
   But should you call his manner Smug
   He'll sigh and give his Branch a Hug;

   Then off again to Sleep he goes,
   Still swaying gently by his Toes,
   And you just *know* he knows he knows.

(''The Sloth,'' Theodore Roethke)

STRESS

If someone were to say to you, in a soft, weak voice, "Pay attention; this is very important," chances are you wouldn't immediately drop what you were doing to listen. If, however, you heard the same command given in a loud, strong voice, you would probably respond immediately. As a rule, in our society, we tend to place more importance on things said loudly than we do on things said softly. This also holds true for the way we customarily *stress* (accent by loudness) the various parts of speech. Nouns, for example, are the primary conveyors of meaning, and as such, we ordinarily give them the most stress. Next come verbs, then adjectives, then adverbs. Those parts of speech getting the least amount of stress, or sometimes no stress at all, include pronouns, articles, prepositions, and conjunctions. In other words, we indicate the relative importance of parts of speech, or the importance of particular things we say by making them louder (we call this stress).

There are, however, certain situations for which you want to give a special twist of meaning to what you are saying. Let's take the sentence, "The boy took his dog to the park" as an example. Spoken as a simple statement, you would stress the nouns boy, dog, and park and the verb took. Using double underlining to indicate primary stress and single underlining to indicate secondary stress, we would indicate the stress pattern of that sentence as:

The boy took his dog to the park.

Suppose you wished to use the very same sentence to answer a series of questions. We can predict the ways in which your stress pattern would vary. Let's ask the questions and listen to the answers:

QUESTION: Did just any boy take his dog to the park?
ANSWER: No, the boy took his dog to the park
QUESTION: Did a girl take a dog to the park?
ANSWER: No, the boy took his dog to the park.
QUESTION: Did the boy take someone else's dog to the park?
ANSWER: No, the boy took his dog to the park.

A whole series of similar questions could be asked, and for each, the word receiving primary stress would change with the change of information asked for in the various questions.

Word Stress

The example above illustrates the way we use word stress, that is, how we make different words louder to transmit special meaning. In the example, each time we said the sentence, using different stress, but not different words, we changed the meaning of the sentence. Try the following:

Word Stress Drill

Following are some simple sentences. Read each one aloud. Begin by stressing the first word of each sentence, then move the stress to the second word, and so on, just as we did with "The <u>boy</u> <u>took</u> his <u>dog</u> to the <u>park</u>."

1. This is my favorite.
2. I'm buying a new car.
3. Where are you going?
4. I don't like him.
5. This is a great book.
6. Do you like my new hat?
7. How much did that cost?
8. Things are sure different around here.
9. Make my day.
10. Don't come home late.

In the following sentences, underline the words to show where you would place primary and secondary stress. Then read the sentences aloud making sure you stress the words the way you planned.

1. Please don't do that again.
2. If I've told you once, I've told you a thousand times.
3. Where are those keys of mine?
4. Which book are you going to buy?
5. I really need a rest.
6. Excuse me, but I believe that seat is mine.
7. I know where I'm going.
8. Tim was certainly not feeling well.
9. Please don't eat the daisies.
10. Just how safe do you think that is?

Syllable Stress

In words of more than one syllable (polysyllabic words), one syllable will receive more stress than the others. The stress pattern is agreed to by the speakers of the language; look up a word in the dictionary and you'll see a diacritical mark indicating stress. Sometimes we stress a different syllable for special emphasis; most of the time, though, a word is considered mispronounced if the wrong syllable stress is used.

When we join two nouns to form a compound word, we usually stress the first noun more than the second. Try the following list.

Compound Word Stress Drill

Read the following words aloud. Place primary stress on the first syllable of each word:

airplane	hothouse	Sunday
flatfoot	beefsteak	downtown
bluefish	notebook	paperback
motorboat	butterfly	forestfire
rubberband	sometime	overcharge
driveway	underpass	football
windchime	textbook	noonday
surfboard	software	grandstand

Polysyllabic words, other than compound words, usually follow a pattern in which the stress moves farther along in the word as the word becomes longer. Try the following:

Polysyllabic Stress Drill

Read the following words aloud, reading *across* the page. Place the primary stress on the appropriate syllable:

major	majority
sacrifice	sacrificial
reference	referee
incident	incidental
continent	continental
simplify	simplification
occupy	occupation
product	productive
beautify	beautification

(more . . .)

converse	conversational	
nominate	nomination	nominee
photograph	photography	photographic
object	objective	objectification
subject	subjective	subjectification
person	personify	personification

Practice Readings for Stress

Read the following selections aloud. It may be helpful for you to under-line words for primary and secondary stress. Remember, there's no right way: interpretation of the authors' words is up to you. Just be aware of how your stress patterns may change the meaning.

1. The idea of <u>you</u> lynching anybody is amusing. The idea of you thinking you had pluck enough to lynch a <u>man</u>! Because you're brave enough to tar and feather poor friend-less cast-out women that come along here, did that make you think you had grit enough to lay your hands on a <u>man</u>? Why, a <u>man's</u> safe in the hands of ten thousand of your kind—as long as it's daytime and you're not behind him.

(*Huckleberry Finn*, Mark Twain)

2. Climb to a thousand feet. Full power straight ahead first, then push over, flapping, to a vertical dive. Then, every time, his left wing stalled on an upstroke, he'd roll violently left, stall his right wing recovering, and flick like fire into a wild tumbling spin to the right.

(*Jonathan Livingston Seagull*, Richard Bach)

3. For a full day and two nights I have been alone. I lay on the beach under the stars at night alone. I made my breakfast alone. Alone I watched the gulls at the end of the pier, dip and wheel and dive for the scraps I threw them. A morning's work at my desk, and then, a late picnic lunch alone on the beach.

(*Gift from the Sea*, Anne Morrow Lindbergh)

4. . . . the boat is caught by the wave and, gathering speed, begins to rush forward. The speedometer needle starts its climb—9, 10, 11 knots. Once in a while, a big one, a real graybeard comes along and we hit 12 and 13 knots.

The helmsman, the wheel vibrating in his hands as the rudder is locked in a fore and aft position by the force of the water rushing by its sides, lets out a howl of triumph. It is almost an animal cry, a natural outlet, welling up in a geyser of exhilaration. He has the feeling of having harnessed the angry forces of nature to beat it at its own game. He has pulled Poseidon's beard.

(On the Wind's Way, William Snaith)

5. Tyger, tyger, burning bright
   In the forests of the night,
   What immortal hand or eye
   Could frame thy fearful symmetry?

   In what distant deeps or skies
   Burnt the fire of thine eyes?
   On what wings dare he aspire?
   What the hand dare seize the fire?

   And what shoulder and what art
   Could twist the sinews of thy heart?
   And, when thy heart began to beat,
   What dread hand and what dread feet?

   What the hammer? What the chain?
   In what furnace was thy brain?
   What the anvil? What dread grasp
   Dare its deadly terrors clasp?

   When the stars threw down their spears,
   And water'd heaven with their tears,
   Did He smile His work to see?
   Did He who made the lamb make thee?

   Tyger, tyger, burning bright
   In the forests of the night,
   What immortal hand or eye
   Dare frame thy fearful symmetry?

("The Tyger," William Blake)

6. The year's at the spring,
   And day's at the morn;
   Morning's at seven;
   The hill-side's dew-pearl'd

The lark's on the wing;
The snail's on the thorn;
God's in His heaven—
All's right with the world!

("Pippa Passes," Part 1, Robert Browning)

7. It seemed to me that I should have to have a desk, even though I had no real need for a desk. I was afraid that if I had no desk in my room my life would seem too haphazard.

The desk looked incomplete when I got it set up, so I found a wire basket and put that on it, and threw a few things in it. This basket, however, gave me a lot of trouble for the first couple of weeks. I had always had TWO baskets in New York. One said IN, the other OUT. At intervals a distribution boy would sneak into the room, deposit something in IN, remove the contents of OUT. Here, with only one basket, my problem was to decide whether it was IN or OUT, a decision a person of some character could have made promptly and reasonably but which I fooled round with for days—tentative, hesitant, trying first one idea then another, first a day when it would be IN, then a day when it would be OUT, then, somewhat desperately, trying to combine the best features of both and using it as a catch-all for migratory papers no matter which way they were headed. This last was disastrous. I found a supposedly out-going letter buried for a week under some broadsides from the local movie house. The basket is now IN. I discovered by test that fully ninety per cent of whatever was on my desk at any given moment were IN things. Only ten per cent were OUT things—almost too few to warrant a special container.

("Incoming Basket," in *One Man's Meat*, E. B. White)

INTONATION

We spoke about pitch in Chapter 7. We also discussed it in Chapter 2. What we've talked about so far is mainly the overall pitch of your voice—pitch range and optimum and habitual pitches. Now we'll look at pitch in a different way: how you use pitch to bring additional meaning to or clarify or reinforce what you say.

Listen to someone whom you consider to be a good speaker. Close your eyes and concentrate mainly on that person's voice, not the actual words. Begin to focus on pitch—not the overall pitch, but the changes in pitch that are occurring. After a while, you should begin to notice a pattern of pitch changes, up and down, that emerges. If you're successful in blocking out the actual words, it will almost seem as though the person is singing rather than speaking.

We *are* singing, to a certain extent, when we speak. Our language, just like every language, has its own unique melody that all native speakers learn from the beginning. We know that the melody adds a lot to the message.

We call the melody of language *intonation*. Intonation refers to the total pattern of pitch changes within an utterance. The intonation patterns we use are familiar and required by our language. For example, say the following sentence five times: *I am going to the store.* Listen closely to the pitch of your voice. You should hear that your voice started off at one pitch, rose slightly during the first couple of words, and then descended gradually during the rest of the utterance. This is a characteristic intonation pattern for a declarative statement. Now try asking some questions aloud. For example, ask "Am I going to the store?" Did you notice a different intonation pattern? You probably noted that rather than a descending pitch pattern at the end, there was a rising pitch. That pattern is characteristic of questioning utterances but not interrogatives. Notice the difference between "Are you going?" and "Why are you going?" The second question actually has a falling pitch.

It's important for you to use the appropriate intonation patterns when you speak. Otherwise, you may be sending messages using intonations that contradict what you want your words to say. Intonation patterns that disagree with the content of the utterance may indicate doubt, sarcasm, or confusion. And speech with a monotone intonation pattern may not be listened to at all. We're going to discuss the types of pitch changes that you make and give you exercises that you can use for practice. The drills and exercises should be helpful to you whether you're a native speaker or have learned English as a second language.

Key

You're most likely aware that there's a relationship between the content and purpose of your utterance and the general pitch level you use. It wouldn't be appropriate for you to, let's say, resign "regretfully" from a job and use the higher notes of your pitch range to tell your boss. Nor would it be appropriate to announce that you just won a million dollar lottery prize using the lower part of your range. Try it: say, "I'm so happy! I just won a million dollars," using a low-pitched voice. You certainly don't sound happy, do you?

What we're talking about is called *key*—the average pitch level of an utterance. Generally, we refer to three keys—*low, middle,* and *high.* The middle key should be comfortable for you because it should correspond to your optimum pitch. Here are some selections for you to read aloud using the different keys. Try reading each sentence five times: first at middle key, then at high key, then back to middle key, then low key, and finally at middle key again:

1. Please take a seat and the dentist will be with you in a few minutes.
2. If I had it to do all over again, I'd do it all over again.
3. An old German proverb says, "It is a bad bridge that is shorter than the stream."
4. "Peace in space will help us nought once peace on Earth is gone." John F. Kennedy
5. "A fool and his money are soon parted." *New York Times,* October 20, 1987.
6. The camel has been called "the ship of the desert," I guess because of seasickness.

The following exercises provide connected passages to read at the three levels.

▼ **Middle Key Readings**

1. Learning is finding out what you already know. Doing is demonstrating that you know it. Teaching is reminding others that they know just as well as you. You are all learners, doers, teachers.

(*Illusions,* Richard Bach)

2. There are two reasons for staining wood. The first is to enhance the surface. In the finishing trade it's called "bringing out the natural beauty." Actually, the idea is not too outlandish. Some fine cabinet woods such as walnut don't look particularly rich in an unadorned state, and so to give them a more luxurious appearance, stain is used on the wood (for example, walnut stain on walnut wood). The grain

becomes vibrant, the richness of the wood becomes apparent, and walnut emerges as real walnut.

The other reason for staining is to upgrade the wood. For example, some people will utilize stain in an effort to upgrade walnut so that it resembles mahogany. In the viewpoint of other craftsmen, this is heresy. However, some woods do make the transition fairly easily.

(*Furniture Refinishing*, W. I. Fischman)

3. Where did I learn to row? How do I know? In the *Emma* I suppose—the narrow, flat bottomed rowboat my grandfather bought at Macy's and stuck off the end of the dock at our summer house on the pond, in case any of the house guests wanted to take a spin around the lake in the evening, or Granny wanted a ride to the cove at the far end of the pond where her old, white-haired friend lived in the big stucco house with a red tile roof that looked as if it belonged in Spain instead of on the eastern tip of Long Island.

(*Striper*, John N. Cole)

4. Use a comma only when you have a definite reason for doing so in accordance with the guidelines below. A safe rule to follow, "When in doubt, leave it out."

(*The Random House Dictionary*)

5. There is an electricity about friendship relationships; they are like no other. Though we might not be able to choose our neighbors, relatives or the people with whom we work, friendships are an act of pure intention. Very few associations allow for such a free exchange of loyalty, trust, affection and, sometimes, doubt, hurt and anger. Friendship not only begins on a voluntary basis, but it continues by choice. The depth and rhythm of the relationship, the desire and willingness to respond to each other are open to negotiation. The process of choice may not be quick nor may it develop spectacularly—the yearning for a good friend is frequently frustrated—but make no mistake about it, most of us are involved in the search: Friendship matters.

(*Friendship: How to Give It, How to Get It*, Joel D. Block)

▼ **Low Key Readings**

1. I leaned on the gate for a moment, breathing in the sweet air. There had been a change during the last week; the harsh winds had dropped, everything had softened and greened and the warming land gave off its scents. On the lower slopes of the fell, in the shade of the pine woods, a pale mist of bluebells drifted among the dead bronze of the bracken and their fragrance came up to me on the breeze.

(*All Things Bright and Beautiful,* James Herriot)

2. "I'm afraid he's dead, Mr. Barnett."
The big man did not change expression. He reached slowly across and rubbed his forefinger against the dark fur in that familiar gesture. Then he put his elbows on the desk and covered his face with his hands.
   I did not know what to say; I watched helplessly as his shoulders began to shake and tears welled between the thick fingers. He stayed like that for some time, then he spoke:
   "He was my friend," he said.

(*The Lord God Made Them All,* James Herriot)

3. The sullen murmur of the bees, shouldering their way through the long, unmown grass, or circling with monotonous insistence round the dusty gilt horns or the straggling woodbine, seemed to make the stillness more oppressive.

(*The Picture of Dorian Gray,* Oscar Wilde)

4. The shell in my hand is deserted. It once housed a whelk, a snaillike creature, and then temporarily, after the death of the first occupant, a little hermit crab, who has run away, leaving his tracks behind him like a delicate vine on the sand. He ran away, and left me his shell.

(*Gift from the Sea,* Anne Morrow Lindbergh)

5. Tears, idle tears, I know not what they mean,
    Tears from the depth of some divine despair
    Rise in the heart, and gather to the eyes,
    In looking on the happy autumn-fields,
    And thinking of the days that are no more.

("The Princess," Alfred Lord Tennyson)

High Key Readings

1.   Realize your youth while you have it. Don't squander the gold of your days, listening to the tedious, trying to improve the hopeless failure, or giving away your life to the ignorant, the common, and the vulgar. These are the sickly aims, the false ideals, of our age. Live! Live the wonderful life that is in you!

(*The Picture of Dorian Gray*, Oscar Wilde)

2.   If you shut your eyes and are a lucky one, you may see at times a shapeless pool of lovely pale colors suspended in the darkness; then if you squeeze your eyes tighter, the pool begins to take shape, and the colors become so livid that with another squeeze they must go on fire. But just before they go on fire you see the lagoon. This is the nearest you ever get to it on the mainland, just one heavenly moment; if there could be two moments you might see the surf and hear the mermaids singing.

(*Peter Pan*, James Barrie)

3.   I spun the periscope. Nothing. Putting it down, I grabbed for the extra earphones and heard it. No doubt about it, O'Brien was right. It sounded very much the same as one of our own torpedoes—the same high-pitched whine I had heard hundreds of times. It crossed our stern, came back up the starboard side, veered to the left as if to cross our bow. That was enough. My hair tingled as I thought of the secret magnetic exploder in the warheads of our torpedoes.

(*Run Silent, Run Deep*, Edward L. Beach)

4.   So let freedom ring—from the prodigious hilltops of New Hampshire, let freedom ring; from the mighty mountains of New York, let freedom ring—from the heightening Alleghenies of Pennsylvania!

Let Freedom ring from the snowcapped Rockies of Colorado. Let freedom ring from the curvaceous slopes of California! But not only that; let freedom ring from Stone Mountain of Georgia.

Let Freedom ring from every hill and mole hill of Mississippi. From every mountainside, let freedom ring.

("I Have a Dream," Martin Luther King, Jr.)

Inflection

Inflectional changes are those changes in pitch that occur within words while you're producing voice. You can think of them as being pitch glides or slides; they are done very smoothly. For example, say the word yes to mean, "Who is it?" You probably said that with a rising inflection. Now say the word no to mean "Absolutely not!" That word probably fell in pitch.

In English, we generally use rising inflection to indicate:

Questions

Incomplete series (Monday, Tuesday, Wednesday, . . .)

Doubt or uncertainty

A stressed word or syllable

We generally use falling inflection to indicate:

Ending or finality—positive statements

End of a phrase

Interrogatives (Where are you?)

A greater amount of stress

Drills for Inflection

Here are some drills for inflection. Doing these with a tape recorder or a fellow student can be helpful. Some of the following sentences have been diagrammed to indicate inflection: ⟋ means rising inflection; ⟍ means falling inflection; → means no change (level pitch). Read the sentences aloud using the inflection indicated by the marks.

Drill for Rising Inflection

Read each of the following words aloud three times, each time asking more of a question. In other words, you're going to read them with a rising pitch, and each time you read a word you're going to exaggerate; make the pitch rise more than the time before.

1. Where?⟋ Where??⟋ Where??? ⟋
2. When?⟋ When??⟋ When??? ⟋
3. Who?⟋ Who??⟋ Who??? ⟋
4. Why?⟋ Why??⟋ Why??? ⟋
5. What?⟋ What??⟋ What??? ⟋

Now read each of the following sentences three times, and each time exaggerate the rise in pitch at the end.

1. Do you have my book? Do you have my book?? Do you have my book???
2. Is that all there is? Is that all there is?? Is that all there is???
3. Are you sure? Are you sure?? Are you sure???
4. Want some coffee? Want some coffee?? Want some coffee???
5. Are we going?   Are we going??   Are we going???

Drill for Falling Inflection

Read each of the following words aloud, three times. Each time make it more of a definite, positive statement. Each time you read the statement, exaggerate the falling inflection.

1. No!   No!!   No!!!
2. Now!   Now!!   Now!!!
3. Sure!   Sure!!   Sure!!!
4. Yes!   Yes!!   Yes!!!
5. Go!   Go!!   Go!!

Now do the same with the following sentences. Read each sentence aloud three times, each time exaggerating the falling pitch more than the time before.

1. Yes, I'm sure! Yes, I'm sure!! Yes, I'm sure!!!
2. That's all there is! That's all there is!! That's all there is!!!
3. I'd like some coffee! I'd like some coffee!! I'd like some coffee!!!
4. Gosh, I'm tired! Gosh, I'm tired!! Gosh, I'm tired!!!
5. You've had it! You've had it!! You've had it!!!

There's another pattern of inflection that we call *circumflex*. It's a combination of rising and falling inflections. Here's an example: Say the word yes to indicate a conspiracy, or say the same word to show sarcasm. You probably said it with rising and falling inflections in the same utterance.

Drill for Circumflex Inflection

Say each of the following words aloud three times, each time exaggerating the rise and fall of pitch more than the time before.

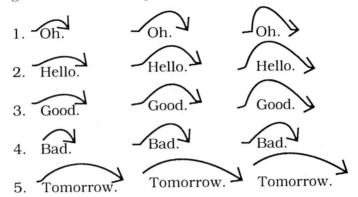

1. Oh. Oh. Oh.
2. Hello. Hello. Hello.
3. Good. Good. Good.
4. Bad. Bad. Bad.
5. Tomorrow. Tomorrow. Tomorrow.

 Practice Sentences

The following sentences contain both rising and falling inflections. Read each sentence using the pattern of inflection indicated by the arrows.

1. Here's your tea.
2. Did you go?
3. I want it now.
4. I bought some books, pens, and ink.
5. Up, up, and away.
6. Are you alone?
7. Can you say please?
8. Do you want a peach, a plum, or a pear?
9. I see.
10. Do you?

We have not marked the following sentences, nor have we provided punctuation. Mark them yourself, being as creative as you like, and then read them according to your directions.

11. Go down that road and make a left
12. Yesterday was hot humid and horrible
13. A word of advice after injury is like a dose of medicine after death

14. Never try to teach a pig to sing—it only wastes your time and makes the pig angry

15. The Greek philosopher Heraclitus said "It is not possible to step into the same river twice"

Steps

We also change pitch *between* utterances. It's an abrupt change, almost a jump, that we call a step. You make this type of change between syllables and words.

Drill for Steps

Read the following phrases and sentences aloud. The steps have been diagrammed as follows:

Example: I can jump up or down. The word *up* steps up to a higher pitch, the word *down* steps down to a lower pitch.

1. He did.
2. What time?
3. Next week.
4. On top of the desk.
5. On top of the desk.
6. The next time.
7. This is a shift.
8. Come here right now!
9. A piece of paper.
10. Do you want it?

Now, diagram the following sentences and say them aloud according to the way you have marked them.

11. Come back tomorrow.
12. Write to me.
13. Ask me a question.
14. Are you hungry?
15. Read this sentence aloud.

16. A man and a woman.
17. Let's take a walk.
18. Do you have today's paper.
19. What time is it?
20. I've got a case of new car fever.

Readings for Intonation

Read the following selections silently first, and decide on the appropriate pitch patterns to use. Plan your readings by marking the selections in advance for overall key, inflectional changes, and steps. Each selection can be read in a number of ways, so make your markings erasable.

1. Sunlight powers the world. It strikes the earth as radiant energy, and as it strikes it is changed into a bewildering variety of other forms. It lifts the waters of the oceans high above the earth, providing a store of potential energy in the clouds. It appears in awesome forms in hurricanes and lightning bolts. It is also a form of chemical energy, stored silently by the green plants of the oceans—chemical energy to be transformed in many ways to serve the energy needs of man. Each of these many pathways—whether in living or in non-living systems—conforms to the law of conservation of energy.

The flashing of a firefly on a hot summer night, the flow of electricity from the generators of Hoover Dam, the surging power of a swordfish, all conform to this same universal law.

(*Into the Ocean World*, Ritchie Ward)

2. I go down.
Rung after rung and still
the oxygen immerses me
the blue light
the clear atoms
of our human air.

I go down.
My flippers cripple me,
I crawl like an insect down the ladder
and there is no one
to tell me when the ocean
will begin.   (*more . . .*)

First the air is blue and then
it is bluer and then green and then
black I am blacking out and yet
my mask is powerful
it pumps my blood with power
the sea is another story
the sea is not a question of power
I have to learn alone
to turn my body without force
in the deep element.

("Diving into the Wreck," Adrienne Rich)

3. A single flow'r he sent me, since we met.
   All tenderly his messenger he chose;
Deep-hearted, pure, with scented dew still wet—
   One perfect rose.

I knew the language of the floweret;
   "My fragile leaves," it said, "his heart enclose."
Love long has taken for his amulet
   One perfect rose.

Why is it no one ever sent me yet
   One perfect limousine, do you suppose?
Ah no, it's always just my luck to get
   One perfect rose.

("One Perfect Rose," Dorothy Parker)

4. To every thing there is a season, and a time to every purpose under the heaven:

A time to be born, and a time to die; a time to plant, and a time to pluck up that which is planted;

A time to kill, and a time to heal; a time to break down, and a time to build up;

A time to weep, and a time to laugh; a time to mourn, and a time to dance;

A time to cast away stones, and a time to gather stones together; a time to embrace, and a time to refrain from embracing;

A time to get, and a time to lose; a time to keep, and a time to cast away;

A time to rend, and a time to sew; a time to keep silence, and a time to speak;

A time to love, and a time to hate; a time of war, and a time of peace.

(Ecclesiastes 3:1–8)

INTEGRATION

Now you can practice putting all the pieces of vocal expression together by integrating them for effective readings. We've provided a number of fiction and nonfiction selections for you to work with. We suggest that you read a piece silently first. Consider the mood, the author's purpose. Determine how you're going to emphasize stress, rate, duration, inflection, pausing, and so on. Mark your directions with arrows, slash marks, and so on the way we've shown you in this chapter. Tape record your readings. Ask for feedback from your instructor or someone in your class.

The selections are organized in three separate groups. The first is general and contains a variety of selections covering a range of materials as well as different subjects. They are all average in level of difficulty. The second group contains selections we considered to be humorous. Since humor is harder to read effectively, we consider these selections to be more difficult than the general selections. The third group is on the Challenge level. These selections may be challenging not only because they have unusual requirements for vocal variety but also because they may contain difficult-to-produce sounds or sounds in intricate combinations.

General

Those who say that we're in a time when there are no heroes—they just don't know where to look. You can see heroes every day going in and out of factory gates. Others, a handful in number, produce enough food to feed all of us and then the world beyond.

You meet heroes across a counter—and they're on both sides of that counter. There are entrepreneurs with faith in themselves and faith in an idea who create new jobs, new wealth and opportunity.

There are individuals and families whose taxes support

the Government and whose voluntary gifts support church, charity, culture, art and education. Their patriotism is quiet but deep. Their values sustain our national life.

(Inaugural Address, Ronald Reagan)

My Fellow Citizens: We observe today not a victory of party but a celebration of freedom—symbolizing an end as well as a beginning—signifying renewal as well as change. For I have sworn before you and almighty God the same solemn oath our forebears prescribed nearly a century and three-quarters ago.

The world is very different now. For man holds in his mortal hands the power to abolish all forms of human poverty and all forms of human life. And yet the same revolutionary beliefs for which our forebearers fought are still at issue around the globe—the belief that the rights of man come not from the generosity of the state but from the hand of God.

We dare not forget today that we are the heirs of that first revolution. Let the word go forth from this time and place, to friend and foe alike, that the torch has been passed to a new generation of Americans—born in this century, tempered by war, disciplined by a hard and bitter peace, proud of our ancient heritage—and unwilling to witness or permit the slow undoing of those human rights to which this nation has always been committed, and to which we are committed today at home and around the world.

Let every nation know, whether it wishes us well or ill, that we shall pay any price, bear any burden, meet any hardship, support any friend, oppose any foe in order to assure the survival and success of liberty.

This much we pledge—and more.

(Inaugural Address, John F. Kennedy)

I looked out over the beautiful expanse, bathed in soft yellow moonlight till it was almost as light as day. In the soft light the distant hills became melted, and the shadows in the valleys and gorges of velvety blackness. The mere beauty seemed to cheer me; there was peace and comfort in every breath I drew. As I leaned from the window my eye was caught by something moving a storey below me, and somewhat to my left, where I imagined, from the lie of the rooms, that the windows of the Count's own room would look out. The window at which I stood was tall and deep, stone-mullioned, and though weather-worn, was still complete; but it was evidently many a day since the case had been there. I drew back behind the stonework, and looked carefully out.

What I saw was the Count's head coming out from the window. I did not see the face, but I knew the man by the neck and the movement of his back and arms. In any case I could not mistake the hands which I had had so many opportunities of studying. I was at first interested and somewhat amused, for it is wonderful how small a matter will interest and amuse a man when he is a prisoner. But my very feelings changed to repulsion and terror when I saw the whole man slowly emerge from the window and begin to crawl down the castle wall over that dreadful abyss, *face down*, with his cloak spreading out around him like great wings. At first I could not believe my eyes, I thought it was some trick of the moonlight, some weird effect of shadow; but I kept looking and it could be no delusion. I saw the fingers and toes grasp the corners of the stones, worn clear of the mortar by the stress of years, and by thus using every projection and inequality move downwards with considerable speed, just as a lizard moves along a wall.

What manner of man is this, or what manner of creature is it in the semblance of man? I feel the dread of this horrible place overpowering me; I am in fear—in awful fear—and there is no escape for me.

(*Dracula*, Bram Stoker)

. . . With tingling nerves but a fixed purpos , I sat in the dark recess of the hut and waited with sombre patience for the coming of its tenant.

And then at last I heard him. Far away came the sharp clink of a boot striking upon a stone. Then another and yet another, coming nearer and nearer. I shrank back into the darkest corner and cocked the pistol in my pocket, determined not to discover myself until I had an opportunity of seeing something of the stranger. There was a long pause which showed that he had stopped. Then once more the footsteps approached and a shadow fell across the opening of the hut.   (*more . . .*)

"It is a lovely evening, my dear Watson," said a well known voice. "I really think that you will be more comfortable outside than in."

(*The Hound of the Baskervilles*, Sir Arthur Conan Doyle)

Willie staggered out past the captain to the open wing. The wind immediately smashed him against the bridge-house, and spray pelted him like small wet stones. He was astounded and peculiarly exhilarated to realize that in the last fifteen minutes the wind had actually become much stronger than before, and would blow him over the side if he exposed himself in a clear space. He laughed aloud, his voice thin against the gutteral "Whooeeee!" of the storm. He inched himself to the door of the radar shack, freed the dogs, and tried to pull the door open, but the wind held it tightly shut. He pounded on the wet steel with his knuckles, and kicked at it, and screamed, "Open up! Open up!"

(*The Caine Mutiny*, Herman Wouk)

The tide rises, the tide falls,
The twilight darkens, the curlew calls;
Along the sea-sands damp and brown
The traveller hastens toward the town,
  And the tide rises, the tide falls.

Darkness settles on roofs and walls,
But the sea, the sea in the darkness calls;
The little waves, with their soft, white hands,
Efface the footprints in the sands,
  And the tide rises, the tide falls.

The morning breaks; the steeds in their stalls
Stamp and neigh, as the hostler calls;
The day returns, but nevermore
Returns the traveller to the shore,
  And the tide rises, the tide falls.

("The Tide Rises, The Tide Falls," Henry Wadsworth Longfellow)

He walked back to the wing, leaned against the windshield, and looked out at the sea and the night; and for the first time he noticed what an incredible night it was. The moon—what an enormous moon! It had risen yellow and round and fat, and now that it was higher it had shrunk a little, but still it was round and full, and no longer yellow, but molten, incandescent silver. The light it spread was daylight with the harshness filtered out, unbelievably pure and even and dimensionless. On the bridge you could have read a newspaper: it was that bright. The moon now was on the port quarter and all the way to the horizon it parted the water in a wide, white glistening path that hurt the eyes; and back where the horizon should be there was really none at all, there was only this pale blue, shimmering haze where sky and water merged without a discernible break. And the sea was even more remarkable: Roberts had never seen the sea quite like this. There wasn't a ripple anywhere; there was only the faintest hint of a ground swell, an occasional bulge of water. The surface, glazed as it was with moonlight, looked heavy, coated, enameled: it was that perfect. The ship slid through the water with an oily hiss, and the bow cut the fabric like a casual knife. At the stern, the wake was a wide, frothing rent, but farther back it was healing and not so wide, and far, far back the fabric was whole and perfect again.

(*Mister Roberts*, Thomas Heggen)

The people will live on.
The learning and blundering people will live on.
They will be tricked and sold and again sold
And go back to the nourishing earth for rootholds,
The people so peculiar in renewal and comeback,
You can't laugh off their capacity to take it.
The mammoth rests between his cyclonic dramas.

The people so often sleepy, weary, enigmatic,
is a vast huddle with many units saying:
"I earn my living.
I make enough to get by
and it takes all my time.
If I had more time
I could do more for myself
and maybe for others.
I could read and study
and talk things over
and find out about things.
It takes time.
I wish I had the time."

(more . . .)

The people is a tragic and comic two-face:
hero and hoodlum: phantom and gorilla twisting to
moan with a gargoyle mouth: "They buy me and
and sell me . . . it's a game . . .
sometime I'll break loose . . ."

("The People, Yes," Carl Sandburg)

The yellow fog that rubs its back upon the window-
panes.
The yellow smoke that rubs its muzzle on the window-
panes,
Licked its tongue into the corners of the evening,
Lingered upon the pools that stand in drains,
Let fall upon its back the soot that falls from chimneys,
Slipped by the terrace, made a sudden leap,
And seeing that it was a soft October night,
Curled once about the house, and fell asleep.

("The Love Song of J. Alfred Prufrock," T. S. Eliot)

In the blue night
frost haze, the sky glows
with the moon
pine tree tops
bend snow-blue, fade
into sky, frost, starlight.
The creak of boots.
Rabbit tracks, deer tracks,
what do we know.

("Pine Tree Tops," Gary Snyder)

Humorous

The sign over a Brooklyn, New York, café reads "Warm Beer—Lousy Food." Hardly inviting at first glance, but after an involuntary double take, one somehow gets a strong feeling that the beer must really be super-cold and the food terrific. It's artful psychology: Aren't chances better you'll remember that place than if its sign read simply, "Cold Beer—Good Food"?

And who couldn't admire the play on words of the Recovery Room, a Salt Lake City upholstery shop, or the San

Francisco eatery specializing in hot dogs called Franks for the Memory. Then there's an auto-rental agency in Mahopac, New York, whose sign hints at a famous movie title: Chariots for Hire.

Unlike their counterparts in most foreign countries, American merchants love to inject humor and sparkle when naming their places of business. All over the United States dealers in products and services have coined odd-ball names for their companies in an effort to make them stand out.

("Sign and Pun-ishment," Fred L. Schroder)

Note from Our Upper West Side Acquaintance With Car:

Justice sometimes does triumph in our town, mostly when least expected. Returning from a weekend in the country the other evening, I found a rare parking space on Central Park West at 68th Street. But just as I was backing into it, another motorist made a lightning U-turn from the other side of the street and stole it away.

Furious, I got out of my car and walked over to his. He was an overwrought yuppie type, the kind Richard Benjamin played some years ago in "Diary of a Mad Housewife." Cheered on by a sidewalk voyeur, I yelled, "That was a rotten thing to do. It was my space and you know it!"

He hollered back: "I was on my way to it before you saw it. And besides, I'm in a big hurry!"

About to give this apology the retort it deserved, I became aware that a large horse had sidled up to me. Astride it was—oh joy of joys!—a policeman. Said the cop to the yuppie: "Show me your license and registration." The yuppie wound up with a summons not only for making an illegal U-turn, but also for not wearing his seat belt.

Deeming it unseemly to gloat in public, I got back into my car, laid my head on the steering wheel and laughed for four delicious minutes. The yuppie got to keep the space, but I blithely wheeled away and found a new one.

(Ron Alexander, "Metropolitan Diary," *The New York Times,* August 24, 1988)

When Radar O'Reilly, just out of high school, left Ottumwa, Iowa, and enlisted in the United States Army it was with the express purpose of making a career of the Signal Corps. Radar O'Reilly was only five feet three inches tall, but he had a long, thin neck and large ears that left his head at perfect right angles. Furthermore, under certain atmospheric, as well as metabolic conditions, and by enforcing complete concentration and invoking unique extra-sensory powers, he was able to receive messages and monitor conversations far beyond the usual range of human hearing.

With this to his advantage, it seemed to Radar O'Reilly that he was a natural for the communications branch of the service, and so, following graduation, he turned down various highly attractive business opportunities, some of them legitimate, and decided to serve his country.

Before his enlistment, in fact, he used to fall asleep at night watching a whole succession of, first, sleeve stripes, and then shoulder insignia, floating by until he would see himself, with four stars on his shoulders, conducting high-level Pentagon briefings, attending White House dinner parties and striding imperiously to ringside tables in New York night clubs.

In the middle of November of the year 1951 A.D., Radar O'Reilly, a corporal in the United States Army Medical Corps, was sitting in the Painless Polish Poker and Dental Clinic of the 4077th Mobile Army Surgical Hospital astride the 38th Parallel in South Korea, ostensibly trying to fill a straight flush.

(*M*A*S*H**, Richard Hooker)

My son, Jaws II, had a habit that drove me crazy. He'd walk to the refrigerator-freezer and fling both doors open and stand there until the hairs in his nose iced up. After surveying two hundred dollars' worth of food in varying shapes and forms he would declare loudly "There's nothing to eat."

(*Aunt Erma's Cope Book*, Erma Bombeck)

Economic Theory: A systematic application and critical evaluation of the basic analytic concepts of economic theory, with emphasis on money and why it's good. Fixed coefficient production functions, cost and supply curves, and nonconvexity comprise the first semester, with the second semester concentrating on spending, making change, and keeping a neat wallet. The Federal Reserve System is analyzed, and advanced students are coached in the proper method of filling out a deposit slip. Other topics include: Inflation and Depression—how to dress for each. Loans, interest, welching.

(*Getting Even*, Woody Allen)

At the age of fifteen Doug and Dinsdale started attending the Ernest Pythagoras Primary School in Clerkenwell. When the Piranhas left school they were called up but were found by an Army Board to be too mentally unstable even for National Service. Denied the opportunity to use their talents in the service of their country, they began to operate what they called "The Operation." . . . They would select a victim and threaten to beat him up if he paid them the so-called protection money. Four months later they started another operation which they called, "The Other Operation." In this racket they selected another victim and threatened not to beat him up if he didn't pay them. One month later they hit upon "The Other Other Operation." In this the victim was threatened that if he didn't pay them, they would beat him up. This for the Piranha brothers was the turning point.

(*Monty Python's Big Red Book*)

There is no question that there is an unseen world. The problem is, how far is it from midtown and how late is it open? Unexplainable events occur constantly. One man will see spirits. Another will hear voices. A third will wake up and find himself running in the Preakness. How many of us have not at one time or another felt an ice-cold hand on the back of our neck while we were home alone? (Not me, thank God, but some have.) What is behind these experiences? Or in front of them, for that matter? Is it true that some men can foresee the future or communicate with ghosts? And after death is it still possible to take showers?

(*Without Feathers*, Woody Allen)

Oh, the slimy, squirmy, slithery eel!
He swallows your hook with malignant zeal,
He tangles your line and he gums your reel,
The slimy, squirmy, slithery eel.   (*more . . .*)

Oh, the slimy, squirmy, slithery eel!
He cannot be held in a grip of steel,
And when he is dead he is hard to peel,
The slimy, squirmy, slithery eel.

Oh, the slimy, squirmy, slithery eel!
The sorriest catch in the angler's creel;
Who said he was fit for a Christian meal—
The slimy, squirmy, slithery eel!

Oh, the slimy, squirmy, slithery eel!
Malevolent serpent! who dares reveal
What eloquent fishermen say and feel
Concerning the slithery, slimy eel?

("Song of Hate for Eels," Arthur Guiterman)

I want something suited to my special needs
I want chrome hubcaps, pin-on attachments
and year round use year after year
I want a workhorse with smooth uniform cut,
dozer blade and snow blade & deluxe steering
wheel
I want something to mow, throw snow, tow, and sow
with
I want precision reel blades
I want a console-styled dashboard
I want an easy spintype recoil starter
I want combination bevel and spur gears, 14
gauge stamped steel housing and
washable foam element air cleaner
I want a pivoting front axle and extrawide turf tires
I want an inch of foam rubber inside a vinyl
covering
and especially if it's not too much, if I
can deserve it, even if I can't pay for it
I want to mow while riding

("Needs," A. R. Ammons)

THERE COMES A TIME in every man's life when, if he
is in Las Vegas alone, he has to call his wife—collect. The
moment came earlier for me than I expected, and the call
went something like this.

"Hello, dear," I said. "I'm calling from Las Vegas."

"I know where you're calling from," she said, the bitterness seeping through the receiver. "What did you do last night?"

"I had a date with a show girl," I told her.

"Don't lie to me. You were gambling."

"Just a little. Nothing much."

"How much did you lose?"

"I love you," I told her.

"I said how much did you lose?"

"I didn't call to talk about that. I called to talk about the children."

"What about the children?" she wanted to know.

"Why do they have to go to college when they grow up? Lots of children don't go to college and turn out to be wonderful parents."

"You didn't lose their college money?" she screamed.

"Only their junior and senior years."

"What else did you lose?"

"Where are you standing now?"

"In our bedroom," she replied.

"Please don't say 'our' bedroom any more."

"You didn't lose the house?" she asked incredulously.

"Just parts of it. I kept title to the basement and the garage."

I could hear sobbing on the other end of the line.

"Now, wait a minute, dear. You said the house was too big for us anyway and you would prefer something smaller. Think of it as a lucky break. Dear, are you there?"

"Yes, I'm here."

"Do me a favor. You know that gold necklace with the pearls I bought you for our anniversary?"

"You lost that?"

"Of course not. Do you think I would do something that low?"

"Well, what about the necklace?"

"I want you to go out and lose it somewhere so we can collect the insurance on it. We'll get a much better price than if we try to sell it."

"I could kill you," she said.

"Don't. It would be a mistake."   *(more . . .)*

"You mean you lost your life insurance, too?"

"They told me a man who plays the way I do will live forever."

"Well, at least you didn't lose my fur coat."

I didn't say anything.

"You *did* lose my fur coat?"

"Who wears a fur coat in Washington?" I replied.

"When are you coming home?"

"That's what I called about. There's a Greyhound bus leaving for Washington at three this afternoon, and if you send me the money I left you for food I'll be on it."

"And what are we going to eat until you get here?"

"Call up the Department of Agriculture. According to the law we're entitled to participate in their surplus food program."

("Collect Call from Las Vegas," in *I Chose Capitol Punishment,*
Art Buchwald)

The coyote is a long, slim, sick and sorry-looking skeleton, with a gray wolf-skin stretched over it, a tolerably bushy tail that forever sags down with a despairing expression of forsakeness and misery, a furtive and evil eye, and a long, sharp face, with slightly lifted lip and exposed teeth. He has a general slinking expression all over. The coyote is a living, breathing allegory of Want. He is *always* hungry. He is always poor, out of luck and friendless. The meanest creatures despise him, and even the fleas would desert him for a velocipede. He is so spiritless and cowardly that even while his exposed teeth are pretending a threat, the rest of his face is apologizing for it. And he is *so* homely!—so scrawny, and ribby, and coarse-haired, and pitiful. When he sees you he lifts his lip and lets a flash of his teeth out, and then turns a little out of the course he was pursuing, depresses his head a bit, and strikes a long, soft-footed trot through the sage-brush, glancing over his shoulder at you, from time to time, till he is about out of easy pistol range, and then he stops and takes a deliberate survey of you; he will trot fifty yards and stop again—another fifty and stop again; and finally the gray of his gliding body blends with the gray of the sage-brush, and he disappears.

(Mark Twain, *Roughing It*)

Challenge

Scientists, like other human beings, have their hopes and fears, their passions and despondencies—and their strong emotions may sometimes interrupt the course of clear thinking and sound practice. But science is also self-correcting. The most fundamental axioms and conclusions may be challenged. The prevailing hypothesis must survive confrontation with observation. Appeals to authority are impermissible. The steps in a reasoned argument must be set out for all to see. Experiments must be reproducible.

(*Broca's Brain*, Carl Sagan)

The plover begin gathering in August. Small flocks of goldens and black-bellieds stand near each other at the ends of sand bars, or cluster on the mud flats at low tide. When clammers approach, the birds take wing, circling, and the crystal whistle of their calls echoes across the marsh—a pure and lonely sound that is Autumn's earliest prelude.

(*Striper*, John N. Cole)

An eel pot or trap is a cylindrical container made of cellar window wire or hardware cloth, about thirty inches long and eight to ten inches in diameter. It has a twine head, called variously a ''funnel'' or ''nozzle,'' at the front end, tied back inside and as wide open as possible. About a third of the way back is another. This one is tied so that the narrow mouth or throat can be pushed open from the front and yet leave no opening apparent when the eel has gone through into the back end or parlor. The head at the far end is tied tight with a pucker string.

(*Cape Cod Fisherman*, Phil Schwind)

. . . and then came, for the hundredth time, the story of his coming ashore at New York, from the *Constellation* frigate, after a cruise of four years round the Horn, —being paid off with over five hundred dollars, —marrying, and taking a couple of rooms in a four-story house, —furnishing the rooms, (with a particular account of the furniture, including a dozen flag-bottomed chairs, which he always dilated upon, whenever the subject of furniture was alluded to,) —going off to sea again, leaving his wife half-pay, like a fool, —coming home and finding her "off, like Bob's horse, with nobody to pay the reckoning"; furniture gone, —flag-bottomed chairs and all; —and with it, his"long togs," the half-pay, his beaver hat, white linen shirts, and everything else.

(*Two Years Before the Mast*, Richard Henry Dana, Jr.)

Engine tune-up is a procedure performed to restore engine performance, deteriorated due to normal wear and loss of adjustment. The three major areas considered in a routine tune-up are compression, ignition, and carburetion, although valve adjustment may be included.

A tune-up is performed in three steps: *analysis*, in which it is determined whether normal wear is responsible for performance loss, and which parts require replacement or service; *parts replacement* or *service*; and *adjustment*, in which engine adjustments are returned to original specifications. Since the advent of emission control equipment, precision adjustment has become increasingly critical, in order to maintain pollutant emission levels.

(*Chilton's Repair & Tune-Up Guide*)

The gas industry continues to forge ahead. The uncertainties of supply that plagued the industry from 1974 until recently have been largely eliminated. Our industry increased gas reserves dramatically last year and the number of wells drilled in 1980 is at an all-time high. There is every reason to believe that higher wellhead prices have stimulated production activity as was anticipated. Canadian and Mexican supplies of gas are increasing and more gas is available to United States users than can be marketed, primarily due to the price of these supplies. The projection of annual supply available to meet the demand by the year 2000 ranges from 23 trillion cubic feet to 33 trillion cubic feet. However, it is clear that the supply can be made available and represents the least-cost energy option for America. The variable part of the demand curve will be largely industrial and will depend a great deal upon governmental policies.

(Annual Report, National Fuel Gas Company)

Jennie: I am sick and tired of running from places and people and relationships. . . . And don't tell me what I want because *I'll* tell you what I want. I want a home and I want a family—and I want a career, too. And I want a dog and I want a cat and I want three goldfish. I want *everything!* There's no harm in wanting it, George, because there's not a chance in hell we're going to get it all, anyway. But if you don't *want* it, you've got even less chance than that. . . .

(*Chapter Two*, Neil Simon)

Mel: You don't know the first thing I'm talking about. . . . You don't know what it is to be in my place. . . . You've never stood on line for two hours waiting for an unemployment check with a shirt and tie, trying to look like you don't need the money. And some fat old dame behind the counter screaming out so everyone can hear, *"Did you look for a job this week?"* "Yes, I looked for a job." *"Did you turn down any work this week?"* "What the hell am I doing here if I turned down work this week?" . . . You never walked into your building and had a ninety-one-year-old doorman with no teeth, asthma and beer on his breath giggle at you because *he's* working. . . .

(*The Prisoner of Second Avenue*, Neil Simon)

You have seen him a thousand times. You have seen him standing on the street corner on Saturday afternoon, in the little county-seat towns. He wears blue jean pants, or overalls washed to a pale pastel blue like the color of sky after a shower in spring, but because it is Saturday he has on a wool coat, an old one, perhaps the coat left from the suit he got married in a long time back. His long wrist bones hang out from the sleeves of the coat, the tendons showing along the bone like the dry twist of grapevine still corded on the stove-length of a hickory sapling you would find in his wood box beside his cookstove among the split chunks of gum and red oak. The big hands, with the knotted, cracked joints and the square, horn-thick nails, hang loose off the wrist bone like clumsy, homemade tools hung on the wall of a shed after work. If it is summer, he wears a straw hat with a wide brim, the straw fraying loose around the edge. If it is winter, he wears a felt hat, black once, but now weathered with streaks of dark gray and dull purple in the sunlight. His face is long and bony, the jawbone long under the drawn-in cheeks. The flesh along the jawbone is nicked in a couple of places where the unaccustomed razor has been drawn over the leather-coarse skin. A tiny bit of blood crusts brown where the nick is. The color of the face is red, a dull red like the red clay mud or clay dust which clings to the bottom of his pants and to the cast-iron-looking brogans on his feet, or a red like the color of a piece of hewed cedar which has been left in the weather. The face does not look alive. It seems to be molded from the clay or hewed from the cedar. When the jaw moves, once, with its deliberate, massive motion on the quid of tobacco, you are still not convinced. That motion is but the cunning triumph of a mechanism concealed within.

But you see the eyes. You see that the eyes are alive. They are pale blue or gray, set back under the deep brows and thorny eyebrows. They are not wide, but are squinched up like eyes accustomed to wind or sun or to measuring the stroke of the ax or to fixing the object over the rifle sights. When you pass, you see that the eyes are alive and are warily and dispassionately estimating you from the ambush of the thorny brows. Then you pass on, and he stands there in that stillness which is his gift.

(*The Patented Gate and the Mean Hamburger*, Robert Penn Warren)

A Appendix A

Dealing with Nervousness

When you first started reading this book, you probably thought about the future; you, making an oral presentation, in front of an audience. You also may have thought back to a time you made a presentation in another class or appeared in a school play. As you thought about those occasions, chances are strange things began to happen to you: your mouth may have begun to feel dry, your stomach a bit shaky, and your hands slightly sweaty and cold. What was happening? You were feeling some of the symptoms of stagefright.

Stagefright goes by a number of names. Some of the more common ones are speechfright, speech anxiety, and just plain nervousness. Whatever we call it, the fact remains that it is the single biggest problem students face in speech classes. Every year in our freshman speech courses we meet graduating seniors who have delayed taking the course for four whole years simply because of their stagefright. Each student, you see, is usually convinced that he or she is the only one with stagefright and is, therefore, abnormal. Since most people believe that stagefright indicates some kind of flaw in a person's personality, a devastating cycle begins: people become *afraid of their stagefright.* Each time they must speak in front of an audience, they get nervous; their nervousness causes them to make the mistakes they were afraid of making, which causes them to be at least as nervous the next time they must speak to an audience.

One of the reasons stagefright is such a problem is that people avoid talking about it; no one wants to admit that he or she has stagefright. We've learned a lot about stagefright over the years, and we would like to share some of what we've learned with you. Let's start by separating fact from fiction.

Fiction: stagefright is abnormal.

Fact: stagefright is normal; almost everyone has it.

Other than those related to health and safety, what's the #1 fear in the nation? That's right; stagefright! Numerous surveys of inexperienced speakers show that, on the average, 75 percent admit to having stagefright and more than 35 percent think it's a serious problem. Surprisingly, stagefright is also considered to be a problem by about 76 percent of experienced speakers—lecturers, politicians, and business people. Those who perform for a living also have stagefright. In a recent *TV Guide* article, Olivia Newton-John told how her stagefright leaves her shaking and crying before a performance. And Jane Fonda has admitted to having "tremendous fear," a sentiment echoed by Sir Laurence Olivier, and many others.

The point we're trying to make is that *stagefright is perfectly normal!* It's so normal, in fact, many speech experts feel that the person who does not have stagefright should be considered *abnormal.*

Fiction: stagefright is always harmful.

Fact: stagefright can be helpful.

You may be surprised to learn that stagefright can actually help you give a better performance. It's true! When you feel the symptoms of stagefright, you become more alert and alive, and you may be better able to listen and adjust to the situation. You are also more "up" and may appear more eager and involved in getting your message across to your listeners. If you don't have stagefright, you run the risk of putting your audience to sleep.

Fiction: stagefright should be eliminated.

Fact: you should understand, expect, accept, control, and use stagefright to make yourself a more effective speaker.

Before we can tell you how to effectively deal with your stage-fright, we should see what stagefright is, what causes it, and how it works.

STAGEFRIGHT DEFINED

Stagefright is a normal state of anxiety and arousal; a combination of fear and excitement. Stagefright usually occurs when you are facing a speaking situation that has an unpredictable outcome. Naturally, the situation that comes to mind is presenting to an audience, but there are other situations in which you may experience stagefright. It's quite common in job interviews, telephone calls, business meetings, class-room reports, club announcements, even meeting your prospective in-laws. What is the ratio of anxiety to arousal in the stagefright you experience at a given moment? It will vary depending on you, the particular situation, and a number of other factors that we will explain in the balance of the chapter.

WHAT CAUSES STAGEFRIGHT?

Stagefright is a speaker's response to a "fight or flight" situation. Here's an example of such a situation. You're taking a walk in the woods on a pleasant autumn afternoon. Strolling around the base of a huge tree, you get the shock of your life! Suddenly, unexpectedly, you come face to face with a giant, hungry, growling grizzly bear! What are you going to do? Whatever you do, you probably won't stop to think about it because at this point your body goes on "automatic pilot." It reacts automatically to prepare itself to either fight the bear or run away as far as is humanly possible. A number of things happen very quickly: your muscles tense; your heartbeat and breathing speed up; glands in your body begin to secrete essential fluids.

Bodily functions that are usually controlled voluntarily are now running on pure emotion. You act now, think later. And you may not become aware of your actions until *after* they have occurred. The mother of one of the authors surprised a burglar in her home in the middle of the night. She bodily threw him out of the house and then sat trembling by the phone for two hours before she could control herself enough to call the police.

The same kind of situation can occur in speech. You may face an audience and experience fear for any number of reasons. Your body interprets the feelings of fear to mean you are facing a real physical threat, such as the bear in the forest or the burglar in the house. As a result, your "automatic pilot" prepares your body to either fight the audience or run away from it, and your mind no longer controls what your body does.

THE PHYSICAL SYMPTOMS OF STAGEFRIGHT

The symptoms of stagefright are easily explained, once you understand what causes it. They all relate to the fact that your body is ready to run or fight. Not everyone experiences all the symptoms, and the symptoms may vary from situation to situation. Which symptoms in the following list of stagefright symptoms have you experienced?

Butterflies in the Stomach

This is one of the first symptoms. Energy in your body needs to be pumped to those parts that are going to get it out of danger. Since the process of digestion requires a lot of energy, that process halts and energy is diverted to the arms and legs. The food you've eaten just sits in your stomach, undigested, until the danger is past.

Dry Mouth

The process of digestion begins in the mouth with the secretion of saliva. Since saliva production has been halted, too, your mouth becomes very dry. And it does not matter how much water you drink; it stays dry.

Rapid Breathing

Increased energy demands mean an increased need for oxygen, so your breathing speeds up accordingly.

Rapid Heart Rate

The heart must circulate the blood through the body more quickly in order to distribute oxygen to the skeletal muscles you'll use in running or fighting.

Trembling Hands, Weak Knees, Unsteady Voice

Almost all your skeletal muscles are under tension. As a result, they begin to tremble. Voice production is controlled by skeletal muscles, too, and you can hear the results of the excess tension.

Perspiration

Even though your mouth becomes dry, your body becomes increasingly wet with perspiration. This is simply an attempt to control body temperature. Because there is more blood circulating near the surface of the body, there is more body heat. Your body sends perspiration to the surface, and as the perspiration evaporates, it cools your body.

These symptoms are the ones most commonly experienced in stagefright. We're sure you can add some of your own to the list.

WHAT CAN YOU DO ABOUT STAGEFRIGHT?

For most people, the symptoms of stagefright can be quite unnerving. Think back to the first time you can remember experiencing stagefright. What frightened you more, the speaking itself or the fact that your body was doing strange, terrible things to you?

The point is this: if you don't understand what's happening to you, more fear can develop. In other words, *stagefright can be fear of fear!*

Let's repeat what we said earlier: you shouldn't try to eliminate stagefright. Instead, you should *understand it, expect it, accept it, control it,* and *use it* to make you a more effective speaker. Don't expect that your fear is going to magically vanish once you learn its secrets. If you think you can be *totally* free from stagefright, you're probably setting yourself up for failure.

Dealing with stagefright involves three treatment stages: long-term, short-term, and what we call "first aid."

Long-term Treatments

UNDERSTAND YOUR STAGEFRIGHT

By learning about the causes and symptoms of stagefright, you take away the fear of the unknown. When you realize that stagefright is perfectly normal, you remove a lot of unnecessary doubt about your sanity.

TALK ABOUT STAGEFRIGHT

Think about times you've had stagefright. Discuss those times with someone who is close to you. You'll find that talking it over clears up some of the mystery about it. You'll also find that the person with whom you're talking will want to share similar experiences with you.

BE REALISTIC ABOUT THE SITUATION

Remember that your audience is nothing like the imaginary bear you faced in the woods. The audience can't cause you any physical harm. In fact, most audiences and listeners are genuinely interested in what you have to say, and they want you to do well. That's especially true in speech classes, where your fellow students would rather listen to you than think about their own cases of stagefright.

PUT THINGS IN PERSPECTIVE

One way to put things in perspective is to play the game we call, "What's the worst that can happen?" Here's what we mean; imagine that when you get up to read in front of the class today, you're going to make a mistake. The professor is going to flunk you, your grade average will drop below 2.00, and you'll be dismissed from college. You probably won't be able to get a job without a college degree and you won't be eligible to collect unemployment. Your parents will throw you out of the house, and then you'll be forced to beg for food in the streets. All because of this one speech assignment.

When playing this game, let your imagination run wild. The result will make your fears seem kind of silly. Once you are able to poke fun at your fears, they will no longer seem more important than they really are.

DEVELOP REALISTIC EXPECTATIONS

The reasons we have heard over the years as to why people are "nervous" about speaking in front of a class tend to fall into two categories: *realistic* and *unrealistic*. Those that are realistic ("I won't be adequately prepared," is a popular one) can be dealt with in realistic ways, and are usually not major problems. The unrealistic fears, strangely enough, cause most of the problems, and cause people to anticipate speaking situations with dread. One such common fear has to do with using notes: "If I have to stop speaking for a moment to collect my thoughts or look at my notes, those one or two seconds of silence will be fatal." The truth of the matter is that, although a few seconds may feel like an eternity to you, they will go largely unnoticed by your listeners. In fact, your listeners may appreciate the opportunity to digest what you're saying, or may think that you've paused for dramatic effect.

Another unrealistic fear has to do with setting standards: "People will be judging me and therefore I can't make any mistakes." Unfortunately, for years most of us have received the message that the only acceptable behavior in an educational setting is perfection. While this may be an appropriate expectation in subject areas where we deal with factual, concrete bits of information, it is not appropriate in areas that deal with human behavior. We believe it is quite unreasonable, even impossible, to expect perfection in any skill. If you were to listen to any number of educated people talk, even professional presenters, you would hear all kinds of behaviors that could be labeled as *non-fluencies*: repeating all or parts of words, hesitating, interjecting sounds like "um," "er," and "like," and even distorting some speech sounds. Although you wouldn't deliberately go out of your way to use them, these are all *normal* aspects of speech behavior. To help you recognize and deal with unrealistic fears about speaking, try the activities below.

Activities

1. Pick a few people you believe to be effective speakers. Listen to their speech. We're sure you can find some of the non-fluencies we described above. Are these behaviors disruptive to the speakers' communication? Probably not. Under most circumstances, you wouldn't even notice most of them.

2. While you are having a conversation with a friend or classmate, deliberately pause for a couple of seconds between phrases or sentences. See if the other person is aware of anything different. If not, lengthen the pauses until the other person notices. You'll be surprised how long a "normal" pause can be.

3. Imagine that you are explaining something to one person. That wouldn't produce too much anxiety, would it? Now, imagine explaining the same thing to two people. That probably wouldn't be any more stressful than with one person. Now, explain to three people. Then four people, then five, and so on. Continue until you reach the number at which you would feel that the situation is becoming stressful. What is that number? Ask yourself why that number of people would be stressful when one person less would not. Can you come up with any acceptable reason?

Now, ask yourself, please, to allow into the group just one more person without getting uptight. Imagine yourself talking to that number of people. Is it getting easier? Repeat this exercise, adding just one more person each time until you reach your absolute limit.

GAIN AS MUCH EXPERIENCE AS POSSIBLE

Try to speak before an audience as often as you can, in as many different types of situations as you can. There are many opportunities for you to make brief presentations where you can "get the feel" of talking to a group. For example, you could make an oral report in one of your classes, introduce a speaker at a seminar, participate in a debate, or speak up at a Board of Education meeting or some other form of public hearing. Each time you speak, you'll feel a little more confident. Experience is really the best teacher.

LEARN TO RELAX

We're sure that, at one time or another, someone has told you to "Relax!" We're also sure that you found it to be easier said than done. You may not be surprised to learn that many people have difficulty deliberately relaxing in stressful situations, but you may be surprised to know that you can *learn* to relax. You can break through much of the tension related to stagefright by regularly practicing a few relaxation exercises.

Because these exercises are also useful when working on breathing for speech, we've placed them in Chapter 7:

Progressive relaxation:	Page 265
Fantasy:	Page 265
Head rolling:	Page 266
Sighing:	Page 266
Yawning:	Page 267

After some consistent practice, you should be able to spend a few minutes getting yourself quickly into a relaxed physical and mental state. Then you'll be able to present yourself and your material in a more confident and effective way.

VISUALIZE YOUR PRESENTATION

Athletes routinely use the technique of *visualization* not only to help them feel more confident, but to actually improve performance. You don't need the type of training that a sports psychologist would administer to use visualization to reduce your nervousness about speaking; the technique is simple.

With your eyes closed, picture yourself getting up to speak and walking to the lectern, podium, or table where your notes will be. Then imagine yourself making your presentation, step by step, point by point, making eye contact with your listeners, gesturing, and moving your body. Imagine that you can hear your voice: loud, strong, and confident. Then imagine the end of the presentation (with applause or congratulations, if appropriate), walking back to your seat, and sitting down.

You can vary your visualizations to fit the specific situation and setting, but the result won't change; your visualization of success will make you feel more confident.

Short-term Treatments

BE PREPARED

Know what you're doing, and you'll feel much more confident and more at ease. Don't worry about how you look or sound; you'll find that your memory seems better and that ideas and words flow more smoothly.

PRACTICE, PRACTICE, PRACTICE!

By "practice" we don't mean a silent reading; we mean saying the words out loud! If you don't practice out loud, you won't have much confidence in yourself. How many times should you practice? There's no magic number; just practice as much as you feel you need. Try to practice in front of another person to get the feeling of saying the words to someone other than yourself. Pick someone who can be objective. We don't recommend brothers or sisters for this because they usually delight in making you feel even worse (if that's possible). If no one is available, use a mirror. And don't forget your trusty tape recorder; it doesn't lie.

Don't practice on the day of your presentation. Chances are you'll be more nervous than usual that day. Nervousness causes errors that cause more nervousness, causing even more errors, causing even more nervousness, causing . . . and so on, reducing you to a mass of quivering jelly. We recommend that your last practice session be on the night before you're due to talk. Last minute preparations really don't help at all.

TALK ABOUT WHAT'S HAPPENING NOW

Explain to yourself, or to others, what's happening to your body. For example, when you feel the first symptoms of stagefright, you might say, "Oh-oh, my mouth is starting to feel dry, and my tongue is like a big ball of cotton. I guess that means my digestion is starting to slow down. Yup, I must be right; I can feel some butterflies starting to fly. I wish I hadn't eaten that pepperoni pizza for lunch. Now my hands are beginning to sweat, and I can feel a slight trembling in my knees. I guess I'm caught in an approach-avoidance conflict. Let's see, what's going to come next? I should start to feel my heart pounding . . . '' When you talk about what's happening to you in such an objective way, the physical feelings seem less frightening and almost become welcome signs of normality. You have removed some of the mystery, and you feel more in control.

CHECK OUT THE ROOM

Look over the room before you speak; it won't feel so strange later on. Make sure everything is set up and works. Do you need a desk or lectern, does the mike work, is the tape recorder plugged in, and so on? If you look over the room before your presentation, things become a little less uncertain.

BURN UP EXCESS ENERGY

Remember, your body begins to go on automatic pilot quite a while before you actually have to speak, and tension builds up in your muscles. There are some things you can do that will help you feel more relaxed: jog around the building, but don't overdo it; get off the bus or subway a few stops early and walk the rest of the way; take the stairs instead of the elevator, and so forth. Engaging in mild forms of exercise will help you get rid of excess energy. Just make sure you don't exhaust yourself.

Relaxation exercises will also help you now. Try the techniques we presented under ''Long-term Treatments.''

GET ENOUGH SLEEP THE NIGHT BEFORE

If you're well rested, you'll feel more sure of yourself and be more in control of your muscles and their movements.

First-aid (On-the-spot) Treatments

THINK ABOUT OTHER THINGS

Look at what's going on in the room around you. Listen carefully to what another speaker has to say. Read a magazine while you're waiting for that job interview. Think about *anything,* except your presentation. Whatever you do, *don't* engage in any last-minute practice sessions.

PAUSE BEFORE YOU SPEAK

You can use that time to expend a little energy and to gather your thoughts. Stand, if possible; it's a lot easier to produce a loud, clear voice while you're standing up than while you're confined to a chair. Standing also uses more energy than sitting.

Take some time to arrange your notes. Move things so that they're to your liking. Each little task uses energy and helps you to shake the jitters.

Make sure you have an adequate supply of air before you start talking. That way you won't rush into your presentation with a low air supply and run out of steam almost immediately.

USE ENERGY WHILE YOU TALK

Use gestures and move your body naturally. If you don't overdo it, you'll look lively, and you'll also be getting rid of useless energy at the same time. Plan some gestures in your practice sessions. You'll feel more comfortable when you use them during the actual presentation.

LOOK FOR FRIENDLY FACES

The audience is not made up of grizzly bears. You'll see smiles of encouragement that will make you feel much better about being there.

Try the things we've suggested, but don't expect instant success. Understanding stagefright means learning to understand yourself, and that takes time. Even we, the authors of this book, have never lost our own cases of stagefright completely; nevertheless, we feel pretty confident about speaking in front of an audience. We're sure that, in time, you will too.

SUGGESTED READINGS

Adler, Ronald B. *Confidence in Communication: A Guide to Assertive and Social Skills.* New York: Holt, Rinehart and Winston, 1977.

Phillips, Gerald M. *Help for Shy People.* Englewood Cliffs, N.J.: Prentice-Hall, Inc., 1981.

Zimbardo, Philip G. *Shyness: What It Is, What to Do About It.* Reading, Mass.: Addison-Wesley, 1977.

B Appendix B

Special Speech Problems

Now that you've studied all the sounds of the language, you probably realize that some of the phonemes are harder to accurately produce than others. Because they are difficult, it's fairly common to find some phonemes misarticulated by children, and it's not unusual to hear the same misarticulations by teenagers and adults. Possibly your speech instructor, or someone else, has told you that you misarticulate one or more of these phonemes. We assume that's why you're reading these pages now; you want to correct your misarticulation.

THE CORRECTION OF DIFFICULT SOUNDS

The phonemes we are talking about include [s] and [z], [ʃ] and [ʒ], [l], [r], and for some people [θ] and [ð]. It is important for you to determine which sounds you misarticulate to get as much information about your productions as possible.

Kinds of Misarticulations

There are three kinds of misarticulations: *omissions, substitutions,* and *distortions.* When you *omit* a phoneme, you're not producing the sound at all where it belongs. For example, a child may say "poon" [pun] instead of "spoon" [spun]. When you *substitute*, you are producing one phoneme in the place of the desired one. Have you ever heard someone utter "thpoon" [θpun] instead of "spoon" [spun] or "mouf" [mauf] instead of "mouth" [mauθ]? These are both forms of substitutions. The third kind of misarticulation, *distortion*, is a bit harder to define, and also to identify. A distorted production of a phoneme is one that resembles the correct production closely enough to be identified as part of the same phoneme but different enough that it sounds incorrect. Perhaps you have heard someone whose [s] sounds were accompanied by a whistle or sounded "mushy" instead of sharp and clear. You knew it was an [s], but it didn't sound right to you.

After you have determined the type of misarticulation you are producing, you should determine the severity and frequency with which it occurs. Is the misarticulation present when you produce the phoneme at the beginning of words? The middle? The ends of words? Does it occur when you say the sound by itself, in a single word, or in a phrase or sentence? Is your misarticulation obvious enough to be noticed by most people? Only a few people? Only by a trained speech person?

In addition to determining the severity and frequency of the misarticulation, you should establish a baseline of production. Use a tape recorder, if possible, and read a list of words containing the target sound. Play it back and, perhaps with the help of another person, determine the percentage of words in which that sound is misarticulated. You can use this baseline figure later to measure your progress as you work on the sound.

At this point, if there is a speech clinic or speech and hearing center at your school, or conveniently located in your community, your instructor may wish to refer you there for an evaluation of your articulation. A hearing test may also be indicated because many misarticulations can be related to a mild-to-moderate loss of hearing, particularly in the high frequency range. Possibly the speech clinic may want to work with you to help eliminate the misarticulations.

If there is no such service available, the following steps may help you to work on correcting the sound or sounds either with the assistance of your instructor or under your own direction.

Steps in Correction

STEP 1

Read Chapter 4 and follow the ear training procedures explained there. Use the sound or sounds you misarticulate until you are able consistently to recognize your own errors.

STEP 2

If possible, ask your instructor to teach you how to make the sound correctly by itself. You might make a tape recording of your instructor producing the sound in a variety of contexts, perhaps using the drill exercises included in this text. Listen to the tape often enough that you get a clear impression of the sound the way that is considered standard. If your instructor can't make the tape for you, ask a member of your speech class who produces the sound correctly.

STEP 3

Begin working on your own correct productions of the sound using the drill exercises you'll find later in this section. Begin by making the sound by itself, then combine it with vowel sounds so that the sound is at the beginning, end, and middle of sound groups. Then put the sound into words in all three positions. Start with beginning, go on to end position, and finally to the middle of words. During the beginning stages, try to have someone listen to you who can tell you whether you are making the sound correctly or not. After a while your ear will be sufficiently trained so that you can make that judgment yourself.

STEP 4

Go on to phrases, sentences, and connected speech. Still use the drill exercises in the text and any other materials you can find using your target sound. For variety, get a partner and make up some games to play using words that contain your target sound; for example, "Scrabble," with every word containing your sound.

Remember, you've probably been misarticulating your target sounds for sixteen or seventeen or more years. You're not going to change the way you produce them overnight. Only after frequent, regular, and conscientious work on your part will you begin to see changes. Short, regular practice sessions will work better than long, infrequent ones. Work on your speech every day and those changes will start to happen.

Frontal and Lateral Distortion of [s] and [z]

If your [s] and [z] sound like your [θ] and [ð], you are probably producing them with the tip of your tongue either against or between your teeth. This is called a *lingual protrusion* or *frontal lisp.* Here are some drills you can use to correct this misarticulation.

STEP 1

Practice making a groove down the center of the tongue, from front to back. You may find it useful to use a thin plastic mixing stick or applicator stick for this. Place the stick along the center of your tongue and wrap the sides of your tongue around the stick. Remove the stick slowly, but keep the sides of your tongue up. Once you are able to do this consistently, you are ready for the next step.

STEP 2

Place your tongue against the alveolar ridge in the position to make the [t] sound. Start to make the [t] sound, but instead of pulling your tongue sharply away, let the tip drop very slightly downward slowly, while keeping the sides up. Keep the teeth almost closed, with a very narrow opening between them. Force air between your teeth, aiming it with your tongue right down the center. You should now be producing a sharp, clear [s].

STEP 3

Place your tongue in position for the [t] sound, but drop the tip slightly before you begin to breathe out. Make sure you maintain the groove down the center of your tongue. You should still be able to produce a sharp, clear sound.

STEP 4

Once you are able to initiate a good, clear [s] sound, practice the following comparisons:

[s]	– [θ]	– [s]	– [θ]	– [s]	– [θ]
sɑ	– θɑ	– sɑ	– θɑ	– sɑ	– θɑ
si	– θi	– si	– θi	– si	– θi
so	– θo	– so	– θo	– so	– θo

Then

θɑ	– sɑ	– θɑ	– sɑ	– θɑ	– sɑ
θi	– si	– θi	– si	– θi	– si
θo	– so	– θo	– so	– θo	– so

Next

sɪn	– θɪn	– sɪn	– θɪn	– sɪn	– θɪn
sʌm	– θʌm	– sʌm	– θʌm	– sʌm	– θʌm
sim	– θim	– sim	– θim	– sim	– θim

Note: make sure there is a sharp distinction between the [θ] and [s] sounds in each pair of sounds, syllables, and words.

You should now be ready to follow the general procedures explained under the heading, "The Correction of Difficult Sounds," on page 334.

Distortion of [l] as in [lɛt]

Sometimes this sound is distorted so that it resembles [w] as in "wet." This happens if you lower the tip of the tongue and purse the lips and produce a bilabial glide instead of the lateral continuant. Another mis-articulation that is less frequent is caused by lowering the tongue tip and raising the *back* of the tongue against, or near, the soft palate. This type of sound resembles the French uvular (trilled) [r].

To produce [l] correctly, raise the tip of the tongue to your alveolar ridge with your mouth open fairly wide. Make sure to keep the back and sides of your tongue low. Now, keeping the tip of the tongue at the alve-olar ridge and the back and sides low, begin to phonate. The sound you are producing should be a fairly accurate [l]. Ask your instructor or a classmate to check your production of the sound. When you are able to produce the sound consistently with your mouth wide open, practice the sound while maintaining a space of one finger between your upper and lower teeth.

You are probably now ready to produce the [l] sound followed by some of the vowels:

> la – la – la
> li – li – li
> lo – lo – lo
> lu – lu – lu

Next produce the vowel before the [l].

> il – il – il
> ɛl – ɛl – ɛl
> ol – ol – ol

Now make the vowel sound before and after the [l].

> ala – ala – ala
> ili – ili – ili
> olo – olo – olo

If you're satisfied with your production so far, try the following comparisons. Make sure there is a marked difference between the consonant sounds.

la – wa – la – wa – la – wa – la
li – we – li – we – li – we – li
lo – wo – lo – wo – lo – wo – lo
la – ga – la – ga – la – ga – la
li – gi – li – gi – li – gi – li
lo – go – lo – go – lo – go – lo

Now go back to the previously outlined procedures for "The Correction of Difficult Sounds," on page 335.

Distortion of [r]

This is one of the most difficult sounds to correct. There are several different misarticulations of this sound. The one that is most troublesome is a substitution of [w] as in "wed" for [r] as in "red." To correct this substitution, try the following procedures.

STEP 1

Ask one of the students in your class to read aloud the following sentence: *The rainbow circled around part of the sky after the rain ended.* Now read the sentence aloud yourself. Do you produce the [r] sounds the same way as your classmate? If your production of "rainbow" or "rain" sounds somewhat like "wainbow" or "wain" you are probably making the [r] sound only with your lips rather than with your tongue *and* your lips.

STEP 2

Produce the [z] sound. See if you can feel where you're placing the tip of your tongue. Produce the [z] sound again. Without stopping, produce the syllable [zra]. Focus your attention on what happens to the tip of your tongue. You will feel, we hope, the tip of the tongue drop slightly away from the gum ridge while the sides remain raised. Repeat the syllable slowly as many times as are necessary for you to get an accurate perception of the correct tongue position for the [r] sound.

STEP 3

Once you have learned the proper tongue position, try making the [r] sound by itself. Ask your speech instructor to check your production of the sound before you proceed. If your instructor is not available, perhaps a classmate with a good ear for sounds can check you out.

STEP 4

Once you are fairly certain that you are producing the sound accurately, follow the procedures outlined in Chapter 4 for ear training and the procedures at the beginning of this Appendix.

Since this is a difficult sound to correct, your instructor may wish to refer you to the college's or university's speech clinic or a community clinic for additional help.

C

Appendix C

Nonverbal Communication

Remember the first day of this class, when you met your instructor for the first time? Perhaps you were already in your seat when the instructor came into the room. Do you remember the things you observed? Maybe you noticed what the person was wearing, that he or she walked in a certain way; maybe you noticed hair color, height, the way he or she looked out over the class, the sound of the person's voice, the way the words were pronounced. You took in all this information, then your mind started to interpret it, and you formed an opinion about your instructor on the spot.

Or, have you ever noticed the conversation that goes on between the pitcher and the catcher in a baseball game? The pitcher looks at the catcher. The catcher makes a sign with his hands. The pitcher shakes his head. The process repeats itself until the catcher makes a sign that's followed by the pitcher nodding his head.

Both the baseball game and the classroom impression are examples of nonverbal communication. By nonverbal communication we mean all the modes of communication that we use other than the symbolic meanings of the actual words. Nonverbal communication provides the accompaniments of spoken language that help make our meanings complete—they help transmit the whole sense of what we want to say.

Most of the modes of nonverbal communication were in existence before the human race developed speech and language. Such things as gesture and facial expressions were commonly used to transmit messages long before humans developed the system of sounds and noises, or the written symbols representing these sounds and noises, that we call language. Because these nonverbal forms of communication have become an innate part of the language system, we tend to derive a great deal of meaning from them, and to respond to them on a deep, often unconscious level. Often the specific meanings of individual nonverbal behaviors vary from culture to culture. For example, a gesture meaning "This is important; you'd better listen to me" in one culture might mean "I give up" in another. So deeply ingrained are nonverbal behaviors in our interpersonal relationships that we place a high value on them.

Mixed Messages

Think back in your experience. Have you ever met someone for the first time and, even though your conversation with that person went smoothly and pleasantly, you came away with a certain amount of dislike for him or her? If so, you may have blamed your dislike on "bad vibes" or some similar expression. In all likelihood, what you were responding to was discordance between the pleasant words that that person used and various physical or vocal behaviors.

In other words, you reacted to a *mixed message*, a segment of communication in which the nonverbal message differs from or contradicts the verbal message. In situations like this, where there is a conflict between what a person's words say and what his or her nonverbal behavior says, you will tend to believe the nonverbal message. The result: the listener often either ends up confused or reacts unfavorably.

For you to be a more effective communicator, you should know about the meanings transmitted by various forms of nonverbal behavior and be sure that all the ways you transmit a message are in harmony with one another. Let's take a look at some of the most common areas of nonverbal communication.

Paralanguage is a collective term for all the audible elements of a person's speech that increase or decrease the meaning of words. It includes such variables as loudness, stress, pitch and pitch variation, rate, rhythm, and voice qualities. Variation in any of these components of spoken speech can cause a listener to interpret the same words in a number of different ways. We discussed these paralinguistic components pretty thoroughly in Chapters 7 and 8, so we won't repeat them here. If you haven't read those chapters yet, we suggest you do so now.

Kinesics

Just as you respond to the many auditory cues in a speaker's message through what you hear (paralanguage), you also respond to a multitude of visual cues. All the behaviors you can observe visually make up the category of nonverbal communication called *kinesics.* Your response to the kinesic elements of communication is probably more unconscious than your response to paralanguage. Yet the role kinesics plays is just as important, if not more important, in your reception and interpretations of others' communicative efforts with you. Remember the "bad vibes" mentioned earlier? If you developed an almost instant dislike to a person, really without knowing why, you were probably responding unconsciously to the other person's kinesics.

Kinesics usually includes gestures, movements of the body or its extremities, facial expressions, the states of muscle tension or relaxation in body parts, postural attitudes, and behaviors involving the eyes, such as winking, blinking, and the direction and duration of eye contact and gaze.

Social and behavioral scientists who make an intensive study of nonverbal behavior have developed a system for examining nonverbal behaviors, including kinesics, in such a way that we can group certain behaviors together into categories. One such system, developed by Ekman and Friesen, includes the categories of *emblems, illustrators, affect displays, regulators,* and *adaptors.*

EMBLEMS

Behaviors that, although not verbalized, can be directly translated into a very specific verbal entity are called *emblems.* Any football fan knows immediately that when an official raises both arms directly overhead, he is indicating that one of the teams has scored; when he stands with his hands on his hips, elbows out, we know that one team was offside. Another example in sports includes the umpire's raised hand, with fingers flexed and thumb extended, meaning "You're out!" And, of course, you know that the very same emblem used outside of the ball park can mean something else when used by a hitchhiker.

We also display emblems on a less formal basis during our everyday communication situations. You may frequently show dislike or displeasure by wrinkling your nose; you may tell someone to approach you by holding out one hand with the palm up and the last three fingers flexed, curling the index finger. These are only a couple of the many emblems we use as individuals and as a culture.

ILLUSTRATORS

Illustrators are behaviors that *accompany* speech and are directly related to it. They are used for emphasis or to clarify or illustrate an idea through the use of body movements. Try to describe, in words alone, a spiral staircase. It's hard, isn't it? It is much easier to use illustrators, gestures with your body and hands, to help your verbal communication.

AFFECT DISPLAYS

Affect displays are the elements of nonverbal communication to which we probably respond most directly and consciously. If you have ever smiled warmly at an attractive member of the opposite sex and received a warm smile in return, you didn't need very much verbal communication to realize that there was a mutuality of feeling between you. We can display affect bodily or facially. The droop of the head and shoulders, for example, can express sadness, weariness, or depression, while shoulders up with head and chin held high can express strong positive feelings of self-confidence. Facial expressions may indicate a wide variety of feelings, ranging from depression and anger on one hand, to joy, delight, and exaltation on the other.

REGULATORS

During any conversation, be it a dialogue between two close friends or a conversation among several people at a party, signals are passed from one person to another or to the group as a whole. We call these signals, or cues, *regulators*. These signals regulate, or control, the back-and-forth flow of the conversation, governing its rate and duration. You give someone permission to speak, encouragement to continue, or a message to stop talking through some nonverbal behavior such as making or avoiding eye contact or head-nodding or head-shaking.

ADAPTORS

An *adaptor* is a nonverbal behavior we use to manifest some of our unconscious needs or drives. Some of these behaviors, such as scratching our heads, rubbing our noses, covering our mouths, or chewing our glasses, are ways of handling anxiety, hostility, or other negative feelings. Most people are not aware of displaying adaptors. Look around your classroom before the next quiz or before a class presentation is to be made. What kind of adaptive behaviors do you see? Probably a lot of foot-tapping, playing with pencils, hand-rubbing, and so on.

In addition to looking at the type of behavior displayed, we can examine the body part we used for the communication, and what we mean to "say." For example, facial expressions may indicate a wide variety of feelings, ranging from depression and anger, on one hand, to such emotions as joy, delight, and exaltation on the other. Specific organs of the face may also play a part in transmitting messages.

EYES

The eyes play a very important role in communication. The length of time that you hold eye contact with another person is generally an indication of the degree and quality of your relationship with that person. Your eye contact with a total stranger or a casual acquaintance is likely to be considerably shorter than eye contact with one of your close friends or family members. If you are angry with someone fairly close to you, you are likely to make your eye contact with that person either very short or much longer than usual. When you're forced into uncomfortably close quarters with someone you don't know intimately, you'll usually compensate by avoiding eye contact. Recall the behavior of people on crowded elevators. Where do they look? Usually at the numbers that indicate the floors. What about on crowded buses or trains? There, people generally look up at the advertising signs or down at their feet.

The eyes may play a role in discouraging relationships. When you avoid eye contact with an acquaintance or friend, you may be saying, "I don't wish to recognize you now or spend time with you." Literature is full of expressions that relate to the wide variety of meanings a person can express in a glance. As Ben Jonson said, "Drink to me only with thine eyes,/And I will pledge with mine."

Eye pupil size expresses another aspect of meaning. When you look at something you find pleasant, your eye pupils tend to enlarge. When you look at something you find unpleasant, your pupils contract. You don't consciously control the size of your pupils, though, and your response to the eye pupil size of others is also largely unconscious. Many experiments have shown that people generally prefer to relate to, be friends with, and work with, people with large eye pupils.

ARMS AND LEGS

The arms and legs also play an important part in conveying either specific meaning or some indication of the communicator's feelings and attitudes.

On one occasion, one of the authors was participating in a group interview of a candidate for a position as counselor. The candidate was very opinionated and outspoken as to her views on a number of subjects and gradually antagonized several of the interviewers, especially the author. After he addressed a couple of questions toward the candidate and received what, to him, were highly unsatisfactory answers, the author's attention was embarrassingly called to his posture by one of the other interviewers. To his surprise and consternation, he found himself leaning way back in his chair, with his arms and legs tightly crossed. Any one of these behaviors would have indicated the interviewer's negative attitude toward the candidate. Together, all of them meant "You don't stand a ghost of a chance with me." The candidate very shortly took the hint, and left. (P.S.: She didn't get the job.)

Attending and Nonattending Exercise

Pair off with another student or a friend. Pick a subject you can discuss for about five minutes. (Possibly what each of you wishes to do to improve your communication effectiveness.) Have one person sit in an *attending position:* leaning slightly forward, arms and legs unfolded but comfortable, with gaze fixed on the other person's face. The other person should sit in a *nonattending position:* slouched back in the chair, arms and legs crossed, gaze averted from partner. Discuss the topic you selected.

At the end of five minutes, reverse your roles so that the former *attender* becomes the *nonattender* and vice versa. Continue to discuss the same topic, or another topic, for another five minutes.

Now discuss with your partner the feelings each of you experienced, both as an attender and as a nonattender, as well as your feelings about being attended to and not being attended to.

What were your feelings about yourself? Were they different in each role? Were your feelings toward your partner different when your partner was assuming a different role with respect to you? Which posture encourages better communication? Which posture encourages better interpersonal relationships? Which role did you find to be more comfortable?

Proxemics

Imagine waking up in the morning, getting out of bed, washing, and dressing. In addition to your usual clothing, this morning you are going to enclose yourself in a transparent plastic bubble. You can see through this bubble, hear through it, smell, touch, and taste through it. As you go through your daily activities, the bubble expands and shrinks, sometimes fitting as tightly as your skin. Most of the time you are quite comfortable with the size of the bubble. Sometimes, though, the bubble is either larger or smaller than you would like it to be, and you feel quite uncomfortable and begin to behave differently than usual.

This imaginary plastic bubble is actually your *personal* space—the distance from another person at which you feel comfortable and at ease. You probably realize that this distance varies considerably depending on the situation and the relationship between the people involved. Generally, as far as communication goes, we can divide personal space into four categories of distance.

PUBLIC DISTANCE

This is the longest distance, usually ranging anywhere from twelve to about twenty feet or more. Public distance is appropriate for highly impersonal situations such as the movies, theater, or sports events such as football or baseball games. At these events, the distance between the spectators and participants indicates that there is little or no *personal* relationship between them. (Except, perhaps, during the World Series, when the wives of the baseball players are frequently shown in the stands. They, however, usually sit in the first row, box seats, as close to the players as possible.)

SOCIAL-CONSULTATIVE DISTANCE

The limits for social-consultative distance range between four feet and twelve feet. This is the range of distance at which impersonal business between two people, or one person and a group, is usually carried out. If you were in a class in which the instructor did some lecturing and spent some time leading class discussions, you would most likely feel more comfortable at a distance between four and twelve feet from the instructor. Closer than four feet, you might feel somewhat threatened and uncomfortable. Farther away than twelve feet, you might feel separated and lose interest in the lecture or discussion.

CASUAL-PERSONAL DISTANCE

This distance may range from one-and-one-half feet to four feet. At this distance, we usually hold conversations with friends, members of our family, and acquaintances with whom we have some sort of working relationship. If you were being interviewed for a position, the interviewer and you would probably sit at a distance in this range. Most of your everyday communication situations take place within this range.

INTIMATE DISTANCE

This is the closest distance, ranging from actual physical contact to about one-and-one-half feet. This distance is usually maintained by two persons who have a very close, personal relationship, and usually is used in a private situation. Husbands and wives, lovers, and close family members are the types of pairs who maintain intimate distance in their communication. If you were forced to be at this distance with a stranger or casual acquaintance in a crowded public situation, you would probably feel a good deal of discomfort and would either avoid eye contact with the other person or use a variety of adaptor behaviors.

Distance Exercise

1. Pair off with a partner. Stand facing one another about twenty feet apart. Start a conversation and continue it for about two minutes. What was your comfort level? What was the topic of conversation? Was it very personal or impersonal? You were at *public distance* during this exercise.

2. Move to a distance of about ten feet from your partner. Continue your conversation for another two minutes. Did your conversation topic change? If so, to what? Was your comfort level any different from the first situation? You were at *social distance.*

3. Move to a distance of three feet from your partner. Continue your conversation for another two minutes. For this distance, answer the same questions asked above. You are now at *personal distance.*

4. Now move close enough to your partner so that you are directly face-to-face, practically touching. Continue your conversation, if you can. Observe your own physical behaviors.

5. Discuss with your partner, or the class, the following questions for each distance:

   What is the effect of distance on feelings of comfort or discomfort?

   What effect does distance have on the topic of conversation and vice versa?

   Does the sex of your partner affect the distance at which you feel comfortable? You may wish to repeat the exercise with a partner of the opposite sex to your original partner and take note of your reactions.

OTHER ASPECTS

Space and human relationships can influence communication situations in other ways, too. Think back to your childhood days and remember, if you can, a situation in which you may have been the only child present in a gathering of adults. The likelihood is that you felt small, insignificant, and unimportant in contrast to all those "giants" surrounding you. Some of that feeling may persist into adulthood when you encounter someone who is considerably taller or at a greater height than you. If you attend a conference or a banquet, you will probably find that the "important" people there, speakers and "honored guests," are seated at tables on a raised platform or dais to indicate their importance in regard to the "ordinary people" seated at a level below them.

In most large organizations that occupy offices on more than one floor in a building, the people with the higher status job titles will occupy offices on the higher floors. An example you may relate to more easily can be found in the classroom. Most of the time the students are seated while the instructor stands and lectures or leads discussion; this is a way of indicating that the teacher is the most important person (has more power) in that classroom and that the seated students should pay close attention.

These are only some of the intentional devices we use to communicate importance in our culture; these devices indicate that we generally associate height directly with importance.

Height Exercise

Pair off with a partner. One of you will be the "persuader" and the other the "persuadee." The persuader will stand and talk to the persuadee, who will be seated. Try to persuade your partner to accept some belief. After two minutes or so, reverse positions but do *not* reverse roles. (The persuader is now seated, the persuadee, standing.) Continue for another two minutes. Now reverse roles and repeat the exercise.

What different feelings did each of you have as persuader when you were standing, as opposed to sitting? What different feelings did each of you have as the person being persuaded while standing as opposed to sitting?

If you were seriously engaged in a persuasive activity, would you choose to be higher or lower than the person or persons you were attempting to persuade?

LOCATION

You can also indicate status or importance through location. If you were to visit a member of a large organization, you would find that the distance to that person's office depends on the person's status within the organization, that is, the higher the status, the farther away the individual would be from "the center of things." In addition, you would find that higher-status persons have larger offices (more personal space) and more barriers separating them from others.

Even through the subtle use of space, humans communicate some piece of information. Space not only plays a part in *what* we communicate, it plays a part in *how* we communicate.

Touch

Our understanding of how we use touch as a form of communication is not as clear or complete as it is of some of the other nonverbal forms, yet there are some principles involved in touch that are important to understand.

We know, for instance, that touch is one of the most important ways for parents to communicate feelings of love and caring to a young child. In fact, children who do not receive a good deal of touching during their early childhood usually show some delays in their emotional development and may develop into adults who are incapable of sensing or expressing very much in the way of feelings. In addition, children who experience little touching behavior usually are found to have very low self-concepts.

In many American cultures, touching is discouraged more and more as we grow older, except in certain formalized, stylistic ways, until we experience very little touching in our daily lives as adults. There are some exceptions, to be sure. If you watch sports you can't help but be aware of all the vigorous touching athletes do to one another. Watch to see what happens to the wide receiver on a professional football team after he catches a long pass and scores a touchdown.

During discussions held in the authors' classes about what makes people feel good about themselves, one of the actions students mentioned most often as a morale booster is a pat on the back (literally!). Another action that makes them feel good is a hug from someone they feel close to. Yet, at the same time, they report that they are reluctant to touch others in the same way they themselves would like to be touched. Unfortunately, as adults we generally associate touching with sexuality and tend to be inhibited about it.

Touching Exercise

(One member of the class may read the directions as the others perform the exercise.)

1. Sit in a circle with other members of your class.
2. Hold hands with your neighbors so that your right hand is *clasping*

the left hand of the person on your right, and your left hand is *being held* by the person on your left.

3. *Close your eyes,* and focus on the feelings in your left hand. How does that hand feel being held? What messages, if any, are you receiving from the person holding that hand? How do you feel about the person holding that hand?

4. Now focus on your right hand. How does that hand feel holding someone else's? What message is being sent to you by the person whose hand you're holding? How do you feel about that person?

5. When you are in touch with all these feelings, open your eyes. (Notice the metaphor—"in touch with"—that we frequently use in regard to being aware of our feelings.)

6. As a group, discuss what you experienced during the exercise. Did you feel differently about holding as opposed to being held? Why? Did you feel differently about the two persons next to you after the hand-holding? Did it matter whether your hand was being held or doing the holding? How comfortable were you while holding hands with your classmates? Was there a difference between touching a member of the same sex as compared to touching a member of the opposite sex? Can you communicate through touch?

Time

There's an old story about a psychiatrist's secretary who informed her boss that she was quitting her job because she didn't want to suffer a nervous breakdown. When her boss asked her why she would have a breakdown on the job, she said that she never knew what time to report to work. Her boss then assured her that she was due at work at 9:00 A.M. every morning. She replied, "Yes, I know that. But when I get here early, you tell me I'm anxious. When I get here late you tell me I'm being hostile. And when I get here on time, you tell me I'm compulsive. There's no way to win!"

Although something of an exaggeration, this anecdote does reflect how people manage and use time to express feelings toward others. Although most of us sit patiently waiting to be seen by doctors or dentists (did you ever wonder about the derivation of the medical use of the term *patient*?), very few of us would casually appear significantly late for an appointment with one of them. Similarly, in job interviews, you'd be more likely to expect that the interviewer might keep the applicant waiting rather than the other way around. We usually think that the person of lower status waits for the person of higher status.

What is your sense of time like? Do you have on-time arrivals and departures? Or, perhaps, do you arrive "fashionably late" to parties and meetings? Do you sometimes punish people by making them wait? What messages do you send through the medium of time? In any case, let us observe a moment of silence in honor of the psychiatrist's secretary in all of us.

Clothing

Imagine that you are a young man or woman preparing for an interview for a position as a junior accountant in a large accounting firm. Which of the following outfits would you be more likely to wear?

1. Jeans, T-shirt, sneakers
2. A well-tailored suit, white shirt (blouse), tie, conservative shoes

At many colleges and universities, the faculty always knows when on-campus job interviews are being held, just by the change in attire worn by many students. The reasons are obvious. Outfit #1 says its wearer is casual, relaxed, informal. Outfit #2, on the other hand, says its wearer is businesslike, serious, mature, hard-working, conforming. The old expression, "Clothes make the man" is not strictly true, but clothes certainly contribute heavily to the impression you make on the rest of the world. Your attire conveys a general impression about you before you have a chance to say a word about yourself.

Other Nonverbal Modes

In the morning when you splash on a dab of perfume or aftershave lotion, you may not be consciously thinking about how other people will react to that particular scent. The odds are, though, that someone has spent some time thinking about that very question. It could be the person who blended the fragrance, the person who named it, the person who planned the advertising campaign, the person (either you or someone else) who purchased it. All those people attempted to associate that perfume or aftershave with a very specific, attractive image, probably one that is attractive to the opposite sex.

Our senses of smell and taste do provide additional channels of nonverbal communication. We don't now know a great deal about those channels, about which research is currently being carried on, but we'll know a lot more in the future.

Caution

At this point, we feel it is important to point out a few cautions. When you interpret and respond to nonverbal behaviors, now that you have become more sensitized to them, try to remember that individual bits of behavior may mean different things in different cultures, in different contexts, and in different people. In interpreting nonverbal behavior, the experienced observer will observe, make a tentative hypothesis about what the behavior means, and observe further to test the hypothesis before arriving at a definite conclusion. We can generalize, however, to the extent that "people watching can be both fun and profitable."

SUGGESTED READINGS

Birdwhistell, Ray L. *Kinesics and Context.* Philadelphia: University of Pennsylvania Press, 1970.

Ekman, Paul, and Friesen, Wallace. "The Repertoire of Nonverbal Behavior: Categories, Origins, Usage and Coding." *Semiotica I* (1969), pp. 49–98.

Knapp, Mark L. *Non-verbal Communication in Human Interaction,* 2nd Edition. New York: Holt, Rinehart and Winston, 1978.

Leathers, Dale. *Non-Verbal Communication Systems.* Boston: Allyn & Bacon, 1978.

Kronkhite, Gary. *Communication and Awareness.* Menlo Park, Calif.: Cummings Publishing Co., 1976.

Rosenfeld, Lawrence, and Civikly, Jean. *With Words Unspoken: Nonverbal Experience.* New York: Holt, Rinehart and Winston, 1976.

D Appendix D

Guide to Dialects

In Chapter 3 we mentioned regional dialects of American English and foreign accents, but we didn't describe their significant features. That's the purpose of this Appendix: to acquaint you with some of the ways in which the major dialects differ, and to show the main differences between certain foreign accents and American English.

REGIONAL DIALECTS

Linguists generally agree that there are four major geographical variations of American English. They are *General American, New England, Eastern,* and *Southern.* Within the Eastern dialect area is a large sub-dialect, *New York.* Because General American is spoken by more people than any of the other dialects, we'll use it as our basis for comparison. The following charts show how each of the regional dialects tends to differ from General American on certain sounds. Within each dialect area, however, there are likely to be wide variations, so don't expect all speakers within a region to sound alike. Even though we are making comparisons with General American, we are not suggesting that General American is preferred over any other dialect; each dialect represents the acceptable standard for its geographical area. See Chapters 5 and 6 for non-standard productions within the dialect areas.

Southern Regional Dialect

Sound	Word	General American	Southern
[ɛ]	pen	[pɛn]	[pɪn]
[ɛ]	red	[rɛd]	[rɛəd]
[ɛ]	yes	[jɛs]	[jɛjəs]
[ɛɚ]	Mary	[mɛɚɪ]	[meɪrɪ]
[ɪ]	hid	[hɪd]	[hɪjəd]
[ɪɚ]	dear	[dɪɚ]	[dɪjə]
[æ]	pass	[pæs]	[pæjəs]
[ɔɚ]	store	[stɔɚ]	[stɔwə]
[u]	Tuesday	[tuzdeɪ]	[tjuzdeɪ]
[aɪ]	time	[taɪm]	[tɑːm]
[aɪ]	tired	[taɪɚd]	[taːd]
[ɑɚ]	car	[kɑɚ]	[kɑː]

Note: Elongation of a vowel is indicated by [ː].

New England Regional Dialect

Sound	Word	General American	New England
[æ]	ask	[æsk]	[ask]
[æ]	ask	[æsk]	[ɑsk]
[u]	Tuesday	[tuzdeɪ]	[tjuzdeɪ]
[ɑ]	hot	[hɑt]	[hɒt]
[ɝ]	third	[θɝd]	[θɜːd]
[ɚ]	father	[fɑðɚ]	[fɑðə]
[ɪɚ]	fear	[fɪɚ]	[fɪə]
[ɛɚ]	hair	[hɛɚ]	[hɛə]
[ɑɚ]	car	[kɑɚ]	[kɑə]
[ɔɚ]	floor	[flɔɚ]	[flɔə]
[uɚ]	poor	[puɚ]	[puə]

Notes: 1. The New England [ɑ] as in *ask* is frequently called the "broad a."
2. [ː] indicates elongation of a vowel.

Eastern Regional Dialect

Sound	Word	General American	Eastern
[æ]	ask	[æsk]	[ask]
[æ]	ask	[æsk]	[ɑsk]
[ɑ]	hot	[hɑt]	[hɒt]
[ɝ]	word	[wɝd]	[wɜːd]
[ɚ]	father	[fɑðɚ]	[fɑðə]
[aʊ]	now	[naʊ]	[nɛaʊ]
[ɪɚ]	here	[hɪɚ]	[hɪə]
[ɛɚ]	pair	[pɛɚ]	[pɛə]
[ɑɚ]	car	[kɑɚ]	[kɑə]
[ɔɚ]	floor	[flɔɚ]	[flɔə]
[uɚ]	poor	[puɚ]	[puə]

Note: Elongation of a vowel is indicated by [ː].

New York Regional Dialect

The New York regional dialect usually includes the features of the Eastern dialect plus the following:

Sound	Word	General American	New York
[æ]	can't	[kænt]	[kɛænt]
[ɔ]	tall	[tɔl]	[tɔəl]
[ɔ]	Florida	[flɔrɪdə]	[flɑrɪdə]
[ɝ]	hurry	[hɝɪ]	[hʌrɪ]
[aɪ]	time	[taɪm]	[tɔɪm]

Note: [ɔ] as in *tall* is diphthongized and has a significant degree of lip-rounding.

FOREIGN ACCENTS

If you learned American English as a second language, there's a good chance that you speak it with an *accent*. That is, the sounds you produce, as well as the stress and intonation patterns you use, vary noticeably from the major regional dialects of American English. The specific variations will depend on the phonemic structure of your first language, and how it differs from American English.

The following charts list some of the significant features of accents that usually result when American English is learned *after* certain other languages. Because stress and intonation features are too complicated to effectively present here, we suggest you read Chapter 8, Vocal Expressiveness, and consult with your instructor if you want to learn more about those aspects of a particular accent.

Interference with American English Consonants According to First Language Learned

	Chinese	French	German	Italian	Japanese	Korean	Pilipino	Russian	Scandinavian	Spanish
[p]	*	*		*		*	*			*
[b]	*					*				*
[t]	*	*	*	*		*	*			*
[d]	*	*		*		*		*		*
[k]	*	*		*		*	*			
[g]	*					*				
[f]	*					*	*			
[v]	*		*		*	*	*		*	*
[θ]	*	*	*	*	*		*	*	*	*
[ð]	*	*	*	*	*	*	*			*
[s]	*		*				*		*	*
[z]	*		*				*			*
[ʃ]	*		*			*				*
[ʒ]	*		*			*				*
[h]		*	*	*						*
[w]			*					*	*	*
[r]	*	*	*	*		*		*	*	*
[j]										*
[l]	*			*	*	*				*
[n]				*						*
[ŋ]	*							*		
[tʃ]		*	*			*	*	*		*
[dʒ]		*	*			*	*	*	*	

Interference with American English Vowels According to First Language Learned

	Chinese	French	German	Italian	Japanese	Korean	Pilipino	Russian	Scandinavian	Spanish
[i]	*	*		*		*		*	*	*
[ɪ]	*	*		*	*	*	*	*	*	*
[e]	*	*								
[ɛ]	*	*							*	
[æ]	*		*		*				*	
[ɔ]			*			*			*	*
[o]	*			*				*		
[ʊ]						*		*	*	*
[u]						*		*	*	*
[ʌ]	*		*	*	*	*		*		
[ə]	*	*		*						
[ɝ]					*	*		*		
[ɚ]					*	*				
[aʊ]			*	*					*	
[ɔ]									*	
[eɪ]									*	*
[oʊ]										

359

First Language Background: Chinese

Sound	Problem	Standard			Non-Standard	Exercise
[p]	[( )]	[dip]	deep	becomes	[di]	(p. 56)
[b]	[( )]	[kæb]	cab	becomes	[kæ]	(p. 61)
[t]	[( )]	[bɛt]	bet	becomes	[bɛ]	(p. 70)
[d]	[( )]	[hæd]	had	becomes	[hæ]	(p. 79)
[k]	[( )]	[tɔk]	talk	becomes	[tɔ]	(p. 86)
[g]	[( )]	[bɪg]	big	becomes	[bɪ]	(p. 90)
[f]	[( )]	[bif]	beef	becomes	[bi]	(p. 99)
[v]	[( )]	[gɪv]	give	becomes	[gɪ]	(p. 103)
[v]	[f/]	[hæv]	have	becomes	[hæf]	(p. 96)
[v]	[w/]	[væn]	van	becomes	[wæn]	(p. 97)
[θ]	[s/]	[θɪk]	thick	becomes	[sɪk]	(p. 111)
[θ]	[f/]	[hɛlθ]	health	becomes	[hɛlf]	(p. 111)
[ð]	[d/]	[ðæt]	that	becomes	[dæt]	(p. 108)
[ð]	[v/]	[smuð]	smooth	becomes	[smuv]	(p. 111)
[s]	[( )]	[haʊs]	house	becomes	[haʊ]	(p. 122)
[z]	[s/]	[ɪz]	is	becomes	[ɪs]	(p. 121)
[z]	[( )]	[hɪz]	his	becomes	[hɪ]	(p. 133)
[ʃ]	[( )]	[fɪʃ]	fish	becomes	[fɪ]	(p. 138)
[ʃ]	[s/]	[ʃu]	shoe	becomes	[su]	(p. 138)
[l]	[r/]	[lɛt]	let	becomes	[rɛt]	(p. 165)
[l]	[( )]	[tɔl]	tall	becomes	[tɔ]	(p. 166)
[l]	[ə+]	[blu]	blue	becomes	[bəlu]	(p. 167)
[tʃ]	[( )]	[ɪntʃ]	inch	becomes	[ɪn]	(p. 184)
[i]	[ɪ/]	[it]	eat	becomes	[ɪt]	(p. 196)
[ɪ]	[i/]	[fɪt]	fit	becomes	[fit]	(p. 196)
[ɛ]	[e/]	[wɛt]	wet	becomes	[wet]	(p. 204)
[æ]	[e/]	sæk]	sack	becomes	[sek]	(p. 209)
[ɔ]	[o/]	[sɔ]	saw	becomes	[so]	(p. 217)
[ʊ]	[u/]	[pʊl]	pull	becomes	[pul]	(p. 225)
[ʌ]	[ɑ/]	[nʌts]	nuts	becomes	[nɑts]	(p. 227)
[ə]	[( )]	[sofə]	sofa	becomes	[sof]	(p. 231)
[ə]	[ɑ/]	[soʊdə]	soda	becomes	[soʊdɑ]	(p. 231)

KEY: / SUBSTITUTION ( ) OMISSION + ADDITION

First Language Background: French

Sound	Problem	Standard			Non-Standard		Exercise
[p]	[(ʰ)]	[pʰaɪ]	pie	becomes	[p⁽ʰ⁾aɪ]	See note 1.	(p. 56)
[t]	[(ʰ)]	[tʰaɪ]	tie	becomes	[t⁽ʰ⁾aɪ]	See note 1.	(p. 66)
[t]	[‿]	[tɛn]	ten	becomes	[t̪ɛn]	See note 2.	(p. 67)
[d]	[‿]	[du]	do	becomes	[d̪u]	See note 2.	(p. 67)
[k]	[(ʰ)]	[kʰæn]	can	becomes	[k⁽ʰ⁾æn]	See note 1.	(p. 84)
[θ]	[s/]	[θɪn]	thin	becomes	[sɪn]		(p. 111)
[ð]	[z/]	[ðɪs]	this	becomes	[zɪs]		(p. 111)
[h]	[()]	[haʊs]	house	becomes	[aʊs]		(p. 144)
[r]	[R/]	[reɪd]	raid	becomes	[Reɪd]	See note 3.	(p. 151)
[tʃ]	[ʃ/]	[watʃ]	watch	becomes	[waʃ]		(p. 138)
[dʒ]	[ʒ/]	[dʒʌdʒ]	judge	becomes	[ʒʌʒ]		(p. 184)
[i]	[ɪ/]	[il]	eel	becomes	[ɪl]		(p. 196)
[ɪ]	[i/]	[bɪt]	bit	becomes	[bit]		(p. 196)
[ɛ]	[æ/]	[lɛnd]	lend	becomes	[lænd]		(p. 209)
[æ]	[ ]	[læmp]	lamp	becomes	[læ̃mp]	See note 4.	(p. 269)
[æ]	[ɑ/]	[tʃæns]	chance	becomes	[tʃans]		(p. 209)
[ə]	[ɔ/]	[əbaut]	about	becomes	[ɔbaut]		(p. 230)
[ou]	[o/]	[koud]	code	becomes	[kod]		(p. 220)

KEY: / SUBSTITUTION ( ) OMISSION   ̪DENTALIZED   ˜NASALIZED

(ʰ) LACKS ASPIRATION

Notes: 1.   Lacks aspirated (explosive) quality of plosive sounds.
   2.   Produced dentally (on the back of the teeth) instead of on the gum ridge.
   3.   Uses [R], a uvular-trilled substitute for the lingua-palatal glide [r].
   4.   Excess nasal resonance.

First Language Background: German

Sound	Problem	Standard			Non-Standard		Exercise
[b]	[v/]	[bot]	boat	becomes	[vot]		(p. 60)
[d]	[t/]	[hæd]	had	becomes	[hæt]		(p. 66)
[v]	[f/]	[lʌv]	love	becomes	[lʌf]		(p. 96)
[θ]	[s/]	[θɪŋk]	think	becomes	[sɪŋk]		(p. 111)
[θ]	[t/]	[θru]	through	becomes	[tru]		(p. 108)
[ð]	[z/]	[ðæt]	that	becomes	[zæt]		(p. 111)
[ð]	[d/]	[ðɪs]	this	becomes	[dɪs]		(p. 108)
[s]	[z/]	[si]	see	becomes	[zi]		(p. 122)

(Continued)

First Language Background: German (*Continued*)

Sound	Problem	Standard		becomes	Non-Standard		Exercise
[s]	[ʃ/]	[spɪn]	spin	becomes	[ʃpɪn]		(p. 126)
[z]	[s/]	[izi]	easy	becomes	[isi]		(p. 121)
[z]	[ts/]	[zɪpɚ]	zipper	becomes	[tsɪpɚ]		(p. 133)
[ʃ]	[tʃ/]	[ʃɪp]	ship	becomes	[tʃɪp]		(p. 138)
[w]	[v/]	[wɛst]	west	becomes	[vɛst]		(p. 148)
[r]	[R/]	[graund]	ground	becomes	[gRaund]	See note.	(p. 151)
[tʃ]	[ʃ/]	[tʃɝtʃ]	church	becomes	[ʃɝʃ]		(p. 183)
[dʒ]	[tʃ/]	[dʒɛli]	jelly	becomes	[tʃɛli]		(p. 187)
[dʒ]	[ʃ/]	[dʒæm]	jam	becomes	[ʃæm]		(p. 187)
[æ]	[ɛ/]	[pæn]	pan	becomes	[pɛn]		(p. 209)
[ʌ]	[ɑ/]	[ʌp]	up	becomes	[ɑp]		(p. 227)
[eɪ]	[e/]	[peɪ]	pay	becomes	[pe]		(p. 201)

KEY: / SUBSTITUTION
Note: Uses [R], a uvular-trilled substitute for the lingua-palatal glide [r].

First Language Background: Italian

Sound	Problem	Standard		becomes	Non-Standard		Exercise
[p]	[(ʰ)]	[stapʰ]	stop	becomes	[stap⁽ʰ⁾]	See note 4.	(p. 56)
[t]	[ʰ]	[sɛnt]	sent	becomes	[sɛntʰ]		(p. 66)
[t]	[̯]	[tɑp]	top	becomes	[t̯ɑp]	See note 1.	(p. 67)
[d]	[̯]	[bæd]	bad	becomes	[bæd̯]	See note 1.	(p. 67)
[k]	[ʰ]	[bæŋk]	bank	becomes	[bæŋkʰ]		(p. 84)
[θ]	[t/]	[θæŋks]	thanks	becomes	[tæŋks]		(p. 108)
[ð]	[d/]	[ðæt]	that	becomes	[dæt]		(p. 108)
[s]	[z/]	[lɔs]	loss	becomes	[lɔz]		(p. 122)
[h]	[()]	[haus]	house	becomes	[aus]		(p. 144)
[r]	[ř/]	[rut]	root	becomes	[řut]	See note 2.	(p. 151)
[n]	[̯]	[naɪs]	nice	becomes	[n̯aɪs]	See note 1.	(p. 173)
[i]	[ɪ/]	[fid]	feed	becomes	[fɪd]		(p. 196)
[ɪ]	[i/]	[skɪd]	skid	becomes	[skid]		(p. 196)
[ʊ]	[u/]	[pʊl]	pull	becomes	[pul]		(p. 225)

(*Continued*)

First Language Background: Italian (*Continued*)

Sound	Problem	Standard			Non-Standard		Exercise
[u]	[ʊ]	[bʊt]	boot	becomes	[bʊt]		(p. 225)
[ʌ]	[ɑ/]	[ʌp]	up	becomes	[ɑp]		(p. 227)
[ə]	[+]	[hɪt]	hit	becomes	[hɪtə]	See note 3.	(p. 230)
[ɝ]	[ɛr]	[bɝd]	bird	becomes	[bɛrd]		(p. 233)
[ɚ]	[ɛr]	[mʌðɚ]	mother	becomes	[mʌðɛr]		(p. 236)

KEY: / SUBSTITUTION   ( ) OMISSION   + ADDITION   ₙDENTALIZED   ʰ ASPIRATED
(ʰ) LACKS ASPIRATION

Notes: 1. Produced dentally (on the back of the teeth) instead of on the gum ridge.
2. Uses [ɾ], a tongue-tap-trilled substitute for the lingua-alveolar glide [r].
3. Frequently added to words ending in consonants.
4. Lacks the aspirated (explosive) quality of plosive sounds.

First Language Background: Japanese

Sound	Problem	Standard			Non-Standard	Exercise
[v]	[b/]	[vaɪn]	vine	becomes	[baɪn]	(p. 97)
[θ]	[s/]	[θɪŋk]	think	becomes	[sɪŋk]	(p. 111)
[ð]	[z/]	[ðɪs]	this	becomes	[zɪs]	(p. 111)
[ð]	[dʒ/]	[ðoʊ]	though	becomes	[dʒoʊ]	(p. 108)
[l]	[r/]	[frɛnd]	friend	becomes	[flɛnd]	(p. 165)
[ɪ]	[i/]	[bɪn]	bin	becomes	[bin]	(p. 196)
[æ]	[ɑ/]	[pæt]	pat	becomes	[pɑt]	(p. 209)
[ʌ]	[ɑ/]	[dʌk]	duck	becomes	[dɑk]	(p. 227)
[ɝ]	[ɑ/]	[hɝ]	her	becomes	[hɑ]	(p. 233)
[ɚ]	[ɑ/]	[fɑðɚ]	father	becomes	[fɑðɑ]	(p. 236)

KEY: / SUBSTITUTION

Note: [n] is the only consonant that may end words in Japanese. Because all other words end in vowels, many speakers of Japanese add the vowels [u] or [ə] to English words ending in consonant sounds. For example, the word *hotel* [hotɛl] may become [hoteru] and *book* [bʊk] may become [bʊkə].

First Language Background: Korean

Sound	Problem	Standard			Non-Standard		Exercise
[p]	[p̃]	[tæp]	tap	becomes	[tæp̃]	See note 1.	(p. 269)
[b]	[b̃]	[rʌb]	rub	becomes	[rʌb̃]	See note 1.	(p. 269)
[t]	[t̃]	[hæt]	hat	becomes	[hæt̃]	See note 1.	(p. 269)
[d]	[d̃]	[rɛd]	red	becomes	[rɛd̃]	See note 1.	(p. 269)
[k]	[k̃]	[pok]	poke	becomes	[pok̃]	See note 1.	(p. 269)
[g]	[g̃]	[hʌg]	hug	becomes	[hʌg̃]	See note 1.	(p. 269)
[v]	[b/]	[gɪv]	give	becomes	[gɪb]		(p. 97)
[v]	[p/]	[hæv]	have	becomes	[hæp]		(p. 97)
[ð]	[dʒ]	[ðɪs]	this	becomes	[dʒɪs]		(p. 108)
[z]	[s/]	[hɪz]	his	becomes	[hɪs]		(p. 121)
[ʃ]	[s/]	[wɪʃ]	wish	becomes	[wɪs]		(p. 138)
[tʃ]	[t/]	[mætʃ]	match	becomes	[mæts]		(p. 184)
[r]	[1/]	[rɔ]	raw	becomes	[lɔ]		(p. 152)
[l]	[r/]	[lɛt]	let	becomes	[rɛt]		(p. 165)
[i]	[ɪ/]	[sit]	seat	becomes	[sɪt]		(p. 196)
[ɪ]	[i/]	[sɪt]	sit	becomes	[sit]		(p. 196)
[u]	[ʊ/]	[sut]	suit	becomes	[sʊt]		(p. 225)
[ʊ]	[u/]	[sʊt]	soot	becomes	[sut]		(p. 225)
[ʌ]	[:]	[sʌn]	son	becomes		See note 2.	(p. 285)
[ɔ]	[:]	[sɔ]	saw	becomes		See note 2.	(p. 285)

KEY: / SUBSTITUTION   ~ CONFUSION   ˜ NASALIZED
    : DURATION

Notes: 1.   Nasalized at the ends of words.
       2.   Confusion of vowel duration (length).

First Language Background: Pilipino

Sound	Problem	Standard			Non-Standard		Exercise
[p]	[(ʰ)]	[ʌpʰ]	up	becomes	[ʌp⁽ʰ⁾]	See note.	(p. 56)
[t]	[(ʰ)]	[tʰu]	too	becomes	[t⁽ʰ⁾u]	See note.	(p. 66)
[k]	[(ʰ)]	[lækʰ]	lack	becomes	[læk⁽ʰ⁾]	See note.	(p. 84)
[f]	[p/]	[kɔfɪ]	coffee	becomes	[kɔpɪ]		(p. 97)
[v]	[b/]	[vɛrɪ]	very	becomes	[bɛrɪ]		(p. 97)
[θ]	[t/]	[θri]	three	becomes	[tri]		(p. 108)
[ð]	[d/]	[ðɪs]	this	becomes	[dɪs]		(p. 108)
[z]	[s/]	[hæz]	has	becomes	[hæs]		(p. 121)

(Continued)

First Language Background: Pilipino (*Continued*)

Sound	Problem	Standard			Non-Standard		Exercise
[ʃ]	[s/]	[ʃu]	shoe	becomes	[su]		(p. 138)
[tʃ]	[ts/]	[mætʃ]	match	becomes	[mæts]		(p. 188)
[dʒ]	[d/]	[ɛdʒ]	edge	becomes	[ɛd]		(p. 187)
[ɪ]	[i/]	[sɪt]	sit	becomes	[sit]		(p. 196)
[ɔ]	[o/]	[lɔ]	law	becomes	[lo]		(p. 217)

KEY: / SUBSTITUTION (ʰ) LACKS ASPIRATION

Note: [p] [t] [k] frequently lack the aspirated (explosive) quality of plosives.

First Language Background: Russian

Sound	Problem	Standard			Non-Standard		Exercise
[t]	[ˌ]	[tu]	too	becomes	[t̪u]	See note 1.	(p. 67)
[d]	[t/]	[sɛd]	said	becomes	[sɛt]	See note 2.	(p. 66)
[d]	[ˌ]	[ædɪŋ]	adding	becomes	[æd̪ɪŋ]	See note 1.	(p. 67)
[f]	[v/]	[kɔfɪ]	coffee	becomes	[kɔvɪ]		(p. 96)
[ð]	[d/]	[ðæt]	that	becomes	[dæt]		(p. 108)
[n]	[ˌ]	[nau]	now	becomes	[n̪au]	See note 1.	(p. 174)
[n]	[j+]	[fʌnɪ]	funny	becomes	[fʌnjɪ]		(p. 174)
[ŋ]	[n/]	[lʌvɪŋ]	loving	becomes	[lʌvɪn]		(p. 175)
[ŋ]	[k+]	[bæŋɪŋ]	banging	becomes	[bæŋkɪŋk]		(p. 178)
[w]	[v/]	[wæks]	wax	becomes	[væks]		(p. 148)
[r]	[r̃/]	[rɛst]	rest	becomes	[r̃ɛst]	See note 3.	(p. 151)
[dʒ]	[ʒ/]	[dʒouk]	joke	becomes	[ʒouk]		(p. 187)
[dʒ]	[tʃ/]	[dʒʌmp]	jump	becomes	[tʃʌmp]		(p. 187)
[i]	[ɪ/]	[sit]	seat	becomes	[sɪt]		(p. 196)
[ɪ]	[i/]	[sɪt]	sɪt	becomes	[sit]		(p. 196)
[o]	[ɔ/]	[kot]	coat	becomes	[kɔt]		(p. 220)
[ʊ]	[u/]	[pʊl]	pull	becomes	[pul]		(p. 225)
[ʌ]	[a/]	[rʌʃən]	Russian	becomes	[raʃan]		(p. 227)
[ɝ]	[ɛr/]	[lɝn]	learn	becomes	[lɛrn]		(p. 233)

KEY: / SUBSTITUTION   + ADDITION   ˌDENTALIZED

Notes: 1. Produced dentally (on the back of the teeth) instead of on the gum ridge.
  2. Problem occurs in word endings.
  3. Uses trilled [r] instead of lingua-palatal glide [r].

First Language Background: Scandinavian

Sound	Problem	Standard		becomes	Non-Standard		Exercise
[θ]	[t/]	[θɪn]	thin	becomes	[tɪn]		(p. 108)
[ð]	[d/]	[ðæt]	that	becomes	[dæt]		(p. 108)
[z]	[s/]	[izi]	easy	becomes	[isi]		(p. 121)
[r]	[r̃]	[rɛd]	red	becomes	[r̃ɛd]	See note 1.	(p. 151)
[w]	[v/]	[wɛst]	west	becomes	[vɛst]		(p. 148)
[ʒ]	[ʃ/]	[beɪʒ]	beige	becomes	[beɪʃ]		(p. 137)
[dʒ]	[j/]	[dʒʌmp]	jump	becomes	[jump]	See note 2.	(p. 184)
[dʒ]	[tʃ/]	[ɛdʒ]	edge	becomes	[ɛtʃ]		(p. 183)
[i]	[j+]	[iɚ]	ear	becomes	[ijɚ]		(p. 192)
[ɪ]	[j+]	[wɪnd]	wind	becomes	[wɪjnd]		(p. 196)
[ɛ]	[j+]	[lɛt]	let	becomes	[lɛjt]		(p. 204)
[eɪ]	[j+]	[eɪm]	aim	becomes	[eɪjm]		(p. 201)
[æ]	[ɛ+]	[bænd]	band	becomes	[bæɛnd]		(p. 210)
[u]	[ʊ/]	[pul]	pool	becomes	[pʊl]		(p. 225)
[ɔ]	[o/]	[kɔl]	call	becomes	[kol]		(p. 217)
[aɪ]	[j+]	[aɪs]	ice	becomes	[aɪjs]		(p. 239)
[ɔɪ]	[j+]	[kɔɪn]	coin	becomes	[kɔɪjn]		(p. 245)

KEY: / SUBSTITUTION   + ADDITION
1.   Uses a trilled [r̃] instead of the lingua-palatal glide [r].
2.   May occur when [dʒ] is represented in written English by the letter *j*.

First Language Background: Spanish

Sound	Problem	Standard		becomes	Non-Standard		Exercise
[p]	[(ʰ)]	[pʰæn]	pan	becomes	[p⁽ʰ⁾æn]	See note 1.	(p. 56)
[t]	[(ʰ)]	[tʰæn]	tan	becomes	[t⁽ʰ⁾æn]	See note 1.	(p. 66)
[t]	[ˌ]	[tu]	too	becomes	[t̪u]	See note 2.	(p. 67)
[d]	[ˌ]	[doʊ]	dough	becomes	[d̪oʊ]	See note 2.	(p. 67)
[k]	[(ʰ)]	[kʰæn]	can	becomes	[k⁽ʰ⁾æn]	See note 1.	(p. 84)
[θ]	[t/]	[θɪn]	thin	becomes	[tɪn]		(p. 108)
[ð]	[d/]	[ðæt]	that	becomes	[dæt]		(p. 108)
[s]	[θ/]	[æskɪŋ]	asking	becomes	[æθkɪŋ]		(p. 111)
[s]	[ɛ+]	[spænɪʃ]	Spanish	becomes	[ɛspænɪʃ]		(p. 122)
[z]	[s/]	[ɪz]	is	becomes	[ɪs]		(p. 121)
[n]	[ŋ/]	[rʌn]	run	becomes	[rʌŋ]		(p. 171)
[n]	[ˌ]	[noʊ]	no	becomes	[n̪oʊ]	See note 2.	(p. 174)

(Continued)

First Language Background: **Spanish** (*Continued*)

Sound	Problem	Standard			Non-Standard		Exercise
[w]	[v/]	[wek]	wake	becomes	[vek]		(p. 148)
[r]	[r̃/]	[rɛd]	red	becomes	[r̃ɛd]	See note 3.	(p. 151)
[ʒ]	[ʃ/]	[beɪʒ]	beige	becomes	[beɪʃ]		(p. 137)
[tʃ]	[ʃ/]	[tʃaɪm]	chime	becomes	[ʃaɪm]		(p. 138)
[j]	[dʒ/]	[jɛs]	yes	becomes	[dʒɛs]		(p. 161)
[i]	[ɪ/]	[sit]	seat	becomes	[sɪt]		(p. 196)
[ɪ]	[i/]	[ʃɪp]	ship	becomes	[ʃip]		(p. 196)
[eɪ]	[e/]	[peɪ]	pay	becomes	[pe]		(p. 201)
[ɔ]	[o/]	[kɔl]	call	becomes	[kol]		(p. 217)
[u]	[ʊ/]	[ʃuz]	shoes	becomes	[ʃʊz]		(p. 225)
[ʌ]	[o/]	[lʌv]	love	becomes	[lov]		(p. 228)

KEY: / SUBSTITUTION   + ADDITION   ₙDENTALIZED   ʰ ASPIRATED
(ʰ) LACKS ASPIRATION

Notes: 1. Lacks aspirated ''explosive'' quality.
 2. Produced dentally (on the back of the teeth) instead of on the gum ridge.
 3. Substitutes trilled [r̃] for linqua-palatal glide [r].

E

Appendix E

Pronunciation List

The words in the following lists are frequently mispronounced. They're all fairly common words, and with a little practice you should be able to pronounce them correctly. We've grouped them according to the type of mispronunciation, so we suggest you work within one type before moving on to the next. Have someone listen to you, or tape your practice session for review later.

A word about the "correct" way to pronounce words; our language is always changing, and a pronunciation that was preferred at one time may not be so widely used today. We used the 1983 *Random House Dictionary* for our guide to preferred pronunciations; you may find that your dictionary shows another. If so, consult your instructor to determine which pronunciation is preferred in your area.

The IPA stress marking system differs from the diacritical system used in dictionaries. Dictionaries place the stress mark to the upper right of the stressed syllable. The IPA system is as follows:

1. Primary stress is shown by a mark at the upper left (in front of) the stressed syllable.
2. Secondary stress is shown by a mark at the lower lefthand side of the syllable.
3. Tertiary (unstressed) syllables are not marked.

REVERSALS

The words in this section are often mispronounced because of the reversal of two sounds. For example, the word *ask*, standardly pronounced [æsk], becomes *ax* when the two consonant sounds are reversed.

Standard Pronunciation

Word	Pronunciation	IPA*	Non-Standard
1. ask	ask	[æsk]	[æks]
2. asked	askt	[æskt]	[ækst]
3. asterisk	as′ tə risk	[ˈæstəˌrɪsk]	[ˈæstəˌrɪks]
4. children	chil′ drən	[ˈtʃɪldrən]	[ˈtʃɪldɚn]
5. hundred	hun′ drid	[ˈhʌndrɪd]	[ˈhʌnɚd]
6. introduction	in′ trə duk′ shən	[ˌɪntrəˈdʌkʃən]	[ˌɪntɚˈdʌkʃən]
7. larynx	lar′ ingks	[ˈlærɪŋks]	[ˈlɑrnɪks]
8. lisp	lisp	[lɪsp]	[lɪps]
9. perform	pər fôrm′	[pɚˈfɔɚm]	[prəˈfɔɚm]
10. perspiration	pûr′ spə ra′ shən	[ˌpɚspəˈreʃən]	[ˌprɛspəˈreʃən]
11. pharynx	far′ingks	[ˈfærɪŋks]	[ˈfɑrnɪks]
12. prescription	pri skrip′ shən	[priˈskrɪpʃən]	[pɚˈskrɪpʃən]
13. pretty	prit′ ē	[ˈprɪti]	[ˈpɚtij]
14. professor	prə fes′ ər	[prəˈfɛsɚ]	[pɚˈfɛsɚ]
15. southern	suth′ ərn	[ˈsʌðɚn]	[ˈsʌðrən]

*IPA transcription of recommended (dictionary) pronunciation.

OMISSIONS

The following words are often mispronounced when people omit one or more of the sounds which should be present. Say these words carefully. Make sure each sound is there that should be there.

Standard Pronunciation

Word	Pronunciation	IPA*	Non-Standard
1. accelerate	ak sel′ ə rat	[ækˈsɛləˌret]	[æˈsɛləˌret]
2. accessory	ak ses′ə rē	[ækˈsɛsəri]	[æˈsɛsəri]

(Continued)

Standard Pronunciation (*Continued*)

Word	Pronunciation	IPA*	Non-Standard
3. antidote	an'ti dōt'	[ˈæntɪˌdot]	[ˈænəˌdot]
4. arctic	ärk'tik	[ˈarktɪk]	[ˈartɪk]
5. basketball	bas'kit bôl'	[ˈbæskətˌbɔl]	[ˈbæskəˌbɔl]
6. candidate	kan'di dāt'	[ˈkændəˌdet]	[ˈkænəˌdet]
7. contact	kon'takt	[ˈkanˌtækt]	[ˈkanˌtæk]
8. correct	kə rekt'	[kəˈrɛkt]	[kəˈrɛk]
9. couldn't	kood'ʰnt	[ˈkʊd nt]	[ˈkʊdn]
10. entertain	en'tər tān'	[ˌɛntɚˈten]	[ˌɛnɚˈten]
11. environment	en vī' rənmənt	[ɛnˈvaɪrənmənt]	[ɛnˈvaɪrəmənt]
12. friendly	frend'lē	[ˈfrɛndli]	[ˈfrɛnli]
13. frustrate	frus'trāt	[ˈfrʌstret]	[ˈfʌstret]
14. library	lī'brer'ē	[ˈlaɪˌbrɛrɪ]	[ˈlaɪˌbɛri]
15. museum	myoo zē'əm	[ˌmjuˈziəm]	[ˌmjuˈzim]
16. orange	or'inj	[ˈarəndʒ]	[ˈaɚndʒ]
17. perhaps	pər haps'	[pɚˈhæps]	[præps]
18. picture	pik'chər	[ˈpɪktʃɚ]	[ˈpɪtʃɚ]
19. poem	po'əm	[ˈpoəm]	[pom]
20. probably	prob'ə blē	[ˈprabəbli]	[ˈprali]
21. professor	prə fes'ər	[prəˈfɛsɚ]	[pəˈfɛsɚ]
22. quiet	kwī' it	[ˈkwaɪət]	[ˈkwaɪt]
23. recognize	rek'əg nīz'	[ˈrɛkəgˌnaɪz]	[rɛkənaɪz]
24. regular	reg'yə lər	[ˈrɛgjəlɚ]	[ˈrɛgəlɚ]
25. robbery	rob'ə rē	[ˈrabəri]	[ˈrabri]
26. scrupulous	skroo'pyə ləs	[ˈskrupjələs]	[ˈskrupələs]
27. skeptical	skep'ti kəl	[ˈskɛptɪkəl]	[ˈskɛpəkəl]
28. slept	slept	[slɛpt]	[slɛp]
29. specific	spi sif'ik	[spəˈsɪfɪk]	[pəˈsɪfɪk]
30. substitute	sub'sti toot'	[ˈsʌbstɪˌtut]	[ˈsʌbsəˌtut]
31. temperature	tem'pər ə chər	[ˈtɛmprətʃɚ]	[ˈtɛmpətʃɚ]
32. throw	thrō	[θrou]	[θou]
33. twenty	twen'tē	[ˈtwɛnti]	[ˈtwɛni]
34. wonderful	wun'dər fəl	[ˈwʌndɚˌful]	[ˈwʌnɚˌful]
35. wouldn't	wood'ənt	[ˈwʊdnt]	[wʊnt]

*IPA transcription of recommended (dictionary) pronunciation.

SUBSTITUTIONS

These words are mispronounced by substituting one sound for another.

Standard Pronunciation

Word	Pronunciation	IPA*	Non-Standard
1. architect	är′ki tekt′	[′arkəˌtɛkt]	[′artʃəˌtɛkt]
2. asphalt	as′fôlt	[′æsfɔlt]	[′æʃfɔlt]
3. attache	at′ə shā′	[ˌætə′ʃe]	[æ′tætʃe]
4. banquet	bang′kwit	[′bæŋkwɪt]	[′bæŋkwɪt]
5. Beethoven	bā′tōv n	[′beˌtovən]	[′biˌθovən]
6. beige	bāzh	[beɪʒ]	[beɪdʒ]
7. brochure	brō shoor′	[bro′ʃuɚ]	[bro′tʃuɚ]
8. charisma	kə riz′mə	[kə′rɪzmə]	[tʃə′rɪzmə]
9. charlatan	shär′lə tən	[′ʃarlətən]	[′tʃarlətən]
10. chasm	kaz′əm	[′kæzəm]	[′tʃæzəm]
11. chef	shef	[ʃɛf]	[tʃɛf]
12. chic	shek	[ʃik]	[tʃɪk]
13. chiropractor	ki′rə prak′tər	[′kaɪrəˌpræktɚ]	[′tʃaɪrəˌpræktɚ]
14. Chopin	sho′pan	[′ʃopæn]	[′tʃopɪn]
15. connoisseur	kon′ə sûr′	[ˌkanə′suɚ]	[ˌkanə′ʃuɚ]
16. crux	kruks	[krʌks]	[krʊks]
17. cuisine	kwi zēn′	[kwɪ′zin]	[kju′zin]
18. cupola	kyoo′ pə lə	[′kjupələ]	[′kʌpələ]
19. data	dā′ tə	[′detə]	[′dætə]
20. deluge	del′yōōj	[′dɛlˌjudʒ]	[′dɛlˌjuʒ]
21. diphthong	dif′thông	[′dɪfθaŋ]	[′dɪpθaŋ]
22. diphtheria	dif thēr′ē ə	[dɪf′θiriə]	[dɪp′θiriə]
23. et cetera	et set′ərə	[ɛt′sɛtərə]	[ˌɛk′sɛtərə]
24. faux pas	fō pä′	[′fo ′pa]	[′fɔks′pæs]
25. filet	fi lā′	[fɪ′leɪ]	[′fɪlɪt]
26. gesture	jes′ch r	[′dʒɛstʃɚ]	[′gɛstʃɚ]
27. gist	jist	[dʒɪst]	[gɪst]
28. harbinger	här′bin jər	[′harbɪndʒɚ]	[′harbɪŋɚ]
29. hearth	härth	[harθ]	[hɜθ]
30. height	hīt	[haɪt]	[haɪθ]
31. heinous	hā′nəs	[′heɪnəs]	[′haɪnəs]

(Continued)

Standard Pronunciation (*Continued*)

Word	Pronunciation	IPA*	Non-Standard
32. heir	âr	[ɛɚ]	[hɛɚ]
33. herald	her′əld	[ˈhɛrəld]	[ˈhærəld]
34. houses	hou′ziz	[ˈhauzɪz]	[ˈhausɪz]
35. indict	in dīt′	[ɪnˈdaɪt]	[ɪnˈdɪkt]
36. indigent	in′di jənt	[ˈɪndɪdʒənt]	[ˈɪndɪgənt]
37. Italian	i tal′yən	[ɪˈtæljən]	[ˌaɪˈtæljən]
38. length	leṉgkth	[lɛŋkθ]	[lɛnθ]
39. longevity	lon jev′i tē	[lɔnˈdʒɛvɪti]	[lɔŋgɛvɪti]
40. longitude	lon′ji too̅d′	[ˈlɔndʒɪˌtud]	[ˈlɔŋgɪˌtud]
41. malingerer	mə ling′gərər	[məˈlɪŋgərɚ]	[məˈlɪndʒərɚ]
42. masochistic	mas′əkis′tik	[mæsəˈkɪstɪk]	[mæsəˈtʃɪstɪk]
43. mocha	mō′kə	[ˈmokə]	[ˈmotʃə]
44. oil	oil	[ɔɪl]	[ɝl]
45. onus	ō′nəs	[ˈounəs]	[ɑnəs]
46. orgy	ôr′jē	[ˈɔrdʒi]	[ˈɔrgi]
47. pathos	pā′thos	[ˈpeθas]	[ˈpæθos]
48. pique	pēk	[pik]	[ˌpiˈke]
49. placard	plak′ärd	[ˈplækɚd]	[ˈplekaɚd]
50. poignant	poin′yənt	[ˈpɔɪnjənt]	[ˈpɔɪgnənt]
51. posthumous	pos′chə məs	[ˈpastʃəməs]	[ˈpasθjuməs]
52. prestige	pre stēzh′	[prɛsˈtiʒ]	[prɛsˈtidʒ]
53. regime	rə zhēm′	[rəˈʒim]	[rəˈdʒim]
54. salient	sāl′lēənt	[ˈseɪliənt]	[ˈsæliənt]
55. strength	streṉgkth	[strɛŋkθ]	[strɛnθ]
56. suave	swäv	[swav]	[sweɪv]
57. suite	swēt	[swit]	[sut]
58. taciturn	tas′i tûrn	[ˈtæsɪˌtɝn]	[ˈtækɪˌtɝn]
59. taupe	tōp	[top]	[tɔp]
60. thyme	tīm	[taɪm]	[θaɪm]
61. tremendous	tri men′dəs	[trɪˈmɛndəs]	[trɪˈmɛndʒuəs]
62. virile	vir′əl	[ˈvɪrəl]	[ˈvaɪrəl]
63. Worcester	woŏs′tər	[ˈwustɚ]	[ˈwɔrsɛstɚ]
64. worsted	woŏs′tid	[ˈwustɪd]	[ˈwɝstɪd]
65. zealot	zel′ət	[ˈzɛlət]	[ˈzilat]
66. zoology	zō ol′ ə jē	[ˌzoˈɑləˌdʒi]	[ˌzuˈɑləˌdʒi]

*IPA transcription of recommended (dictionary) pronunciation.

INTRUSIONS

The words in this list are mispronounced by adding sounds that don't belong there.

Standard Pronunciation

Word	Pronunciation	IPA*	Non-Standard
1. across	əkrôs′	[ə'krɔs]	[ə'krɔst]
2. almond	ä′mənd	['amənd]	['almənd]
3. athlete	ath′lēt	['æθlit]	['æθəˌlit]
4. balk	bôk	[bɔk]	[bɔlk]
5. balmy	bä′mē	['bami]	['balˌmi]
6. burglar	bûr′glər	['bɝglɚ]	['bɝgjələ]
7. business	biz′nis	['bɪznɪs]	['bɪzɪnɪs]
8. calm	käm	[kam]	[kalm]
9. chimney	chim′nē	[tʃɪmni]	['tʃɪmbli]
10. column	kol′əm	['kaləm]	['kaljəm]
11. condominium	kon′də min′ēəm	[ˌkandə'miniəm]	[ˌkamndə'miniəm]
12. consonant	kon′sə nənt	['kansənənt]	['kanstənənt]
13. corps	kôr	[kɔɚ]	[kɔɚps]
14. drowned	dround	[draund]	['draundəd]
15. electoral	i lek′tər əl	[ɪ'lɛktərəl]	[ɪlɛk'tɔriəl]
16. escalator	es′kə lā′tər	['ɛskəletɚ]	['ɛskjəletɚ]
17. escape	e skāp′	[ɛs'kep]	[ɛk'skep]
18. evening	ēv′ning	['ivnɪŋ]	['ivənɪŋ]
19. facetious	fəsē′shəs	[fə'siʃəs]	[fə'siʃiəs]
20. film	film	[fɪlm]	['fɪləm]
21. grievous	grē′vəs	['grivəs]	['griviəs]
22. momentous	mō men′təs	[mo'mɛntəs]	[mo'mɛnˌtʃuəs]
23. monstrous	mon′strəs	['manstrəs]	['manstərəs]
24. nuclear	noo′klē ər	['nukliɚ]	['nukjələ]
25. often	ô′fən	[ɔfən]	[ɔftən]
26. once	wuns	[wʌns]	[wʌnst]
27. psalm	säm	[sam]	[salm]
28. righteous	rī′chəs	['raɪtʃəs]	['raɪtʃuəs]
29. schism	siz′əm	['sɪzəm]	['skɪzəm]
30. soften	sô′fən	['sɔfən]	['sɔftən]

(Continued)

Standard Pronunciation (*Continued*)

Word	Pronunciation	IPA*	Non-Standard
31. sophomore	sof′môr	[ˈsɑfmɔɚ]	[ˈsɑfəmɔɚ]
32. statistics	stə tis′tiks	[stəˈtɪstɪks]	[stəˈstɪstɪks]
33. subtle	sut′əl	[ˈsʌtl]	[ˈsʌbtl]
34. sword	sōrd	[sɔɚd]	[swɔɚd]
35. tremendous	tri men′dəs	[trɪˈmɛndəs]	[trɪˈmendʒəs]

*IPA transcription of recommended (dictionary) pronunciation.

MISPLACED STRESS

The following words are all frequently mispronounced due to misplaced syllable stress; that is, emphasizing the wrong syllable.

Standard Pronunciation

Word	Pronunciation	IPA*	Non-Standard
1. abdomen	ab′də mən	[ˈæb dəmən]	[ˌæbˈdomən]
2. absurd	ab sûrd′	[æbˈsɚd]	[ˈæbsɚd]
3. admirable	ad′mər ə bəl	[ˈædˌmərəbəl]	[ˌædˈmaɪrəbəl]
4. applicable	ap′lə kə bəl	[ˈæpləkəbəl]	[ˌəˈplɪkəbəl]
5. bravado	brə vä′dō	[ˌbrəˈvado]	[ˈbravədo]
6. Caribbean	kar′ə bē′ən	[ˌkærəˈbiən]	[kəˈrɪbiən]
7. cement	si ment′	[sɪˈmɛnt]	[ˈsimɛnt]
8. chagrin	shə grin′	[ʃəˈgrɪn]	[ˈʃʌgrɪn]
9. conduit	kon′doo it	[ˈkɑndʊit]	[kənˈdʊit]
10. delight	di līt′	[dɪˈlaɪt]	[ˈdilaɪt]
11. deluge	del′yooj	[ˈdɛljudʒ]	[dəˈludʒ]
12. guitar	gi tär′	[gɪˈtɑɚ]	[ˈgɪtɑɚ]
13. impotent	im′pə tant	[ˈim pətənt]	[ˌimˈpotənt]
14. incomparable	in kom′pər ə bəl	[inˈkɑmpərəbəl]	[inkamˈpɛrəbəl]
15. incongruous	in kong′groo ə s	[inˈkɑŋˌgruəs]	[inkənˈgruəs]
16. infamous	in′fə məs	[ˈin fəməs]	[ˌinˈfeməs]
17. inquiry	inkwiər′ē	[inˈkwaɪri]	[ˈinkwaɪri]
18. irreparable	i rep′ər ə bəl	[ɪˈrɛpərəbəl]	[ˌɪriˈpɛɚəbəl]
19. maintenance	mān′tənəns	[ˈmeɪnˌtənəns]	[menˈteɪnəns]

(*Continued*)

Standard Pronunciation (*Continued*)

Word	Pronunciation	IPA*	Non-Standard
20. mischievous	mis′chə vəs	[′mɪs t∫əvəs]	[mɪs′t∫iviəs]
21. omnipotent	om nip′ə tənt	[ɑm′nɪpətənt]	[ɑmnɪ′potənt]
22. police	pə lēs	[pə′lis]	[′polis]
23. preclude	pri klo͞od′	[pri′klud]	[′priklud]
24. preferable	pref′ərə bəl	[′prɛfərəbəl]	[ˌprə′fɜrəbəl]
25. preference	pref′ərəns	[′prɛfər əns]	[prə′fɜrəns]
26. respite	res′pit	[′rɛspɪt]	[rəs′paɪt]

*IPA transcription of recommended (dictionary) pronunciation.

Appendix F

Glossary

This is an informal glossary of words that are used in this book. We have given definitions that could be considered to be "working definitions," and they might not always be the best definitions in other contexts.

abdomen The belly; contains the stomach.

abdominal breathing A pattern of breathing that is typified by controlled movements of the abdominal muscles.

accent 1. A pattern of pronunciation, stress, and intonation typical of the speech of a particular person, group, or geographical area. See **dialect, standard, non-standard, regionalism,** and **foreign accent.** 2. Stress given to a syllable in a word. See **stress.**

acoustic Pertaining to sound, or the qualities of a sound.

"adam's apple" A noticeable prominence on the front edge of the thyroid cartilage. See **thyroid cartilage.**

adaptors Gestures that we learn early in life, such as scratching our heads, rubbing our noses, chewing our glasses, and so on. It is generally thought that adaptors reflect our unconscious needs or drives.

affect display Gestures or facial expressions that reflect a person's emotional state.

affricate   A single consonant sound produced by following a plosive closely with a fricative. The first sound in the word *chew* is an affricate.

allophone   A variation of a phoneme. Although the variation may be noticeable, it is slight enough that it would not affect the meaning of a word. See **phoneme.**

alveolar ridge   The gum ridge just behind the upper front teeth.

amplify   To increase the loudness of a sound.

articulation   Movements of the speech organs to produce speech sounds.

articulators   The organs of speech used to produce speech sounds: tongue, lips, soft palate, hard palate, alveolar ridge, teeth, glottis.

arytenoid cartilage   Triangular-shaped cartilages in the larynx to which the vocal folds attach.

assimilation   The process by which speech sounds become part of the sounds around them. For example *"Jeet?"* (Did you eat?)

audition   The process of hearing.

back vowel   A vowel sound produced when the tongue is arched in the back part of the mouth, with the lips rounded. The vowel in the word *so* is a back vowel.

bi-labial sounds   Consonants produced using both lips to block the breathstream, such as the first and last sounds in the word *pub*.

blend   A sound that is the result of joining two consonants closely and smoothly together. For example the *sw* in *swan*.

breath control   Regulating the rate of exhalation during speech and voice production.

breathiness   An excessive loss of air while speaking. A breathy voice has a "whispery" quality.

breathing   The process of moving air in and out of the lungs for respiration.

breathstream   Air released from the lungs that is used to start vocal fold vibration for vowels and also to produce consonants.

casual-personal distance   The distance at which we hold conversations with friends, family members, and others with whom we have working relationships. Ranges from 1½ feet to 4 feet. See **proxemics.**

central nervous system   The part of the human nervous system composed of the brain and spinal cord.

circumflex   See **inflection.**

cluster   A grouping of consonants in the same syllable, with no vowel between them. For example, the first three consonants in the word *straw* form a cluster.

cochlea   The snail-shaped portion of the inner ear containing the end-organ of hearing.

cognate sounds   Two consonant sounds that are made in the same place and in the same manner. The only difference is that one is voiced and the other is voiceless. See **place of production, method of production,** and **voiced and voiceless consonants.**

communication   The process by which an idea, thought, or feeling that arises in the mind of one person is conveyed to the mind of someone else.

complex tone   A sound wave having more than two frequencies. See **frequency, wave form.**

consonant   A type of speech sound that is produced by completely or partially blocking the breathstream using the articulators. The first and last sounds in the word *kiss* are consonants.

cricoid cartilage   The ring-shaped cartilage at the base of the larynx.

decibel   The measurement unit of sound intensity.

defective speech   Speech that results in a noticeable communication deficit for the speaker. The speaker may not be able to produce a particular sound in a standard manner without assistance from a teacher or speech pathologist.

denasality   Too little nasal resonance resulting in a voice that sounds as if the speaker has a stuffed nose. See **nasality.**

dialect   A form of a language that is spoken in a specific geographical area that differs from the official language of the larger area. See **accent, regionalism,** and **foreign accent.**

diaphragm   The main muscle of respiration. It is located between the chest and abdominal cavities.

diction   The production of the sounds of a particular language, and the selection of words of the language when speaking.

diphthong   A glide composed of two vowels, blended together, produced in a single syllable.

distortion   Defective production of a speech sound due to faulty placement, timing, pressure, direction, movement, or integration of the articulators. The sound produced can be readily identified, but is not accurate enough to be considered standard.

duration   The length of a sound; how long it is held when produced.

emblem   A gesture that has a direct verbal translation. For example, if while standing at the side of a highway you face traffic and make a fist with the thumb extended and pointing upward, you are indicating to drivers that you want a ride.

emphasis   Stress given to a word in a phrase. See **stress.**

excessive nasality   A voice quality resulting from too much nasal resonance. See **nasality.**

external auditory canal   A canal leading from the external ear to the tympanic membrane (ear drum).

facial nerve   The seventh cranial nerve. Its fibers travel to the face and muscles of the tongue.

force   In sound production, the energy that activates a vibrator.

foreign accent   A pattern of pronunciation, stress, and intonation in a person's second language (or foreign language) that reflects the phonetic traits of the person's first (native) language.

frequency   When referring to sound, the number of vibrations per second. The unit of frequency is Hz (Hertz).

fricative   A type of consonant sound produced when the breath-stream is forced through a narrow opening between two articulators. The first sound in the word *see* is a fricative.

front vowel   A vowel sound produced with the tongue arched in the front part of the mouth, with the lips slightly spread. The vowel sound in the word *see* is a front vowel.

glide   A consonant sound produced while the articulators are in motion. The first sound in *wet* is a glide.

glottal fry   A rough, bubbly, cracking voice quality that usually occurs in the lower part of the pitch range.

glottis   The opening between the vocal folds.

gum ridge   See **alveolar ridge.**

habitual pitch   The pitch level at which a person usually begins production.

hard glottal attack   A way of producing vowel sounds. The vocal folds are very tense, and the vowels begin very abruptly. The vowels have a hard, explosive quality.

hard palate   The roof of the mouth, lying between the alveolar (gum) ridge and the soft palate.

harsh voice   A rough-sounding voice that results from irregular vibration of the vocal folds.

hoarse voice   A voice that sounds both harsh and breathy. The vocal folds are not able to close completely.

Hz (Hertz)   The unit of measurement of frequency, named for the physicist Heinrich Hertz.

illiteracy   The lack of the ability to read and write.

illustrator   A gesture that accompanies speech and is directly related to what is being said, but cannot stand alone. For example, the gestures used while explaining the shape of a spiral staircase add to the explanation, but would be meaningless without the speech they accompany.

incus The middle bone of the ossicular chain connecting the tympanic membrane to the cochlea. Because of its shape, it is also called the *anvil*. See **ossicles.**

inflection Pitch changes that occur *during* phonation. They may be rising, falling, or circumflex (a combination of both).

innervation The process of supplying nerve impulses to muscles.

intensity The power of a sound.

International Phonetic Alphabet (I.P.A.) An alphabet that uses a special set of symbols to represent the sounds of a language. Because the I.P.A. has one distinct symbol to represent each sound of the language, there may be little correlation with spelling using the conventional alphabet where a symbol may represent more than one sound.

intimate distance The distance maintained in private situations by two persons having a close, personal relationship. Intimate distance ranges from contact to about 1½ feet.

intonation The pattern of pitch changes in connected speech; the "melody" of a language.

I.P.A. See **International Phonetic Alphabet.**

key The average pitch level of a segment of connected speech. See **pitch.**

kinesics The study of body movement, gestures, posture, and facial expression as a means of communication.

kinesthetics One's awareness of the movements of one's own speech muscles and structures.

labio-dental sounds Consonant sounds produced by using the lower lip and upper teeth. The first sound in *first* is a labio-dental consonant.

language An agreed upon set of symbols, written and/or spoken, used in a uniform way by a number of people in order to communicate with each other.

larynx The structure for producing voice. Composed of cartilage and muscle, it is the uppermost part of the trachea.

lateral consonant The first sound in the word *leaf*. It is produced with the gum ridge and tongue. Air is emitted at the sides of the mouth (laterally).

lingua-alveolar consonant Consonant sounds that are produced with the tongue touching or near the gum ridge. The first and last sounds in *sit* are lingua-alveolar consonants.

lingua-dental consonants   Consonant sounds that are produced with the tongue touching the front teeth. The first sound in the word *thumb* is a lingua-dental consonant.

lingua-palatal consonants   Consonant sounds that are produced with the middle and back of the tongue raised toward the hard palate. The first sound in *ship* is a lingua-palatal consonant.

linguistics   The study of language, in general, or the study of the sounds and structure of a particular language.

literacy   The ability to read and write.

loudness   The psychological sensation of sound intensity.

malleus   The largest bone of the ossicular chain in the middle ear connecting the tympanic membrane to the cochlea. Because of its shape, it is also called the *hammer.* See **ossicles.**

mass   Thickness, when referring to a vibrating object, such as the vocal folds.

medium   A substance capable of and necessary for transmitting sound vibrations. For example, sound travels easily through air and water.

metallic voice   A usually high-pitched voice that sounds both strident and harsh. See **harsh** and **strident.**

method of articulation   The physical processes used to produce a consonant sound. For example, the method of articulation of the *plosive* that is the first sound in the word *too* involves stopping the breathstream by pressing the tongue against the alveolar ridge, building up air pressure, and letting the air "explode." Other methods of articulation are *fricative, glide, nasal, lateral,* and *affricate.*

mid vowel   A vowel sound produced when the tongue is arched in the middle part of the mouth. The first sound in the word *up* is a mid vowel.

misarticulation   Inaccurate or imprecise production of a phoneme.

mixed message   A contradiction or conflict between the verbal and nonverbal portions of a message. In the United States, such a conflict would occur if a speaker agrees verbally by saying "Yes," but shakes his head back and forth sideways at the same time.

muscle tension   The amount of contraction of the muscles of the tongue when producing vowel sounds. The degree of muscle tension varies with each vowel, and vowels are said to be either *tense* or *lax.*

nasal   Consonant sounds produced with air emitted from the nose rather than the mouth as in *mor<u>n</u>ing.* Also refers to resonance of sounds in the nasal cavities. See **nasality** and **resonance.**

nasal cavity Passageway to the pharynx from the nostrils. See **pharynx.**

nasality The quality of voice that results from the degree of resonance by the nasal cavities.

nasopharynx The nasal portion of the pharynx. See **pharynx.**

noise A barrier to communication, which may take one or more of the following forms

> **acoustic** Unwanted sounds which may block out speech or make hearing difficult.

> **environmental** Factors in the communication situation, such as poor lighting and distracting movements, which may distort speech between the speaker and listener.

> **linguistic** Noise-caused language misuse, faulty grammar, syntax, incorrect word choice, faulty sound production, and so on.

> **listener generated** Psychological and perceptual factors within the listener that may reduce communication effectiveness. For example, if you dislike or fear a particular person, you may not listen objectively to that person's message.

> **paralinguistic** Interference caused by factors other than language itself, such as uneven loudness, rate, or rhythm; inappropriate pitch or stress factors.

nonstandard speech Speech which is considered to be significantly different from the speech generally considered to be "standard." See **standard speech.**

nonverbal All the modes and behaviors of communication, either intentional or unintentional, other than the symbolic meanings of the words themselves.

objective characteristics Qualities that are observable and measurable with instruments, and are not subject to interpretation.

optimum pitch The pitch level at which a particular person can produce the loudest voice and best vocal quality with the least effort; producing the pitch your body was "designed" to produce. See **pitch, larynx,** and **frequency.**

oral cavity The portion of the mouth extending as far back as the pharynx. See **pharynx.**

oropharynx The portion of the pharynx immediately behind the mouth, below the nasopharynx, and above the pharynx. See **mouth, nasopharynx,** and **pharynx.**

ossicles The three smallest bones in the body, collectively called the ossicles. They serve as part of the hearing mechanism, and connect the middle ear with the cochlea. Individually, the bones are the *malleus* (hammer), *incus* (anvil), and *stapes* (stirrup).

ossicular chain See **ossicles.**

paralanguage All the audible elements that accompany speech and increase or decrease the meanings of words: loudness, stress, pitch, pitch variation, rate, rhythm, and voice quality. *How* you say something, rather than *what* you say.

pause A temporary stop in speech.

pausing Using pauses at the end of thought groups or utterances to enhance meaning and to provide opportunities for inhalation. See **phrasing.**

peripheral nervous system Nerves and ganglia outside of the brain and spinal cord. It conducts impulses to and from the central nervous system.

pharynx The throat.

phonation The production of vocal sounds using the vocal folds.

phoneme A "family" of sounds in a language, acoustically very similar. We generally recognize the entire sound family as one sound, different from all the other phonemes of the language. The phoneme functions in a language to signal a difference in meaning.

phonemics The study of the distinctive meaningful units of a language.

phonetics The study of the individual sounds of a language; their production and transcription into written symbols of the *International Phonetic Alphabet.*

phrasing Grouping words for better understanding or meaning. Not necessarily a complete sentence, and may not follow written punctuation. See **pausing** and **thought-group.**

pinna The outer, most visible portion of the ear.

pitch The subjective perception of the highness or lowness of a sound.

pitch range The difference between the highest and lowest pitched sounds a given individual can produce. Most people have a range of about two octaves. See **pitch.**

place of articulation The point at which the breathstream is obstructed to produce a consonant sound. The place of articulation of the first sound in the word *bee* is *bi-labial* (both lips). Other places of articulation are *labio-dental* (lip-teeth), *lingua-dental* (tongue-teeth), *lingua-alveolar* (tongue-gum ridge), *lingua-alveolo/palatal* (tongue-gum ridge/palate), *lingua-palatal* (tongue-palate), and *glottal* (vocal folds). See **articulation, articulators,** and **consonant.**

place of production The part of the tongue primarily responsible for production of a given vowel. For example, the vowel in the word *bee* is produced with the front of the tongue.

plosive A consonant sound produced by blocking the airstream completely, building up pressure, and suddenly exploding the air. The first and last sounds in *top* are plosives.

primary stress Applying more force to one syllable of a word than to the other syllables. The result is to make the syllable receiving primary stress noticeably the loudest in the word. See **stress.**

projection To use enough vocal force to be heard by all your listeners or to be heard at a distance. See **loudness.**

proxemics The study of the use, and perception, of space by humans.

public distance The distance usually appropriate for impersonal communication situations, where the distance indicates the lack of a personal relationship between the communicators. Public distance usually ranges from 12 to 20 feet or more. See **proxemics.**

pure-tone A sound consisting of only one frequency of vibration.

quality The subjective interpretation of a sound, based on frequency, intensity, phase, etc.

rate The number of words spoken per minute.

recurrent laryngeal nerve A branch of a cranial nerve supplying most of the nerve impulses to the larynx.

regional dialect See **regionalism** and **accent.**

regionalism That type of speech used and accepted in a particular area; similar to a dialect See **accent.**

regulator A nonverbal cue, such as eye contact or head nodding, that regulates the back-and-forth nature of conversation.

resonance Amplification and modification of sound either by an air-filled chamber (such as the cavities of the vocal tract) or by another object that vibrates sympathetically.

rest breathing Breathing when not talking. The rate and depth of inhalation and exhalation are roughly equal.

rising inflection See **inflection.**

schwa The neutral, unstressed mid-vowel. It is produced with the least energy of any of the vowels, and is typical of unstressed syllables in spoken English. It is the most common vowel sound in English. See **unstressed.**

secondary stress A degree of force (loudness) applied to a syllable greater than unstressed, but less than the syllable receiving primary stress. For example, the middle syllable in the word *regional* receives secondary stress, the first syllable receives primary stress, and the last syllable is unstressed.

sensory feedback   Awareness of the structure and muscles of the speech mechanism through kinesthetics and the sense of touch.

sinus   A cavity or hollow in a bone. There are several sinus cavities in the face near the nose and eyes.

social-consultative distance   The range of about 2 to 4 feet at which impersonal business is carried out.

soft-palate   The soft, muscular, movable, rearmost portion of the roof of the mouth.

sound   Vibrations in a medium (such as air) that stimulate the organs of hearing and produce the sensation of hearing.

spectrum   The graphic display of a sound, showing the component frequencies and their relative intensities.

standard speech   The way the majority of educated speakers in a large area speak. The generally ''correct'' style of speaking.

stapes   The smallest bone of the ossicular chain in the middle ear connecting the tympanic membrane to the cochlea. Because of its shape, it is also called the *stirrup*. See **ossicles.**

step   An abrupt pitch change between syllables or words.

stress   Making a syllable or word appear to be ''larger'' and louder by applying more force.

stridency   A high-pitched, tense, metallic vocal quality.

syllable stress   See **stress.**

synesthesia   A confusion of modalities or senses, such as picturing a certain color when hearing a particular sound.

syntax   The pattern or structure of word order in a sentence or phrase.

tenseness   A vocal quality resulting from excess tension in the larynx.

tension   In voice production, refers to the act of making the edges of the vocal folds thinner and tighter to produce a higher pitched sound.

tertiary stress   See **unstressed.**

thorax   The chest.

thought group   A grouping of words in a phrase or sentence that is complete in meaning and can stand by itself. A thought group is usually distinguished by pauses, and is similar to a written sentence or phrases set off by punctuation. See **pausing** and **phrasing.**

throaty   A vocal quality that seems lacking in resonance and strength; it seems to come from the back of the throat.

thyroid cartilage   The largest cartilage of the larynx, shaped like a shield and forming the front wall.

tongue height The distance the tongue is moved from the floor of the mouth toward the roof in the production of vowels. For example, the vowel in the word *bee* is a *high* vowel, while the vowel in the word *on* is a *low* vowel.

trachea A tube composed mainly of cartilage, connecting the lungs with the pharynx. Commonly called the "windpipe."

transcription Using the written symbols of the International Phonetic Alphabet to record speech sounds as they are *heard*, rather than as they are spelled.

trigeminal nerve The fifth cranial nerve, with fibers traveling to and from the jaw, face, and tongue.

tympanic membrane A fibrous membrane, commonly called the ear drum, located at the end of the external auditory canal. The malleus attaches to the inside surface. See **ossicles.**

unstressed Applying the least amount of force (loudness) possible to a syllable. An unstressed syllable is noticeably weaker and lower pitched than syllables receiving primary and secondary stress. The last sound in the word *regional* is unstressed. See **schwa, stress, primary stress,** and **secondary stress.**

velum The soft palate.

vibrator An object, which when set into vibration transmits its energy to the molecules of the medium around it, resulting in the production of sound. For example, the vocal folds are set into vibration in the process of phonation. See **sound, medium, phonation.**

vocal expression The use of rate, phrasing, intonation, and stress to make speech meaningful, gain attention, and add interest.

vocal folds Two small bands of tissue located in the larynx. They can be made to vibrate in the airstream from the lungs and create voice.

vocal fry See **glottal fry.**

vocal tract The part of the speech mechanism above the level of the vocal folds. It is where speech sounds generated by the vocal folds are modified and amplified. The vocal tract includes the *pharynx, oral cavity,* and the *nasal cavity.*

voice Sound produced by the vibration of the vocal folds.

voiced consonant A consonant sound produced with voice. The first sound in *back* is voiced; the last is voiceless.

voiceless consonant A consonant sound produced without voice. The first sound in *kid* is voiceless; the last sound is voiced.

vowel Voiced sounds produced without blocking the breathstream.

waveform A graphic representation of a sound wave, showing amplitude (intensity) over a period of time.

word stress See **stress.**

G Appendix G

Diagnostic Materials

 1: Sentences—Long List

Each of the following sentences emphasizes one sound or blend in American English. Approximate reading time: 4½ minutes.

[p] 1. Put the plastic cup on top of the pile of paper plates.

[b] 2. The baby's bathtub was filled to the brim with bubbles.

[t] 3. Tom took great delight in telling how fast he typed two letters.

[d] 4. The murderer did the dreadful deed with a dirty, old dagger.

[k] 5. Ken quit his job rather than work an extra weekend shift.

[g] 6. Peg used to gargle vigorously after eating garlic.

[f] 7. It's a fifty dollar fine if you don't file your tax form.

[v] 8. "A hand of iron in a velvet glove" was his favorite saying.

[θ] 9. Both authors used themes found in three Greek myths.

[ð] 10. Place the leather belt with the other clothing.

[s] 11. "Pass the syrup," said the first trombonist, "so I can play sweetly."

[z] 12. The busiest bee wisely zeroes in on his options.

[ʃ] 13. The magician wished he hadn't rushed to shine his shoes.

[ʒ] 14. The explosion occurred after the collision near the garage.

[h] 15. Perhaps it's not as humid in the western half of Ohio.

[ʍ] 16. Which wheel fell off when the white car hit the curb?

[w] 17. Wait until you see the new watch I was awarded.

[r] 18. Rosalie saw a red robin yesterday near her brook.

[j] 19. In my opinion, the view of that yacht is spectacular.

[l] 20. Laura left the yellow pillow in the third-floor hallway.

[m] 21. I may start writing my term paper during the summer semester.

[n] 22. Nancy was offered a chance to spend her vacation in Norway.

[ŋ] 23. Playing some guessing games requires counting on your fingers.

[tʃ] 24. Charlie had two chances to win a matching watch and chain.

[ʤ] 25. Does Virginia enjoy wearing her jeans in July?

[str] 26. The district attorney and the magistrate met near the construction barrier on the street.

[tl] 27. Littleton is a better place than Tottenville to buy
[tn]   antique bottles and buttons.

[i] 28. We were required to read *East of Eden* and also to see the movie.

[ɪ] 29. It was difficult to distinguish the pens from the pins.

[eɪ] 30. The train was delayed eight hours due to a break
[e]   in the rails.

[ɛ] 31. It doesn't make any sense to bet with your friends.

[æ] 32. Alan went to California to enhance his acting career.

[ɑ] 33. The honest guard calmly parked his car in the hot courtyard.

[ɔ] 34. Paul knocked for an awfully long time at the wrong door.

[oʊ] [o] 35. "No soap, radio" is the punch line of a very old joke.

[ʊ] 36. I couldn't find a good recipe for sugar cookies in that book.

[u] 37. It was too late to go on the cruise to Liverpool, so he flew.

[ʌ] 38. Hungry ducklings dive underwater to find their lunch.

[ə] 39. The camera-shy panda was not in the parade.

[ɝ] 40. At first, Herb only heard every third word.

[ɚ] 41. Oh brother, exclaimed the barber, I'd rather be a butcher.

[aɪ] 42. If I have enough time, I'll try to buy some ice cream.

[aʊ] 43. People who go around saying "How now, brown cow?" should be hounded out of town.

[ɔɪ] 44. Olive Oyl took great joy in avoiding Popeye's noisy toys.

2: Sentences—Short List

Each of the following sentences emphasizes two or more sounds or blends in American English. Approximate reading time: 2 minutes.

1. The puppy bumped his paws and stopped bouncing.
2. It takes daring to be a detective in today's world.
3. The caretaker took his gardening with a grain of salt.
4. Frank sent a Valentine's gift to Vivian on February fourteenth.
5. Without thinking, Theo's brother bothered him for the thirtieth time.
6. Sandy was observing zebras in zoology classes last semester.

7. Fresh fish are unusually delicious when served with sausage and relish.

8. Harry said the heat bothers him only half as much as the humidity.

9. The wild, wet weather kept me awake on Wednesday night.

10. The whetstone whirred and whined while it spun around.

11. Roy was surprised to receive three waterproof raincoats as graduation presents.

12. The yellow lion stretched lazily and yawned loudly.

13. Megan began knitting a new cardigan last month.

14. Driving on the Long Island Expressway is like being in the world's longest parking lot.

15. James and Virginia won the matched set of luggage, jewelry, and Chippendale furniture.

16. I asked them why there was so much construction machinery in the street.

17. Little by little Benton analyzed the contents of the bottle.

18. It's easier to swallow a bitter pill with something sweet to drink.

19. I'll bet I can make every second Wednesday seem like a vacation from Broadway matinees.

20. Alan honestly planned to drive calmly to the grandstand.

21. I ought to buy that dog from my lawyer.

22. Roy was a piano hoister who took great joy in his toil.

23. Sarah's oatmeal cookbook is a bestseller from coast to coast.

24. You should never do unto others what you don't want them to do to you.

25. The price of bananas sunk again, but bubble gum blew sky high.

26. Whether you call it soda or pop, you purchase more of it in warm summer weather.

27. Nine mountain climbers went through the clouds up one side and down the other.

3. Connected Speech

The following has been used for many years as a diagnostic and research passage. It contains all the sounds of American English in about the same proportion as they occur in everyday speech. Approximate reading time: 2 minutes.

The Rainbow Passage

When the sunlight strikes raindrops in the air, they act like a prism and form a rainbow. The rainbow is a division of white light into many beautiful colors. These take the shape of a long round arch, with its path high above, and its two ends apparently beyond the horizon. There is, according to legend, a boiling pot of gold at one end. People look, but no one ever finds it. When a man looks for something beyond his reach, his friends say he is looking for the pot of gold at the end of the rainbow.

Throughout the centuries men have explained the rainbow in various ways. Some have accepted it as a miracle without physical explanation. To the Hebrews it was a token that there would be no more universal floods. The Greeks used to imagine that it was a sign from the gods to foretell war or heavy rain. The Norsemen considerd the rainbow as a bridge over which the gods passed from earth to their home in the sky. Other men have tried to explain the phenomenon physically. Aristotle thought that the rainbow was caused by reflection of the sun's rays by the rain. Since then physicists have found that it is not reflection, but refraction by the raindrops which causes the rainbow. Many complicated ideas about the rainbow have been formed. The difference in the rainbow depends considerably upon the size of the water drops, and the width of the colored band increases as the size of the drops increases. The actual primary rainbow observed is said to be the effect of superposition of a number of bows. If the red of the second bow falls upon the green of the first, the result is to give a bow with an abnormally wide yellow band, since red and green lights when mixed form yellow. This is a very common type of bow, one showing mainly red and yellow, with little or no green or blue.

Appendix H

Speech Check Lists

SPEECH CHECK LIST

Name _____   Course _____

Rater _____   Date _____

Articulation

Consonants
Reading

		1	2
p	pat	_____	_____
b	boat	_____	_____
t	top	_____	_____
d	dog	_____	_____
k	key	_____	_____
g	go	_____	_____
f	four	_____	_____
v	very	_____	_____
θ	thin	_____	_____
ð	the:	_____	_____
s	snake	_____	_____
z	zoo	_____	_____
ʃ	she	_____	_____
ʒ	beige	_____	_____
h	hot	_____	_____
ʍ	where	_____	_____
w	wet	_____	_____
r	red	_____	_____
j	yes	_____	_____
l	left	_____	_____
m	man	_____	_____
n	no	_____	_____
ŋ	sing	_____	_____
tʃ	chair	_____	_____
dʒ	judge	_____	_____

Blends

		1	2
str	street	_____	_____
skr	scratch	_____	_____
tl	little	_____	_____

Vowels
Reading

		1	2
i	see	_____	_____
ɪ	sit	_____	_____
e	ate	_____	_____
ɛ	bet	_____	_____
æ	pat	_____	_____
a	ask	_____	_____
ɑ	calm	_____	_____
ɔ	awful	_____	_____
o	so	_____	_____
ʊ	book	_____	_____
u	too	_____	_____
ʌ	up	_____	_____
ə	banana	_____	_____
ɝ-ɚ	early	_____	_____
ɚ	father	_____	_____

Diphthongs
Reading

		1	2
aɪ	ice	_____	_____
aʊ	how	_____	_____
ɔɪ	coin	_____	_____
eɪ	day	_____	_____
oʊ	glow	_____	_____
ɔɚ	pour	_____	_____
ɛɚ	share	_____	_____
ɑɚ	car	_____	_____
iɚ	here	_____	_____
uɚ	poor	_____	_____

Other Articulatory Features:

	1	2
Consonant omissions	_____	_____
Consonant additions	_____	_____
dentalized d, t	_____	_____
intrusive r	_____	_____
final unvoicing	_____	_____
lisp (type)	_____	_____
excess sibilance	_____	_____
assimilation	_____	_____
dialect (type)	_____	_____
other	_____	_____
	_____	_____
	_____	_____
	_____	_____

Voice

Reading #1:

Pitch:	Appropriate	Too High	Too Low	Patterned	Monotonous	Other ____
Volume:	Appropriate	Too Loud	Too Weak	Uncontrolled	Monotonous	Other ____
Rate:	Appropriate	Too Fast	Too Slow	Hesitant	Monotonous	Other ____
Quality:	Appropriate	Nasal	Denasal	Breathy	Hoarse	Other ____

Reading #2:

Pitch:	Appropriate	Too High	Too Low	Patterned	Monotonous	Other ____
Volume:	Appropriate	Too Loud	Too Weak	Uncontrolled	Monotonous	Other ____
Rate:	Appropriate	Too Fast	Too Slow	Hesitant	Monotonous	Other ____
Quality:	Appropriate	Nasal	Denasal	Breathy	Hoarse	Other ____

Comments: _____

SPEECH CHECK LIST

Name _____ Course _____

Rater _____ Date _____

Articulation

Consonants Reading			Vowels Reading			Diphthongs Reading		
	1	2		1	2		1	2
p pat	____	____	i see	____	____	aɪ ice	____	____
b boat	____	____	ɪ sit	____	____	aʊ how	____	____
t top	____	____	e ate	____	____	ɔɪ coin	____	____
d dog	____	____	ɛ bet	____	____	eɪ day	____	____
k key	____	____	æ pat	____	____	oʊ glow	____	____
g go	____	____	a ask	____	____	ɔɚ pour	____	____
f four	____	____	ɑ calm	____	____	ɛɚ share	____	____
v very	____	____	ɔ awful	____	____	ɑɚ car	____	____
θ thin	____	____	o so	____	____	iɚ here	____	____
ð the:	____	____	ʊ book	____	____	uɚ poor	____	____
s snake	____	____	u too	____	____			
z zoo	____	____	ʌ up	____	____			
ʃ she	____	____	ə banana	____	____			
ʒ beige	____	____	ɜ-ɝ early	____	____			
h hot	____	____	ɚ father	____	____			
ʍ where	____	____						
w wet	____	____						
r red	____	____						
j yes	____	____						
l left	____	____						
m man	____	____						
n no	____	____						
ŋ sing	____	____						
tʃ chair	____	____						
dʒ judge	____	____						

Other Articulatory Features:

	1	2
Consonant omissions	____	____
Consonant additions	____	____
dentalized d, t	____	____
intrusive r	____	____
final unvoicing	____	____
lisp (type)	____	____
excess sibilance	____	____
assimilation	____	____
dialect (type)	____	____
other	____	____
	____	____
	____	____
	____	____

Blends

	1	2
str street	____	____
skr scratch	____	____
tl little	____	____

Voice

Reading #1:

Pitch:	Appropriate	Too High	Too Low	Patterned	Monotonous	Other ____
Volume:	Appropriate	Too Loud	Too Weak	Uncontrolled	Monotonous	Other ____
Rate:	Appropriate	Too Fast	Too Slow	Hesitant	Monotonous	Other ____
Quality:	Appropriate	Nasal	Denasal	Breathy	Hoarse	Other ____

Reading #2:

Pitch:	Appropriate	Too High	Too Low	Patterned	Monotonous	Other ____
Volume:	Appropriate	Too Loud	Too Weak	Uncontrolled	Monotonous	Other ____
Rate:	Appropriate	Too Fast	Too Slow	Hesitant	Monotonous	Other ____
Quality:	Appropriate	Nasal	Denasal	Breathy	Hoarse	Other ____

Comments: _____

Reading: _____

SPEECH CHECK LIST

Name _____ Course _____
Rater _____ Date _____

Articulation

Consonants
Reading

		1	2
p	pat	_____	_____
b	boat	_____	_____
t	top	_____	_____
d	dog	_____	_____
k	key	_____	_____
g	go	_____	_____
f	four	_____	_____
v	very	_____	_____
θ	thin	_____	_____
ð	the:	_____	_____
s	snake	_____	_____
z	zoo	_____	_____
ʃ	she	_____	_____
ʒ	beige	_____	_____
h	hot	_____	_____
ʍ	where	_____	_____
w	wet	_____	_____
r	red	_____	_____
j	yes	_____	_____
l	left	_____	_____
m	man	_____	_____
n	no	_____	_____
ŋ	sing	_____	_____
tʃ	chair	_____	_____
dʒ	judge	_____	_____

Blends

str	street	_____	_____
skr	scratch	_____	_____
tl	little	_____	_____

Vowels
Reading

		1	2
i	see	_____	_____
ɪ	sit	_____	_____
e	ate	_____	_____
ɛ	bet	_____	_____
æ	pat	_____	_____
a	ask	_____	_____
ɑ	calm	_____	_____
ɔ	awful	_____	_____
o	so	_____	_____
ʊ	book	_____	_____
u	too	_____	_____
ʌ	up	_____	_____
ə	banana	_____	_____
ɜ-ɝ	early	_____	_____
ɚ	father	_____	_____

Diphthongs
Reading

		1	2
aɪ	ice	_____	_____
aʊ	how	_____	_____
ɔɪ	coin	_____	_____
eɪ	day	_____	_____
oʊ	glow	_____	_____
ɔɚ	pour	_____	_____
ɛɚ	share	_____	_____
ɑɚ	car	_____	_____
iɚ	here	_____	_____
uɚ	poor	_____	_____

Other Articulatory Features:

	1	2
Consonant omissions	_____	_____
Consonant additions	_____	_____
dentalized d, t	_____	_____
intrusive r	_____	_____
final unvoicing	_____	_____
lisp (type)	_____	_____
excess sibilance	_____	_____
assimilation	_____	_____
dialect (type)	_____	_____
other	_____	_____
	_____	_____
	_____	_____

Voice

Reading #1:

Pitch:	Appropriate	Too High	Too Low	Patterned	Monotonous	Other _____
Volume:	Appropriate	Too Loud	Too Weak	Uncontrolled	Monotonous	Other _____
Rate:	Appropriate	Too Fast	Too Slow	Hesitant	Monotonous	Other _____
Quality:	Appropriate	Nasal	Denasal	Breathy	Hoarse	Other _____

Reading #2:

Pitch:	Appropriate	Too High	Too Low	Patterned	Monotonous	Other _____
Volume:	Appropriate	Too Loud	Too Weak	Uncontrolled	Monotonous	Other _____
Rate:	Appropriate	Too Fast	Too Slow	Hesitant	Monotonous	Other _____
Quality:	Appropriate	Nasal	Denasal	Breathy	Hoarse	Other _____

Comments: _____

SPEECH CHECK LIST

Name _____   Course _____

Rater _____   Date _____

Articulation

Consonants
Reading

		1	2
p	pat	_____	_____
b	boat	_____	_____
t	top	_____	_____
d	dog	_____	_____
k	key	_____	_____
g	go	_____	_____
f	four	_____	_____
v	very	_____	_____
θ	thin	_____	_____
ð	the:	_____	_____
s	snake	_____	_____
z	zoo	_____	_____
ʃ	she	_____	_____
ʒ	beige	_____	_____
h	hot	_____	_____
ʍ	where	_____	_____
w	wet	_____	_____
r	red	_____	_____
j	yes	_____	_____
l	left	_____	_____
m	man	_____	_____
n	no	_____	_____
ŋ	sing	_____	_____
tʃ	chair	_____	_____
dʒ	judge	_____	_____

Blends

		1	2
str	street	_____	_____
skr	scratch	_____	_____
tl	little	_____	_____

Vowels
Reading

		1	2
i	see	_____	_____
ɪ	sit	_____	_____
e	ate	_____	_____
ɛ	bet	_____	_____
æ	pat	_____	_____
a	ask	_____	_____
ɑ	calm	_____	_____
ɔ	awful	_____	_____
o	so	_____	_____
ʊ	book	_____	_____
u	too	_____	_____
ʌ	up	_____	_____
ə	banana	_____	_____
ɜ-ɝ	early	_____	_____
ɚ	father	_____	_____

Diphthongs
Reading

		1	2
aɪ	ice	_____	_____
aʊ	how	_____	_____
ɔɪ	coin	_____	_____
eɪ	day	_____	_____
oʊ	glow	_____	_____
ɔɚ	pour	_____	_____
ɛɚ	share	_____	_____
ɑɚ	car	_____	_____
iɚ	here	_____	_____
uɚ	poor	_____	_____

Other Articulatory Features:

	1	2
Consonant omissions	_____	_____
Consonant additions	_____	_____
dentalized d, t	_____	_____
intrusive r	_____	_____
final unvoicing	_____	_____
lisp (type)	_____	_____
excess sibilance	_____	_____
assimilation	_____	_____
dialect (type)	_____	_____
other	_____	_____
	_____	_____
	_____	_____

Voice

Reading #1:

Pitch:	Appropriate	Too High	Too Low	Patterned	Monotonous	Other ____
Volume:	Appropriate	Too Loud	Too Weak	Uncontrolled	Monotonous	Other ____
Rate:	Appropriate	Too Fast	Too Slow	Hesitant	Monotonous	Other ____
Quality:	Appropriate	Nasal	Denasal	Breathy	Hoarse	Other ____

Reading #2:

Pitch:	Appropriate	Too High	Too Low	Patterned	Monotonous	Other ____
Volume:	Appropriate	Too Loud	Too Weak	Uncontrolled	Monotonous	Other ____
Rate:	Appropriate	Too Fast	Too Slow	Hesitant	Monotonous	Other ____
Quality:	Appropriate	Nasal	Denasal	Breathy	Hoarse	Other ____

Comments: _____

SPEECH CHECK LIST

Name _____   Course _____

Rater _____   Date _____

Articulation

	Consonants Reading			Vowels Reading			Diphthongs Reading	
	1	2		1	2		1	2
p	pat _____	_____	i	see _____	_____	aɪ	ice _____	_____
b	boat _____	_____	ɪ	sit _____	_____	aʊ	how _____	_____
t	top _____	_____	e	ate _____	_____	ɔɪ	coin _____	_____
d	dog _____	_____	ɛ	bet _____	_____	eɪ	day _____	_____
k	key _____	_____	æ	pat _____	_____	ou	glow _____	_____
g	go _____	_____	a	ask _____	_____	ɔɚ	pour _____	_____
f	four _____	_____	ɑ	calm _____	_____	ɛɚ	share _____	_____
v	very _____	_____	ɔ	awful _____	_____	ɑɚ	car _____	_____
θ	thin _____	_____	o	so _____	_____	iɚ	here _____	_____
ð	the: _____	_____	ʊ	book _____	_____	uɚ	poor _____	_____
s	snake _____	_____	u	too _____	_____			
z	zoo _____	_____	ʌ	up _____	_____			
ʃ	she _____	_____	ə	banana _____	_____			
ʒ	beige _____	_____	ɜ-ɝ	early _____	_____			
h	hot _____	_____	ɚ	father _____	_____			
ʍ	where _____	_____						
w	wet _____	_____						
r	red _____	_____						
j	yes _____	_____						
l	left _____	_____						
m	man _____	_____						
n	no _____	_____						
ŋ	sing _____	_____						
tʃ	chair _____	_____						
dʒ	judge _____	_____						

Other Articulatory Features:

	1	2
Consonant omissions	_____	_____
Consonant additions	_____	_____
dentalized d, t	_____	_____
intrusive r	_____	_____
final unvoicing	_____	_____
lisp (type)	_____	_____
excess sibilance	_____	_____
assimilation	_____	_____
dialect (type)	_____	_____
other	_____	_____
	_____	_____
	_____	_____
	_____	_____

Blends

	1	2
str	street _____	_____
skr	scratch _____	_____
tl	little _____	_____

Voice

Reading #1:

Pitch:	Appropriate	Too High	Too Low	Patterned	Monotonous	Other _____
Volume:	Appropriate	Too Loud	Too Weak	Uncontrolled	Monotonous	Other _____
Rate:	Appropriate	Too Fast	Too Slow	Hesitant	Monotonous	Other _____
Quality:	Appropriate	Nasal	Denasal	Breathy	Hoarse	Other _____

Reading #2:

Pitch:	Appropriate	Too High	Too Low	Patterned	Monotonous	Other _____
Volume:	Appropriate	Too Loud	Too Weak	Uncontrolled	Monotonous	Other _____
Rate:	Appropriate	Too Fast	Too Slow	Hesitant	Monotonous	Other _____
Quality:	Appropriate	Nasal	Denasal	Breathy	Hoarse	Other _____

Comments: _____

SPEECH CHECK LIST

Name _____ Course _____

Rater _____ Date _____

Articulation

	Consonants Reading 1	2		Vowels Reading 1	2		Diphthongs Reading 1	2
p	pat _____	_____	i	see _____	_____	aɪ	ice _____	_____
b	boat _____	_____	ɪ	sit _____	_____	aʊ	how _____	_____
t	top _____	_____	e	ate _____	_____	ɔɪ	coin _____	_____
d	dog _____	_____	ɛ	bet _____	_____	eɪ	day _____	_____
k	key _____	_____	æ	pat _____	_____	ou	glow _____	_____
g	go _____	_____	a	ask _____	_____	ɔɚ	pour _____	_____
f	four _____	_____	ɑ	calm _____	_____	ɛɚ	share _____	_____
v	very _____	_____	ɔ	awful _____	_____	ɑɚ	car _____	_____
θ	thin _____	_____	o	so _____	_____	iɚ	here _____	_____
ð	the: _____	_____	ʊ	book _____	_____	uɚ	poor _____	_____
s	snake _____	_____	u	too _____	_____			
z	zoo _____	_____	ʌ	up _____	_____			
ʃ	she _____	_____	ə	banana _____	_____			
ʒ	beige _____	_____	ɝ-ɚ	early _____	_____			
h	hot _____	_____	ɚ	father _____	_____			
ʍ	where _____	_____						
w	wet _____	_____						
r	red _____	_____						
j	yes _____	_____						
l	left _____	_____						
m	man _____	_____						
n	no _____	_____						
ŋ	sing _____	_____						
tʃ	chair _____	_____						
dʒ	judge _____	_____						

Blends

		1	2
str	street	_____	_____
skr	scratch	_____	_____
tl	little	_____	_____

Other Articulatory Features:

	1	2
Consonant omissions	_____	_____
Consonant additions	_____	_____
dentalized d, t	_____	_____
intrusive r	_____	_____
final unvoicing	_____	_____
lisp (type)	_____	_____
excess sibilance	_____	_____
assimilation	_____	_____
dialect (type)	_____	_____
other	_____	_____
	_____	_____
	_____	_____
	_____	_____

Voice

Reading #1:

Pitch:	Appropriate	Too High	Too Low	Patterned	Monotonous	Other _____
Volume:	Appropriate	Too Loud	Too Weak	Uncontrolled	Monotonous	Other _____
Rate:	Appropriate	Too Fast	Too Slow	Hesitant	Monotonous	Other _____
Quality:	Appropriate	Nasal	Denasal	Breathy	Hoarse	Other _____

Reading #2:

Pitch:	Appropriate	Too High	Too Low	Patterned	Monotonous	Other _____
Volume:	Appropriate	Too Loud	Too Weak	Uncontrolled	Monotonous	Other _____
Rate:	Appropriate	Too Fast	Too Slow	Hesitant	Monotonous	Other _____
Quality:	Appropriate	Nasal	Denasal	Breathy	Hoarse	Other _____

Comments: _____

SPEECH CHECK LIST

Name _____   Course _____
Rater _____   Date _____

Articulation

	Consonants Reading				Vowels Reading				Diphthongs Reading	
	1	**2**			**1**	**2**			**1**	**2**
p	pat _____	_____	i	see _____	_____		aɪ	ice _____	_____
b	boat _____	_____	ɪ	sit _____	_____		aʊ	how _____	_____
t	top _____	_____	e	ate _____	_____		ɔɪ	coin _____	_____
d	dog _____	_____	ɛ	bet _____	_____		eɪ	day _____	_____
k	key _____	_____	æ	pat _____	_____		ou	glow _____	_____
g	go _____	_____	a	ask _____	_____		ɔɚ	pour _____	_____
f	four _____	_____	ɑ	calm _____	_____		ɛɚ	share _____	_____
v	very _____	_____	ɔ	awful _____	_____		ɑɚ	car _____	_____
θ	thin _____	_____	o	so _____	_____		iɚ	here _____	_____
ð	the: _____	_____	ʊ	book _____	_____		uɚ	poor _____	_____
s	snake _____	_____	u	too _____	_____				
z	zoo _____	_____	ʌ	up _____	_____				
ʃ	she _____	_____	ə	banana _____	_____				
ʒ	beige _____	_____	ɝ-ɚ	early _____	_____				
h	hot _____	_____	ɚ	father _____	_____				
ʍ	where _____	_____							
w	wet _____	_____							
r	red _____	_____							
j	yes _____	_____							
l	left _____	_____							
m	man _____	_____							
n	no _____	_____							
ŋ	sing _____	_____							
tʃ	chair _____	_____							
dʒ	judge _____	_____							

Other Articulatory Features:

	1	2
Consonant omissions	_____	_____
Consonant additions	_____	_____
dentalized d, t	_____	_____
intrusive r	_____	_____
final unvoicing	_____	_____
lisp (type)	_____	_____
excess sibilance	_____	_____
assimilation	_____	_____
dialect (type)	_____	_____
other	_____	_____
	_____	_____
	_____	_____
	_____	_____

Blends

str	street _____	_____
skr	scratch _____	_____
tl	little _____	_____

Voice

Reading #1:

Pitch:	Appropriate	Too High	Too Low	Patterned	Monotonous	Other ____
Volume:	Appropriate	Too Loud	Too Weak	Uncontrolled	Monotonous	Other ____
Rate:	Appropriate	Too Fast	Too Slow	Hesitant	Monotonous	Other ____
Quality:	Appropriate	Nasal	Denasal	Breathy	Hoarse	Other ____

Reading #2:

Pitch:	Appropriate	Too High	Too Low	Patterned	Monotonous	Other ____
Volume:	Appropriate	Too Loud	Too Weak	Uncontrolled	Monotonous	Other ____
Rate:	Appropriate	Too Fast	Too Slow	Hesitant	Monotonous	Other ____
Quality:	Appropriate	Nasal	Denasal	Breathy	Hoarse	Other ____

Comments: _____

Permissions
Acknowledgments

Daniloff/Schuckers/Feth, *The Physiology of Speech and Hearing: An Introduction,* Copyright © 1980, p. 87. Reprinted by permission of Prentice-Hall, Inc., Englewood Cliffs, N.J.

"Respiratory Function In Speech" by Thomas J. Hixon in *Normal Aspects of Speech, Hearing, and Language* edited by Minifie/Hixon/Williams, Copyright © 1973, p. 76. Reprinted by permission of Prentice-Hall, Inc., Englewood Cliffs, N.J.

The lines from "The Supper After Last" from *Mortal Acts, Mortal Words* by Galway Kinnell. Copyright © 1980 by Galway Kinnell. Reprinted by permission of the Houghton Mifflin Company.

From *Come Blow Your Horn* by Neil Simon. Copyright © 1961 by Neil Simon. Reprinted by permission of Random House, Inc. and the author.

Excerpt from "Ars Poetica" by Archibald MacLeish from *New and Collected Poems, 1917–1976* by Archibald MacLeish. Copyright © 1976 by Archibald MacLeish. Reprinted by permission of the Houghton Mifflin Company.

From *Don't Drink the Water* by Woody Allen, Samuel French, Inc., Copyright © 1967 by Woody Allen. By permission of the author's agent.

"The Sloth," copyright 1950 by Theodore Roethke from the book *The Collected Poems of Theodore Roethke* by Theodore Roethke. Reprinted by permission of Doubleday & Company, Inc.

James M. Barrie, *Peter Pan.* Copyright © 1911, 1921 Charles Scribner's Sons: copyright renewed 1939, 1949 by Lady Cynthia Asquith and Peter L. Davies. Reprinted with the permission of Charles Scribner's Sons.

From *The Little Foxes* by Lillian Hellman. Copyright © 1939 and renewed 1967 by Lillian Hellman. Reprinted by permission of Random House, Inc.

Excerpt from *Another Part of the Forest* by Lillian Hellman. Copyright © 1947 by Lillian Hellman. Copyright renewed 1975 by Lillian Hellman. Reprinted by permission of Viking Penguin Inc.

From *California Suite* by Neil Simon. Copyright © 1977 by Neil Simon. Reprinted by permission of the author and Random House, Inc.

From *Chapter Two* by Neil Simon. Copyright © 1978, 1979 by Neil Simon. Reprinted by permission of the author and Random House, Inc.

From *The Prisoner of Second Avenue* by Neil Simon. Copyright © 1972 by Nancy Enterprises, Inc. Reprinted by permission of the author and Random House, Inc.

From *Getting Even* by Woody Allen. Copyright © 1971 by Woody Allen. Reprinted by permission of Random House, Inc.

From *Without Feathers* by Woody Allen. Reprinted by permission of Random House, Inc.

"Song of Hate for Eels" by Arthur Guiterman (1923). Reprinted by permission of Louise H. Sclove.

The lines from "Diving into the Wreck," from *Diving into the Wreck, Poems, 1971–1972,* by Adrienne Rich, are reprinted by permission of the author and publisher, W.W. Norton & Company, Inc. Copyright © 1973 by W.W. Norton & Company, Inc.

"One Perfect Rose" by Dorothy Parker from *The Portable Dorothy Parker.* Copyright 1926, renewed copyright 1954 by Dorothy Parker. Reprinted by permission of Viking/Penguin, Inc.

"Needs" is reprinted from *Collected Poems, 1951–1971,* by A.R. Ammons, by permission of W.W. Norton & Company, Inc. Copyright © 1972 by A.R. Ammons.

From "The Love Song of J. Alfred Prufrock" in *Collected Poems 1909–1962* by T.S. Eliot, copyright 1936 by Harcourt Brace Jovanovich, Inc., copyright © 1963, 1964 by T.S. Eliot. Reprinted by permission of the publisher.

From *The People, Yes* by Carl Sandburg, copyright 1936 by Harcourt Brace Jovanovich, Inc.; renewed 1964 by Carl Sandburg. Reprinted by permission of the publisher.

From "The Patented Gate and the Mean Hamburger" in *The Circus in the Attic and Other Stories* by Robert Penn Warren, copyright 1968 by Harcourt Brace Jovanovich, Inc. Reprinted by permission of the publisher.

"Pine Tree Tops" by Gary Snyder, *Turtle Island.* Copyright © 1972, 1974 by Gary Snyder. Reprinted by permission of New Directions Publishing Company.

Index

409